Instructor's Manual/Test Item File

INTERMEDIATE MICROECONOMICS

Instructor's Manual
by
Hal Varian

Test Item File
by
Theodore C. Bergstrom

W·W·Norton & Co.
New York/London

ISBN 0-393-95675-X

W. W. Norton & Company, Inc., 500 Fifth Avenue, New York, N.Y. 10110
W. W. Norton & Company Ltd., 27 Great Russell Street, London WC1B 3NU

1 2 3 4 5 6 7 8 9 0

Part II: Test Item File

Part III: Answers to *Workouts in Intermediate Microeconomics*

Part I
CHAPTER HIGHLIGHTS

Chapter 1

The Market

This chapter was written so I would have something to talk about on the first day of class. I wanted to give students an idea of what economics was all about, and what my lectures would be like, and yet not have anything that was really critical for the course. (At Michigan, students are still shopping around on the first day, and a good number of them won't necessarily be at the lecture.)

I chose to discuss a housing market since it gives a way to describe a number of economic ideas in very simple language and gives a good guide to what lies ahead. In this chapter I was deliberately looking for *surprising results*—analytic insights that wouldn't arise from "just thinking" about a problem. The two most surprising results that I presented are the condominium example and the tax example in Section 1.6. It is worth emphasizing in class just why these results are true, and how they illustrate the power of economic modeling.

It also makes sense to describe their limitations. Suppose that every condominium conversion involved knocking out the walls and creating two apartments? Then what would happen to the price of apartments? Suppose that the condominiums attracted suburbanites who wouldn't otherwise consider renting an apartment? In each of these cases, the price of remaining apartments would rise when condominium conversion took place.

The point of a simple economic model of the sort considered here is to focus our thoughts on what the relevant effects are, not to come to a once-and-for-all conclusion about the urban housing market. The real insight that is offered by these examples is that you have to consider both the supply *and* the demand side of the apartment market when you analyze the impact of this particular policy.

The only concept that the students seem to have trouble with in this chapter is the idea of Pareto efficiency. I usually talk about the idea a little more than is in the book and rephrase it a few times. But then I tell them not to worry about it too much, since we'll look at it in great detail later in the course.

The workbook problems here are pretty straightforward. The biggest problem is getting the students to draw the true (discontinuous) demand curve, as in Figure 1.1, rather than just to sketch in a downward sloping curve as in Figure 1.2. This is a good point to emphasize that when they are given numbers describing a curve they have to use them—they can't just sketch in any old shape.

The Market

A. Example of an economic model — the market for apartments
   1. models are simplifications of reality
   2. for example, assume all apartments are identical
   3. some are close to University, others are far away
   4. price of far away apartments is **exogenous** — determined outside the model
   5. price of close-in apartments in **endogenous** — determined within the model

B. Two principles of economics
   1. **optimization principle** — people choose actions that are in their interest.
   2. **equilibrium principle** — peoples' actions must eventually be consistent with each other

C. Constructing the demand curve
   1. line up the people by willingness-to-pay. See Figure 1.1.
   2. for large numbers of people, this is essentially a smooth curve as in Figure 1.2.

D. Supply curve
   1. depends on time frame
   2. but we'll look at the **short run** — when supply of apartments is fixed.

E. Equilibrium
   1. when demand equals supply
   2. price that clears the market

F. Comparative statics
   1. how does equilibrium adjust when economic conditions change?
   2. "comparative" — compare two equilibria
   3. "statics" — only look at equilibria, not at adjustment
   4. example — increase in supply lowers price; see Figure 1.5.
   5. example — create condos which are purchased by renters; no effect on price; see Figure 1.6.

G. Other ways to allocate apartments
   1. discriminating monopolist
   2. ordinary monopolist
   3. rent control

H. Comparing different institutions
   1. need a criterion to compare how efficient these different allocation methods are.

    2. an allocation is **Pareto efficient** if there is no way to make some group of people better off without making someone else worse off.

    3. if something is *not* Pareto efficient, then there *is* some way to make some people better off without affecting any other people.

    4. if something is not Pareto efficient, then there is some kind of "waste" in the system.

I. Checking efficiency of different methods
    1. free market — efficient
    2. discriminating monopolist — efficient
    3. ordinary monopolist — not efficient
    4. rent control — not efficient

J. Equilibrium in long run
    1. supply will change
    2. can examine efficiency in this context as well

Chapter 2

Budget Constraint

Most of the material here is pretty straightforward. Drive home the formula for the slope of the budget line, emphasizing the derivation on page 23. Try some different notation to make sure that they see *idea* of the budget line, and don't just memorize the formulas. In the workbook, we use a number of different choices of notation for precisely this reason. It is also worth pointing out that the slope of a line depends on the (arbitrary) choice of which variable is plotted on the vertical axis. It is surprising how often confusion arises on this point.

Students sometimes have problems with the idea of a numeraire good. They understand the algebra, but they don't understand when it would be used. One nice example is in foreign currency exchange. If you have English pounds and American dollars, then you can measure the total wealth that you have in either dollars or pounds by choosing one or the other of the two goods as numeraire.

In the workbook, students sometimes get thrown on Exercise 2.8 where one of the goods has a negative price, so the budget line has a positive slope. This comes from trying to memorize formulas and figures rather than thinking about the problem. This is a good exercise to go over in order to warn students about the dangers of rote learning!

Chapter 2: Budget Constraint

A. Consumer theory: consumers choose the best bundles of goods they can afford.
   1. this is virtually the entire theory in a nutshell
   2. but this theory has many surprising consequences

B. Two parts to theory
   1. "can afford" — **budget constraint**
   2. "best" — according to consumers **preferences**

C. What do we want to do with the theory?
   1. test it — see if it is adequate to describe consumer behavior
   2. predict how behavior changes as economic environment changes
   3. use observed behavior to estimate underlying values
      a) cost-benefit analysis

b) predicting impact of some policy

D. Consumption bundle
1. (x_1, x_2) — how much of each good is consumed
2. (p_1, p_2) — prices of the two goods
3. m — money the consumer has to spend
4. budget constraint: $p_1 x_1 + p_2 x_2 \leq m$
5. all (x_1, x_2) that satisfy this constraint make up the **budget set** of the consumer.

E. Two goods
1. theory works with more than two goods, but can't draw pictures
2. often think of good 2 (say) as a composite good, representing money to spend on other goods.
3. budget constraint becomes $p_1 x_1 + x_2 \leq m$. "money spent on good 1 $(p_1 x_1)$ plus the money spent on good 2 (x_2) has to be less than amount available (m).

F. Budget line
1. $p_1 x_1 + p_2 x_2 = m$
2. Also written as $x_2 = m/p_2 - (p_1/p_2)x_1$.
3. budget line has slope of $-p_1/p_2$ and vertical intercept of m/p_2.
4. set $x_1 = 0$ to find vertical intercept (m/p_2); set $x_2 = 0$ to find horizontal intercept (m/p_1).
5. slope of budget line measures opportunity cost of good 1 — how much of good 2 you must give up in order to consume more of good 1.

G. Changes in budget line
1. increasing m makes parallel shift out
2. increasing p_1 makes budget line steeper
3. increasing p_2 makes budget line flatter
4. just see how intercepts change
5. multiplying all prices by t is just like dividing income by t
6. multiplying all prices and income by t doesn't change budget line
    a) "a perfectly balanced inflation doesn't change consumption possibilities"

H. The numeraire
1. can arbitrarily assign one price a value of 1 and measure other price relative to that
2. useful when measuring relative prices; e.g. English pounds per dollar, 1987 dollars vs. 1974 dollars, etc.

I. Taxes, subsidies and rationing
1. quantity tax — tax levied on units bought $p_1 + t$
2. value tax — tax levied on dollars spent $p_1 + \tau p_1$. Also known as *ad valorem* tax
3. subsides — opposite of a tax
    a) $p_1 - s$
    b) $(1 - \sigma)p_1$

      4. lump sum tax or subsidy — amount of tax or subsidy is independent of consumer's choices. Also called a head tax or a poll tax.

      5. rationing — can't consume more than a certain amount of some good.

J. Example — food stamps

    1. before 1979 was an *ad valorem* subsidy on food

      a) paid a certain amount of money to get food stamps which were worth more.

      b) some rationing component — could only buy a maximum amount of food stamps

    2. after 1979 got a straight lump sum grant of food coupons. Not the same as a pure lump sum grant since could only spend the coupons on food.

Chapter 3

Preferences

This chapter takes a move up in terms of abstraction and needs somewhat more motivation than the previous chapters. It might be a good idea to talk about relations in general before introducing the particular idea of preference relations. Try the relations of "taller," and "heavier," and "taller and heavier." Point out that "taller and heavier" isn't a complete relation, while the other two are. This general discussion can motivate the general idea of preference relations.

Make sure that the students learn the specific examples of preferences described in Section 3.4. They will use those ideas many, many times in the next few weeks!

When describing the ideas of perfect substitutes, emphasize that the defining characteristic is that the slope of the indifference curves is constant, not that it is -1. In the text, I always stick with the case where the slope is -1, but in the workbook, we often treat the general case. The same warning goes with the perfect complements case. I work out the symmetric case in the text and try to get the student to do the asymmetric case in the workbook.

The definition of the marginal rate of substitution is fraught with "sign confusion." Should the MRS be defined as a negative or a positive number? I've chosen to give the MRS its natural sign in the book, but I warn the students that many economists tend to speak of the MRS in terms of absolute value. Example: diminishing marginal rate of substitution refers to a situation where the *absolute value* of the MRS decreases as we move along an indifference curve. The actual value of the MRS (a negative number) is *increasing* in this movement!

Students often begin to have problems with the workbook exercises here. The first confusion they have is that they get mixed up about the idea that indifference curves measure the directions where preferences are constant, and instead draw lines that indicate the directions that preferences are increasing. The second problem that they have is in knowing when to draw just arbitrary curves that qualitatively depict some behavior or other, and when to draw exact shapes. Problems 3.5 and 3.6 are especially good ones to illustrate this distinction. Problem 3.5 has an exact answer—perfect substitute indifference curves with a slope of -2, while problem 3.6 has a qualitative answer.

Try asking your students to draw their indifference curves between five dollar bills and one dollar bills. Offer to make them trades based on what they draw. In addition to getting them to think, this is a good way to supplement your faculty salary.

Chapter 3: Preferences

A. Preferences are relationships between bundles.
   1. if a consumer would choose bundle (x_1, x_2) when (y_1, y_2) is available, then it is natural to say that bundle (x_1, x_2) is preferred to (y_1, y_2) by this consumer.
   2. preferences have to do with the entire *bundle* of goods, not with individual goods.

B. Notation
   1. $(x_1, x_2) \succ (y_1, y_2)$ means the x-bundle is **strictly preferred** to the y-bundle
   2. $(x_1, x_2) \sim (y_1, y_2)$ means that the x-bundle is regarded as **indifferent** to the y-bundle.
   3. $(x_1, x_2) \succeq (y_1, y_2)$ means the x-bundle is **at least as good as** (preferred to or indifferent to) the y-bundle

C. Assumptions about preferences
   1. complete — any two bundles can be compared
   2. reflexive — any bundle is at least as good as itself
   3. transitive — if $X \succeq Y$ and $Y \succeq Z$ then $X \succeq Z$.
      a) transitivity necessary for theory of *optimal* choice

D. Indifference curves
   1. graph the set of bundles that are indifferent to some bundle
   2. indifference curves are like contour lines on a map
   3. note that indifference curves describing two distinct levels of preference can not cross
      a) proof — use transitivity

E. Examples of preferences
   1. perfect substitutes
      a) red pencils and blue pencils; pints and quarts
      b) constant rate of trade-off between the two goods
   2. perfect complements
      a) always consumed together
      b) right shoes, left shoes; coffee and cream
   3. bads
   4. neutrals
   5. satiation or bliss point

F. Well-behaved preferences
   1. monotonicity — more of either good is better
      a) implies indifference curves have negative slope
   2. convexity — averages are preferred to extremes

   a) slope gets flatter as you move further to right
   b) example of non-convex preferences

G. Marginal rate of substitution
   1. slope of the indifference curve
   2. $MRS = \Delta x_2 / \Delta x_1$ along an indifference curve
   3. sign problem — natural sign is negative, since indifference curves
      will generally have negative slope
   4. measures how the consumer is willing to trade off consumption of
      good 1 for consumption of good 2
   5. measures marginal willingness to pay (give up)
      a) not the same as how much you have to pay
      b) but how much you would be *willing* to pay

Chapter 4

Utility

In this chapter, the level of abstraction kicks up another notch. Students often have trouble with the idea of utility. It is sometimes hard for trained economists to sympathize with them sufficiently, since it seems like such an obvious notion to us.

Here is a way to approach the subject. Suppose that we return to the idea of the "heavier than" relation discussed in the last chapter. Think of having a big balance scale with two trays. You can put someone in each side of the balance scale and which person is heavier, but you don't have any standardized weights. Nevertheless you have a way to determine whether x is heavier than y.

Now suppose that you decide to establish a scale. You get a bunch of stones, check that they are all the same weight, and then measure the weight of individuals in stones. It is clear that x is heavier than y if x's weight in stones is heavier than y's weight in stones.

Somebody else might use different units of measurements—kilograms, or pounds, or whatever. It doesn't make any difference in terms of deciding who is heavier. At this point it is easy to draw the analogy with utility—just as pounds give a way to represent the "heavier than" order numerically, utility gives a way to represent the preference order numerically. Just as the units of weight are arbitrary, so are the units of utility.

This analogy can also be used to explore the concept of a positive monotonic transformation, a concept that students have great trouble with. Tell them that a monotonic transformation is just like changing units of measurement in the weight example.

However, it is also important for students to understand that nonlinear changes of units are possible. Here is a nice example the illustrate this. Suppose that wood is always sold in piles shaped like cubes. Think of the relation, "one pile has more wood than another." Then you can represent this relation by looking at the measure of the sides of the piles, the surface area of the piles, or the volume of the piles. That is, x, x^2, or x^3 give exactly the same comparison between the piles. Each of these numbers is a different representation of the utility of a cube of wood.

Be sure to go over carefully the examples here. The Cobb-Douglas example is an important one, since we use it so much in the workbook. Emphasize that it is just a nice functional form that gives convenient expressions. Be sure to elaborate on the idea that $x_1^a x_2^b$ is the general form for Cobb-Douglas preferences, but various monotonic transformations (e.g., the log) can make it look quite different. It's a good idea to calculate the MRS for a few representations of the Cobb-Douglas utility function in class so that people can see how to do them, and, more importantly, that the MRS doesn't change as you change the representation of utility.

The example at the end of the chapter, on commuting behavior, is very nice one. If you present it right, it will convince your students that utility is an operational concept. Talk about how the same methods can be used in marketing surveys, surveys of college admissions, etc.

The exercises in the workbook for this chapter are very important since they drive home the ideas. A lot of times, students *think* that they understand some point, but they don't, and these exercises will point that out to them. It is a good idea to let the students discover for themselves that a sure-fire way to tell whether one utility function represents the same preferences as another is to compute the two marginal rate of substitution functions. If they don't get this idea on their own, you can pose it as a question and lead them to the answer.

Chapter 4: Utility

A. Two ways of viewing utility
   1. old way
      a) measures how "satisfied" you are
         1) not operational
         2) many other problems
   2. new way
      a) summarizes preferences
      b) a utility function assigns a number to each bundle of goods so that more preferred bundles get higher numbers
      c) that is, $u(x_1, x_2) > u(y_1, y_2)$ if and only if $(x_1, x_2) \succ (y_1, y_2)$.
      d) only the ordering of bundles counts, so this is a theory of **ordinal utility**
      e) advantages
         1) operational
         2) gives a complete theory of demand

B. Utility function are not unique
   1. if $u(x_1, x_2)$ is a utility function that represents some preferences, and $f(\cdot)$ is any increasing function, then $f(u(x_1, x_2))$ represents the same preferences
   2. Why? Because $u(x_1, x_2) > u(y_1, y_2)$ only if $f(u(x_1, x_2)) > f(u(y_1, y_2))$.
   3. So if $u(x_1, x_2)$ is a utility function then any positive monotonic transformation of it is also a utility function that represents the same preferences.

C. Constructing a utility function
   1. can do it mechanically using the indifference curves
   2. can do it using the "meaning" of the preferences

D. Examples
 1. utility to indifference curves
    a) easy — just plot all points where the utility is constant
 2. indifference curves to utility
 3. Examples
    a) perfect substitutes — all that matters is total number of pencils, so $u(x_1, x_2) = x_1 + x_2$ does the trick.
       1) can use any monotonic transformation of this as well, such as $log(x_1 + x_2)$.
    b) perfect complements — what matters is the minimum of the left and right shoes you have, so $u(x_1, x_2) = \min\{x_1, x_2\}$ works.
    c) quasilinear preferences — indifference curves are vertically parallel
       1) utility function has form $u(x_1, x_2) = v(x_1) + x_2$
    d) Cobb-Douglas preferences
       1) utility has form $u(x_1, x_2) = x_1^b x_2^c$
       2) convenient to take transformation $f(u) = u^{\frac{1}{b+c}}$ and write $x_1^{\frac{b}{b+c}} x_2^{\frac{c}{b+c}}$
       3) or $x_1^a x_2^{1-a}$, where $a = b/(b+c)$.

E. Marginal utility
 1. extra utility from some extra consumption of one of the goods, holding the other good fixed.
 2. this is a derivative, but a special kind of derivative — a *partial* derivative.
 3. this just means that you look at the derivate of $u(x_1, x_2)$ keeping x_2 fixed — treating it like a constant.
 4. Examples
    a) if $u(x_1, x_2) = x_1 + x_2$, then $MU_1 = \partial u/\partial x_1 = 1$
    b) if $u(x_1, x_2) = x_1^a x_2^{1-a}$, then $MU_1 = \partial u/\partial x_1 = ax_1^{a-1} x_2^{1-a}$.
 5. Note that marginal utility depends on which utility function you choose to represent preferences.
    a) If you multiply utility times 2 you multiply marginal utility times 2.
    b) thus it is not an operational concept
    c) however, MU is closely related to MRS, which is an operational concept
 6. Relationship between MU and MRS
    a) $u(x_1, x_2) = k$ where k is constant, describes an indifference curve.
    b) we want to measure slope of indifference curve, the MRS
    c) so consider a change (dx_1, dx_2) that keeps utility constant. Then

$$MU_1 dx_1 + MU_2 dx_2 = 0$$

$$\frac{\partial u}{\partial x_1} dx_1 + \frac{\partial u}{\partial x_2} dx_2 = 0$$

    d) Hence

$$\frac{dx_2}{dx_1} = -\frac{MU_1}{MU_2}.$$

    e) So we can compute MRS from knowing the utility function.

F. Example
1. take a bus or take a car to work?
2. let x_1 be the time of taking a car, y_1 be the time taking bus. Let x_2 be cost of car, etc.
3. suppose utility function takes linear form $U(x_1, \ldots, x_n) = \beta_1 x_1 + \ldots + \beta_n x_n$
4. we can observe a number of choices and use statistical techniques to estimate the parameters β_i that best describe choices.
5. One study that did this could forecast the actual choice over 93% of the time.
6. Once we have the utility function we can do many things with it:
   a) calculate the marginal rate of substitution between two characteristics
      1) how much money would the average consumer give up in order to get a shorter travel time?
   b) forecast consumer response to proposed changes
   c) estimate whether proposed change is worthwhile in a benefit-cost sense.

Chapter 5

Choice

This is the chapter where we bring it all together. Make sure that students understand the *method* of maximization and don't just memorize the various special cases. The problems in the workbook are designed to show the futility of memorizing special cases, but often students try it anyway.

The material in section 5.4 is very important—I introduce it by saying "Why should you *care* that the MRS equals the price ratio?" The answer is that this allows economists to determine something about peoples' tradeoffs by observing market prices. Thus it allows for the possibility of benefit-cost analysis.

The material in section 5.5 on choosing taxes is the first big non-obvious result from using consumer theory ideas. I go over it very carefully, to make sure that students understand the result, and emphasize how this analysis uses the techniques that we've developed. Pound home the idea that the analytic techniques of microeconomics have a big payoff—they allow us to answer questions that we wouldn't have been able to answer without these techniques.

If you are doing a calculus based course, be sure to spend some time on the appendix to this chapter. Emphasize that to solve a constrained maximization problem, you must have two equations. One equation is the constraint, and one equation is the optimization condition. I usually work a Cobb-Douglas and a perfect complements problem to illustrate this. In the Cobb-Douglas case, the optimization condition is that the MRS equals the price ratio. In the perfect complements case, the optimization condition is that the consumer chooses a bundle at the corner.

Again, working the problems in *Workouts* is very important to get these ideas down. Problem 5.7 is a nice one, but we really should have provided 5 different graphs, since plotting all those lines on one graph gets quite messy.

Chapter 5 — Choice

A. Optimal choice
   1. Move along budget line until preferred set doesn't cross the budget set.

2. Note that tangency occurs at optimal point — necessary condition for optimum. In symbols: MRS = price ratio = p_1/p_2.
   a) Exception — kinky tastes
   b) Exception — boundary optimum
3. Tangency is not sufficient
   a) Unless indifference curves are convex.
   b) Unless optimum is interior.
4. Optimal choice is demanded bundle
   a) As we vary prices and income, we get demand functions.
   b) Want to study how optimal choice — the demanded bundle — changes as price and income changes.

B. Examples
   1. Perfect substitutes: $x_1 = m/p_1$ if $p_1 < p_2$, 0 otherwise.
   2. Perfect complements: $x_1 = m/(p_1 + p_2)$.
   3. Neutrals and bads: $x_1 = m/p_1$.
   4. Concave preferences: just like perfect substitutes. Note that tangency doesn't work.
   5. Cobb-Douglas preferences: $x_1 = am/p_1$. Note constant budget shares, a = budget share of good 1.

C. Implications of MRS condition
   1. Why do we care that MRS = price ratio?
   2. If everyone faces same prices, then everyone has the same local tradeoff between the two goods. This is independent of income and tastes.
   3. Since everyone locally values the tradeoff the same, we can make policy judgements. Is it worth sacrificing one good to get more of the other? Prices serve as a guide to relative marginal valuations.

D. Application — choosing a tax. Which is better, a commodity tax or an income tax?
   1. Can show an income tax is always better in the sense that given any commodity tax, there is an income tax that makes the consumer better off.
   2. Go through proof, page 81-82.
      a) original budget constraint: $p_1 x_1 + p_2 x_2 = m$
      b) budget constraint with tax: $(p_1 + t)x_1 + p_2 x_2 = m$
      c) optimal choice with tax: $(p_1 + t)x_1^* + p_2 x_2^* = m$
      d) revenue raised is tx_1^*
      e) income tax that raises same amount of revenue leads to budget constraint: $p_1 x_1 + p_2 x_2 = m - tx_1^*$
         1) this line has same slope as original budget line
         2) also passes through (x_1^*, x_2^*)
         3) proof: $p_1 x_1^* + p_2 x_2^* = m - tx_1^*$
         4) so (x_1^*, x_2^*) is affordable under the income tax, so the optimal choice under the income tax must be even better than (x_1^*, x_2^*).
   3. Caveats
      a) only applies for one consumer — for each consumer there is an income tax that dominates.

b) income is exogenous — if income responds to tax, problems.

c) no supply response — only looked at demand side.

E. Appendix — solving the for the optimal choice

1. Calculus problem — constrained maximization.

2. max $u(x_1, x_2)$ s.t. $p_1 x_1 + p_2 x_2 = m$

3. method 1: write down $MRS = p_1/p_2$ and budget constraint and solve.

4. method 2: substitute from constraint into objective function and solve.

5. method 3: Lagrange's method

   a) Write Lagrangian: $L = u(x_1, x_2) - \lambda(p_1 x_1 + p_2 x_2 - m)$.

   b) Differentiate with respect to x_1, x_2, λ.

   c) Solve equations

6. Another example: quasilinear preferences

   a) max $u(x_1) + x_2$ s.t. $p_1 x_1 + x_2 = m$

   b) easiest to substitute, but works each way.

Chapter 6

Demand

This is a very important chapter, since it unifies all the materials in the previous chapter. It is also the chapter that separates the sheep from the goats. If the student has been paying attention for the previous 5 chapters and has been religiously doing the homework, then it is fairly easy to handle this chapter. Alas, I have often found that students have developed a false sense of confidence after seeing budget constraints, drift through the discussions of preference and utility, and come crashing down to earth at Chapter 6.

So, the first thing to do is to get them to review the previous chapters. Emphasize how each chapter builds on the previous chapters, and how Chapter 6 represents a culmination of this building. In turn Chapter 6 is a foundation for further analysis, and must be mastered in order to continue.

Part of the problem is that there are just a large number of new concepts in this chapter: offer curves, demand curves, Engel curves, inferior goods, Giffen goods, etc. A list of these ideas along with their definitions and page references is often helpful just for getting the concepts down pat.

I introduce the idea of elasticity and the various elasticity identities derived from the budget constraint in this chapter, but I don't really do very much with these ideas at this point. I introduce the idea of elasticity again in Chapter 16 and give a much more thorough treatment.

If you are doing a calculus based course, the material in the Appendix on quasilinear preferences is quite important. We will refer to this treatment later on when we discuss consumer's surplus, so it is a good idea to go through it carefully now.

Students usually have a rough time with the workbook problems. In part, I think that this is due just to the fact that we have now got a critical mass of ideas, and that it has to percolate a bit before they can start brewing some new ideas. A few words of encouragement help a lot here, as well as drawing links with the earlier chapters. Most students will go back on their own and see what they missed on first reading, if you indicate that is a good thing to do. Remember: the point of the workbook problems is to show the students what they *don't* understand, not to give them a pat on the back. The role of the professor is to give them a pat on the back, or a nudge in the behind, whichever seems more appropriate.

Chapter 6 — Demand

A. Demand functions — relate prices and income to choices

B. How do choices change as economic environment changes?
1. Changes in income
   a) this is a parallel shift out of budget line
   b) increase in income increases demand — **normal** good
   c) increase in income decreases demand — **inferior** good
   d) as income changes the optimal choice moves along the **income expansion path.**
   e) the relationship between the optimal choice and income, with prices fixed, is called the **Engel curve.**

C. Changes in price
1. this is a tilt or pivot of the budget line
2. decrease in price increases demand — **ordinary** good
3. decrease in price decreases demand — **Giffen** good
4. as price changes the optimal choice moves along the **offer curve.**
5. the relationship between the optimal choice and a price, with income and the other price fixed, is called the **demand curve.**

D. Substitutes and complements
1. increase in p_2 increases demand for x_1 — substitutes
2. increase in p_2 decreases demand for x_1 — complements

E. Inverse demand curve
1. usually think of demand curve as measuring quantity as a function of price — but can also think of price as a function of quantity
2. this is the **inverse demand curve**
3. same *relationship* but just represented differently

F. Elasticity
1. how responsive is demand to price?
2. absolute numbers don't make much sense
3. better to use proportional changes
4. **price elasticity of demand** is defined by

$$\epsilon = \frac{\Delta x / x}{\Delta p / p}$$

5. For small changes in price, this becomes

$$\epsilon = \frac{\partial x}{\partial p} \frac{p}{x}$$

6. Example: $x = 10p^{-2}$. Then $\epsilon = -2$.
7. Example: $x = 10 - 3p$. Then $\epsilon = -3p/(10 - 3p)$.

Chapter 7

Revealed Preference

This is a big change of pace, and usually a welcome one. The basic idea of revealed preference, as described in Section 7.1 is a very intuitive one. All I want to do in this chapter is give the students the tools to express that intuition algebraically.

I think that the material in section 7.3, on recovering preferences, is very exciting. Start out with the idea of indirect revealed preference, as depicted in Figure 7.2. Point out that the optimization model allows us to predict how this person would behave when faced with a choice between (x_1, x_2) and (z_1, z_2), *even though we have never observed the person when faced with this choice!* This is a *big* idea, and a very important one. Again, drive home how the economic model of optimization allows us to make strong predictions about behavior.

Figure 7.3 is the natural extension of this line of reasoning. Given the idea of revealed preference, and more importantly the idea of *indirect* revealed preference, we can determine the shape of underlying indifference curves from looking at choice data. I motivate this in terms of benefit-cost issues, but you could also choose to think about forecasting demand for products in a marketing survey, or similar applications.

Once students understand the idea of revealed preference, they can usually understand the Weak Axiom right away. However, they generally have difficulty in actually checking whether the weak axiom is satisfied by some real numbers. I added section 7.5 for this reason; it just outlines one systematic way to check WARP. The students can omit this in their first reading, but they might want to come back to it when they start to do the exercises. If your students know a little computer programming, you might ask them to think about how to write a computer program to check WARP.

The same comments go for the treatment of the Strong Axiom and checking SARP. This is probably overkill, but I found that students couldn't really handle problem 7.5 in the workbook without some guidance about how to systematically check SARP. Speaking of the workbook, the problems in this section are really fun. I am especially fond of 7.6 and 7.7. Problem 7.9 had some wrong numbers in it in early printings of *Workouts*, so people with old books should be warned.

Finally, the material on index numbers is very worthwhile. It is probably a good idea to indicate that year s is the "base" year and year t is the "comparison" year.

Chapter 7 — Revealed Preference

A. Motivation
1. Up until now we've started with preference and then described behavior
2. Revealed preference is "working backwards" — start with behavior and describe preferences.
3. Recovering preferences — how to use observed choices to "estimate" the indifference curves.

B. Basic idea
1. if (x_1, x_2) is chosen when (y_1, y_2) is affordable, then we know that (x_1, x_2) is at least as good as (y_1, y_2).
2. in equations: if (x_1, x_2) is chosen when prices are (p_1, p_2) and $p_1 x_1 + p_2 x_2 \geq p_1 y_1 + p_2 y_2$ then $(x_1, x_2) \succeq (y_1, y_2)$
3. see Figure 7.1.
4. if $p_1 x_1 + p_2 x_2 \geq p_1 y_1 + p_2 y_2$ we say that (x_1, x_2) is **directly revealed preferred** to (y_1, y_2).
5. if X is directly revealed preferred to Y and Y is directly revealed preferred to Z (etc.) then we say that X is **indirectly revealed preferred** to Z. See Figure 7.2.
6. the "chains" of revealed preference can give us a lot of information about the preferences. See Figure 7.3.
7. the information revealed about tastes by choices can be used in formulating economic policy.

C. Weak Axiom of Revealed Preference
1. recovering preferences makes sense only if consumer is actually maximizing
2. what if we observed a case like Figure 7.4?
3. in this case X is revealed preferred to Y and Y is also revealed preferred to X!
4. in equations, we have (x_1, x_2) purchased at prices (p_1, p_2) and (y_1, y_2) purchased at prices (q_1, q_2) and $p_1 x_1 + p_2 x_2 > p_1 y_1 + p_2 y_2$ and $q_1 y_1 + q_2 y_2 > q_1 x_1 + q_2 x_2$.
5. this kind of behavior is inconsistent with the optimizing model of consumer choice.
6. the Weak Axiom of Revealed Preference (WARP) rules out this kind of behavior.
7. WARP: if (x_1, x_2) is directly revealed preferred to (y_1, y_2) then (y_1, y_2) can not be directly revealed preferred to (x_1, x_2).
8. WARP: if $p_1 x_1 + p_2 x_2 \geq p_1 y_1 + p_2 y_2$ then it must happen that $q_1 y_1 + q_2 y_2 \leq q_1 x_1 + q_2 x_2$.
9. this condition can be checked by hand or by computer

D. Strong Axiom of Revealed Preference

1. WARP is only a necessary condition for behavior to be consistent with utility maximization.
2. Strong Axiom of Revealed Preference: if (x_1, x_2) is directly or *indirectly* revealed preferred to (y_1, y_2) then (y_1, y_2) can not be directly or indirectly revealed preferred to (x_1, x_2)
3. SARP is a *necessary and sufficient* condition for utility maximization.
4. this means that if the consumer is maximizing utility then his behavior must be consistent with SARP, and ...
5. if his observed behavior is consistent with SARP, then we can always find a utility function that explains the behavior of the consumer as maximizing behavior
6. can also be tested by a computer

E. Index numbers
1. given consumption and prices in two years, base year s and some other year t.
2. how does consumption in year t compare to base year consumption?
3. general form of a consumption index:

$$\frac{w_1 x_1^t + w_2 x_2^t}{w_1 x_1^s + w_2 x_2^s}$$

4. natural to use prices as weights
5. get two indices depending on whether you use period t or period s prices
6. Paasche index uses period t (current period) weights

$$\frac{p_1^t x_1^t + p_2^t x_2^t}{p_1^t x_1^s + p_2^t x_2^s}$$

7. Laspeyres index uses period s (base period) weights:

$$\frac{p_1^s x_1^t + p_2^s x_2^t}{p_1^s x_1^s + p_2^s x_2^s}$$

8. Note connection with revealed preference: if Paasche index is greater than 1, then period t must be better than period s:
   a)
$$\frac{p_1^t x_1^t + p_2^t x_2^t}{p_1^t x_1^s + p_2^t x_2^s} > 1$$

   b)
$$p_1^t x_1^t + p_2^t x_2^t > p_1^t x_1^s + p_2^t x_2^s$$

   c) so period t is revealed preferred to period s
9. Same sort of thing can be done with Laspeyre's index — if Laspeyres index is less than 1 consumer is worse off.

Chapter 8

Slutsky Equation

Most books talk about income and substitution effects, but then they don't do anything with the ideas. My view is that you have to give the student enough of an understanding of an idea to be able to compute with it; otherwise, why bother?

The Slutsky decomposition is an analytical tool that allows us to understand how demand changes when a price changes. It does this by breaking the total change in demand up into smaller pieces. The sign of the overall effect depends on the sign of the pieces, but sign of the pieces is easier to determine.

I have used the Slutsky definition of substitution effect in this chapter. This is because it is much, much easier to compute examples using this definition. The Hicksian definition is theoretically more elegant, but students can't compute with it until they have more advanced mathematical tools.

A large part of getting this material across is just convincing the students to read the book. The change in income necessary to compensate for a change in price is neither a difficult concept nor a difficult calculation, but it has to be repeated a few times before the students grasp it.

One way to describe income and substitution effects is to give an example based on their own consumption patterns. Talk about a student who spends all of her allowance on food and books. Suppose that the price of books drops in half, but her parents find out about it and cut her allowance. How much do they cut her allowance if they want her to keep her old consumption level affordable?

Once they grasp the idea of the substitution and income effect, it isn't hard to put them together in section 8.4. The next real hurdle is expressing the Slutsky equation in terms of rates of change, as is done in section 8.5. This is the way that we usually refer to the Slutsky equation in later chapters, so it is worthwhile going through the algebra so they can see where it comes from. However, if you don't want to go through the algebraic computations, just make sure that they get the basic point: the change in demand can be decomposed into a substitution effect (always negative, i.e., opposite the direction of price change) and an income effect

(positive or negative depending on whether we have a normal or inferior good.)

I usually skip the Optional sections in this chapter, but they are there for reference if needed. I like the tax rebate section, but it is a little sophisticated. Emphasize the idea that even if you give the money from the tax back to the consumers the demand for the good will go down and consumers will be left worse off.

Chapter 8 — Slutsky Equation

A. We want way to decompose the effect of a price change into "simpler" pieces.
   1. that's what *analysis* is all about
   2. break up into simple pieces to determine behavior of whole

B. Break up price change into a **pivot** and a **shift** — see Figure 8.2.
   1. these are hypothetical changes
   2. we can examine each change in isolation and look at sum of two changes

C. Change in demand due to pivot is the **substitution effect**
   1. this measures how demand changes when we change prices, keeping purchasing power fixed.
   2. how much would person demand if he just had enough money to consume the original bundle?
   3. this isolates the pure effect from changing the relative prices.
   4. substitution effect *must* be negative due to revealed preference.
      a) "negative" means quantity moves opposite the direction of price

D. Change in demand due to shift is the **income effect**
   1. increase income, keep prices fixed
   2. income effect can increase or decrease demand depending on whether we have a normal or inferior good

E. Total change in demand is substitution effect plus the income effect.
   1. if good is normal good the substitution effect and the income effect reinforce each other
   2. if good is inferior good, total effect is ambiguous
   3. see Figure 8.3

F. Specific examples
   1. perfect complements — Figure 8.4
   2. perfect substitutes — Figure 8.5
   3. quasilinear — Figure 8.6

G. Application — rebating a tax
   1. put a tax on gasoline and return the revenues
   2. original budget constraint: $px^* + y^* = m$
   3. after tax budget constraint: $(p + t)x' + y' = m + tx'$
   4. so consumption after tax satisfies $px' + y' = m$
   5. so (x', y') was affordable originally and rejected in favor of (x^*, y^*)
   6. consumer must be worse off

H. Rates of change
   1. can also express Slutsky effect in terms of *rates of change*
   2. takes the form
$$\frac{\partial x}{\partial p} = \frac{\partial x^s}{\partial p} - \frac{\partial x}{\partial m} x.$$
   3. can interpret each part just as before

Buying and Selling

The idea of an endowment is an important one, and I wanted to devote a whole chapter to it rather than give it the cursory treatment it gets in most books. It is somewhat unnatural in a two-good context, so it is worth pointing out to students that artificiality and that it does make perfectly good sense in a more general context.

Emphasize the statement in section 9.3 that an increase in the value of the endowment allows for greater consumption possibilities of both goods. You'll be happy you did this when you discuss present value! Be sure to explain why a consumer would necessarily prefer an endowment with higher value, while she may or may not prefer a consumption bundle with higher value.

The section on price changes is a very nice application of revealed preference arguments. Students often appreciate this idea a lot more after seeing these applications.

The Slutsky equation treatment in this chapter is quite neat, but a trifle involved. Point out that in the original treatment of the Slutsky equation money income didn't change when prices changed—only the purchasing power of the money changed. In this chapter, where consumers get their money from selling their endowments, money income *does* change when purchasing power changes, and this effect has to be accounted for.

I have found that blowing up Figure 9.7 and carefully stepping through the movements is a big help in seeing this point. Point out that if we take away the budget line through point C we have the standard diagram of the previous chapter. The movement from D to C is the only new thing that has been added in this chapter.

If you've got a group that is pretty comfortable with abstraction, the treatment in the appendix to this chapter will be of interest. It gives an *exact* derivation of the Slutsky equation in this case.

Section 9.7 gives a very short example of the Slutsky equation when an endowment is present. Point out how the result comes solely from the maximization hypothesis, and how hard it would be to figure this out without some analytic tools. That's the point of analytic tools like the Slutsky equation: they make this kind of calculation mechanical so that you don't have to reproduce a complicated path of reasoning in each particular case.

Chapter 9 — Buying and Selling

A. Up until now, people have only had money to exchange for goods. But in reality, people sell things they own (e.g., labor) to acquire goods. Want to model this idea.

B. Net and gross demands
   1. Endowment, (ω_1, ω_2), is what you have before you enter the market.
   2. Gross demands: (x_1, x_2) — what you end up consuming
   3. Net demands: $(x_1 - \omega_1, x_2 - \omega_2)$ — what you actually buy (positive) and sell (negative).
   4. For economists gross demands are the more important; for laypeople, net demands are more important.

C. Budget constraint
   1. Value of what you consume = value of what you sell.
   2. $p_1 x_1 + p_2 x_2 = p_1 \omega_1 + p_2 \omega_2$
   3. $p_1(x_1 - \omega_1) + p_2(x_2 - \omega_2) = 0$
   4. Budget line depicted in Figure 9.1; note endowment is always affordable.
   5. With two goods, the consumer is always a net demander of one good, net supplier of the other.

D. Comparative statics
   1. Changing the endowment
      a) normal and inferior
      b) increasing the value of the endowment makes the consumer better off. Note that this is different from increasing the value of the consumption bundle. Need access to market.
   2. Changing prices
      a) if the price of a good the consumer is selling goes down, and the consumer decides to remain a seller, then welfare goes down. Figure 9.3
      b) if the consumer is a net buyer of a good and the price decreases, then the consumer will remain a net buyer. Figure 9.4.
      c) etc.
   3. Offer curves and demand curves
      a) offer curves
      b) gross demand curve
      c) net demand curves (and net supply curves)

E. Slutsky equation
   1. When prices change we now have three effects
      a) ordinary substitution effect
      b) ordinary income effect
      c) endowment income effect — change in the value of the endowment affects demand.
   2. Figure 9.7 depicts the three effects.
   3. the income effect depends on the *net demand*

4. Slutsky equation now takes the form

$$\frac{\partial x_1}{\partial p_1} = \frac{\partial x_1^s}{\partial p_1} + (\omega_1 - x_1)\frac{\partial x_1}{\partial m}$$

5. Read through proof in appendix.

Chapter 10

Labor Supply

In this chapter and the next one we get the payoff for all that theory—a deeper insight into some real-world choice problems. Some people skip these chapters to save time, but I think that this is a big mistake. At the least, have the students read the chapters so they can see some real applications of the theoretical ideas they have been studying.

The first thing that we do in this chapter is to manipulate the budget constraint so it fits into the framework studied earlier. Emphasize that this is a common strategy for analysis: arrange the problem at hand so that it looks like something we've seen before. Also, it is useful to emphasize the interpretation of the endowment in this context: the endowment is what you end up consuming if you don't engage in any market transactions.

Once the labor supply problem has been put in the standard framework, we can apply all the tools that we have at our disposal. The first one is the Slutsky equation. In section 10.2 I first go through a mistaken analysis, and then correct it to give the right analysis. I think that this is appropriate in this case, since so many people get the labor supply analysis wrong. A backwards-bending labor supply curve is not a Giffen phenomenon. The supply curve of labor slopes backwards because the endowment of leisure is worth more when the wage rate rises, and this can lead to an increased consumption of leisure due to the income effect.

The overtime example is really a dandy illustration of substitution effects. I sometimes introduce the idea by considering the following paradox: if an employer increases a flat wage by some amount, and pays a higher wage for all hours worked, his employees could easily end up choosing to work less. But if the employer pays the *same* increased wage as an overtime wage, the employees will never choose to work less, and will likely choose to work more. Isn't it paradoxical that giving the workers more money (via the flat wage increase) results in less labor forthcoming? Seen in terms of substitution effects and revealed preference it all makes very good sense, but without those ideas, this common phenomenon can seem very confusing.

The analysis of progressive and regressive taxation is also useful in emphasizing the importance of the marginal wage. The examples in Figure 10.5 of the impact of taxing labor and non-labor income are also worth some class discussion.

Chapter 10 — Labor Supply

A. Two goods
   1. consumption (C)
   2. labor (L) — maximum amount you can work is $\bar{L}$
   3. money (M)

B. Budget constraint for labor supply
   1. $pC = M + wL$
   2. define $\bar{C} = M/p$
   3. $pC + w(\bar{L} - L) = p\bar{C} + w\bar{L} = p\bar{C} + w\bar{R}$.
   4. define leisure $R = \bar{L} - L$. Note $\bar{R} = \bar{L}$
   5. $pC + wR = p\bar{C} + w\bar{L}$
   6. this is just like ordinary budget constraint
   7. supply of labor is like demand for leisure
   8. w/p is price of leisure

C. See Figure 10.1

D. Comparative statics
   1. apply Slutsky equation to demand for leisure to get

$$\frac{\partial R}{\partial w} = \text{substitution effect} + (\bar{R} - R) \times \text{ income effect.}$$

   2. Increase in the wage rate has an ambiguous effect on supply of labor. Depends on how much labor is supplied already.
   3. Backwards bending labor supply curve.

E. Overtime
   1. Offer someone a higher straight wage, may work less.
   2. Offer them a higher overtime wage, they must work at least as much.
   3. See Figure 10.2.
   4. Overtime is a way to get at the substitution effect.

F. Taxes
   1. what matters in labor supply is the after-tax wage, $(1 - t)w$.
   2. nonlinear taxation
      a) progressive and regressive (Fig. 10.3 and 10.4)
      b) may be perfectly rational to be indifferent about working a lot or a little.

Intertemporal Choice

This is one of my favorite topics, since it uses consumer theory in such fundamental ways, and yet has many important and practical consequences.

The intertemporal budget constraint is pretty straightforward. I sometimes draw the kinked shape that results from different borrowing and lending rates, just to drive the point home. It is good to spell out the importance of convexity and monotonicity for intertemporal preferences. Ask your students what savings behavior would be exhibited by a person with *convex* intertemporal preferences.

The difference between the present value and the future value formulation of the budget constraint can be seen as a choice of numeraire.

The comparative statics is simply relabelled graphs we've seen before, but it still is worth describing in detail as a concrete example.

I think that it is worth repeating the conclusion of Section 11.6 several times, as students seem to have a hard time absorbing it. An investment that shifts the endowment in a way that increases its present value is an investment that *every* consumer must prefer (as long as they can borrow and lend at the same interest rate.) It is a good idea to express this point in several different ways. One especially important way is to talk explicitly about investments as changes in the endowment $(\Delta m_1, \Delta m_2)$, and then point out that any investment with positive present value is worthwhile.

Emphasize that present value is really a linear operation, despite appearances. Given a table of present values, as Table 11.1, show how easy it is to calculate present values.

The installment loan example is a very nice one. It is good to motivate it by first considering a person who borrows $1,000 and then pays back $1,200 a year later. What rate of interest is he paying? Show that this rate can be found by solving the equation

$$1000(1 + r) = 1200,$$

or

$$1000 = \frac{1200}{1 + r}.$$

It is then very natural to argue that the monthly rate of interest for the installment loan is given by the i that solves the equation

$$1000 = \frac{100}{1+i} + \frac{100}{(1+i)^2} + \ldots + \frac{100}{(1+i)^{12}}.$$

Finally, the equivalent yearly rate is $r = 12i$.

The workbook problems for this chapter are also quite worthwhile. Problem 11.1 is a nice example of present value analysis, using the perpetuity formulas. Problem 11.6 illustrates the budget constraint with different borrowing and lending rates.

Chapter 11 — Intertemporal Choice

A. Budget constraint
1. (m_1, m_2) money in each time period is endowment
2. allow the consumer to borrow and lend at rate r
3. $c_2 = m_2 + (1+r)(m_1 - c_1)$
4. Note that this works for both borrowing and lending, as long as it is at the same interest rate.
5. Various forms of the budget constraint
   a) $(1+r)c_1 + c_2 = (1+r)m_1 + m_2$ — future value
   b) $c_1 + c_2/(1+r) = m_1 + m_2/(1+r)$ — present value
   c) choice of numeraire
   d) see Fig. 11.2
6. Preferences — convexity and monotonicity are very natural

B. Comparative statics
1. If consumer is initally a lender and interest rate increases, he remains a lender. Fig. 11.4
2. A borrower is made worse off by an increase in the interest rate. Fig. 11.5.
3. Slutsky allows us to look at effect of increasing the price of today's consumption (increasing the interest rate)
   a) change in consumption today when interest rate increases = substitution effect $+(m_1 - c_1)$ income effect.
   b) assuming normality, increase in interest rate lowers current consumption for a borrower, ambiguous for lender
   c) provide intuition

C. Inflation
1. Put in prices, $p_1 = 1$ and p_2
2. budget constraint takes the form

$$p_2 c_2 = m_2 + (1+r)(m_1 - c_1)$$

3. or,

$$c_2 = \frac{m_2}{p_2} + \frac{(1+r)}{p_2}(m_1 - c_1)$$

4. If π is rate of inflation, then $p_2 = (1+\pi)p_1$
5. $1 + \rho = (1+r)/(1+\pi)$ is the real interest rate
6. $\rho = (r - \pi)/(1+\pi)$ or $\rho \approx r - \pi$

D. Present value — a closer look
  1. Future value and present value — what do they mean?
  2. If the consumer can borrow and lend freely, then she would always prefer a consumption pattern with a greater present value.

E. Present value works for any number of periods.

F. Use of present value
  1. The one correct way to rank investment decisions.
  2. Linear operation, so relatively easy to calculate.

G. Bonds
  1. coupon x, maturity date T, face value F
  2. consols
  3. the value of a console is given by $PV = x/r$
     a) proof: $r = x \times PV$

H. Installment loans
  1. borrow some money and pay it back over a period of time
  2. what is true rate of interest?
  3. example: borrow $1,000 and pay back 12 equal installments of $100.
  4. have to value a stream of payments of $1,000, -100, \ldots -100$.
  5. turns out that the true interest rate is about 35%!

Chapter 12

Asset Markets

This chapter fits in very nicely with the present value calculations in the last chapter. The idea that all riskless assets should earn the same rate of return in equilibrium is a very powerful idea, and generally receives inadequate treatment in intermediate micro texts.

I especially like the arbitrage argument, and showing how it is equivalent to all assets selling for their present values. The applications of the Hotelling oil price model and the forest management model are quite compelling to students.

One interesting twist that you might point out in the forestry problem is that the *market* value of the standing forest will always be its present value, and that present value will grow at the rate of interest—like any other asset. However, the value of the *harvested* forest will grow more rapidly than the interest rate until we reach the optimal harvest time, and then grow less rapidly.

The problems in *Workouts* are quite practical in nature, and it is worth pointing this out to students. Emphasize that present value calculations are the meat-and-potatoes of investment analysis.

Chapter 12 — Asset Markets

A. Consider a world of perfect certainty. Then all assets must have the same rate of return.
  1. If one asset had a higher rate of return than another, who would buy the asset with the lower return?
  2. How do asset prices adjust? Answer: **Riskless arbitrage.**
    a) Two assets. Bond earns r, other asset costs p_0 now.
    b) Invest \$1 in bond, get $1 + r$ dollars tomorrow.
    c) Invest $p_0 x = 1$ dollars in other asset, get $p_1 x$ dollars tomorrow.
    d) Amounts must be equal, which says that $1 + r = p_1/p_0$.
  3. This is just another way to say present value.
    a) $p_0 = p_1/(1 + r)$.
  4. Think about the process of adjustment.

B. Example from stock market
  1. Index futures and underlying assets that make up the futures.

2. No risk in investment, even though asset values are risky, because there is a fixed relationship between the two assets at time of expiration.

C. Adjustments for differences in characteristics
   1. liquidity and transactions cost
   2. taxes
   3. form of returns — consumption return and financial return

D. Applications
   1. Depleteable resource — price of oil
      a) let p_t = price of oil at time t
      b) oil in the ground is like money in the bank, so $p_{t+1} = (1 + r)p_t$.
      c) demand equals supply over time
      d) let T = time to exhaustion, D = demand per year, and S = available supply. Hence $T = S/D$.
      e) let C = cost of next best alternative (e.g., liquified coal.)
      f) arbitrage implies $p_0 = C/(1 + r)^T$.
   2. Harvesting a forest
      a) $F(t)$ = value of forest at time t.
      b) natural to think of this increasing rapidly at first and then slowing down
      c) harvest when rate of growth of forest = rate of interest.

E. This theory tells you relationships that have to hold between asset prices, given the interest rate.

F. But what determines the interest rate?
   1. Answer: aggregate borrowing and lending behavior
   2. Or: consumption and investment choices over time.

G. What do financial institutions do?
   1. adjust interest rate so that amount people want to borrow equals amount they want to lend.
   2. change pattern of consumption possible over time. Example of college student and retiree.
   3. example of entrepeneur and investors.

Chapter 13

Uncertainty

This chapter begins with the idea of contingent consumption and an insurance market example. Make sure that you define "contingent" since a lot of students don't know the term. (The definition is given in the book on page 213.) The emphasis in this first section is on the idea that exactly the same tools that we have used earlier can be used to analyze choice under uncertainty, so it is worth talking about what happens to the budget line when the price of insurance changes, etc.

The expected utility discussion is reasonably elementary. However, it is often hard to motivate the expected utility hypothesis without seeing a lot of applications. I put it in since some schools might want to have an elementary treatment of the subject for use in other courses, such as finance courses.

The easiest application of expected utility theory that I could think of was the result that expected utility maximizers facing actuarially fair insurance would fully insure. In the next edition of the book I'm going to talk about moral hazard and adverse selection in insurance markets, and those might be fun ideas to touch on in class discussion.

The last three sections on diversification, risk spreading, and the role of the stock market are important economic ideas. I usually discuss those ideas in verbal terms and skip the details of the expected utility material. This seems like a reasonable compromise for a general purpose intermediate micro course.

Chapter 13 — Uncertainty

A. Contingent consumption
1. what consumption or wealth you will get in each possible outcome of some random event.
2. Example: rain or shine, car is wrecked or not, etc.
3. Consumer cares about pattern of contingent consumption: $U(c_1, c_2)$.
4. Market allows you to trade patterns of contingent consumption — insurance market. Insurance premium is like a relative price for the different kinds of consumption.
5. Can use standard apparatus to analyze choice of contingent consumption.

B. Utility functions
   1. preferences over the consumption in different events depends on the probabilities that the events will occur.
   2. So $u(c_1, c_2, \pi_1, \pi_2)$ will be the general form of the utility function.
   3. Under certain plausible assumptions, utility can be written as being linear in the probabilities, $p_1 u(c_1) + p_2 u(c_2)$. That is, the utility of a pattern of consumption is just the expected utility over the possible outcomes.

C. Risk aversion
   1. Shape of expected utility function describes attitudes towards risk.
   2. Draw utility of wealth and expected utility of gamble. Note that person prefers sure thing to expected value.
   3. Diversification and risk sharing

D. Role of the stock market
   1. Aids in diversification and in risk sharing.
   2. Just as entrepeneur can rearrange his consumption patters through time by going public, he can also rearrange his consumption across states of nature.

Chapter 14

Risky Assets

The first part of this chapter is just notation and review of the concepts of mean and standard deviation. If your students have had some statistics, these ideas should be pretty standard. If they haven't had any statistics, then be sure to get the basics down before proceeding.

The big idea here is in Figure 14.2. In mean-standard deviation space, the "budget constraint" is a straight line. Again, all of the technical apparatus of consumer theory can be brought to bear on analyzing this particular kind of choice problem. Ask what happens to the "price of risk" when the risk free rate goes down. What do students think this will do to the budget line, and the portfolio choice? Don't let them guess—make them give reasons for their statements.

Section 14.2 is a little bit of a fudge. I do give the actual definition of beta in the footnote on page 236, but I don't really go through the calculations for the Capital Asset Pricing Model. I may do the algebra in an appendix to this chapter in the next edition if people are interested.

The idea of the risk adjusted interest rate and the story of how returns adjust is a nice one, and should be accessible to most students who understood the case of adjustment with certainty.

It might be worth pointing out that participants in the stock market take all this stuff very seriously. There are consulting services that sell their estimates of beta for big bucks, and use them as measures of risk all the time.

Chapter 14 — Risky Assets

A. Utility depends on mean and standard deviation of wealth.
   1. utility = $u(\mu_w, \sigma_w)$
   2. this form of utility function describes tastes.

B. Invest in risky portfolio (with expected return r_m) and a riskless asset (with return r_f)
   1. suppose you invest a fraction x in the risky asset
   2. expected return = $xr_m + (1-x)r_f$
   3. standard deviation of return = $x\sigma_m$
   4. this relationship gives "budget line" as in Figure 14.2

C. At optimum we must have the price of risk equal slope of budget line:
$MRS = (r_m - r_f)/\sigma_m$
  1. the observable value $(r_m - r_f)/\sigma_m$ is the price of risk
  2. can be used to value other investments, like any other price

D. Measuring risk of a stock — depends on how it contributes to the risk of the overall portfolio.
  1. β_i = covariance of asset i with the market portfolio/standard deviation of market portfolio
  2. roughly speaking, β_i measures how sensitive a particular asset is to the market as a whole
  3. assets with negative betas are worth a lot, since they reduce risk
  4. how returns adjust — plot the market line

E. Equilibrium
  1. risk adjusted rates of return should be equalized.
  2. in equations:

$$r_i - \beta_i(r_m - r_f) = r_j - \beta_j(r_m - r_f)$$

  3. suppose asset j is riskless, then

$$r_i - \beta_i(r_m - r_f) = r_f$$

  4. this is called the Capital Asset Pricing Model (CAPM)

F. Examples of use of CAPM
  1. how returns adjust — see Figure 14.4
  2. public utility rate of return choice
  3. ranking mutual funds
  4. investment analysis, public and private

Chapter 15

Consumer's Surplus

The basic idea of consumer's surplus is given in Section 15.1 for those who just want the standard intuitive discussion. But since we've spent so much time in this book doing consumer theory carefully, I wanted to give a careful treatment of this confusing topic for people who really wanted to get it right.

One thing that I should point out is that I use a slightly non-standard terminology on page 244. What I call "total consumer's surplus" is usually called "total benefits." The standard terminology is more descriptive, and I intend to remove the "total surplus" term in the next edition.

The big problem in most treatments is that authors talk about utility when they first introduce consumer theory and talk about consumer's surplus at the end of their treatment of consumers, and never say *anything* about the connection between the two ideas. I want to make it clear that consumer's surplus *is* a utility measure (in a special case) and is an approximation to a utility function in general.

The best way to do this, in my opinion, is to introduce the idea of money metric utility. Students get the geometric idea pretty easily, but the algebra poses some hurdles. Be sure to do the examples so that the students can see some concrete calculations.

If the student understands the idea of the money metric utility, the ideas of the compensating and equivalent variation are easy. I use the example of a tax, but another example that is somewhat closer to home is the idea of cost-of-living indexes for various places to live. Take an example of an executive in New York who is offered a job in Tucson. Relative prices differ drastically in these two locations. How much money would the executive need at the Tucson prices to make him as well off as he was in New York? How much money would his New York company have to pay him to make him as well off in New York as he would be if he moved to Tucson?

The next section, section 15.5, shows that the compensating and the equivalent variation are the same in the case of quasilinear utility. We then go on to calculate the money metric utility function in this case. The big calculation here is the one illustrated in Figure 15.5—why it is that the height of the intercept of the indifference curve in part *A* is given by the area under the demand curve in *B*.

The algebraic treatment really is optional. It is essentially repeating the proof of the fundamental theorem of calculus. In the next edition, I think that this will go in the appendix, along with an expanded calculus treatment.

Chapter 15 — Consumer's Surplus

A. Basic idea of consumer's surplus
1. Want a measure of how much a person is willing to pay for something. How much a person is willing to sacrifice of one thing to get something else.
2. price measures marginal willingness to pay, so add up over all different outputs to get total willingness to pay.
3. Total consumer's surplus, net consumer's surplus, change in consumer's surplus. See Figure 15.1.

B. How do we relate this to utility theory?
1. Willingness to pay in general depends on prices — how much money you are willing to sacrifice to get something depends on what the prices are.
2. Money metric utility
   a) how much money would you need at one set of prices to be as well off as you would be consuming some particular bundle?
   b) See Figure 15.2.
   c) in general depends on prices
   d) compensating and equivalent variations — Figure 15.3
3. How do we recover money metric utility (willingness to pay) from the demand curve?
   a) In quasilinear case differences don't depend on prices — can measure difference between indifference curves at any prices.
   b) In particular use prices that reduce demand to zero. See Figure 15.4.
   c) Special case of quasilinear preferences $v(x) + y = v(0) + y'$, so $y' = v(x) - v(0) + y$.
4. In special case of quasilinear preferences $p(x) = v'(x)$. So just integrate the demand curve.
5. That is, by fundamental theorem of calculus:

$$v(x) - v(0) = \int_0^x v'(t)\, dt = \int_0^x p(t)\, dt$$

C. Area under the demand curve measures quasilinear utility — good approximation to money metric utility in general.

D. Also can argue by areas of rectangles — Figure 15.5.

E. Producer's surplus — area above supply curve. Change in producer's surplus. etc.
1. Figure 15.8.
2. Intuitive interpretation.

Chapter 16

Market Demand

It would be logical to proceed directly to discussing the theory of the firm, but I wanted to take a break from pure optimization analysis, and discuss instead some ideas from equilibrium analysis. I think that this switch of gears helps students to see where they are going and why all this stuff is useful.

The most important idea in this chapter is elasticity. Elasticity was introduced earlier in Chapter 6, but I never did anything much with it there. Here we can really put it through it's paces. The calculations here are all pretty standard, but I'm more careful than usual to distinguish between elasticity and the absolute value of elasticity.

If you use calculus, make sure that you compute elasticities for the linear and log-linear cases.

I love the Laffer curve example in the Appendix. Here are some totally trivial elasticity calculations that give a major insight into a big policy issue. I really push on this example in class to show people how what they have learned can really help in making informed judgments about policy.

Chapter 16 — Market Demand

A. To get market demand, just add up individual demands.
  1. add horizontally
  2. properly account for zero demands; Figure 16.2

B. Often think of market behaving like a single individual
  1. **representative consumer** model
  2. not true in general, but OK for this course

C. Inverse of aggregate demand curve measures the MRS for each individual.

D. Reservation price model
  1. appropriate when one good comes in large discrete units
  2. reservation price is price that just makes person indifferent
  3. defined by $u(0, m) = u(1, m - p_1^*)$
  4. see Figure 16.3

5. add up demand curves to get aggregate demand curve
6. see Figure 16.4

E. Elasticity
1. measures responsiveness of demand to price
2.
$$\epsilon = \frac{p}{q}\frac{dq}{dp}$$

3. example for linear demand curve
   a) for linear demand, $q = a - bp$, so $\epsilon = -bp/q = -bp/(a - bp)$
   b) note that $\epsilon = -1$ when we are halfway down the demand curve.
   c) see Figure 16.5
4. suppose demand takes form $q = Ap^{-b}$.
5. then elasticity is given by

$$\epsilon = -\frac{p}{q}bAp^{-b-1} = \frac{-bAp^{-b}}{Ap^{-b}} = -b$$

6. thus elasticity is constant along this demand curve
7. note that $\log q = \log A - b\log p$
8. What does elasticity depend on? In general how many and how close substitutes a good has.

F. How does revenue change when you change price?
1. $R = pq$, so $\Delta R = (p + dp)(q + dq) = pq + pdq + qdp + dpdq$.
2. last term is very small relative to others
3. $dR/dp = q + pdq/dp$.
4. See Figure 16.6.
5. $dR/dp > 0$ when $|e| < 1$.

G. How does revenue change as you change quantity?
1. Marginal revenue $= MR = dR/dq = p + qdp/dq = p[1 + 1/\epsilon]$.
2. **elastic:** absolute value of elasticity greater than 1.
3. **inelastic:** absolute value of elasticity less than 1.
4. Application: Monopolist never sets a price where $|\epsilon| < 1$ — because could always make more money by reducing output.

H. Marginal revenue curve
1. Always the case that $dR/dq = p + qdp/dq$.
2. In case of linear (inverse) demand, $p = a - bq$, $MR = dR/dq = p - bq = (a - bq) - bq = a - 2bq$.

I. Laffer curve
1. How does *tax revenue* respond to changes in tax rates?
2. Idea of Laffer curve: Figure 16.9.
3. Theory is OK, but what do the magnitudes have to be?
4. Model of labor market, Figure 16.10.
5. Tax revenue $= T = t\bar{w}S(w(t))$ where $w(t) = (1 - t)\bar{w}$.
6. When is $dT/dt < 0$?

7. Calculate derivative to find that Laffer curve will have negative slope when

$$\frac{dS}{dw}\frac{w}{S} > \frac{1-t}{t}$$

8. So if tax rate is .50, would need labor supply elasticity greater than 1 to get Laffer effect.

9. Very unlikely to see magnitude this large

Chapter 17

Equilibrium

Some people have suggested that it would make more sense to save this chapter until after deriving supply curves, but I still feel that it is better position here. After all, the students have seen labor supply curves and net supply curves earlier in the course, and it isn't any shock to see demand and supply treated together now.

The first part of the chapter is pretty standard, although I go to extra pains to be clear to emphasize the idea of the inverse demand and supply curves. I tell the students that the inverse functions describe the same relationship, but just from a different viewpoint.

The treatment of taxes is more thorough than is usually the case. I like the idea of looking at taxation in several different ways. It is a good idea to emphasize that there are really *four* different variables in a taxation problem: the demand price, p_d, the supply price p_s, the amount demanded, q_d, and the amount supplied, q_s. When confronted with a tax problem, the *first* thing you should do is write down the relationships between these four variables.

The most typical set of relationships is

$$p_d = p_s + t$$
$$q_d = q_s.$$

But other relationships are possible. For example, if a tax-in-kind is levied, as in the King Kanuta problem in the workbook, then the amount demanded will be *different* than the amount supplied. In fact the only systematic way to work out King Kanuta it to be very careful about writing down the relationships among the four variables.

You should emphasize that the incidence of the tax doesn't depend on the legal requirements of who is responsible for paying the tax. The Social Security tax is a really nice example for this. The Social Security tax is based on 15% of the nominal wage. The employer "pays" half of the tax and the worker "pays" the other half. But of course, this is a fiction. Show the students how we could redefine the nominal wage so that the worker paid all the tax or the employer paid all the tax, and leave the take-home pay of the worker unchanged.

This leads naturally to a discussion of the real incidence of a tax, the ideas of "passing along a tax," and so on.

I like to use the old red pencil-blue pencil example at this point. If red pencils and blue pencils are perfect substitutes in consumption and production, what is the impact of a tax on red pencils? There is a big output effect—consumption and production of red pencils would drop to zero. But what is the effect on consumer utility and producer profits? Zero—consumers and producers just substitute to other activities. This leads naturally to the idea of measuring the impact of a tax via consumer and producer surplus, as is done in Section 17.8.

The two examples that end the chapter, the market for loans and the food subsidies, are really wonderful examples and deserve careful discussion. I like to point out to the students how confused they would be in trying to understand these examples without the analytic methods of economics.

Chapter 17 — Equilibrium

A. Supply curves — measure amount the supplier wants to supply at each price
   1. net supply from Chapter 9.
   2. supply of labor from Chapter 10.

B. Equilibrium
   1. competitive market — each agent takes prices as outside of his or her control.
      a) many small agents
      b) a few agents who think that the others keep fixed prices
   2. equilibrium price — that price where desired demand equals desired supply
      a) $D(p) = S(p)$
   3. special cases — Figure 17.1
      a) vertical supply — quantity determined by supply, price determined by demand
      b) horizontal supply — quantity determined by demand, price determined by supply
   4. an equivalent definition of equilibrium: where inverse demand curve crosses inverse supply curve
      a) $P_d(q) = P_s(q)$
   5. Examples with linear curves

C. Comparative statics
   1. Shift each curve separately
   2. Shift both curves together

D. Taxes — nice example of comparative statics
   1. Demand price and supply price — different in case of taxes
   2. $p_d = p_s + t$
   3. Equilibrium happens when $D(p_d) = S(p_s)$
   4. Put equations together:
      a) $D(p_s + t) = S(p_s)$
      b) or $D(p_d) = S(p_d - t)$

5. Also can solve using inverse demands:
   a) $P_d(q) = P_s(q) + t$.
   b) or, $P_d(q) - t = P_s(q)$.
6. Pictures — Figure 17.3 and Figure 17.4

E. Passing along a tax — Figure 17.5
   1. flat supply curve
   2. vertical supply curve

F. Deadweight loss of a tax — Figure 17.7
   1. Benefits to consumers
   2. Benefits to producers
   3. Value of lost output

G. Market for loans
   1. Tax system subsidizes borrowing, tax lending.
   2. With no tax: $D(r^*) = S(r^*)$
   3. With tax: $D((1-t)r') = S((1-t)r')$
   4. Hence, $(1-t)r' = r^*$. Quantity transacted is same.
   5. See Figure 17.8.

H. Food subsidies
   1. buy up harvest and resell at half price.
   2. before program: $D(p^*) + K = S$
   3. after program: $D(\hat{p}/2) + K = S$
   4. so, $\hat{p} = 2p^*$.
   5. Subsidized mortgages — unless the housing stock changes, no effect on cost.

I. Pareto efficiency
   1. efficient output is where demand equals supply
   2. because that is where demand price equals supply price
   3. that is, the marginal willingness to buy equals the marginal willingess to sell.
   4. deadweight loss measures loss due to inefficiency

Chapter 18

Technology

Here we start our discussion of firm behavior. This chapter discusses the concepts that economists use to describe technologies. Almost all of the material here is quite straightforward, especially given all of the exposure that the students have had to indifference curves, utility functions, etc.

Since students are by now quite familiar with Cobb-Douglas utility functions you should be sure to emphasize that monotonic transformations are no longer warranted, since now the value of the production function represents some real, physical amount of output. Of course, you could choose to measure the output in different units, in which case the parameters of the production function would change. But given the units of measurement, we don't have any choice about how to measure production.

The new ideas are the ideas of the short and long run, and the idea of returns to scale. These ideas will show up several times in the next few chapters, so the initial discussion is rather brief. In the workbook we give several examples of technologies and ask about their return-to-scale properties. It's a good idea to work one or two examples to show the students what is going on.

Chapter 18 — Technology

A. Need a way to describe the technological constraints facing a firm
  1. what patterns of inputs and outputs are feasible?

B. Inputs
  1. factors of production
  2. classifications: Labor, land, raw materials, capital
  3. usually try to measure in flows
  4. financial capital vs. physical capital

C. Describing technological constraints
  1. production set — combinations of inputs and outputs that are feasible patterns of production
  2. production function — upper boundary of production set
  3. see Figure 18.1

    4. isoquants — all combinations of inputs that produce constant level of output

    5. isoquants (constant output) are just like indifference curves (constant utility)

D. Examples of isoquants
1. fixed proportions — one man one shovel
2. perfect substitutes — pencils
3. Cobb-Douglas — $y = Ax_1^a x_2^b$
4. can't take monotonic transformations any more!

E. Well-behaved technologies
1. monotonic — more inputs produce more output
2. convex — averages produce more than extremes

F. Marginal product
1. MP_1 is how much extra output you get from increasing the input of good 1
2. holding good 2 fixed.
3. $MP_1 = \partial f(x_1, x_2)/\partial x_1$

G. Technical rate of substitution
1. like the marginal rate of substitution
2. given by the ratio of marginal products
3.
$$TRS = \frac{dx_2}{dx_1} = -\frac{\partial f/\partial x_1}{\partial f/\partial x_2}$$

H. Diminishing marginal product
1. more and more of a single input produces more output, but at a decreasing rate. See Figure 18.5.
2. the "law of diminishing returns"

I. Diminishing technical rate of substitution
1. equivalent to convexity
2. note difference between diminishing MP and diminishing TRS

J. Long run and short run
1. All factors varied — long run
2. Some factors fixed — short run

K. Returns to scale
1. constant returns — baseline case
2. increasing returns
3. decreasing returns

Chapter 19

Profit Maximization

I start out the chapter with a careful definition of profits: you must value each output and input at its *market* price, whether or not the good is actually sold on a market. This is because the market price measures the price at which you *could* sell the input, and thus measures the true opportunity cost of using the factor in this production process rather than in some other use.

I give some commonplace examples of this idea, but more examples won't hurt. It's good to get this idea across carefully now, since it will make it much easier to discuss the idea of zero long run profits when it comes up. This idea is usually a stumbling block for students and a careful examination about just what it is that goes into the definition of economic profits helps a lot in getting the point across.

The material on stock market value is something that is left out of most texts, but since we have had a careful discussion of asset markets, we can draw the link between maximizing profits and maximizing stock market value.

The rest of the material in the chapter is fairly standard. The one novel feature is the revealed profitability approach to firm behavior. This section, Section 19.10, shows how you can use the fact that the firm is maximizing profits to derive comparative statics conclusions. If you have treated revealed preference in consumption carefully, students should have no trouble with this approach.

Chapter 19 — Profit Maximization

A. Profits defined to be revenues minus costs
1. value each output and input at its market price — even if it is not sold on a market.
2. It could be sold, so using it in production rather than somewhere else is an **opportunity cost**.
3. measure in terms of flows. In general, maximize present value of flow of profits

B. Stock market value

    1. in world of certainty, stock market value equals present value of stream of profits

    2. so maximizing stock market value is the same as maximizing pv of profits

    3. uncertainty — more complicated, but still works

C. Short run and long run maximization

    1. fixed factors — plant and equipment

    2. quasi-fixed factors — can be eliminated if operate at zero output (advertising, lights, heat, etc.)

D. Short run maximization

    1. max $pf(x) - wx$

    2. $pf'(x^*) - w = 0$

    3. in words: the value of the marginal product equals wage rate

    4. comparative statics: change w and p and see how x and $f(x)$ respond

E. Long run profit maximization

    1. $p\partial f/\partial x_1 = w_1$, $p\partial f/\partial x_2 = w_2$

F. Profit maximization and returns to scale

    1. constant returns to scale implies profits are zero

        a) note that this doesn't means that economic factors aren't all appropriately rewarded

        b) use examples

    2. increasing returns to scale implies competitive model doesn't make sense

G. revealed profitability

    1. simple, rigorous way to do comparative statics.

    2. observe two choices, at time t and time s

    3. (p^t, w^t, y^t, x^t) and (p^s, w^s, y^s, x^s)

    4. if firm is profit maximizing, then must have:

$$p^t y^t - w^t x^t \geq p^t y^s - w^t x^s$$
$$p^s y^s - w^s x^s \geq p^s y^t - w^s x^t$$

    5. write these equations as

$$p^t y^t - w^t x^t \geq p^t y^s - w^t x^s$$
$$-p^s y^t + w^s x^t \geq -p^s y^s + w^s x^s$$

    6. add these two inequalities:

$$(p^t - p^s)y^t - (w^t - w^s)x^t \geq (p^t - p^s)y^s - (w^t - w^s)x^s$$

    7. rearrange:

$$(p^t - p^s)(y^t - y^s) - (w^t - w^s)(x^t - x^s) \geq 0$$

    8. or

$$\Delta p \Delta y - \Delta w \Delta x \geq 0$$

    9. implications for changing output and factor prices.

Chapter 20

Cost Minimization

The treatment in this chapter is pretty standard, except for the material on revealed cost minimization. However, by now the students have seen this kind of material three times, so they shouldn't have much difficulty with it.

It is worthwhile emphasizing the difference between the unconditional factor demand functions of Chapter 19 and the conditional factor demands of Chapter 20. Here we are looking at the best input choice holding the physical level of output fixed. In chapter 19 we looked for the best input choice holding the price out output fixed, where the level of output adjusted to its most profitable level.

The material on returns to scale and the cost function is important to get across, as we will refer in future chapters to cases of increasing average cost, decreasing average cost, etc. It is important to be able to link these ideas to the returns-to-scale ideas discussed in earlier chapters.

The material in sections 20.4 and 20.5 are laying groundwork for ideas that will be further explored in the next chapter. Both sections are just exploring various definitions. Section 20.4 will be used in discussing the shapes of short-run and long-run cost curves. Section 20.5 will be used to distinguish between two different concepts of fixed costs in the short and long run.

Chapter 20 — Cost Minimization

A. Cost minimization problem

  1. minimize cost to produce some given level of output:

$$\min_{x_1, x_2} \ w_1 x_1 + w_2 x_2$$

$$\text{s.t. } f(x_1, x_2) = y.$$

  2. see Figure 20.1 for geometric solution: slope of isoquant equals slope of isocost curve.

  3. in equations, $w_1/w_2 = MP_1/MP_2$

  4. optimal choices of factors are the **conditional factor demand functions**

5. optimal cost is the **cost function**.
6. Examples
    a) if $f(x_1, x_2) = x_1 + x_2$, then $c(w_1, w_2, y) = \min\{w_1, w_2\}y$
    b) if $f(x_1, x_2) = \min\{x_1, x_2\}$, then $c(w_1, w_2, y) = (w_1 + w_2)y$
    c) can calculate other answers using calculus

B. Revealed cost minimization
    1. suppose we hold output fixed and observe choices at different factor prices.
    2. when prices are (w_1^s, w_2^s) choice is (x_1^s, x_2^s) and when prices are (w_1^t, w_2^t) choice is (x_1^t, x_2^t).
    3. If choices minimize cost, then we must have:

    $$w_1^t x_1^t + w_2^t x_2^t \leq w_1^t x_1^s + w_2^t x_2^s$$
    $$w_1^s x_1^s + w_2^s x_2^s \leq w_1^s x_1^t + w_2^s x_2^t$$

    4. This is the **Weak Axiom of Cost Minimization (WACM)**
    5. Multiply the second equation by -1 and get:

    $$w_1^t x_1^t + w_2^t x_2^t \leq w_1^t x_1^s + w_2^t x_2^s$$
    $$-w_1^s x_1^t - w_2^s x_2^t \leq -w_1^s x_1^s - w_2^s x_2^s$$

    6. Add these two inequalites:

    $$(w_1^t - w_1^s)(x_1^t - x_1^s) + (w_2^t - w_2^s)(x_2^t - x_2^s) \leq 0$$
    $$\Delta w_1 \Delta x_1 + \Delta w_2 \Delta x_2 \leq 0$$

    7. Roughly speaking, "factor demands move opposite changes in factor prices."
    8. In particular, *factor demand curves must slope downward.*

C. Returns to scale and the cost function
    1. increasing returns to scale implies decreasing AC
    2. constant returns implies constant AC
    3. decreasing returns implies increasing AC

D. Long run and short run costs
    1. long run: all inputs variable
    2. short run: some inputs fixed

E. Fixed and quasifixed costs
    1. fixed: must be paid, whatever the output level
    2. quasifixed: only paid when output is positive. (heating, lighting, etc.)

Cost Curves

Now we get to the standard meat-and-potatoes of undergraduate microeconomics. The first sections lays out the rationale behind U-shaped average cost curves. To me the most natural rationale is constant fixed costs and increasing average variable costs.

The link between marginal costs and variable costs is left out of a lot of books, but is important for understanding producer's surplus.

I am very keen on the cost function $c(y) = y^2 + 1$, and use it in a lot of the examples. Be sure to go over its derivation and show how it gives rise to the various cost curves.

The material on how to get the long-run cost curve from the short-run cost curve is pretty straightforward. It may be a little easier to first do section 21.5, and then draw in a lot of extra short-run curves to get to the diagram in Figure 21.7.

Chapter 21 — Cost curves

A. Family of cost curves
  1. total cost: $c(y) = c_v(y) + F$
  2.
$$\frac{c(y)}{y} = \frac{c_v(y)}{y} + \frac{F}{y}$$
$$AC = AVC + AFC$$

  3. See Figure 21.1
  4. marginal costs are change in costs due to change in output $c'(y) = dc(y)/dy = dc_v(y)/dy$.
     a) marginal costs equals AVC at zero units of output
     b) goes through minimum point of AC and AVC
        1)
$$\frac{d}{dy}\frac{c(y)}{y} = \frac{yc'(y) - c(y)}{y^2}$$

        2) this is negative (for example), when $c'(y) < c(y)/y$.

c) fundamental theorem of calculus implies that

$$c_v(y) = \int_0^y c'(t)\, dt$$

d) geometrically: the area under the marginal cost curve gives the total variable costs

e) intuitively: the maginal cost curve measures the cost of each additional unit. So adding up the MCs gives the variable costs.

B. Example $c(y) = y^2 + 1$
  1. $AC = y + 1/y$
  2. $AVC = y$
  3. $MC = 2y$

C. Long run costs from short run costs
  1. average costs Figure 21.8
  2. marginal costs: Figure 21.9

Chapter 22

Firm Supply

After all that material on technology and optimization problems, it is fun to get back to the behavior of "real" economic units. I devote a fair amount of time to laying out the idea of a purely competitive market. It is important to distinguish between the definition of a competitive market and the rationale for that definition. The *definition* is that it is a market where firms take the market price as being given, independent of the actions of any particular firm. The usual rationale for this assumption is that each firm is a negligible part of the market.

However, it is also important to emphasize that even markets with a middling number of firms may act in a reasonably competitive fashion. For example, if each firm believes that the other firms will keep their prices fixed no matter what price it charges, we would have a model where each firm would face an essentially flat demand curve for it's product. This idea—the distinction between the market demand curve and the demand curve facing a firm—is an important one to get across. Economists often talk about a quantity-setting firm or a price-setting firm, but these ideas are really rather unnatural. Real firms set both variables. But a firm in a highly competitive market has no real choice about what price to set—it has to meet the price at which everyone else is selling if it wants to make any sales at all. For a competitive firm, the only real choice variable is how much it wants to sell at the going market price.

The treatment on producer surplus is correct, but it may help to point out one additional fact. In Figure 22.6, producer's surplus can also be represented as the area to the left of the marginal cost/supply curve between p_1 and p_2. This is because the area of the box in the diagram gives the producer's surplus up to y_1 and the area of the "triangle" gives the producer's surplus between y_1 and y_2, as depicted.

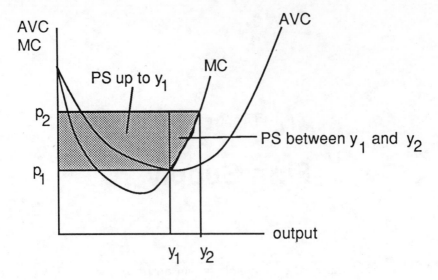

Chapter 22 — Firm Supply

A. Firms face two sorts of constraints
  1. technological constraints — summarize in cost function
  2. market constraints — how will consumers and other firms react to a given firm's choice?

B. Pure competition
  1. formally — takes market price as given, outside of any particular firm's control
  2. example: many small price-takers
  3. demand curve facing a competitive firm — Figure 22.1

C. Supply decision of competitive firm
  1. $\max_y py - c(y)$
  2. first order condition: $p = c'(y)$
  3. price equals marginal cost determines supply as function of price
  4. second order condition: $-c''(y) \leq 0$, or $c'(y) \geq 0$.
  5. only upward sloping part of marginal cost curve matters
  6. is it profitable to operate at all?
    a) compare $py - c_v(y) - F$ to $-F$
    b) profits from operating will be greater when $p > c_v(y)/y$
    c) operate when price covers average variable costs

D. So supply curve is upward sloping part of MC curve that lies above the AVC curve
  1. see Figure 22.3

E. Inverse supply curve
  1. $p = c'(y)$ measures the marginal cost curve directly

F. Example $c(y) = y^2 + 1$
  1. $p = 2y$ gives the (inverse) supply curve
  2. is $p \geq AVC$?
    a) yes, since $2y \geq y$ for all $y \geq 0$.
  3. See Figure 22.8

G. Producer's surplus

    1. producer's surplus is defined to be $py - c_v(y)$

    2. since $c_v(y)$ = area under marginal cost curve

    3. producer's surplus is also the area above the marginal cost curve

    4. see Figure 22.7

    5. and Figure 22.3 again

H. Long run supply — use long run MC. In long run price must be greater than AC

I. Special case — constant AC (CRS): flat supply curve

    1. see Figure 22.11

Chapter 23

Industry Supply

The treatment of industry supply in the case of free entry given in this chapter is more satisfactory than that one typically sees. I simply draw the supply curves for different numbers of firms and look for the lowest intersection that allows for nonnegative profits. After drawing a few examples of this sort, students are quite ready to believe that the equilibrium price can never get very far above minimum average cost. This naturally leads to the standard approximation of taking the supply curve of a competitive industry as being flat at price equals minimum average cost.

The idea that long-run profits are zero in sections 23.4 and 23.5 is a very important one, and often misunderstood. Be sure to emphasize the exact sense in which it is true.

The other big idea in this chapter is the idea of economic rent. I like to express the relationship between the two ideas this way:

Long run profits in competitive industries are always zero. If there are no barriers to entry, then entry competes profits away to zero. If there are specific factors that prevent entry, then competition to acquire those factors forces profits to zero. In a sense, it is always the attempt to enter an industry that forces profits to zero: new firms either enter an industry by adding firms to the industry or by buying out existing firms. The first form of entry increases supply and decreases prices; the second form of entry doesn't affect supply, but simply pushes up the factor prices and costs. But either way, profits get driven to zero.

I like the discussion of economic rent and of the politics of rent quite a bit. One great example of rent seeking is to discuss the social costs of theft. It's not the transfer of property that represents a social loss, it's all the expense that one has to go to *prevent* theft that represents the social loss. The true social cost of theft is not the lost TVs, but the cost of the locks on the doors! If students appreciate the insight in this sentence, they are well on their way to becoming real economists. (If they don't appreciate the insight, they'll just think you're nuts.)

A. Short run industry supply
   1. sum of the MC curves
   2. equilibrium in short run
      a) look for point where $D(p) = S(p)$
      b) can then measure profits of firms
      c) see Figure 23.2

B. Long run industry supply
   1. change to long run technology
   2. entry and exit by firms
      a) look at curves with different number of firms
      b) find lowest curve consistent with nonnegative profits
      c) see Figure 23.3

C. Long run supply curve
   1. exact — see Figure 23.4
   2. approximate — flat at $p =$ minimum AC
   3. like replication argument

D. Taxation in long and short run
   1. see Figure 23.6
   2. in industry with extry and exit
   3. part of tax is borne by each side
   4. long run — all borne by consumers

E. Meaning of zero profits
   1. pure economic profit means anyone can get it
   2. a mature industry may show accounting profits, but economic profits are probably zero

F. Economic rent
   1. what if some factors are scarce in long run?
      a) licenses — liquor, taxicab
      b) raw materials, land, etc.
   2. fixed from viewpoint of industry, variable from viewpoint of firm
   3. in this case, industry can only support a certain number of firms
   4. whatever factor is preventing entry earns rents
      a) always the possibility of entry that drives profits to zero
      b) if profits are being made, firms enter industry by
         1) bringing in new resources
         2) bidding up prices of existing resources
   5. see Figure 23.7
   6. discount flow of rents to get asset value
   7. politics of rent
      a) rents are a pure surplus payment
      b) but people compete for those rents
      c) taxicab licenses — current holders want very much to prevent entry. Rent seeking.
      d) subsidies and rents — incidence of subsidy falls on the rents
         1) tobacco subsidies
         2) farm policy in general

Chapter 24

Markets

This is an examples chapter—a lot of fun examples of economic analysis. The capsule history of energy economics in the seventies contains some *wonderful* examples of the application (or misapplication) of economic ideas. Students really like it, so be sure to go over these ideas.

The parrot smuggling example is also very nice since it leads to a surprising conclusion: making an activity illegal may induce criminals to adopt inferior technologies and end up causing more harm than if the activity weren't illegal in the first place. If you are brave, you might like to talk about prostitution in this context.

In the first three printings there is a typo in the middle of page 410 that can cause problems. The probability of getting caught should be π, not πx.

Chapter 24 — Markets

A. Discuss some examples of economic analysis of markets

B. Oil markets
   1. In 1974 OPEC raised the price of oil
   2. Congress thought gasoline prices would rise and attempted to hold them down by creating 2 tiered oil pricing system
      a) foreign oil sold for $10 a barrel
      b) domestic oil sold for $5 a barrel
   3. effect on supply of gasoline
      a) what did MC curve look like?
         1) takes jump when domestic supply is exhausted.
         2) see Figure 24.1
      b) equilibrium price is not affected since cost of marginal barrel (the foreign oil) doesn't change.
   4. price controls
      a) so Dept. of Energy set prices in relation to costs
      b) gasoline shortages due to regional misallocations
   5. entitlement program
      a) each barrel of foreign oil entitled one to buy a barrel of cheap domestic oil

  b) this was a subsidy of imported oil!

  c) see Figure 24.2

6. windfall profits tax

  a) $p = (1 - t)c'(y)$

  b) discouraged full extraction of oil

C. Parrot smuggling

  1. birds sell for a lot. Make export illegal has two effects

    a) raises costs

    b) reduces supply due to poor smuggling technology

  2. number of birds exported $= x$

  3. probability of getting caught is π

  4. fine is F, so expected fine is $\pi x F$

  5. $kx =$ number of birds that survive shipment

  6. Profit maximization problem is:

$$\max_x p(1 - \pi)kx - c(x) - \pi F x$$

  7. First order condition is

$$p(1 - \pi)k - \pi F = c'(x).$$

  8. Or,

$$p = \frac{c'(x)}{(1 - \pi)k} + \frac{\pi F}{(1 - \pi)k}.$$

  9. shift and tilt of supply curve. See Figure 24.5.

  10. Equilibrium condition: Demand $= (1 - \pi)kS(p)$

  11. result: could be more birds taken from wild than before

Monopoly

This rather long chapter discusses the theory of monopoly and compares it to that of competition. The big idea here is the inefficiency of monopoly. The first way to drive it home is to use the fundamental definition of Pareto improvement: whenever price exceeds marginal cost, there must be a whole set of transactions that are Pareto improving. The second way is to add up the consumer and producer surpluses to measure the deadweight loss of monopoly.

The example of an optimal patent life is a nice way to illustrate the why society might want to allow certain kinds of monopolies. I usually talk about the current hot topic of software manufacturers wanting to protect the "look and feel" of their software.

I have very minimal treatment of monopsony in this chapter since I think that it is such a slight variation on the ideas of monopoly that it isn't worth all that much discussion. But you can take some of the ideas I have used in the treatment of monopoly and discuss these in a monopsony context. For example: is monopsony inefficient? Why? What does price discrimination look like in a monopsony market?

Chapter 25 — Monopoly

A. Profit maximization
1. max $r(y) - c(y)$ implies $r'(y) = c'(y)$
2. max $p(y)y - c(y)$ implies $p(y) + p'(y)y = c'(y)$
3. can also write this as

$$p(y)\left[1 + \frac{dp}{dy}\frac{y}{p}\right] = c'(y).$$

4. or, $p(y)[1 + 1/\epsilon] = c'(y)$
5. linear case
   a) in case of linear demand, $p = a - by$, marginal revenue is given by $MR = a - 2by$
   b) see Figure 25.1
6. constant elasticity, $q = Ap^\epsilon$
   a) in this case, $MR = p[1 + 1/\epsilon]$

    b) so, optimal condition is $p[1 + 1/\epsilon] = c'(y)$

    c) markup on marginal cost

    d) see Figure 25.2.

B. Taxes

    1. linear case — price goes up by half of tax. Figure 25.3

    2. log case — price goes up by more than tax, since price is a markup on MC.

C. Inefficiency of monopoly.

    1. Pareto efficient means no way to make some group better off without hurting some other group.

    2. Pareto *in*efficient means that there *is* some way to make some group better off without hurting some other group.

    3. Monopoly is Pareto inefficient since $P > MC$

    4. Measure the deadweight loss — value of lost output

    5. See Figure 25.5.

D. Patents

    1. sometimes we want to pay this cost of inefficiency

    2. patents: tradeoff of innovation against monopoly losses

E. Natural monopoly

    1. public utilities (gas, electricity, telephone) are often thought of as **natural monopolies**.

    2. occurs when $p = mc$ is unprofitable — decreasing AC

    3. Figure 25.6

    4. often occurs when fixed costs are big and marginal costs are small

    5. how to handle

        a) government operates and covers deficit from general revenues

        b) regulate and price at set price $= AC$

F. Cause of monopoly

    1. MES large relative to size of market

    2. collusion

    3. law (oranges, sports, etc.)

    4. trademarks, copyrights, brand names, etc.

G. Price discrimination

    1. first degree — perfect price discrimination

        a) gives Pareto efficient output

        b) same as take it or leave it offer

        c) producer gets all surplus

    2. second degree – nonlinear pricing

        a) hard problem to solve

        b) biggest purchaser pays MC

    3. third degree – most common

        a)

$$\max\ p_1(y_1)y_1 + p_2(y_2)y_2 - c(y_1 + y_2)$$

b) gives us the first order conditions

$$p_1 + p_1'(y_1)y_1 = c'(y_1 + y_2)$$
$$p_2 + p_2'(y_2)y_2 = c'(y_1 + y_2)$$

c) or,

$$p_1[1 - 1/|\epsilon_1|] = MC$$
$$p_2[1 - 1/|\epsilon_2|] = MC$$

d) result: if $p_1 > p_2$, then $\epsilon_1 < \epsilon_2$.

e) more elastic users pay lower prices

H. Monopolistic competition
   1. rare to see pure monopoly
   2. product differentiation – so some market power
   3. free entry
   4. result — excess capacity theorem
      a) see Figure 25.9
      b) (but is it really?)

Chapter 26

Oligopoly

This chapter is a serious attempt to convey some of the standard models of strategic interaction to intermediate microeconomics students. This is an ambitious goal, but with some motivation it can be done. I have pursued a middle ground in this chapter between the traditional approach to oligopoly and the more modern game theoretic approach.

The first model analyzed is the standard Cournot model. I have been careful to phrase the concept of a Cournot equilibrium as an equilibrium in beliefs as well as actions—each firm is maximizing given its beliefs about the other firm's choices, and each firm finds that it's beliefs are confirmed in equilibrium. I find that it is very useful to calculate out an equilibrium example, so that students can see the richness of the idea involved. The graphical treatment is also very helpful.

Section 26.3, on adjustment to equilibrium, is a little bit of a cheat. This is not really consistent with a thoroughgoing game theoretic analysis, but I put it in anyway since the students seem to like it. It shows in a graphic way how an apparently sensible adjustment process can lead to the Cournot equilibrium.

Section 26.4, on many firms, is a very nice illustration of what the idea of a "demand curve facing a firm" looks like. The idea that a Cournot equilibrium approaches the competitive equilibrium as market shares goes to zero is a useful one, and the calculations in this section motivate this idea quite powerfully.

Section 26.5 on collusion is also very important. I usually motivate this using OPEC as an example. Each firm negotiates to set a quota that maximizes overall cartel profits ... and then each firm goes home and tries to cheat on the cartel. It is worth pointing out that equation 26.3 implies that the smaller firm 1's output is, relative to firm 2, the more incentive firm 2 has to cheat on the cartel agreement. This is true since

$$\frac{\Delta \pi_1}{\Delta y_1} = -\frac{\Delta p}{\Delta Y} y_2^*.$$

If the output of firm 2 is large, then $\Delta \pi_1 / \Delta y_1$ will be large.

In Figure 26.3 it is useful to point out that the reason that we get a whole range of outputs that maximize industry profits is that we have assumed that marginal costs are identical—in fact, we have assumed that they are zero for both firms. If the marginal costs were different, we would most likely get a unique cartel solution.

I usually motivate the Stackelberg solution by talking about an industry with a dominant firm such as IBM. Another example is to use Saudi Arabia trying to act as a dominant firm to stabilize the oil market. The Stackelberg solution is easy to present graphically, as in Figure 26.4. The algebraic details are somewhat messier, but still worth going into.

The Bertrand model is best viewed as a Cournot equilibrium in prices. It leads to a somewhat paradoxical solution, namely, that the only Nash equilibrium in prices is the competitive equilibrium. On the other hand, there is a reasonable amount of work in industrial organization that suggests that industries with only a few firms turn out to act quite competitively. Perhaps the Bertrand equilibrium suggests why this is.

Another model that I want to add to the next edition is the model of price leadership, which is like a Stackelberg equilibrium, but in prices. The idea is that there is a dominant firm that sets a price, p, and then a competitive fringe that supplies output as a function of the price set. The dominant firm has to take into account its rivals' behavior when it sets its own price.

If $S(p)$ is the supply function by the competitive fringe, $D(p)$ is market demand, and $c(y)$ is the cost function for the dominant firm, then the profit maximization function facing the dominant firm is

$$\max_p p[D(p) - S(p)] - c(D(p)).$$

The bracketed expression is called the *residual demand curve* and represents the demand curve actually facing the monopolist, once the competitive supply has been subtracted off. Thus the problem facing the dominant firm is just maximizing profits given the residual demand curve that it faces, and this has a standard graphical solution.

I view conjectural variations as a reasonable way to classify the behavioral assumptions underlying the various models presented in this chapter. I understand the "bastardized" nature of this idea, but I think that its aid as an organization tool outweighs the somewhat sloppy dynamic notion that is involved here.

The first three problems in the workbook are the three cases examined in the text: Cournot, Stackelberg, and collusion. Problems 26.7 and 26.8 are examples of the price leadership model described above. Problem 26.9 is a somewhat heroic attempt to analyze a Hotelling type oligopoly model; this is a nice problem for advanced students, but is too hard for the average undergraduate.

Chapter 26 — Oligopoly

A. Oligopoly is the study of the interaction of a small number of firms
   1. duopoly, triopoly and so on
   2. duopoly is simplest case
   3. unlikely to have a general solution; depends on market structure and specific details of how firms interact.

B. Cournot equilibrium
   1. Each firm makes a choice of output, given its forecast of the other firm's output.
   2. Let y_1 be the output choice of firm 1 and y_2^e be firm 1's beliefs about firm 2's output choice.
   3. maximization problem $\max_{y_1} \ p(y_1 + y_2^e)y_1 - c(y_1)$
   4. Let $Y = y_1 + y_2^e$ first order condition is

$$p(Y) + p'(Y)y_1 = c'(y_1)$$

   5. this gives firm one's reaction curve — how it chooses output given its beliefs about firm 2's output
   6. see Figure 26.1
   7. Look for Cournot equilibrium — where each firm finds its beliefs confirmed in equilibrium
   8. see Figure 26.2.

C. Example
   1. assume zero costs
   2. linear demand function $p(Y) = a - bY$
   3. profit function: $[a - b(y_1 + y_2)]y_1 = ay_1 - by_1^2 - by_1y_2$
   4. isoprofit lines
   5. derive reaction curve
      a) maximize profits
      b) $a - 2by_1 - by_2 = 0$
      c) calculate to get $y_1 = (a - by_2)/2b$
      d) do same sort of thing to get reaction curve for other firm
   6. look for intersection of reaction curves
   7. adjustment to equilibrium; see Figure 26.2.
   8. many firms in a Cournot equilbrim
      a) $p(Y) + \frac{dp}{dY}y_i = MC_i$
      b) $p(Y)[1 + \frac{dp}{dY}\frac{Y}{p}\frac{y_i}{Y}] = MC_i$
      c) $p(Y)[1 + s_i/\epsilon] = MC$
      d) as market share goes to zero, Cournot approaches competition

D. Collusion
   1. firms get together to maximize joint profits
   2. marginal impact on joint profits from selling output of either firm must be the same
   3. see Figure 26.3
   4. note instability — if firm 1 believes 2 will keep its output fixed, it will always pay it to increase its own output
   5. problems with OPEC
   6. if it doesn't believe other firm will keep its output fixed, it will cheat first!
   7. illustrate using the isoprofit curves

E. Stackelberg behavior
   1. asymmetry — one firm gets to move first
      a) time — incumbent and entrant

b) size — IBM, etc.
2. maximize profits, given the reaction behavior of the other firm
3. take into response that the other firm will follow my lead
4. graphical solution in Figure 26.4.

F. Bertrand competition
   1. keep price fixed
   2. competition is result

G. Conjectural variations
   1. how will other firm's output choice vary if I change my output choice?
   2. classify equilibria

Game Theory

This is a fun chapter. Students like it a lot, and faculty usually like teaching it. Game theory is hot stuff in economics these days, and this chapter tries to convey some of the reasons why.

The first two equilibrium concepts, that of a dominant strategy equilibrium and a Nash equilibrium, are reasonably easy to convey. The idea of a Nash equilibrium in mixed strategies is a little harder. Here's an example that will motivate the idea.

Consider the game of Baseball. The pitcher has two strategies: pitch high or pitch low. Likewise, the batter has two strategies, swing high or swing low. If the batter connects, he gets a payoff of 1 and the pitcher gets zero. If the batter misses, the pitcher gets a payoff of 1.

What are the Nash equilibria in this game? If the pitcher always pitches high, the batter will always swing high, and if the pitcher always pitches low, then the batter will always swing low. It is clear from this observation—and from observing baseball games—that the equilibrium strategy must involved a *mixed strategy*. The pitcher will flip a coin and decide whether to pitch high or low, and the batter flips a coin to decide whether to swing high or low. The batter will connect 50% of the time. Here students are very willing to accept that the optimal strategy must involve randomization.

If you really want to get them buzzing, you can talk about the following paradox. If the batter really believes that the pitcher will really randomize 50–50, then he might as well swing high all the time. But of course, once the pitcher detects this departure from randomizing, he will modify his own behavior to exploit the batter's sloppiness. This example drives home the important point that what keeps the players at the Nash equilibrium is the desire to avoid being psyched out by their opponents.

Most students have heard of the prisoner's dilemma by now, but they haven't seen the analysis of the repeated game. The reason why the repeated game is different from the one-shot game is that in the repeated game, the strategy choice at time t can depend on the entire history of the game up until t. Thus choices at time $t - 1$ may have some influence on choices at time t. This opens the possibility of tit-for-tat and other strategies that can allow for cooperative solutions.

The analysis of the sequential games, and especially the game of entry deterrence. Students really get excited about this kind of analysis since they think that it will help them be better businessmen. (Well, who knows, maybe it will!)

It is fun to describe Schelling's game of the kidnapper with cold feet—this has a plot line very similar to the movie *Nasty People*. A kidnapper grabs a victim and then gets cold feet. The problem is that if he releases his victim, the rational strategy for the victim is to go to the polices and identify the kidnapper. The problem with this sequential game is that the victim has no way to precommit to staying away from the police.

Schelling's solution is characteristically inventive: he suggests that the victim allow the kidnapper to photograph him in some unspeakably disgusting act. This gives the kidnapper a threat—if the victim ever exposes the kidnapper, the kidnapper can release the photo. The students think that this game is great fun. You can ask them to suggest various "unspeakably disgusting acts" that the victim might suggest.

Chapter 27 — Game Theory

A. Game theory studies strategic interaction. Developed by von Neumann and Morgenstern around 1950.

B. How to depict payoffs of game from different strategies
   1. Two players
   2. Two strategies
   3. Example: Figure 27.1
      a) this depicts a **dominant strategy**
      b) each person has a strategy that is best no matter what the other person does
      c) nice when it happens, but doesn't happen that often

C. Nash equilibrium
   1. what if there is no dominant strategy?
   2. in this case, look for strategy that is best if the other player plays his best strategy.
   3. note the "circularity" of definition
   4. appropriate when you are playing against a "rational" opponent
   5. each person is playing the best given his expectations about other person's play and expectations are actually confirmed.
   6. Example: Figure 27.2.
      a) Note (top, left) is Nash; (bottom, right) is also Nash
   7. Nash equilibrium in pure strategies may not exist
   8. But if allow mixed strategies, and people care about expected payoff then Nash will always exist.

D. Prisoner's dilemma
   1. 2 prisoners, each may confess (and implicate other) or deny
   2. Gives payoff matrix in Figure 27.4
   3. Note that (confess, confess) is unique dominant strategy equilibrium. But (deny, deny) is Pareto efficient.
   4. Example: cheating in a cartel

5. Example: agreeing to get rid of spies
6. Problem — no way to communicate and make binding agreements

E. Repeated games
   1. if game is repeated with same players, then there may be ways to enforce a better solution to prisoner's dilemma.
   2. Suppose PD is repeated 10 times and people know it.
      a) then backwards inductions says it is a dominant strategy to cheat every round.
   3. Suppose that PD is repeated an indefinite number of times
      a) then may pay to cooperate.
   4. Axelrod's experiment: tit-for-tat

F. Example – enforcing cartel and price wars

G. Sequential game — time of choices matters.

H. Example: Figure 27.5 and Figure 27.6
   1. (top, left) and (bottom, right) are both Nash equilibria
   2. but in extensive form (top, left) is not reasonable
   3. to solve game, start at end and work backwards
   4. (top, left) is not an equilibrium, since the choice of "top" is not a credible choice

I. Example: entry deterrence
   1. Stay out and fight
   2. excess capacity to prevent entry — change payoffs
   3. see Figure 27.7
   4. strategic inefficiency

Chapter 28

Exchange

This chapter starts out with a relatively standard treatment of trade in an Edgeworth box. This leads naturally to the idea of Pareto efficient allocations as the outcome of a voluntary trading process. Given the many possibilities that can result from unstructured voluntary trade, I then turn to examining a particular mechanism for trade, the competitive market mechanism.

It is important to emphasize that if there are really only two players, the market mechanism isn't very plausible. We assume that our two players take prices as given; this is sensible only in a model with many players. One way out of this problem is to suppose that there are a hundred A players and a hundred B players, and that the Edgeworth box depicts the bundle that each type has. If there are two hundred small consumers in the Edgeworth box, then there is no problem with them behaving competitively.

The rest of the treatment here is fairly standard. The *reductio ad absurdum* proof in 28.10 throws a few students—they've generally forgotten any logic they've learned by the time they get to college. So if you want to go over this proof, you should remind them of the logic that it uses.

The main problem with presenting the two welfare theorems is that the students don't have anything to compare them to. That's why I like the monopoly in the Edgeworth box example. A standard monopolist in the Edgeworth box gives an example of a market based resource allocation system that results in a Pareto inefficient allocation. A perfectly discriminating monopolist gives an example of a market based resource allocation scheme other than pure competition that results in Pareto efficiency. These two examples help to illustrate the richness of the idea of Pareto efficiency, as well as some of its limitations.

The implications of the first and second welfare theorems are profound, but it is sometimes hard to convey that profundity. It helps people to see the various aspects of these ideas if they can discuss them a little.

Chapter 28 — Theory of Exchange

A. Partial equilbrium — theory of single market

B. General equilibrium — interactions among many markets
    1. complements and substitutes
    2. prices affect income affects prices

C. We do pure exchange first, then production

D. Edgeworth box
    1. Figure 28.1
    2. allocation
    3. feasible allocation
    4. consumption bundles
    5. initial endowment
    6. final allocation

E. Trade
    1. move to Pareto preferred point
    2. keep going until no more mutually preferred trades

F. Pareto efficient allocations
    1. where trade stops — no mutual improvement possible
    2. Pareto efficient — no way to make both people better off
    3. indifference curves must be tangent
    4. Pareto set, or contract curve — locus of all PE points

G. Market trade
    1. specific way to trade — using price system
    2. gross demands and net demands; Figure 28.3
    3. market equilibrium — where supply equals demand
    4. see Figure 28.4

H. Algebra
    1. only one of the markets needs to clear
    2. Walras's law: if each individual satisfies his or her budget constraint,
       then the market as a whole must satisfy its budget constraint
    3. existence of equilibrium?

I. Efficiency
    1. does the market exhaust all the gains from trade?
    2. is the market outcome efficient?
    3. First theorem of welfare economics — yes
    4. is any efficient allocation a market equilbrium? — yes, if things are
       appropriately convex
    5. see Figure 28.8

J. Meaning of First Welfare Theorem
    1. implicit assumptions — no externalities
    2. competitive behavior
    3. existence
    4. shows that there is a general mechanism that will achieve efficient
       outcomes
    5. can decentralize decisions

K. Meaning of Second Welfare Theorem

1. prices play allocative and distributive role
2. use market for allocation, income redistribution for distributive
3. but problems in production economy
   a) how to measure endowments?
   b) how to redistribute endowments?

Chapter 29

Production

In this chapter I describe a general equilibrium model of production, the classical Robinson Crusoe economy. I usually start my lecture by apologizing for the two-good, one-person nature of this example, since this is a context where a two-good treatment seems quite unnatural. On the other hand, there isn't much way to avoid this unnatural discussion and still stick to a graphical treatment.

The fundamental idea is that the price systems serves as a way to decentralize resource allocation problems. Robinson, the consumer, only has to know the public prices, his own income, and his own tastes. Robinson, the producer, only has to know the prices. The consumer doesn't have to know anything about what is technologically feasible, and the firm doesn't have to know anything about tastes. All of the relevant information about tastes and technology end up being summarized in the equilibrium prices.

This decentralization role of the price system isn't very interesting in the one- or two-person economy, but if there are thousands of people it can be extremely important. Thus it is important to understand those cases where the price system works well as a decentralization device, and when it works poorly.

In this chapter, the efficacy of the price system depends on the nature of the technology—everything works out just dandy if there are decreasing or constant returns to scale, but if there are increasing returns to scale, it all breaks down. It is a good idea to compare the problems with the increasing returns to scale technology discussed here with the problems with the decreasing average costs technology discussed in the chapter on monopoly. These are just two different ways of depicting the same phenomena—marginal cost pricing is not viable since it results in negative profits.

In section 29.10 I describe the basic idea of comparative advantage. This is a very important idea in economics, but unless students take international trade they probably won't see it after the standard treatment in their principles course.

Production

A. Want to study production in a general equilibrium context

1. two-good model is somewhat artificial
2. but necessary for a graphical treatment

B. Robinson Crusoe economy
   1. Robinson is both consumer and producer
   2. consumes leisure and coconuts
   3. can make leisure-consumption choice directly as in Figure 29.1
   4. ... or can make it indirectly via the market

C. Crusoe, Inc. — the firm's choices
   1. firm looks at prices and chooses profit maximizing plan
   2. generates some profits π^*. See Figure 29.2.

D. Robinson the consumer
   1. Robinson collects profits as nonlabor income
   2. looks at price and wage and decides how much to work
   3. chooses optimal consumption point. See Figure 29.3.

E. In equilibrium, demand equals supply
   1. demand for labor equals supply of labor
   2. demand for consumption equals supply of consumption

F. Decentralization
   1. each "agent" in the economy only has to look at the prices and make his own decisions
   2. the consumer doesn't have to know anything about the production problem
   3. the producer doesn't have to know anything about the consumer's problem
   4. all information is conveyed in prices
   5. in a one-person economy, this is silly
   6. but in many-person, there can be great savings

G. Different kinds of technologies
   1. constant returns to scale — zero profits
   2. decreasing returns to scale — positive profits
   3. increasing returns to scale — competitive markets don't work. Natural monopoly problem.

H. Welfare theorems
   1. First welfare theorem — competitive markets are Pareto efficient
   2. Second welfare theorem — any Pareto efficient outcome can be achieved by competitive markets

I. Production possibilities
   1. If there is more than one good, we can illustrate the production set. Figure 29.7.
   2. if more than one way to produce output can exploit comparative advantage. Figure 29.8.
   3. Production possibilities and the Edgeworth box. Figure 29.9.

Chapter 30

Welfare

I like to describe the aggregation of preference issues in terms of manipulation. Majority voting is bad because the outcome can depend on the order in which the vote is taken and this can lead to agenda manipulation. Rank-order voting is bad because introducing a new alternative can change the outcome of the process, again offering a way to manipulate the political process. Arrow's theorem can be interpreted to say that there is no way to avoid such manipulation possibilities.

However, that being said, we typically resort to looking at simple ways to aggregate preferences through the use of welfare functions. The essential point to get across here is the connection between Pareto efficiency and welfare maximization—every welfare maximum is efficient, and subject to the usual convexity conditions, every efficient allocation is a welfare maximum for *some* welfare function.

The fair allocation stuff is fun. Students like it, since it addresses problems of equity in a nice way. I sometimes talk about other methods of fair division, such as one person cuts and the other chooses, etc.

Welfare

A. Incorporate distributional considerations into the analysis

B. Need some way to compare individual preferences or utilities

C. Aggregation of preferences
  1. majority voting
  2. paradox of voting; see Table 30.1
  3. rank order voting
  4. dependence of irrelevant alternatives; see Table 30.2

D. Arrow's impossibility theorem

E. Social welfare fuctions
  1. add together utilities in some way
  2. classical utilitarian: $\sum_{i=1}^{n} u_i$
  3. weighted-sum-of-utilities: $\sum_{i=1}^{n} a_i u_i$
  4. minimax: $\min\{u_1, \ldots, u_n\}$

F. Maximizing welfare
  1. every welfare maximum is Pareto efficient. Figure 30.1.
  2. every Pareto efficient allocation is welfare maximum (if utility possibilities set is convex).

G. Fair allocations
  1. generalized the idea of symmetric treatment
  2. if $u_i(x_j) > u_i(x_i)$ then we say that i **envies** j.
  3. typically will be possible to find allocations that are envy-free and efficient
  4. proof: start out with equal division and let people trade using a competitive market.
  5. end up with equal incomes; if someone envies someone else, then they couldn't have purchased the best bundle they could afford.

Chapter 31

Externalities

I really like the smokers and nonsmokers example in the Edgeworth box. I think that it gets the main points about externalities across very simply. Students sometimes get confused about the vertical axis. Emphasize that this is the total amount of smoke in the apartment, not how much each person smokes. Only one person generates the smoke—but both people have to consume it.

This presentation shows how special it is when there is a unique optimal level of the externality. Essentially that only occurs when preferences are quasilinear, as shown in Figure 31.2. By the way, Figure 31.2 is a great optical illusion; the Pareto efficient allocations form a horizontal line, although it looks like the line slants from right to left.

Quasilinear preferences make a lot of sense in the production context; after all, profit functions are quasilinear. I treat the standard Pigouvian tax in section 31.4, but the deeper idea in that section is the idea that the efficient outcome is independent of the assignment of property rights. Students resist the idea that a polluter could have the right to pollute, and its victim would have to buy back clean water from it. But if they understand that idea, they will understand externalities a lot better.

Section 31.5 is an important one too, since it shows that if there is a productive externality involving only a few firms, then there is a natural market signal to internalize the externality. There was a wonderful example of this on *L.A. Law* a few weeks ago. A water company was polluting the groundwater of a neighboring trailer park. The nasty businessman from the water company said that it was reasonable for the water company to make a million dollar damage settlement every few years since it would cost 30 million to clean up their technology. This provided a lot of drama on the T.V. but it was terrible economics. The sensible thing to do was for the water company to buy up the trailer park—certain to cost a lot less than one million—and evict the tenants. This way they could internalize the externality, and make everyone better off. Unfortunately, the L.A. lawyers didn't suggest this to the waterworks. Perhaps they thought that they would lose their fees.

Chapter 31 — Externalities

A. Consumption externality occurs when an agent cares directly about another agent's consumption or production of some good.
1. playing loud music
2. smoking cheap cigar

B. Production externality occurs when a firm's production function depends on choices of another firm or consumer.
1. apple orchard and honeybees
2. pollution

C. Example: smokers and nonsmokers
1. 2 roommates who consume smoke and money, one likes smoke, the other doesn't
2. preferences
3. endowment
   a) each has $100
   b) but what is initial endowment of smoke?
   c) endowment depends on legal system — just like rights to private property
   d) right to clean air
   e) right to smoke
   f) Pareto efficient amounts of smoke and money
   g) contract curve; how to trade
   h) Figure 31.1.
   i) price mechanism generates a "price of smoke"
   j) problems arise because property rights are poorly determined.
4. Under some conditions, the amount of smoke is independent of the assignment of property rights. Figure 31.2.

D. Production externalities
1. S, a steel firm and F, a fishery
2. steel: $\max_s \ p_s s - c_s(s, x)$
3. fishery:$\max_f \ p_f f - c_f(s, x)$
4. FOC for fishery:
$$p_s = MC_s(s, x)$$
$$0 = MC_x(s, x)$$

5. FOC for fishery:
$$p_f = MC_f(s, x)$$

E. Efficient solution
1. merge and maximize joint profits
2. **internalize** the externality
3.
$$\max_{s,f} p_s s + p_f f - c_s(s, x) - c_f(s, x).$$

4. get $p_s = MC_s$, $p_f = MC_f$ and
$$0 = \Delta c_s / \Delta x + \Delta c_f / \Delta x$$

5. joint firm takes into account interaction
6. private costs and social costs
7. how to get firms to recognize social cost
   a) Pigouvian tax — set price of pollution to equal social cost
   b) market pollution rights
   c) assign property rights and let firms bargain over amount of pollution

Chapter 32

Public Goods

I start by introducing the basic idea of a public good—a good that lacks exclusion in consumption. The standard textbook treatment leaps right into the Samuelson conditions, but I think that it makes much more sense to look at the public provision of a discrete good. I derive the optimality condition in this context, namely that the sum of the reservation prices exceeds the cost of the good. Once students are armed with this example the Samuelson case is a relatively easy extension.

I then turn to a discussion of free riding, and relate it to the prisoner's dilemma. The example there is a little bit forced, but tends to get the point across: if each person makes his decision about the public good independently, there may be under provision of the public good. It is fun to talk about other kinds of free-riding; e.g., who cleans up the living room?

I next look at the classical Samuelson conditions for efficiency when the public good can be provided at different levels of output. I treat the free rider problem in section 32.6. Figure 32.2 is really quite a nice diagram and repays careful study.

The next topic for discussion is how to "solve" the public goods problem. Students have been taught democratic ideals in high school civics classes, so it might come as a shock to them that voting isn't that good a mechanism for making decisions about public goods. Here it is worthwhile giving some examples where one person cares a lot about something and would be willing to compensate others, but voting won't be able to reach the Pareto efficient decision. You might talk about ways that real-life political processes get around this problem–e.g., logrolling–but that may tend to confuse them unless they've had some political science.

Finally I discuss the Clarke tax — a way that really "solves" the public goods problem, at least for a special case. The best way to get students to understand the Clarke tax is to actually have them use it. One faculty member I know had his class use a Clarke tax procedure to determine the date of the midterm exam. This is certainly a public goods problem, and the students really understood what was going on when they actually participated. But even if you can't determine the provision of a real public good, like the date of the midterm, it is still of interest to run through a numerical example, such as the one given in the book.

Chapter 32 — Public Goods

A. A particular kind of externality — where everyone has to consume some good in the same amount

B. Examples: national defense, street lights, roads, etc. — same amount must be provided by all.

C. When should a public good be provided? What institutional arrangements will actually provide a public good?

D. Example: a TV for 2 roommates. Roommate i will contribute g_i. TV will be provided if $g_1 + g_2 \geq C$.
   1. consider the reservation prices r_1 and r_2. It will be Pareto efficient to provide the TV if $r_1 \geq g_1$, $r_2 \geq g_2$ and $g_1 + g_2 \geq C$.
   2. So condition for efficiency is that the sum of the willingnesses to pay must exceed the cost of provision
   3. In case of divisible good (e.g., how much to spend on TV), the the optimum occurs when the sum of the willingness to pay equals marginal cost
   4. But will this be satisfied?
      a) consider special problem: $\max_x \ x + a_i f(\sum g_i)$. Assume $f''(G) < 0$. First order condition is $a_i f'(G) = 1$. Only one person will satisfy this — everyone will free ride on the person with the largest value of the good.
      b) So voluntary contributions don't work well because of free riding.
      c) Voting — median voter where half prefer more and half prefer less. But for efficiency want to maximize the utility of the sum of the voters — i.e., the average utility.
      d) Are there ways to get the efficient amount provided? Sort of, but it has a cost. Have to impose social costs on the individuals who change the social decisions.

Part II

TEST QUESTIONS*

Chapter 2
BUDGET CONSTRAINT

Multiple-Choice Questions

Difficulty: 2
Correct: B

1. If she spends all of her income on apples and pineapples, Sally can just afford 8 apples and 15 pineapples per day. Sally could also use her entire budget to buy 12 apples and 3 pineapples per day. The price of apples is 12 pesos each. How much is Sally's income per day?
    a) Her income is 146 pesos per day.
    b) Her income is 156 pesos per day.
    c) Her income is 7 pesos per day.
    d) Her income is 301 pesos per day.
    e) None of the above.

Difficulty: 1
Correct: C

2. Harry thrives on two goods, paperback novels and bananas. The cost of paperback novels is 4 dollars each. The cost of bananas is 3 dollars per bunch. If Harry spent all of his income on bananas, he could afford 12 bunches of bananas per week. How many paperback novels could he buy if he spent all of his income on paperback novels?
    a) 36
    b) 48
    c) 9
    d) 16
    e) None of the above.

Difficulty: 2
Correct: B

3. Archie lives on pizza and seafood salads. Pizzas cost him two dollars each. Seafood salads cost him 4 dollars each. Archie allows himself to spend no more than 20 dollars a day on food. Archie also restricts his consumption to 4000 calories per day. Archie's pizzas contain 850 calories each and his seafood salads contain 200 calories each. One day Archie spends his entire budget of $20 on food and also consumes his entire calorie limit of 4000. How many pizzas did Archie consume?
    a) 3 pizzas
    b) 4 pizzas
    c) 10 pizzas
    d) The problem doesn't give enough information to determine how many.
    e) None of the above.

Difficulty: 1
Correct: A

4. Sheila spends her entire budget and consumes 3 units of x and 5 units of y. The price of x is twice the price of y. Her income doubles and the price of y doubles but the price of x stays the same. If she continues to buy 5 units of y, whatis the largest number of units of x that she can afford?
    a)   6
    b)   3
    c)   2
    d)   There is not enough information to say.
    e)   None of the above

Difficulty: 1
Correct: E

5. Suppose that the prices of good x and good y both double and income triples. On a graph where the budget line is drawn with x on the horizontal axis and y on the vertical axis
    a)   the budget line becomes steeper and shifts inward.
    b)   the budget line becomes flatter and shifts outward.
    c)   the budget line becomes flatter and shifts inward.
    d)   the new budget line is parallel to the old budget and lies below it.
    e)   none of the above

Difficulty: 1
Correct: D

6. Suppose that the price of good x triples and the price of good y doubles while income remains constant. On a graph where the budget line is drawn with x on the horizontal axis and y on the vertical axis, the new budget line
    a)   is flatter than the old one and lies below it.
    b)   is flatter than the old one and lies above it.
    c)   crosses the old budget line.
    d)   is steeper than the old one and lies below it.
    e)   is steeper than the old one and lies above it.

Difficulty: 1
Correct: E

7. The initial price of good x is 1, the initial price of good y is 2 and initial income is 70. The price of x changes to 3, the price of y changes to 6, and income remains at 70. On a graph with x on the horizontal axis and y on the vertical, the new budget line is
    a)   flatter than the old one and lies below it.
    b)   flatter than the old one and lies above it.
    c)   steeper than the old one and lies below it.
    d)   steeper than the old one and lies above it.
    e)   none of the above.

Difficulty: 3
Correct: C

8. While traveling abroad, Tammy spent all of the money in her purse to buy 5 plates of spaghetti and 6 oysters. Spaghetti costs 8 currency units per plate and she had 82 units of the local currency in her purse. If s denotes the number of plates of spaghetti and o denotes the number of oysters purchased, which equation describes the commodity bundles that she could just afford with the money in her purse?
   a) $8s+6o=82$
   b) $6s+8o=82$
   c) $16s+14o=164$
   d) $5s+6o=82$
   e)   none of the above

Difficulty: 2
Correct: B

9. Billy Bob wants to gain some weight so that he can play football. Billy eats only milkshakes and spinach. Milkshakes cost him $1 each and spinach costs $2 per serving. A milkshake has 850 calories and a serving of spinach has 200 calories. Billy Bob never spends more than $20 a day on food and he always consumes at least 8000 calories per day. Which of the following is necessarily true?
   a)   Billy Bob consumes at least 9 milkshakes a day.
   b)   Billy Bob never consumes more than 6 servings of spinach a day.
   c)   Billy Bob never consumes positive amounts of both goods.
   d)   Billy Bob consumes only milkshakes.
   e)   none of the above

Difficulty: 2
Correct: D

10. Lars consumes only potatoes and herring. The price of potatoes is 9 crowns per sack and the price of herring is 5 crowns per crock. He used to spend his entire income to buy 5 sacks of potatoes and 10 crocks of herring per month. Now the government subsidizes potatoes. Market prices haven't changed, but consumers get a subsidy of 5 crowns for every sack of potatoes consumed. To pay for this subsidy, the government introduced an income tax. Lars pays an income tax of 20. If s is the number of sacks of potatoes and c is the number of crocks of herring what is Lars' NEW budget?
   a) $9s+5c=100$
   b) $9s+5c=95$
   c) $4s+5c=95$
   d) $4s+5c=75$
   e)   none of the above

Difficulty: 1
Correct: C

11. If you spent your entire income, you could afford either 4 units of x and 9 units of y or 9 units of x and 4 units of y. If you spent your entire income on x, how much x could you buy?
    a) 25 units
    b) 36 units
    c) 13 units
    d) Since the problem doesn't give us either prices or income, there is not enough information to say.
    e) none of the above

Difficulty: 1
Correct: C

12. Bella's budget line for x and y depends on all of the following except
    a) the amount of money she has to spend on x and y.
    b) the price of x.
    c) her preferences between x and y.
    d) the price of y.

Difficulty: 1
Correct: D

13. Your budget constraint for the two goods G and B is $10G + 2B = 80$. You are currently consuming 4 units of G and 20 units of B. In order to get 3 more units of G, how many units of B would you have to give up?
    a) 3
    b) 9
    c) 12
    d) 15
    e) none of the above

True or False Questions

Difficulty: 1
Correct: T

1. Increasing the price of one of the goods while leaving income and other prices constant reduces the size of the budget set.

Difficulty: 1
Correct: F

2. If good 1 is measured on the horizontal axis and good 2 is measured on the vertical axis, and if the price of good 1 is p1 and the price of good 2 is p2, then the slope of the budget line is -p2/p1.

Difficulty: 1
Correct: F

3. If all prices are doubled and income left the same, the budget set does not change because relative prices don't change.

Short-Answer Questions

Difficulty: 1

1. Perry lives on avocados and beans. The price of avocados is 10 and the price of beans is 5. Perry's income is 40. Draw a graph showing Perry's budget line. Put avocados on the horizontal axis and beans on the vertical axis. Label the point where the budget line hits the horizontal axis "A" and the point where the budget line hits the vertical axis "B". Next to these labels, write down the number of avocados purchased at A and the number of beans purchased at B. Draw another budget line showing what Perry's budget would be if his income doubled, the price of avocados doubled, and the price of beans stayed the same. Label the point where this line hits the vertical axis "C" and the point where it hits the horizontal axis "D". Next to these labels write the number of avocados at C and the number of beans at D.

At A there are 4 avocados. At B there are 8 units of beans.
At C there are 4 avocados. At D there are 16 units of beans.

Difficulty: 2

2. Brenda likes hot dogs and Coca-Cola. Hot dogs cost $1 each and Cokes cost $.50 per bottle. (She only drinks bottled Coke.) Brenda finds out about a special promotion for Coke that will last for one month. If Brenda sends in the bottle tops from the Cokes she drinks during the next month, she will get a refund of $.20 for every bottlecap beyond the first 12 that she returns. For example, if she returns 25 bottle caps she will get back $2.60 = $.20(25 - 12). Brenda has $40 to spend on hot dogs and Coke during the next month. Draw her budget line with Coke on the horizontal axis and hot dogs on the vertical axis. Find the points where the budget line hits the axes and the point where it has a kink. At each of these three points write down the quantities of each good consumed.

The budget line runs from (0,40) on the vertical axis to a kink point (12,34) and from (12,34) to about (125.3,0).

Difficulty: 2

3. Felicity is studying economics and political science. She can read 30 pages of political science per hour but only 5 pages of economics per hour. This week she has a 50 page assignment in economics and a 150 page assignment in political science. Because of sorority rush, she can not devote more than 10 hours to studying these subjects this week. She realizes she can not complete all of her assignments but is determined to complete at least 30 pages of her economics reading. Draw a graph with pages of economics on the horizontal axis and pages of political science on the vertical axis. On this graph, show the possibilities that are consistent with the constraints that Felicity has imposed on herself. (She is allowed to read ahead in either subject.) Label key points on your graph with their numerical values.

Anything in the triangle bounded by (0,300), (30,120) and (30,0) satisfies these constraints.

Difficulty: 3

4. Ed Moore and his family live in a city with many private schools and one public school. The Moores are thinking of sending their only child to private school because they would like a school that has more teachers and other resources per student than the local public school. The Moores must pay taxes to support local public schools whether or not their child goes to private school. There is such a variety of private schools that the Moores can get just about any level of inputs per student by choosing the appropriate private school. Tuition in the private schools equals expenditure per student. Draw a diagram to show the Moores budget constraint. Put expenditures per student in the child's school on the horizontal axis and other goods on the vertical.

One point is (x,d) where x is expenditures per pupil in public school and d is disposable income. The rest of the budget is a line with slope -1 from (2s,d-x) to the x axis.

Chapter 3
PREFERENCES

Multiple-Choice Questions

Difficulty: 1
Correct: E

1. If two goods are both desirable and preferences are convex, then
   a) there must be a kink in the indifference curves.
   b) indifference "curves" must be straight lines.
   c) if two bundles are indifferent, then an average of the two bundles is worse than either one.
   d) the marginal rate of substitution is constant along any indifference curve.
   e) none of the above

Difficulty: 2
Correct: B

2. If there are only two goods, if more of good one is always preferred to less and less of good two is always preferred to more, then
   a) indifference curves must be convex toward the origin.
   b) indifference curves must slope upward to the right.
   c) indifference curves may cross.
   d) indifference curves could take the form of ellipses.
   e) none of the above

Difficulty: 2
Correct: E

3. If two goods are perfect complements
   a) then there is a bliss point and the indifference curves surround this point.
   b) consumers must buy the same amount of both goods.
   c) peoples' preferences are influenced by the choices of others.
   d) indifference curves have a positive slope.
   e) none of the above

Difficulty: 2
Correct: C

4. The relation "is preferred to" between commodity bundles is just one example of a binary relation. Another example is the relation "is a full brother of" defined over the set of all human beings. Let xRy mean person x is a full brother of person y.
   a) The relation R is reflexive, transitive, and complete.
   b) The relation R is transitive and complete but not reflexive.
   c) The relation R is transitive but not complete or reflexive.
   d) The relation R is complete but not transitive or reflexive.
   e) The relation R is neither reflexive, transitive, nor complete.

Difficulty: 1
Correct: C

5. Preferences are said to be monotonic if
   a) all goods must be consumed in fixed proportions.
   b) all goods are perfect substitutes.
   c) more is always preferred to less.
   d) there is diminishing marginal rate of substitution.
   e) none of the above

True or False Questions

Difficulty: 1
Correct: F

1. If preferences are transitive, then more is always preferred to less.

Difficulty: 1
Correct: F

2. A person with reflexive preferences is someone who does not shop carefully.

Difficulty: 2
Correct: T

3. If someone has the utility function $U = 2\min\{x,y\}$ then x and y are perfect complements for that person.

Difficulty: 1
Correct: T

4. A consumer with convex preferences who is indifferent between the bundles (1,4) and (9,2) will like the bundle (5,3) at least as well as either of the first two bundles.

Difficulty: 2
Correct: T

5. If preferences are monotonic and there is diminishing marginal rate of substitution, then preferences are convex.

Difficulty: 1
Correct: F

6. If preferences are convex, then for any commodity bundle, x, the set of commodity bundles that are worse than x is a convex set.

Short-Answer Questions

Difficulty: 3

1. Draw graphs with quantities of pepperoni pizza on the horizontal axis and anchovy pizza on the vertical axis to illustrate the following situations. In each case draw two different indifference curves and make a little arrow pointing in the direction of greater preference.
    a) Marvin loves pepperoni pizza and hates anchovy pizza. b) Mavis hates anchovy pizza and is completely indifferent about pepperoni pizza.

    a) Indifference curves slopes up and to the right. Arrow points down and to the left. b) Indifference curves are horizontal lines. Arrow points down.

Difficulty: 3   2.   Coach Steroid likes his players to be big, fast, and obedient. If player A is better than player B in two of these three characteristics, Steroid will prefer A to B. Three players try out for quarterback. Wilbur Westinghouse weighs 320 pounds, runs very slowly and is quite obedient. Harold Hotpoint weighs 240 pounds, runs extremely fast and is extremely disobedient. Jerry Jacuzzi weighs 150 pounds, runs at average speed and is extremely obedient. Does Coach Steroid have transitive preferences? Explain your answer.

No. Steroid prefers W to H because W is heavier and more obedient. He preferes H to J because H is heavier and faster. But he prefers J to W because J is more obedient and faster than W. Since his preferences have a cycle, they cannot be transitive.

Difficulty: 3   3.   Belinda loves chocolate and always thinks that more is better than less. Belinda thinks that a few piano lessons would be worse than none at all but if she had enough piano lessons to get good at playing the piano, she would prefer more lessons to less. Draw a graph with piano lessons on the horizontal axis and chocolate on the vertical axis. On your graph sketch two indifference curves for Belinda that would be consistent with this story. Label the better of the two indifference curves AA and the worse one BB.

The indifference curves would look something like inverted U's. (The area under these curves needn't be necessarily convex.) The better of the two curves drawn is the higher one.

Difficulty: 3   4.   Mac Rowe doesn't sweat the petty stuff. In fact, he just cannot detect small differences. He consumes two goods, x and y. He prefers the bundle (x,y) to the bundle (x',y') if and only if $xy - x'y' > 1$. Otherwise he is indifferent between the two bundles. Show a) that the relation of indifference is not transitive for Mac. (Hint: Give an example.) b) that the preferred relation is transitive for Mac.

Consider the bundles A = (1,1), B = (1,1.75), C = (1,2.5). Then A is indifferent to B and B to C but C is preferred to A. To see that strict preference is transitive, suppose we have any three bundles, (x,y), (x',y') and (x'',y''). If the first is preferred to the second and the second to the third, then $xy - x'y' > 1$ and $x'y' - x''y'' > 1$. Simple algebra shows that $xy - x''y'' > 1$. Therefore the first must be preferred to the third.

Difficulty: 3

5. Blanche Carter has devised a system for rating the males in her economics class. She cares about their intelligence and their looks. She has ranked each male s on a scale of 1 to 5 for intelligence and 1 to 3 for looks. She defines a preference relation, R, as follows xRy if boy x scores at least as high as boy y in either looks or in intelligence. Give an example to show that Blanche's method of determining preferences might not lead to transitive preferences.

Suppose boy x has rankings 1 and 2, boy y has rankings 3 and 1 and boy z has rankings 2 and 3. Then xRy because x is better looking than y and yRz because y is smarter than z. But it is not true that xRz. In fact z is both smarter and better looking than x.

Difficulty: 2

6. Explain how it would be possible to cheat someone who had intransitive preferences. Be explicit about what you would offer him if you were trying to exploit his intransitivity and what he would do in response.

Suppose that he has bundle C right now and prefers A to B, B to C, and C to A. If you offer him a trade that leaves him at B instead of C he will accept the deal. If you now offer him a trade that leaves him at A instead of B he will accept that. But now he would prefer to be back where he originally was to where he is. So you could offer to give him back his original bundle, minus a reward to you for your efforts and he would accept the deal.

Difficulty: 1

7. If good X is measured on the horizontal axis and good Y on the vertical, what can you say about the preferences of someone whose indifference curves are a) parallel to the Y axis b) positively sloped with more desirable indifference curves as one moves to the right c) negatively sloped with more desirable indifference curves as one moves to the left.

a) This person doesn't care how much X he has. b) This person likes X but hates Y. c) This person hates both goods.

Difficulty: 2

8. Suppose that there are two commodities and a consumer prefers more to less of each good. If the consumer has transitive preferences, can her indifference curves cross? Sketch a brief proof of your answer, illustrating with a diagram.

See the textbook.

Chapter 4
UTILITY

Multiple-Choice Questions

1. Mac's utility function is $U(x,y) = \max\{2x-y, 2y-x\}$.
   a) Mac's preferences are quasi-linear.
   b) If Mac has more x than y, any increase in his consumption of y would lower his utility.
   c) If Mac has more x than y, a decrease in his consumption of y would raise his utility.
   d) Mac has convex preferences.
   e) More than one of the above are true.

2. Charles' utility function is $U(x,y) = xy$. Anne's utility function is $U(x,y) = 1000xy$. Diana's utility function is $U(x,y) = -xy$. Elizabeth's utility function is $U(x,y) = -1/(xy+1)$. Fergie's utility function is $U(x,y) = xy-10000$. Margaret's utility is $U(x,y) = x/y$. Philip's utility function is $U(x,y) = x(y+1)$. (The goods x and y are two very expensive goods--we leave you to speculate about what they are.) Which of these people have the same preferences as Charles?
   a) Everybody except Diana.
   b) Anne and Fergie.
   c) Anne, Fergie and Elizabeth.
   d) None of them.
   e) All of them.

3. Raymond's preferences are represented by the utility function $U(x,y) = x/y$ if $y > 0$ and $U(x,y) = 0$ if $y = 0$.
   a) Raymond's indifference curves are rectangular hyperbolas.
   b) Raymond has monotonic preferences.
   c) Raymond has quasi-linear preferences.
   d) Raymond has a bliss point.
   e) none of the above

4. Molly's utility function is $U(x,y) = y + 4\sqrt{x}$. She has 25 units of x and 12 units of y. If her consumption of x is lowered to 0, how many units of y would she have to have to be exactly as well off as before?
   a) 48 units
   b) 37 units
   c) 32 units
   d) 112 units
   e) none of the above

Difficulty: 2
Correct: C

5. Jack's utility function is $U(x,y) = 98xy$. He has 24 units of good x and 4 units of good y. Bart's utility function for the same two goods is $U(x,y) = 5x + 2y$. Bart has 5 units of x and 24 units of y.
    a) Jack prefers Bart's bundle to his own bundle.
    b) Bart prefers Jack's bundle to his own.
    c) Each prefers the other guy's bundle to his own.
    d) Neither prefers the other guy's bundle to his own.
    e) There is not enough information to determine who envies whom since they have different preferences.

Difficulty: 2
Correct: C

6. Hans has the utility function $U(x,y) = \min\{3x+y, 2x+3y\}$. If x is on the horizontal axis and y is on the vertical axis, what is the slope of his utility function at the point (6,2)?
    a) The slope is -3.
    b) The slope is -1/3.
    c) The slope is -2/3.
    d) The slope is -3/2.
    e) The slope is not well-defined at (6,2).

Difficulty: 2
Correct: E

7. Mort's utility function is $U(x,y) = xy$. Mort consumes 6 units of x and 2 units of y.
    a) Mort would be willing to make small exchanges of x for y in which he gives up 4 units of x for every unit of y he gets.
    b) Mort would be willing to trade away all of his x for y so long as he gets more than 3 units of y for every unit of x he gives up.
    c) Mort likes x and y equally well so he will always be willing to change 1 unit of either good for more than one unit of the other.
    d) Mort will always be willing to make trades at any price if he does not have equal amounts of the two goods.
    e) None of the above.

Difficulty: 2
Correct: B

8. Henry's utility function is $x^2 + 16xw + 64w^2$ where x is his consumption of x and w is his consumption of w.
    a) Henry's preferences are nonconvex.
    b) Henry's indifference curves are straight lines.
    c) Henry has a bliss point.
    d) Henry's indifference curves are hyperbolas.
    e) None of the above.

Difficulty: 1
Correct: D

9. Josephine says, "My utility function is $U(x,y) = y + 5\sqrt{x}$." She has one unit of x and two units of y. If her consumption of x is lowered to zero, how much y must she have in order to be exactly as well off as before?
   a) 14 units
   b) 9 units
   c) 11 units
   d) 7 units
   e) none of the above

True or False Questions

Difficulty: 2
Correct: F

1. If someone has quasilinear preferences, then the slope of indifference curves is constant along all rays through the origin.

Difficulty: 2
Correct: F

2. Wanda Lott has the utility function $U(x,y) = Max\{x,y\}$. Wanda's preferences are convex.

Short-Answer Questions

Difficulty: 1

1. Jim's utility function is $U(x,y) = xy$. Jerry's utility function is $U(x,y) = 1000xy + 2000$. Tammy's utility function is $U(x,y) = xy(1-xy)$. Oral's utility function is $U(x,y) = -1/(10 + 2xy)$. Marjoe's utility function is $U(x,y) = x(y + 1000)$. Pat's utility function is $U(x,y) = .5xy-10000$. Billy's utility function is $U(x,y) = x/y$. Francis's utility function is $U(x,y) = -xy$. a) Who has the same preferences as Jim? b) Who had the same indifference curves as Jim? c) Explain why the answers to a) and b) differ.

   Jerry, Pat and Oral have the same preferences as Jim since their utility functions are monotonic transformations of Jim's. Jerry, Pat, Oral, Tammy and Francis have the same indifference curves as Jim, but Tammy and Francis have different preferences. Francis's utility function is a decreasing transformation of Jim's so he orders his indifference curves in the opposite way. Tammy's utility function is a transformation of Jim's but is sometimes increasing, sometimes decreasing.

Difficulty: 3

2. A consumer has a utility function of the form $U(x,y) = x^a + y^b$. Suppose that both a and b are nonnegative. What additional restrictions on the values of the parameters a and b are imposed by each of the following assumptions? i) Preferences are quasi-linear, convex, and x is a normal good. ii) Preferences are homothetic. iii) Preferences are homothetic and convex. iv) Goods x and y are perfect substitutes.

   i) a = 1, b is between 0 and 1. ii) a = b iii) a = b and a is between 0 and 1. iv) a = b = 1

Difficulty: 3   3.   Victor Finick likes to have the same amount of x as he has of y. His utility function is $U(x,y) = \min\{2x-y, 2y-x\}$. a) Draw the indifference curve for Victor that passes through the bundle (0,0) and the indifference curve that passes through (4,4). (Hint: Each indifference curve is the intersection of two line segments.) b) If Victor has a bundle that he likes better than (0,0) and his consumption of both goods is doubled, is Victor better off? c) Does Victor always prefer more of either good to less?

Victor's indifference curves are V-shaped. The one through the origin consists of the two rays, $y = 2x$ and $x = 2y$. The one through (2,2) has two rays going out from (2,2)--one with slope 1/2, and the other with slope 2. b) Yes c) No. If $x > y$, then an increase in x by itself makes him worse off and if $y > x$, an increase in y by itself makes him worse off.

Difficulty: 1   4.   Use separate graphs to sketch two indifference curves for people with each of the following utility functions. a) $U(x,y) = x + 2y$ b) $U(x,y) = \text{Min}\{x, 2y\}$ c) $U(x,y) = \text{Max}\{x, 2y\}$

a) These are straight lines with slope -1/2. b) These are L-shaped. The corners lie along the locus $x = 2y$. c) A typical indifference curve consists of a horizontal line from the y axis to the locus $x = 2y$ and then a vertical line to the x axis from the point where the horizontal line met the line $x = 2y$.

Difficulty: 2   5.   Use separate graphs to draw indifference curves for each of the following utility functions: a) $U(x,y) = \text{Min}\{2x+y, 2y+x\}$ b) $U(x,y) = \max\{2x+y, 2y+x\}$ c) $U(x,y) = x + \min\{x,y\}$. In which of these cases are preferences convex?

If you take a point on the line $x = y$ and draw two lines through it, one with a slope of -1/2 and the other with a slope of -2, the outer envelope of these lines will be an indifference curve for a) and the inner envelope will be an indifference curve for b). The indifference curves for c) passing through a point on the line $x = y$ consist of a line segment going down and to the right with slope -1 and a line segment going up and to the left with slope -2. Cases a) and c) display convex preferences and case b) does not.

Chapters 5 and 6
CHOICE AND DEMAND

Multiple-Choice Questions

Difficulty: 3
Correct: C

1. Mary Granola consumes grapefruits and avocados. Let G be the number of grapefruits she consumes and A the number of avocados. Mary's indifference curves are kinky. When G > A, she is just willing to trade 2 grapefruits for 1 avocado. When G < A, she is just willing to trade 2 avocados for 1 grapefruit. Let Pa be the price of avocados and Pg the price of grapefruits. Sketch one of Mary's indifference curves and use it to determine which of these is true.
   a) When Pa > Pg, she consumes only grapefruits.
   b) When Pa > Pg, she consumes twice as many grapefruits as avocados.
   c) Whe Pa > 2Pg, she will consume only grapefruits.
   d) When Pa > Pg, she will consume only avocados.
   e) She must consume equal amounts of both.

Difficulty: 3
Correct: D

2. Janet consumes two commodities x and y. Her utility function is U(x,y) = min{x + 2y, y + 2x}. She chooses to buy 10 units of good x and 20 units of good y. The price of good x is 1. Which of the following is true?
   a) Janet's income is 40.
   b) Janet's income is 50.
   c) Janet's income is 30.
   d) Janet's income is 20.
   e) There is not enough information in the problem to determine her income because we are not told the price of y.

Difficulty: 2
Correct: D

3. Frank consumes 6-packs of Miller Lite and cases of Bud Light. His budget for these two commodities is described by the equation 5x + 25y = 300 where x is 6-packs of Miller Lite and y is cases of Bud Light. Frank considers two cases of Bud Light to be perfect substitutes for 6 6-packs of Miller Lite. Which of the following is true?
   a) He will consume 12 cases of Bud Light.
   b) He will consume 12 6-packs of Miller Lite.
   c) He will consume 60 cases of Bud Light.
   d) He will consume 60 6-packs of Miller Lite.
   e) He is indifferent between any two bundles that use up his entire income.

Difficulty: 2
Correct: A

4.   Martha's utility function is $U(x,y) = \min\{x+2y, 2x+y\}$. George's utility function is $U(x,y) = \min\{2x+4y, 4x+2y\}$. If George and Martha have the same income and face the same prices for the goods x and y
a)   George and Martha will both demand the same amount of y.
b)   Martha will always prefer George's consumption bundle to her own.
c)   George will always prefer Martha's consumption bundle to his own.
d)   George will demand more x than Martha demands.
e)   none of the above

Difficulty: 3
Correct: C

5.   Badger Madison consumes only beer and sausages. His income is 100. Beer costs him $.50 per can and sausages cost $1 each. Where x is the number of cans of beer and y the number of sausages he consumes per week, Badger's utility function is $U(x,y) = -\{(x50)^2 + (y-40)^2\}$.
a)   Badger must always be unhappy since whatever he consumes his utility is negative.
b)   He has monotonic preferences.
c)   If his income increases, he won't change the commodity bundle that he buys.
d)   If the price of beer goes down, he will buy more beer.
e)   More than one of the above statements is true.

Difficulty: 2
Correct: C

6.   Howard has the utility function $U(x,y) = x-1/y$.
a)   Howard does not like good y.
b)   Howard has a bliss point.
c)   If the price of x is 4 and the price of y is 1, Howard will buy 2 units of y, no matter what his income is.
d)   Howard will buy good y only if it is cheaper than good x.
e)   None of the above.

Difficulty: 2
Correct: B

7.   Julius has a utility function $U(x,y) = x(y+1)$. The price of x is 1 and the price of y is 1.
a)   Julius consumes exactly as much x as y.
b)   Julius consumes one more unit of x than he consumes of y.
c)   Julius consumes one more unit of y than he consumes of x.
d)   Julius consumes twice as much x as y.
e)   None of the above.

Difficulty: 1
Correct: E

8. The inverse demand for x
    a) expresses 1/x as a function of prices and income.
    b) expresses demand for x as a function of 1/px and income where px is the price of x.
    c) expresses demand for x as a function of 1/px and 1/m where px is the price of x and m is income.
    d) specifies 1/x as a function of 1/px and 1/m.
    e) none of the above

Difficulty: 3
Correct: A

9. If there are two goods and if income and the price of good 1 doubles, while the price of good 2 stays constant
    a) demand for good 2 must increase if good 2 is a normal good.
    b) demand for good 2 will increase only if demand for good 1 falls.
    c) demand for good 2 will increase or decrease depending on whether the price elasticity of good 1 is greater or smaller than one in absolute value.
    d) more than one of the above
    e) none of the above

Difficulty: 3
Correct: A

10. If there are only two goods, an increase in the price of good 1 will increase the demand for good 2
    a) if and only if the price elasticity of demand for good 2 is greater than one in absolute value.
    b) whenever both goods are normal goods.
    c) only if the two goods are perfect substitutes.
    d) never.
    e) none of the above

Difficulty: 2
Correct: B

11. Richie Strait's demand function for comic books is x=30-10p where p is the price in dollars and x is the quantity he demands. If the price of comic books is $.50, what is Richie's price elasticity of demand for comic books?
    a) -10
    b) -1/5
    c) -1/10
    d) -1/3
    e) none of the above

Difficulty: 3
Correct: A

12. Minnie Applesauce is shopping for a summer lake cottage. Minnie hates mosquito bites, but the cheapest lake cottages have the most mosquitos. The price of a lake cabin is related to the number of mosquito bites you can expect per hour, b, according to the formula $p = \$20,000 - 100b$. Minnie's utility function is $u = x - 5b^2$ where x is her expenditure on all goods other than her lake cabin. If Minnie makes her best choice of lake cabin, how many mosquito bites per hour will she get?
   a) 10
   b) 5
   c) 20
   d) 25
   e) none of the above

Difficulty: 2
Correct: C

13. Jake's utility is $\min\{x, y + 2z\}$. The price of x is 1, the price of y is 2, the price of z is 3. Jake's income is 20. How much x does Jake demand?
   a) 10
   b) 12
   c) 6
   d) 8
   e) none of the above

Difficulty: 2
Correct: D

14. Regardless of his income and regardless of prices, Smedley always spends 25% of his income on housing, 10% on clothing, 30% on food, 15% on transportation and 20% on recreation. From this we can conclude that
   a) all goods are perfect substitutes.
   b) Smedley's demand is inelastic both to price and income.
   c) Smedley is not maximizing his utility.
   d) Smedley's price elasticity is -1 and his income elasticity is 1.
   e) all goods are consumed in fixed proportions.

Difficulty: 2
Correct: B

15. Mickey is considering buying a tape recorder. His utility function is $U(x,y,z) = x + f(y)\sqrt{z}$ where x is the amount of money he spends on other goods, y is the number of tape recorders he buys and z is the number of tapes he buys. Let $f(y) = 0$ if $y < 1$ and $f(y) = 8$ if y is greater than or equal to 1. The price of tape recorders is 20, the price of tapes is 1, and he can easily afford to buy a tape recorder and several tapes. Will he buy a tape recorder?
   a) Yes
   b) No
   c) He is indifferent about buying a tape recorder or not.
   d) There is not enough information here for us to be able to tell.

Difficulty: 1
Correct: D

16. Walt consumes strawberries and cream but only in the fixed ratio of three boxes of strawberries to two cartons of cream. At any other ratio, the excess goods are totally useless to him. The cost of a box of strawberries is 10 and the cost of a carton of cream is 10. Walt's income is 200. Which of the following is true?
a)   Walt demands 10 cartons of cream.
b)   Walt demands 10 boxes of strawberries.
c)   Walt considers strawberries and cream to be perfect substitutes.
d)   Walt demands 12 boxes of strawberries.
e)   none of the above

Difficulty: 2
Correct: B

17. The prices of goods 1 and 2 are each $1. Jane has $20 to spend and is considering choosing 10 units of x and 10 units of y. Jane has nice convex preferences. Where x is drawn on the horizontal axis and y is drawn on the vertical axis, the slope of her indifference curve at the bundle (10,10) is -2. From these facts we can conclude that
a)   the bundle (10,10) is the best she can afford.
b)   she would be better off consuming more of good x and less of good y.
c)   she would be better off consuming more of good y and less of good x.
d)   she must dislike one of the goods.
e)   more than one of the above is true

Difficulty: 2
Correct: A

18. Daisy received a tape recorder as a birthday gift and is not able to return it. Her utility function is $U(x,y,z) = x + f(y)\sqrt{z}$ where z is the number of tapes she buys, y is the number of tape recorders she has and x is the amount of money she has left to spend on other goods. Let $f(y) = 0$ if $y < 1$ and $f(y) = 12$ if y is greater than or equal to 1. If the price of tapes is 3 and she can easily afford to buy dozens of tapes, how many tapes will she buy?
a)   4
b)   3
c)   5
d)   6
e)   We need to know the price of tape recorders to solve this problem.

Difficulty: 1
Correct: D

19.   Seppo consumes brandy and saunas. Neither is an inferior good. Seppo has a total of $30 a day and 6 hours a day to spend on brandy and saunas. Each brandy costs $2 and takes half an hour to consume. Each sauna costs $1 and takes 1 hour to consume. (It is, unfortunately, impossible to consume a brandy in the sauna.) Seppo suddenly inherits a lot of money and now has $50 a day to spend on brandy and saunas. Since Seppo is a rational consumer he must have
a)   increased brandy consumption only.
b)   increased sauna consumption only.
c)   increased consumption of both.
d)   consumed the same amounts of both goods as before.
e)   We can't tell since we are told nothing about his indifference curves.

Difficulty: 1
Correct: A

20.   Clarissa's utility function is $U(r,z) = r + 50z - z^2$ where r is the number of rose plants she has in her garden and z is the number of zinnias. She has 600 square feet to allocate to roses and zinnias. Roses each take up 4 square feet and zinnias each take up 1 square foot. She gets the plants for free from a generous friend. If she acquires another 100 square feet of land for her garden and her utility function remains unchanged she will
a)   plant 25 more roses and no more zinnias.
b)   plant 100 more zinnias and no more roses.
c)   plant 20 more roses and 20 more zinnias.
d)   plant 10 more roses and 60 more zinnias.
e)   plant 13 more roses and 48 more zinnias.

Difficulty: 1
Correct: C

21.   Coke and Pepsi are perfect substitutes for Mr. Drinker and the slope of his indifference curves is -1. One day he bought 2 cans of Coke and 20 cans of Pepsi. (The cans of both drinks are the same size.)
a)   Coke is less expensive than Pepsi.
b)   Coke is more expensive than Pepsi.
c)   Coke and Pepsi cost the same.
d)   Mr. Drinker prefers Pepsi to Coke.
e)   none of the above

True or False Questions

Difficulty: 1
Correct: T

1.   If preferences are quasilinear, then for very high incomes the income offer curve is a straight line parallel to one of the axes.

Difficulty: 1
Correct: F

2.   In economic theory, the demand for a good must depend only on income and its own price and not on the prices of other goods.

Difficulty: 1
Correct: F

3.   If two goods are substitutes, then an increase in the price of one of them will reduce the demand for the other.

Difficulty: 1
Correct: T

4. If consumers spend all of their income, it is impossible for all goods to be inferior goods.

Difficulty: 1
Correct: F

5. An Engel curve is a demand curve with the vertical and horizontal axes reversed.

Difficulty: 2
Correct: F

6. If the demand curve is a straight line, then the price elasticity of demand is constant all along the demand curve.

Difficulty: 2
Correct: T

7. If the own price elasticity of demand for a good is -1, then doubling the price of that good will leave total expenditures on that good unchanged.

Difficulty: 2
Correct: T

8. If preferences are homothetic, then the income elasticity of demand for all goods is 1.

Difficulty: 1
Correct: T

9. A good is a luxury good if the income elasticity of demand for it is greater than 1.

Difficulty: 2
Correct: T

10. Prudence was maximizing her utility subject to her budget constraint. Then prices changed. After the price change she is better off. Therefore the new bundle costs more at the old prices than the old bundle did.

Difficulty: 2
Correct: F

11. If income is doubled and all prices are doubled, then the demand for luxury goods will more than double.

Difficulty: 1
Correct: T

12. If preferences are homothetic and all prices double while income remains constant, then demand for all goods is halved.

Difficulty: 1
Correct: F

13. An inferior good is less durable than a normal good.

Short-Answer Questions

Difficulty: 3

1. Is the following statement true or false? Write a brief but convincing explanation of your answer. "If consumers spend their entire incomes, it is impossible for the income elasticity of demand for every good to be bigger than one."

    True. If income elasticities of demand for all goods exceed 1, then a 1% increase in income would result in a more than 1% increase in expenditures for every good. Therefore total expenditures would rise by more than 1%. But this is impossible if the entire budget is spent both before and after the income increase.

Difficulty: 2

2. Harold consumes chardonnay and quiche. His utility function is $U(c,q) = \min\{c, q^2\}$. Draw a diagram showing three or four of Harold's indifference curves. If the price of chardonnay is 10 and the price of quiche is 3 and if Harold is consuming 4 units of quiche, how many units of chardonnay is he consuming?

    The diagram has fixed coefficients indifference curves, but their corners line up along the locus $c = q$ squared rather than along a straight line. 16 units of chardonnay.

Difficulty: 3

3. Wanda Lott's utility function is $U(x,y) = \max\{2x, y\}$. Draw some of Wanda's indifference curves. If the price of x is 1, the price of y is p and her income is m, how much y does Wanda demand?

    Wanda's indifference curves are rectangles that are twice as high as they are wide. If $p > .5$, Wanda demands no y. If $p < .5$, Wanda demands m/p units of y. If $p = .5$ Wanda is indifferent to her two best options, which are buying m units of x and no y or 2m units of y and no x.

Difficulty: 3   4.   Ray Starr has the utility function $U(x,y) = y/(100-x)$. a) Does Ray prefer more to less of both goods? b) Draw a diagram showing Ray's indifference curves corresponding to the utility levels $U = 1/2$, $U = 1$, and $U = 2$. c) How can you describe the set of indifference curves for Ray? d) If the price of x is 1 and the price of y is 1, find Ray's demand for x as a function of his income and draw a diagram showing his Engel curve for x.

a) yes b) These curves are straight lines with the equations $x/2 + y = 50$, $x + y = 100$, $2x + y = 200$. c) The indifference curve through any bundle is the straight line passing through that point and through the point (100,0). The set of all indifference curves is the star-shaped set of rays passing through the point (100,0) (to be more precise, the part of that set that is in the nonnegative quadrant). d) If Ray's income is less than 100 he buys y and no x. If his income is more than 100 he buys x and no y.

Difficulty: 2   5.   Les has the utility function $U(x,y) = (x+1)(y+4)$. The price of y is 1. Les spends all of his income to buy 6 units of y and no x. From these facts we can tell that the price of x must be at least how much? Explain your answer and draw a diagram to illustrate it.

Price of x must be at least 10. His marginal rate of substitution at the bundle (6,0) is 10. If the price of x is 10 or greater he will choose that corner.

Difficulty: 2   6.   With some services, e.g. checking accounts, phone service, pay T.V., a consumer is offered a choice of two or more payment plans. You can either pay a high "entry fee" and get a low price per unit of service or you pay a low entry fee and a high price per unit of service. Suppose you have an income of $100. There are two plans. Plan A has an entry fee of $20 with a price of $2 per unit. Plan B has an entry fee of $40 with a price of $1 per unit for using the service. Let x be expenditure on other goods and y be consumption of the service. a) Write down the budget equation that you would have after you paid the entry fee for each of the two plans. b) If your utility function is xy, how much y would you choose in each case? c) Which plan would you prefer? Explain.

a) $x + 2y = 80$, $x + y = 60$. b) 20, 30 c) Plan B. The utility of the bundle chosen with A is $20*40 = 800$ and the utility from the Plan B bundle is $30*30 = 900$.

Difficulty: 2   7.   Marie's utility function is $U(x,y) = \min\{3x+2y, 2x+5y\}$ where x is the number of units of sugar she consumes and y is the number of units of spice she consumes. She is currently consuming 12 units of sugar and 40 units of spice and she is spending all of her income. Draw a graph showing her indifference curve through this point. The price of spice is 1. In order for this to be her consumption bundle, what must be the price of sugar and what must her income be?

Her indifference curve is a broken line consisting of the outer envelope of the two lines $3x+2y=116$ and $2x+5y=116$. The point (12,40) is on the line $3x+2y=116$. The price of sugar is 1.5 and her income is 58.

Difficulty: 3   8.   Martha has the utility function $U = \min\{4x, 2y\}$. Write down her demand function for x as a function of the variables m, px, and py, where m is income, px is the price of x and py is the price of y.

$x = m/(px + 2py)$

Difficulty: 3   9.   Murphy's utility function is $U(x,y) = \min\{4x+y, 2x+2y, x+4y\}$. Murphy is consuming 12 units of x and 6 units of y. Draw the indifference curve through this point. At what points does this indifference curve have kinks? The price of good x is 1. What is the highest possible price for y? What is the lowest possible price for y?

The indifference curve is a broken line extending from (36,0) to (12,6) to (6,12) to (0,36). The price of y must be between 1 and 4.

Difficulty: 1   10.   Briefly explain in a sentence or two how you could tell a) whether a good is a normal good or an inferior good. b) whether a good is a luxury or a necessity. c) whether two goods are complements or substitutes.

a) If prices are left constant and income rises, demand for a normal good will rise, demand for an inferior good will fall. b) If income rises, expenditure on it will rise more or less than proportionately depending on whether the good is a luxury or a necessity respectively. c) Two goods are complements or substitutes depending on whether a rise in the price of one of them increases or decreases demand for the other.

Difficulty: 1   11.   Define each of the following: a) Inverse demand function. b) Engel curve.

The inverse demand function expresses for any quantity the price at which that quantity can be sold. It is simply the inverse function corresponding to the demand function. An Engel curve is the graph of the function that expresses quantity demanded as a function of income.

Difficulty: 2   12.   Max has the utility function $U(x,y) = x(y+1)$. The price of x is 2 and the price of y is 1. Income is 10. How much x does Max demand? How much y? If his income doubles and prices stay unchanged, will Max's demand for both goods double?

To set his MRS equal to the price ratio, Max sets $(y+1)/x = 2$. His budget constraint is $2x + y = 10$. Solve these two equations to find that $x = 11/4$ and $y = 9/2$. If his income doubles and prices stay unchanged, his demand for both goods does not double. A quick way to see this is to note that if quantities of both goods doubled, the MRS would not stay the same and hence would not equal the price ratio which has stayed constant.

Difficulty: 3   13.   Casper consumes cocoa and cheese. Cocoa is sold in an unusual way. There is only one supplier and the more cocoa you buy from him the higher the price you have to pay per unit. In fact y units of cocoa will cost Casper y^2 dollars. Cheese is sold in the usual way at a price of 2 dollars per unit. Casper's income is 20 dollars and his utility function is $U(x,y) = x + 2y$ where x is his consumption of cheese and y is his consumption of cocoa. a) Sketch Casper's budget set and shade it in. b) Sketch some of his indifference curves and label the point that he chooses. c) Calculate the amount of x and the amount of y that Casper demands at these prices and this income.

This problem is different from those in the text and is designed to see whether student can use the tools presented there in a creative way. The budget set is a convex set and the solution is a point of tangency. Casper demands 2 units of y and 16 units of x.

Difficulty: 1   14.   Is the following statement true or false? Briefly explain your answer. "A utility maximizer will always choose a bundle at which his indifference curve is tangent to his budget line."

False. At a corner solution the indifference curve need not be tangent to the budget line.

Difficulty: 2   15.   Max has a utility function $U(x,y) = 2xy + 1$. The prices of x and y are both $1 and Max has an income of $20. a) How much of each good will he demand? b) A tax is placed on x so that x now costs Max 2 dollars while his income and the price of y stay the same. How much good x does he now demand? c) Would Max be as well off as he was before the tax if, when the tax was imposed, his income rose by an amount equal to $1 times the answer to part b?

a) 10 x and 10 y. b) 5x c) No.

Chapter 7
REVEALED PREFERENCE

Multiple-Choice Questions

Difficulty: 2
Correct: D

1. Twenty years ago, Dmitri consumed bread which cost him 10 kopeks a loaf and potatoes which cost him 13 kopeks a bag. With his income of 286, he bought 13 loaves of bread and 12 sacks of potatoes. Today he has an income of 410. Bread now costs him 10 kopeks a loaf and potatoes cost him 24 kopeks a bag. Assuming his preferences haven't changed (and the size of loaves and bags haven't changed), when was he better off?
   a) twenty years ago
   b) today
   c) He was equally well off in the two periods.
   d) From the information given here we are unable to tell.
   e) none of the above

Difficulty: 1
Correct: B

2. At prices (4,12), Harry chooses the bundle (2,9). At the prices (8,4) Harry chooses the bundle (6,6). Is this behavior consistent with the weak axiom of revealed preference?
   a) yes
   b) no
   c) It depends on his income.
   d) We would have to observe a third choice to be able to say.
   e) none of the above

Difficulty: 1
Correct: C

3. When prices are (4,20), Goldie chooses the bundle (11,5) and when prices are (12,4) she chooses the bundle (7,3). Which of the following is true?
   a) She prefers the bundle (7,3) to the bundle (11,5).
   b) She violates SARP.
   c) She prefers (11,5) to (7,3).
   d) She violates WARP.
   e) none of the above

Difficulty: 2
Correct: A

4. Maria consumes strawberries which cost her 10 pesos a box and bananas which cost her 9 pesos a bunch. With her income of 192 pesos she buys 12 boxes of strawberries and 8 bunches of bananas. Daphne, with an income of 170 shillings consumes strawberries at a cost of 6 shillings per box each and bananas at a cost of 12 shillings per bunch each. Assuming their preferences are identical,
a) Maria would prefer Daphne's consumption bundle to her own.
b) Daphne would prefer Maria's consumption bundle to her own.
c) they would both be indifferent between their own bundles and the other person's bundle.
d) each prefers her own bundle to the other's.
e) We can't make any of the above statements without more information.

Difficulty: 2
Correct: B

5. In 1971, good x cost 5 and good y cost 1. They now cost 9 and 5 respectively. In 1971 the consumption bundle of x and y was 4 x's and 5 y's. It is now 9 x's and 7 y's. Calculate the Laspeyres index of current prices relative to 1971 prices rounded to one decimal place. (Remember the Laspeyres index uses the old quantities for weights.)
a) .5
b) 2.0
c) 2.5
d) 2.2
e) none of the above

Difficulty: 2
Correct: B

6. Carlos has at one time or another lived in Argentina, Bolivia, and Colombia. He buys only two goods, x and y. In Argentina the prices were (9,3) and he consumed the bundle (6,7). In Bolivia he consumed (9,2). In Colombia he consumed the bundle (6,5) at the prices (3,3). Which of the following is true?
a) The Argentine bundle is directly revealed preferred to the Bolivian bundle.
b) The Argentine bundle is indirectly revealed preferred to the Bolivian bundle.
c) The Colombian bundle is directly revealed preferred to the Argentine one.
d) There is not enough information to enable us to tell whether he likes the Argentine or the Bolivian bundle better.
e) none of the above

Difficulty: 1
Correct: E

7. Let A stand for the bundle (7,9), B stand for the bundle (10,5) and C stand for the bundle (6,6). When prices are (2,4) Betty chooses C and when prices are (12,3) she chooses A. Which of the following is true?
a) A is directly revealed preferred to B.
b) A is indirectly revealed preferred to B.
c) C is directly revealed preferred to A.
d) B is directly revealed preferred to A.
e) none of the above

Difficulty: 2
Correct: A

8.   Prudence plans ahead. She is going to Paris next year to study. To protect herself from exchange rate fluctuations she bought a futures contract for the number of francs she plans to spend next year, given current prices. When she arrives in Paris she can cash in her contract for this many francs no matter what the exchange rate is. If the value of the franc relative to the dollar should happen to fall before she gets to Paris

.   a)   she will be at least as well off and probably better off than if the exchange rate hadn't changed.

   b)   she will be worse off than if exchange rates hadn't changed.

   c)   she will be exactly as well off as if exchange rates hadn't changed.

Difficulty: 2
Correct: B

9.   Jose consumes rare books which cost him 8 pesos each and pieces of antique furniture which cost him 10 pesos each. He spends his entire income to buy 9 rare books and 11 pieces of antique furniture. Nigel has the same preferences as Jose but faces different prices and has a different income. Nigel has an income of 162 pounds. He buys rare books at a cost of 4 pounds each and pieces of antique furniture at a cost of 11 pounds each.

   a)   Nigel would prefer Jose's bundle to his own.

   b)   Jose would prefer Nigel's bundle to his own.

   c)   Neither would prefer the other's bundle to his own.

   d)   We can't tell whether either would prefer the other's bundle without knowing what quantities Nigel consumes.

Difficulty: 2
Correct: D

10.   Twenty years ago, Amanda consumed cans of motor oil which cost her 6 pesos each and gallons of gasoline which cost her 14 pesos each. With her income of 112 pesos, she bought 7 cans of motor oil and 5 gallons of gasoline. Today she has an income of 230 pesos. Cans of motor oil now cost 10 pesos each and gallons of gasoline now cost 32 pesos each. Assuming her preferences haven't changed, when was she better off?

   a)   now

   b)   twenty years ago

   c)   no change

   d)   There is not enough information to tell.

Difficulty: 1
Correct: B

11. When prices are (2,4), Ms. Consumer chooses the bundle (7,9) and when prices are (15,3) she chooses the bundle (10,3). Is her behavior consistent with the weak axiom of revealed preference?
   a) yes
   b) no
   c) We would have to observe a third choice to be able to say.
   d) We can't tell because we are not told her income in the two cases.
   e) none of the above

Difficulty: 1
Correct: B

12. Stan Ford currently spends $100 a week on entertainment. A rich uncle offers him a choice between a $50 a week allowance and the opportunity to buy all of his entertainment at half price. Stan would:
   a) prefer the $50 allowance.
   b) prefer the half-price subsidy.
   c) be indifferent between the allowance and the subsidy.
   d) prefer the subsidy if entertainment is a normal good and otherwise be indifferent.
   e) prefer the allowance if entertainment is an inferior good but otherwise prefer the subsidy.

Difficulty: 2
Correct: C

13. When prices are (2,10) Emil chooses the bundle (1,6) and when prices are (12,4), he chooses the bundle (7,2). Which of the following is true?
   a) Emil violates WARP.
   b) Emil prefers (7,2) to (1,6).
   c) Emil prefers (1,6) to (7,2).
   d) Emil violates SARP.
   e) none of the above

Difficulty: 2
Correct: B

14. Desmond has lived in Australia, Belgium and Canada. His tastes never changed but his income and prices did. In Australia his commodity bundle was (x1,x2) = (7,8), in Belgium it was (9,4) and in Canada it was (7,5). Prices in Canada were (p1,p2) = (3,3) and in Australia prices were (p1,p2) = (16,4).
   a) Desmond's consumption in Australia is directly revealed preferred to his consumption in Belgium.
   b) His consumption in Australia is indirectly revealed preferred to his consumption in Belgium.
   c) His consumption in Australia is indirectly but not directly revealed preferred to his consumption in Canada.
   d) We can't tell if he was better off in Belgium or in Australia.
   e) none of the above

Difficulty: 2
Correct: B

15. Remember that the Laspeyres price index uses the old quantities for the weights. In 1971, good x cost 5 and good y cost 1. They now cost 7 and 5 respectively. In 1971 the consumption bundle was $(x,y) = (2,6)$. It is now $(x,y) = (9,7)$. The Laspeyres index of current prices relative to 1971 prices is a number
   a) between .3 and .4
   b) between 2.7 and 2.8.
   c) between 1.8 and 1.9
   d) between 3.2 and 3.3
   e) none of the above

Difficulty: 1
Correct: D

16. If all prices increase by 20%,
   a) the Paasche price index increases by more than 20% and the Laspeyres price index increases by less than 20%.
   b) the Laspeyres price index increases by more than 20% and the Paasche price index increases by less than 20%.
   c) both the Paasche and the Laspeyres price index increase by more than 20%.
   d) both the Paasche and the Laspeyres price index increase by exactly 20%.
   e) both the Paasche and the Laspeyres price index increase by less than 20%.

True or False Questions

Difficulty: 2
Correct: T

1. The strong law of revealed preference says that if a consumer chooses x when he can afford y and y when he can afford z, then he will not choose z when he can afford x.

Difficulty: 1
Correct: T

2. Rudolf Rational obeys the weak axiom of revealed preferences and they don't change over time. One year he could afford bundle x but bought bundle y. If another year he buys bundle y, then he can't afford bundle x.

Difficulty: 2
Correct: T

3. If a consumer maximizes a utility function subject to a budget constraint, then his behavior will necessarily satisfy the weak axiom of revealed preference and the strong axiom of revealed preference.

Difficulty: 1
Correct: T

4. The Laspeyres index of prices in period 2 relative to period 1 tells us the ratio of the cost of buying the period 1 bundle at period 2 prices to the cost of buying the period 1 bundle at period 1 prices.

Difficulty: 1
Correct: F

5. The Laspeyres price index differs from the Paasche price index because the Laspeyres index holds prices constant and varies quantities while the Paasch index holds quantities constant and varies prices.

Difficulty: 2
Correct: F

6. Patience was maximizing her utility subject to her budget constraint. Prices changed and Patience was less well off than before. Therefore at the old prices, her new bundle must cost less than her old bundle.

Difficulty: 1
Correct: F

7. The strong axiom of revealed preference states that if a consumer chooses x when he could afford y and chooses y when he could afford x, then his income must have changed between the two observations.

Difficulty: 2
Correct: F

8. The strong axiom of revealed preference says that if a consumer bought x when he could have afforded y and y when he could have afforded z, then he will buy x whenever he can afford z.

Difficulty: 1
Correct: F

9. An increase in the price of an inferior good makes the people who consume that good better off.

Chapter 8
SLUTSKY EQUATION

Multiple-Choice Questions

1. Ernest's income elasticity of demand for natural gas is .4. His price elasticity of demand for natural gas is -.3, and he spends 10% of his income on natural gas. What is his substitution price elasticity?
   a) -.26
   b) -.34
   c) .20
   d) -.12
   e) none of the above

2. Suppose that bananas are a normal good and Woody is currently consuming 100 bananas at a price of $.10 each.
   a) His Slutsky compensated demand curve going through this point is steeper than his ordinary demand curve.
   b) His ordinary demand curve going through this point is steeper than his Slutsky compensated demand curve.
   c) His ordinary demand curve is steeper to the left and his compensated demand curve is steeper to the right of this point.
   d) Which is steeper depends on whether his price elasticity is greater than 1.
   e) none of the above

3. The following can be said about income and substitution effects:
   a) The former is always positive and the latter is always negative.
   b) Both can be either positive or negative.
   c) While the latter is always negative, the former can be either positive or negative.
   d) While the former is always negative, the latter can be either positive or negative.
   e) The former can at times be negative, but it will never overwhelm the latter.

Difficulty: 1
Correct: C

4. Nigel consumes fish and ale. The price of ale is fixed at half a quid per pint. Nigel's demand for fish is determined by the function, q = .03m-4p. If his income, m, is 1000 and the price of a sack of fish is 3, find the income and substitution effects when the price of a sack of fish goes to 4.
    a) Income effect reduces q by 1 and substitution effect reduces q by 4.
    b) Income effect reduces q by 3.46 and substitution effect reduces q by .54.
    c) Income effect reduces q by .54 and substitution effect reduces q by 3.46.
    d) Income effect reduces q by .54 and substitution effect reduces q by .54.
    e) There is not enough information to tell.

Difficulty: 1
Correct: E

5. When the price of x rises, Marvin responds by changing his demand for x. The substitution effect is the part of this change that represents his change in demand
    a) holding the prices of substitutes constant.
    b) if he is allowed to substitute as much x for y as he wishes.
    c) if his money income is held constant when the price of x changes.
    d) if the prices of all other goods are held constant.
    e) none of the above

Difficulty: 1
Correct: B

6. Polly consumes crackers and fruit. The price of fruit rose and the price of crackers stayed constant. The income effect on Polly's demand is
    a) 0 because Polly's income didn't change.
    b) the change in Polly's demand if her income is decreased by the change in the price of fruit times the amount of fruit she used to buy.
    c) the change in Polly's demand if her income is decreased by the amount she used to spend on crackers.
    d) the change in Polly's demand if her income is increased by the amount she used to spend on fruit.
    e) the change in Polly's demand if her income is increased by the change in the price of fruit times the amount of fruit she used to buy.

True or False Questions

Difficulty: 1
Correct: T

1. A Giffen good must be an inferior good.

Difficulty: 1
Correct: F

2. If a good is an inferior good, then an increase in its price will increase the demand for it.

Difficulty: 1
Correct: F

3. The compensated demand function refers to the demand function of someone who is adequately paid for what he or she sells.

Difficulty: 2
Correct: F

4. The Slutsky compensation effect measures the movement between two points on the same indifference curve.

Difficulty: 2
Correct: F

5. In the case of homothetic preferences the entire change in demand from a price change is due to the substitution effect.

Difficulty: 1
Correct: T

6. If two goods x and y are perfect complements, then if the price of x falls, the entire change in the demand for x is due to the income effect.

Difficulty: 1
Correct: T

7. If the Engel curve slopes up, then the demand curve slopes down.

Difficulty: 1
Correct: F

8. If a rational consumer prefers more of good x to less and if the price of good x rises and the prices of all other goods remain constant, then the consumer must necessarily demand less of x.

Difficulty: 1
Correct: F

9. When the price of a good rises and income remains constant there is a substitution effect on demand but no income effect.

Difficulty: 2
Correct: T

10. Ivan spends his entire income on two goods. One of them is a Giffen good. If the price of the Giffen good rises, demand for the other good must fall.

Short-Answer Questions

Difficulty: 1

1. Suggest at least one reason why it might be worth the trouble it takes to learn how to decompose the effects of a price change into an income effect and a substitution effect.

    One reason is that we know that the substitution effect of a price change in a good moves the demand for the good in the opposite direction. We also know that if demand for the good increases as income increases, then the income effect works in the same direction as the substitution effect. Therefore the decomposition into income and substitution effects allows one to prove that the demand curve slopes down whenever the Engel curve slopes up. A second reason is that someone who has already purchased his planned consumption bundle faces only a substitution effect and not an income effect when prices change, since in this case his budget line just pivots around the current consumption.

Difficulty: 2

2. A taxpayer says "Sure I pay a lot of income tax, but I don't mind because I get back just as much money as I pay in." Assuming that his facts are correct, explain why the taxpayer's reasoning is faulty. Use a diagram to show that an income tax can make a person worse off even if he is rebated an amount of money equal to what he paid in.

    See page 148 of Varian.

Difficulty: 3

3. Use a diagram to prove that in case there are two goods, the substitution effect of an increase in the price of good x reduces the demand for good x.

    A good way to proceed is to suppose that the price of x increases and the substitution effect increases demand for x. Draw the pivoted budget and notice that the new bundle would have to be a bundle that was previously rejected in favor of the old bundle. Since the pivoted budget still allows the old purchase, the weak axiom of revealed preference would be violated.

Difficulty: 2

4. Draw two different diagrams, one illustrating the Slutsky version of income and substitution effects and the other illustrating the Hicks version of income and substitution effects. How do these two notions differ?

    The diagrams can be found in Varian's book. The Slutsky version of the substitution effect has income adjusted so the consumer is just able to afford the old bundle at the new prices. The Hicks version has the consumer's income adjusted so he is exactly as well off as he was at the old prices.

Difficulty: 1

5. What conditions ensure that the quantity of a good demanded increases as its price falls? Explain your answer, using diagrams.

    The standard Slutsky analysis is called for here. See the text.

Chapter 9
BUYING AND SELLING

Multiple-Choice Questions

Difficulty: 1
Correct: C

1. Marsha Mellow is very flexible. She consumes x and y. She says "Give me x or give me y", I don't care. She is currently endowed with 15 units of x and 7 units of y. The price of x is 3 times the price of y. Marsha can trade x and y at the going prices, but has no other source of income. How much y will Marsha consume?
    a) 0 units
    b) 12 units
    c) 52 units
    d) 13 units
    e) none of the above

Difficulty: 2
Correct: C

2. Woody Crotchet insists on consuming x and y in the ratio of 2 y's for every x. He will consume them in no other ratio. The price of x is 3 times the price of y. Woody has an endowment of 20 x's and 10 y's which he can trade at the going prices. He has no other source of income. What is Woody's gross demand for x?
    a) 20
    b) 10
    c) 14
    d) There is not enough information here to be able to tell.
    e) none of the above

Difficulty: 1
Correct: C

3. Mabel consumes commodities x and y and her utility function is $U(x,y) = xy^2$ where y is her consumption of y and x is her consumption of x. Good y costs $1 per unit and good x costs $3 per unit. If she is endowed with 6 units of y and 1 unit of x, find her consumption of good y.
    a) 3
    b) 1
    c) 6
    d) 0
    e) none of the above

Difficulty: 2
Correct: A

4. Donald consumes goods x and y. His utility function is $U(x,y) = y^3$ where x is the number of units of x he consumes and y is the number of units of y he consumes. He is endowed with 8 units of x and 10 units of y. Find his consumption of y.
    a) 66
    b) 2
    c) 18
    d) 75
    e) none of the above

Difficulty: 1
Correct: D

5. Jackie's net demands for x and y are (6,-6) and her gross demands are (15,15). What is her initial endowment of x?
    a) 16
    b) 13
    c) 5
    d) 9
    e) none of the above

Difficulty: 1
Correct: C

6. Doreen consumes x and y. The price of x is 5 and the price of y is 5. Doreen has no outside income but she has an endowment of 11 units of x and 11 units of y which she can buy or sell at the going prices. She plans to consume 12 units of x and 10 units of y. If the prices change to 9 for x and 9 for y, which of the following is true?
    a) She is better off.
    b) She is worse off.
    c) There is no change in her well-being.
    d) We can't tell whether she is better or worse off.

Difficulty: 1
Correct: D

7. Milton consumes two commodities in a perfect market system. The price of x is 4 and the price of y is 1. His utility function is U(x,y) = xy. He is endowed with 28 units of good x and no y. Find his consumption of good y.
    a) 65
    b) 32
    c) 70
    d) 56
    e) none of the above

True or False Questions

Difficulty: 2
Correct: T

1. If a rational utility maximizer is a net demander of a good and if an increase in its price causes him to buy more of it, then it must be an inferior good.

Difficulty: 2
Correct: F

2. If a person is a net supplier of a normal good and its price increases while all other prices stay the same, then his demand for the good must decrease.

Difficulty: 1
Correct: T

3. If a consumer is a buyer of some goods and a seller of others, then a change in prices will generate an extra income effect in the Slutsky equation due to the revaluation of the consumer's endowment.

Difficulty: 1
Correct: T

4. If a consumer is initially endowed with a positive amount of two goods and sells some of one to get more of the other, and if she has no other sources of income, her budget line will pass through her endowment point.

Difficulty: 2
Correct: F

5. If a utility maximizer is a net seller of something and the price of that good rises, the person might possibly be made so much better off that she becomes a net buyer.

Difficulty: 1
Correct: T

6. If a person is a net seller of something and the price of that decreases she might possibly become a net buyer.

Short-Answer Questions

Difficulty: 3

1. Mr. and Mrs. Brauer owned their own home. There was a real estate boom in their town and the price of housing doubled. Their income and other prices stayed constant. The Brauer's complained that "we are being driven from our home, we can't afford to live here any more." a) Draw a diagram illustrates what happened to the Brauer's budget constraint. b) Could they have been made worse off by the change? Could they have been made better off? Explain why or why not.

A good diagram would show their budget line between housing and other goods pivoting around their current consumption. They can't be made worse off because they can still afford their old consumption bundle. They might be better off because they might choose to consume less housing and more other goods.

Difficulty: 1

2. Harvey's net demands for goods 1 and 2 are (2,-3) and his endowment is (6,5). a) What are his gross demands? b) Draw a diagram illustrating his budget line, his endowment, and his consumption. (Put good 1 on the horizontal axis.) c) Draw a dotted line to show what his budget line would be if the price of good 1 doubled and the price of good 2 stayed the same.

Harvey's gross demands are (8,2). The graph is pretty straightforward. Check the text for similar graphs.

Difficulty: 2   3.   Is it ever possible that if someone is a net seller of a good, and the price of the good he sells falls, the consumer could wind up better off than he was before by switching from being a seller to being a buyer? Draw a graph to justify your answer.

Yes, it is possible. For example, one can draw a budget line and an indifference curve for a person who is a net seller of the good on the horizontal axis. The price decrease pivots the budget line around his initial endowment which is located below and to the right of his consumption. Draw the pivoted line so that it crosses the indifference curve. The consumer can now benefit by becoming a net buyer of the good on the horizontal axis.

Difficulty: 1   4.   Is it ever possible that an increase in the price of a good for which a person is a net seller can make him worse off? Use a diagram to illustrate your answer.

No, it is not. If one is a net seller of a good and its price rises, one can still afford the old consumption bundle and hence can't be made worse off.

Difficulty: 1   5.   Peter has an endowment of 3 units of good x and 5 units of good y. He can buy and sell x at a price of $100 and y at a price of $200. He receives an income of $700 as alimony from a former spouse. a) Draw Peter's budget line for x and y. Show his initial endowment of x and y on your diagram. b) Calculate the amount of x that he could afford if he bought only x and of y he could afford if he bought only y. c) Write an equation for Peter's budget.

He could afford 20 units of x and no y or 10 units of y and no x. His budget is $100x + 200y = 2000$.

Chapter 10
LABOR SUPPLY

Multiple-Choice Questions

Difficulty: 2
Correct: A

1. Jack earns $5 per hour. He has 100 hours per week available for either labor or leisure. The government installs a plan in which each worker receives a $100 payment from the government, but has to pay 50% of his or her labor income in taxes. If his utility function is $U(c,r) = cr$ where c is dollars worth of consumption of goods and r is hours of leisure per week, how many hours per week will Jack choose to work?
    a)   30
    b)   40
    c)   26
    d)   20
    e)   none of the above

Difficulty: 1
Correct: E

2. Aristotle earns $5 per hour. He has 110 hours per week available for either labor or leisure. In the old days he paid no taxes and received nothing from the government. Now he gets a $200 payment per week from the government and he must pay half of his labor income in taxes. (His before-tax wages are the same as they were before, and he has no other source of income than wages and payments from the government.) He notices that with the government payment and his taxes, he can exactly afford the combination of leisure and consumption goods that he used to choose. How many hours per week did he work in the old days?
    a)   100
    b)   20
    c)   45
    d)   60
    e)   none of the above

Difficulty: 2
Correct: C

3. Rhoda takes a job with a construction company. She earns $5 an hour for the first 40 hours of each week and then gets "double-time" for overtime. That is, she is paid $10 an hour for every hour beyond 40 hours a week that she works. Rhoda has 70 hours a week available to divide between construction work and leisure. She has no other source of income, and her utility function is $U = cr$ where c is her income to spend on goods and r is the number of hours of leisure that she has per week. She is allowed to work as many hours as she wants to. How many hours will she work?
    a)   50
    b)   25
    c)   45
    d)   35
    e)   none of the above

Difficulty: 2
Correct: C

4. Wendy and Mac work in fast-food restaurants. Wendy is paid $4 an hour for the first 40 hours a week that she works and $6 an hour for every hour beyond 40 hours per week. Mac gets $5 an hour no matter how many hours he works. Each has 110 hours per week to allocate between work and leisure. Each has a utility function $U = cr$ where c is expenditure per week on consumption and r is hours of leisure per week. Each can choose the number of hours to work. If Wendy works W hours and Mac works M hours, then

   a) W=1.5M.
   b) W<M.
   c) W-M=6 2/3.
   d) W-M=10.
   e) none of the above

Difficulty: 2
Correct: B

5. Heather and Myrtle have the same tastes. Heather is paid $10 an hour and chooses to work 9 hours a day. Myrtle is paid $9 an hour for the first 8 hours she works and $18 an hour for any time she works beyond 8 hours a day.

   a) Since she has the same tastes as Heather and can earn the same income as Heather by working 9 hours a day, that is what Myrtle will choose.
   b) Unless there is a kink in her indifference curve, Heather would be better off if she faced the same pay schedule as Myrtle.
   c) Myrtle would prefer Heather's pay schedule to her own.
   d) Myrtle will work less than 9 hours a day.
   e) none of the above

Difficulty: 1
Correct: C

6. Mike Teevee likes to watch television and to eat candy. In fact his utility function is $U(x,y) = x^2 y$ where x is the number of hours he spends watching television and y is the number of dollars per week he spends on candy. Mike's mother doesn't like him to watch so much television. She limits his television watching to 36 hours a week and in addition she pays him $1 an hour for every hour that he reduces his television watching below 36 hours a week. If this is Mike's only source of income to buy candy, how many hours of television does he watch per week?

   a) 36
   b) 12
   c) 24
   d) 18
   e) 16

Difficulty: 1
Correct: B

7. Minnie earns $5 an hour. She has 120 hours a week available for either labor or leisure. If her utility function is $U(c,r) = cr$ where c is dollars worth of goods and r is hours of leisure, how many hours per week will she work?
    a) 80
    b) 60
    c) 40
    d) 24
    e) none of the above

True or False Questions

Difficulty: 2
Correct: F

1. If all goods are normal goods, then an increase in the wage rate will make people want to work more hours.

Difficulty: 2
Correct: T

2. If someone has a Cobb-Douglas utility function and no income from any source other than labor earnings, an increase in wages will not change the amount that person chooses to work.

Difficulty: 1
Correct: T

3. If leisure is a normal good, then an increase in non-labor income will reduce labor supply.

Difficulty: 1
Correct: F

4. A person's full income is how much income he or she would have if there were no taxes.

Difficulty: 1
Correct: F

5. An increase in wages causes the budget line between leisure and other goods to shift outward in a parallel fashion.

Difficulty: 1
Correct: T

6. If leisure is an inferior good, then an increase in the wage rate will make a person work more.

Short-Answer Questions

Difficulty: 2

1. Dudley's utility function for goods and leisure is $U(G,L) = G-(20-L)(20-L)$ where G is consumption of goods and L is the number of hours of leisure per day. Goods cost $1 per unit. a) If Dudley has an income from nonlabor sources of $25 per day and could work as much as he chose to but gets zero wages, how much would he work? b) Sketch Dudley's indifference curves on a graph with leisure on the horizontal axis and income on the vertical axis. If Dudley's non-labor income were $25 a day and he could work as much as he wished for $10 an hour, how many hours a day would he choose to work?

    a) 4 hours a day. b) 9 hours a day.

Difficulty: 2   2.   Marilyn is a journalist. She is considering two possible jobs. One job is as an editor for a magazine. The other job is writing "free-lance" articles and selling them to whoever buys them. If she works for the magazine, she must spend 10 hours a day at work and commuting. She will be paid $130 a day net of commuting costs and taxes if she takes this job. If she writes free-lance articles, she can work at home and work as many hours a day as she pleases. She estimates that she would earn $10 an hour after taxes if she does this. Her utility function is $U = (R^3)C$ where R is the number of hours a day she spends not working or commuting and C is her earnings.
a) If Marilyn chooses to free-lance, how many hours will she work?
b) Calculate her utility in each job and tell which she will choose.

a) 6 hours. b) If she freelances, U=349,920. If she works for the magazine U=356,720. She should choose the magazine.

Difficulty: 1   3.   Ernie's wage rate is $10 an hour. He has no earnings other than his labor income. His utility function is $U(C,L) = C(R^2)$ where C is the amount of money he spends on consumption, and R is the number of hours a day he spends NOT working. a) Write an equation that describes Ernie's budget constraint. b) How many hours does Ernie choose to work per day? c) How much money does he spend on consumption per day?

a) C+10R=240 b) 8 c) 80

Difficulty: 1   4.   This problem concerns Ernie from the previous problem. Suppose that Ernie has to pay an income tax of 20% of his earnings. a) Write Ernie's budget constraint. b) How many hours a day will he choose to work? c) How much taxes will he pay per day? d) How much will he spend per day on consumption?

a) C+8R=192 b) 8 c) $16 a day d) $64

Difficulty: 2   5.   This question also concerns Ernie from the previous question. Suppose that the government spends the money from the taxes it collects to make lump sum "income support payments." The government pays Ernie a lump sum of $16 a day and taxes his income at 20%. a) Write down Ernie's budget equation. b) How many hours will he work per day? c) How much taxes does he pay per day?

a) 8R+C=208 b) 7 and two thirds c) 15 and one third dollars per day.

Difficulty: 3   6. This question asks more about Ernie from the previous question. The government decides to introduce a progressive tax system. It taxes Ernie nothing for the first $40 a day that he earns and then taxes him at 40% on everything that he earns beyond $40 a day. a) Draw a diagram depicting Ernie's budget with leisure on the horizontal axis and consumption on the vertical axis. b) At what point does the budget have a kink? c) Write equations for the two lines that bound his budget constraint. d) How many hours per day will Ernie choose to work? e) How much tax will he pay per day?

a), b), and c) The budget set is the area lying below the two lines $10R + C = 240$ and $6R + C = 160$. The kink is at the point $R = 20$, $C = 40$. d) 6.222 hours a day. e) 12.888 dollars per day.

Difficulty: 3   7. May's utility function is $U = C + 14\sqrt{D} - .5(H + J)^2$ where C is dollars spent on goods other than housecleaning, D is the number of hours per day that somebody spends cleaning her house, H is the number of hours per day May spends cleaning her house, and J is the number of hours per day May spends working at her job. All May's income comes from her job. She can work as many hours a day as she wishes at a wage of $7 an hour. a) If she cannot hire anyone to do her housecleaning, how many hours will she spend on the job and how many hours will she spend housecleaning? b) If she can hire a housecleaner at $5 an hour, how many hours will she work on her job, how many hours of housecleaning will she hire, and how many hours will she clean house?

a) 6 hours, 1 hour b) 7 hours, 49/25, 0

Difficulty: 2   8. Leo thinks leisure and goods are perfect complements. Goods cost $1 per unit. Leo wants to consume 5 units of goods per hour of leisure. Leo can work as much as he wants to at the wage rate of $15 an hour. He has no other source of income. a) How many hours a day will Leo choose to spend at leisure? b) Draw a diagram showing Leo's budget and his choice of goods and leisure. c) Will Leo work more or less if his wage rate increases?

a) 18 hours a day c) less

Difficulty: 2 9.   Lucetta changes light bulbs. She is paid $10 an hour. She can work as many hours as she wishes. Lucetta works only 6 hours a day. But she says she loves her job and is happier working at this job than she would be if she made the same income without working at all. Though this may sound strange, Lucetta is perfectly rational. Draw a graph showing leisure on the horizontal axis and income on the vertical axis. Draw a budget line and some indifference curves for Lucetta that are consistent with Lucetta's words and actions. Explain in words what happens.

Work for Lucetta is desirable on average but undesirable at the margin when she is working 6 hours a day. The diagram will work if you draw a U-shaped indifference curve tangent to her budget line at 6 hours. Make sure that this indifference curve intersects the horizontal line through her consumption choice somewhere to the right of her choice but to the left of where she doesn't work at all.

Multiple-Choice Questions

Difficulty: 2
Correct: B

1. If current and future consumption are both normal goods, an increase in the interest rate will necessarily
    a) cause savers to save more.
    b) cause borrowers to borrow less.
    c) reduce everyone's current consumption.
    d) more than one of the above
    e) none of the above

Difficulty: 2
Correct: E

2. Harvey Habit has a utility function $U(c_1,c_2) = \min\{c_1,c_2\}$ where c_1 and c_2 are his consumption in periods 1 and 2 respectively. Harvey earns $210 in period 1 and he will earn $55 in period 2. Harvey can borrow or lend at an interest rate of 10%. There is no inflation.
    a) Harvey will save $77.50.
    b) Harvey will borrow $77.50.
    c) Harvey will neither borrow nor lend.
    d) Harvey will save $132.50.
    e) none of the above

Difficulty: 2
Correct: D

3. O. B. Kandle will live for only two periods. In the first period he will earn $100,000. In the second period he will retire and live on his savings. Mr. Kandle has a Cobb-Douglas utility function $U(c_1,c_2) = (c_1)^2(c_2)$ where c_1 is his period 1 consumption and c_2 is his period 2 consumption. The real interest rate is r.
    a) If the interest rate rises, Mr. Kandle will save more.
    b) If the interest rate rises, Mr. Kandle will save less.
    c) The effect of the interest rate is ambiguous, but we can tell that Mr. Kandle will arrange so that he consumes the same amount in each period.
    d) A change in the interest rate won't affect his saving.
    e) none of the above

Difficulty: 2
Correct: B

4. Suppose that a person can borrow and lend at an interest rate of 10%. But there is a 5% rate of inflation and one has to pay an income tax of 30% on all interest income. If you borrow money, you can deduct interest as an expense. Where current consumption is on the horizontal axis and future consumption is on the vertical axis,
    a) the budget line will have a kink at the point of no saving or lending.
    b) the budget line will be a straight line with a slope of about -1.02.
    c) the budget line will be a straight line with a slope of about -1.05.
    d) the budget line will be a straight line with a slope of about -1.35.
    e) none of the above

Difficulty: 2
Correct: B

5. For every two boxes of strawberries that she consumes, Millicent insists on having one pitcher of cream. She does not, however, insist on consuming the same amount every week. Her utility function is $U = \min\{2s_1, c_1\}\min\{2s_2, c_2\}$ where s_1 and s_2 are the number of boxes of strawberries she consumes this week and next week and c_1 and c_2 are the number of pitchers of cream she consumes this week and next. Strawberries cost $2 a box and cream costs $1 a pitcher. The present value of the money she has to spend on strawberries and cream in the next two weeks is $100. The weekly interest rate is 1%. How many boxes of strawberries will she buy this week?
    a) 10
    b) 20
    c) 22
    d) 14.1
    e) 6.06

Difficulty: 2
Correct: A

6. Roger's utility function is $U = \min\{a_1, a_2\}\min\{b_1, b_2\}$ where a_1 and a_2 are the number of piano lessons he consumes this year and next and b_1 and b_2 are the number of ice skating lessons he consumes this year and next. The price of piano lessons is $10 each and the price of ice skating lessons is $4 each. The prices won't change, but the interest rate is 7%. If Roger consumes 20 piano lessons this year, how many ice-skating lessons will he consume next year?
    a) 50
    b) 20
    c) 40
    d) 30
    e) There is not enough information for us to tell.

Difficulty: 1
Correct: B

7. If a consumer viewed a unit of consumption in period 1 as a perfect substitute for a unit of consumption in period 2 and if the real interest rate were positive, the consumer would
    a) consume only in period 1.
    b) consume only in period 2.
    c) consume equal amounts in each period.
    d) consume more in the first period than the second if income elasticity exceeds one, but otherwise would consume more in the second period than in the first.
    e) would equalize expenditures but not consumption in the two periods.

True or False Questions

Difficulty: 1
Correct: T

1. An increase in the interest rate cannot make a lender who satisfies WARP become a borrower.

Difficulty: 1
Correct: T

2. If the real interest rate is positive, then a unit of future consumption can be had for the sacrifice of less than one unit of current consumption.

Difficulty: 1
Correct: F

3. The real interest is the interest rate that one receives net of brokerage costs or fees imposed by financial intermediaries.

Difficulty: 2
Correct: T

4. The present value of a given stream of income necessarily decreases as the interest rate increases.

Difficulty: 1
Correct: T

5. In a graph that has current consumption on the horizontal axis and future consumption on the vertical axis, the horizontal intercept of the budget line is the present value of all one's income in the two periods.

Difficulty: 1
Correct: T

6. If a consumer can borrow and lend at the interest rate, then he can exactly afford a consumption plan if the present value of his consumption equals the present value of his income.

Difficulty: 1
Correct: F

7. It would be a mistake to choose the investment that maximizes the present value of your income stream unless you planned to spend your entire wealth in the present.

Difficulty: 2
Correct: T

8. If the interest rate you can borrow at is higher than the interest rate you can lend at, your budget for current and future consumption is still a convex set.

Difficulty: 2
Correct: F

9. If apples today are perfect substitutes for bananas today, then apples today must also be perfect substitutes for bananas tomorrow.

Short-Answer Questions

Difficulty: 2

1. Ophelia says "If I could lend money at the rates I must pay to borrow, I would. And if I could borrow money at the rates I receive when I lend, I would again. But forsooth, although I spend, I neither borrow nor lend." Contrary to common belief, Ophelia is entirely rational. Draw a diagram to show how Ophelia's remarks can be consistent with rational behavior and smooth convex preferences if she pays a different interest rate when she borrows than she gets when she lends. Explain what happens in words.

    Ophelia's budget between current and future consumption is kinked at the point where her consumption in each period equals her income. The highest indifference curve to touch her budget touches at the kink. The extensions of each of the lines that meet at the kink pass above this indifference curve for a ways. These lines are the lines she could move along if she could borrow at the lending rate and lend at the borrowing rate, respectively.

Difficulty: 3

2. Patience has the utility function $U(c_1,c_2) = \sqrt{c_1} + 2\sqrt{c_2}$ where c_1 is her consumption in period 1 and c_2 is her consumption in period 2. She will earn 100 units of the consumption good in period 1 and 100 units of the consumption good in period 2. She can borrow or lend at an interest rate of 10%. a) Write an equation that describes Patience's budget. b) If Patience neither borrows nor lends, what will be her marginal rate of substitution between current and future consumption? c) If Patience does the optimal amount of borrowing or saving, what will be the ratio of her period 2 consumption to her period 1 consumption?

    a) $c_1 + c_2/1.1 = 100 + 100/1.1$. b) 2 c) She will consume 4.84 times as much in period 2 as in period 1.

Difficulty: 2   3.   Buzz is a chicken farmer. His earnings will be 100 this year and 100 next year. He can lend money at an interest rate of 20%. Because of a subsidized loan program for chicken farmers he can borrow money at an interest rate of 10%. No matter what he borrows or lends, his earnings will still be 100 each year. a) If he is not allowed to both borrow and lend, draw a graph showing his budget between consumption this year and consumption next year. Put numerical labels on the vertical and horizontal intercepts of the budget set. b) Suppose that Buzz is allowed to borrow up to the present value of next year's earnings at 10% and is also allowed to make loans. Draw Buzz's budget constraint in this case.

a) Budget line is kinked at 100,100. Vertical intercept is 220. Horizontal intercept is $100+100/1.1$. b) Budget constraint is a straight line with slope -1.2 passing through horizontal intercept of previous budget line.

Difficulty: 2   4.   Ymir Larson farms near Niffleheim, Minnesota. He works 80 hours a week. He can either grow rutabagas or pigs. Every hour that he spends growing rutabagas gives him $2 of income this year. Every hour that he spends with the pigs this year will add $4 to his income next year. In fact, next year's weekly income will be $100+4H$ dollars where H is the number of hours he spends with the pigs this year. Ymir's utility function is $U(c1,c2)=\min\{c1,c2\}$ where c1 and c2 are his consumption expenditures this year and next year. Ymir doesn't believe in banks and will neither lend money nor borrow money. a) Draw Ymir's budget line for current and future consumption, labeling key points on it. b) How many hours a week will he choose to spend with the pigs? c) How much money will he spend per week on consumption in each year?

a)Budget set is bounded by a line from (0,420) to (160,100) and a vertical line from (160,100) to the horizontal axis. b)10 c)170

Difficulty: 2   5.   This question concerns Ymir Larson from the previous question. Ymir could borrow money at the bank in Niffleheim at an interest rate of 10%. He could lend money to the bank at 5%. a) Draw a diagram to show Ymir's budget line if he was willing to borrow and lend. b) If Ymir was willing to deal with bankers, how much time would he spend with the pigs? c) How much would he consume per week in each period?

a) Budget line is a line with slope -1.1 touching the vertical axis at (0,420). b) 80 hours a week. c) 200

Difficulty: 2   6.   Luella has to pay an interest rate of 50% to borrow. She only gets an interest rate of 5% if she lends. She is currently endowed with $1000 in period 1 and $1050 in period 2. She considers two alternative investment projects. She can only choose one of them. For project A she would HAVE TO PAY $500 in period 1 and would BE PAID BACK $630 in period 2. For project B, she would BE PAID $500 in period 1 and would HAVE TO PAY BACK $525 in period 2. a) Diagram her budget set if she chooses project A. Also show her budget if she chooses project B. b) If she neither borrows nor lends, which project has the higher present value at the interest rate 50%? Which has the higher present value at an interest rate of 5%? c) Draw indifference curves such that she should choose A. d) With different preferences might she choose B?

b) B,A d) yes

Difficulty: 2   7.   In an isolated peasant village, the only crop is corn. Good harvests alternate with bad harvests. This year the harvest will be 1000 bushels. Next year it will be 150 bushels. There is no trade with the outside world. Corn can be stored, but rats will eat 25% of what is stored in a year. The villagers have the Cobb-Douglas utility function $U(c1,c2) = c1c2$ where c1 is consumption this year and c2 is consumption next year. a) Draw a budget line for the village with this year's consumption on the horizontal axis and next year's consumption on the vertical axis. On your graph show the quantities at which the budget line intercepts the vertical and horizontal axes. b) How much will the villagers consume this year? c) How much will the rats eat? d) How much will the villagers consume next year?

b)600 c) 100 d) 450

Difficulty: 2   8.   This question concerns the peasant village of the previous question. Suppose that the village is opened up to trade with the rest of the world. Suppose that the world price of corn does not change from year to year. The villagers are able to sell their corn at the world price and to borrow and lend at an interest rate of 10%. For this problem suppose that transportation costs are zero. a) Draw the appropriate budget line for the villagers now. b) Solve for the amount they would consume in the first period and in the second period.

b) 568, 624 (rounded)

Difficulty: 3

9.   This problem refers to the peasant village of the previous two problems. Suppose that there is a transportation cost equal to 5% of the value of corn shipped into or out of the village. Rework the previous problem under this assumption.

The budget line would have a kink at the point (1000, 150). Moving up and to the right, the slope would be -1. Moving down to the left, the slope would be -1.1. The villagers would choose to consume 575 in period 1. They would sell 475 units and invest the proceeds at 10% interest. But they would have to pay a 5% transportation cost both when they sold this year's crop and again when they imported corn next year. The interest rate that they get for waiting equals the cost of hauling in and out so that one unit of next year's consumption costs exactly one unit of this year's consumption.

Chapter 12
ASSET MARKETS

Multiple-Choice Questions

Difficulty: 2
Correct: A

1. Vincent Smudge's paintings are unappreciated now. Nobody is willing to pay anything to have them on the walls. In 5 years Smudge's work will gain enduring popularity. People will suddenly be willing to pay $1000 a year to have an original Smudge on their walls and will continue to be willing to do so ever after. If investors realize that this is the case, and if the interest rate is and always will be r, a painting by Smudge will currently be worth about
   a) $(1000/r)(1/(1+r)^5$
   b) $1000/r-5000/r$
   c) $1000(1+r)^5$
   d) $1000(1/r)^5$
   e) $200/r$

Difficulty: 1
Correct: C

2. If the interest rate is r percent and will remain r percent forever, then a bond that will pay 25 dollars a year forever is worth
   a) $25/(1+r)$.
   b) $25(1+r)$.
   c) $25/r$.
   d) $25/(1+r+r^2+...+r^n+...)$.
   e) none of the above

Difficulty: 2
Correct: B

3. If the nominal interest rate is 80% and the rate of inflation is 50%, then the exact real rate of interest is
   a) 10%.
   b) 20%.
   c) 30%.
   d) 40%.
   e) none of the above

Difficulty: 1
Correct: C

4. The interest rate is 10%. A certain piece of land can be used either for a parking lot, in which case it will yield a net return of $5,000 per year forever or it can have a house built on it. Building the house would cost $50,000. If a house is built on the lot, it will yield a stream of net income equal to $12,000 per year. No other uses are contemplated. The theory of asset markets predicts that
   a) The lot will sell for $120,000 and a house will be built on it.
   b) The lot will sell for $50,000 and a parking lot will be built on it.
   c) The lot will sell for $70,000 and a house will be built on it.
   d) The lot will sell for $13,200 and a house will be built on it.

Difficulty: 1
Correct: D

5.   The interest rate is 8% and investors are convinced it will stay at 8% for the next 10 years. A corporate bond comes on the market that will pay $160 a year to whoever owns it for each of the next 7 years. At the end of 7 years, the issuer of the bond will "redeem" the bond by buying it back from the bondholder for $2000. What should this bond sell for?
a) $3120
b) $2160
c) $1600
d) $2000
e) $2780

Difficulty: 2
Correct: B

6.   The interest rate will be 10% for one more year, but a year from now, it will fall to 5% and stay at 5% forever. What is the market value of an investment that is sure to pay $110 a year forever, starting two years from today?
a) $2200
b) $2300
c) $115
d) $1260
e)   none of the above

Difficulty: 2
Correct: B

7.   A certain wine costs $3 a bottle to produce. It improves in taste if stored properly for a period of time. When it is newly bottled, people are willing to pay only $2 a bottle to drink it. But the amount that people are willing to pay to drink a bottle of this wine will rise by $3 a year for the next 50 years. Storage costs, not including interest, are $.50 per year. If the interest rate is 5% and it is kept by rational investors, how old will it be when it is drunk and what will be its price at that time?
a)   50 years old and $152
b)   16 years old and $50
c)   50 years old and $153
d)   20 years old and $63
e)   4 years old and $14

Difficulty: 2
Correct: B

8. A wine costs $3 a bottle to produce. The amount people are willing to pay to drink it when it is t years old is $2+3t. It costs $.50 a bottle per year to store it. The interest rate is 5%. If the annual cost of storing the wine rises to $1, what will happen eventually to the price of this kind of wine when it is drunk and to the length of time for which it is stored?
   a) Both will rise.
   b) Both will fall.
   c) The price would rise and the time for which it is stored would fall.
   d) The price would not change but the time for which it is stored would fall.
   e) The price would rise and the time for which it is stored would stay constant.

Difficulty: 2
Correct: D

9. You buy a painting for $1280. Its market value will rise by $80 per year for the next 30 years. It is worth $80 a year to you to have it hanging on the wall. The interest rate is 10%. In how many years will you sell it?
   a) 30
   b) Immediately
   c) 8
   d) 4
   e) 5

Difficulty: 3
Correct: D

10. Art Dreck's paintings are terribly unpopular now. In fact nobody would pay a dime to have one of his paintings on the wall now. But experts believe that 10 years from now there will be a craze for Dreck paintings. The craze will last for 2 years and then nobody will ever want to see a Dreck again. During this 2 year period, people will be willing to pay $1100 a year to have an original Dreck on the wall. The interest rate is r. If the experts' belief is widely held among investors, today's market value of a Dreck should be about:
   a) $2200/r$
   b) $2200/(1+r)$
   c) $1100(1+r)^{10}+1100(1+r)^{11}$
   d) $1100/(1+r)^{10}+1100/(1+r)^{11}$
   e) $1100r +1100r^2$

Difficulty: 2
Correct: B

11. A large (subterranean) pool of oil lies in a remote region of Ohio. Oil companies have explored this region and know how much oil there is. They have purchased the rights to drill and extract oil when they wish to do so. Because of the extremely forbidding geography and the savagery of the natives, the companies have decided to postpone extraction until the price of oil is higher. The theory of intertemporal arbitrage predicts that the
    a) companies are behaving irrationally.
    b) price of rights to this oil must rise at the interest rate.
    c) oil companies will not drill unless production costs fall.
    d) price of rights to this oil will stay constant until it pays to extract.
    e) none of the above

Difficulty: 2
Correct: B

12. Suppose that a dispute in the Persian Gulf halts the sale of oil from the Persian Gulf for 1 year. At the same time an important new oil field is found in a place where nobody expected there to be oil. What does economic theory predict will be the effect on the futures price of oil to be delivered 2 years from now?
    a) It will fall if the new pool is larger than the stock of oil in the Persian Gulf and rise otherwise.
    b) It will fall.
    c) It will rise unless the new pool can be brought into production before the Persian Gulf supply is resumed.
    d) It will rise.
    e) It will rise if the cost of extraction for the new oil is higher than the cost of extraction in the Persian Gulf and fall otherwise.

True or False Questions

Difficulty: 1
Correct: F

1. If the interest rate is 10%, then an asset that returns $1 a year forever is worth $1/1.1.

Difficulty: 2
Correct: F

2. Because there is a fixed stock of diamonds in the world, the inter-temporal arbitrage condition implies that the price of diamonds should rise at the interest rate.

Short-Answer Questions

Difficulty: 2

1   The interest rate is 10% and will remain 10% forever. Suppose that you do not drink wine but are interested in buying it for investment purposes. How much would you be willing to pay for each of the following? i) A bottle of wine that will be worth $22 a year from now and will then go bad and be worthless. ii) A bottle of wine that will be worth $22 a year from now and will rise in value by $1 a year forever? Explain your answer.

Both are worth $20. Each will be sold and drunk in 1 year. The increase in value of $1 per year on a $22 bottle of wine is not a high enough rate of return for anyone to want to hold it another year.

Difficulty: 3

2.   A certain wine costs $3 a bottle to produce. The amount that people are willing to pay to drink it t years after it has been bottled is $2+3t. Storage costs, not including interest, are $.50 per year. If the interest rate is 5%, how much would a rational investor be willing to pay for it at the time it is bottled? Explain how you get your answer. Feel free to write formulas for present value calculations without working out the numerical answer if it involves long calculations. (Hint: How long would the wine be kept before it is drunk? At what price would it sell?)

Wine would be kept for 16 years and sold for $50. The present value of this is $50/(1.05)^{16}$. From this number we have to subtract the present value of storage costs which is the present value of paying $.50 a year for 16 years. This is the cost of paying $.50 a year forever, starting now minus the cost of paying $.50 a year forever starting in 16 years or $.50(1/r)(1-1/(1+r)^{16})$.

Difficulty: 2

3.   Suppose that the cost of personal computers falls by 20% per year. To make this problem relatively easy, we will assume that their quality does not change and that computers never wear out. You plan to get one sometime. What is the rational way to decide when to buy one?

Figure out what it is worth to you to have the computer for one year. Notice that the cost to you of having it is approximately the difference between the price of a computer at the beginning of the year and the price at the end of the year. If the value to you is V and the current price is P, you buy if V > .2P. Otherwise you wait. Eventually, .2P will be smaller than V. Then you buy.

Difficulty: 2

4. According to a recent story in the New York Times, the South African gold strike has been costing South African mining companies about $7.5 million per day. Assuming that this number is the value of the gold that was not mined because of the strike, minus the labor costs (and other operating costs) that are saved by shutting down the mines, what is wrong with this calculation?

The gold that is not mined now will still be there and can be extracted later. The figure that was reached would be the cost if the gold that would have been mined had somehow been destroyed by the strike. The actual costs would be more closely measured by the interest cost of postponement of the net revenues from the gold mines until the strike is settled.

Chapter 13
UNCERTAINTY

Multiple-Choice Questions

Difficulty: 1
Correct: C

1. Prufrock is risk averse. He is offered a gamble in which with probability 1/4 he will lose $1000 and with probability 3/4, he will win $500. Will Prufrock take the gamble?
    a) yes
    b) no
    c) There is not enough information for us to tell.

Difficulty: 3
Correct: B

2. Timmy Qualm's uncle gave him a lottery ticket. With probability 1/2 the ticket will be worth $100 and with probability 1/2 it will be worthless. Let x be Timmy's wealth if the lottery ticket is a winner and y his wealth if it is a loser. Timmy's preferences over alternative contingent commodity bundles are represented by the utility function $U(x,y) = \min\{2x-y, 2y-x\}$. He has no risks other than the ticket.
    a) Timmy would sell his lottery ticket for $25 but not for less.
    b) Timmy hates risk so much that he'd be willing to throw away the lottery ticket rather than worry about whether he won.
    c) Timmy satisfies the expected utility hypothesis.
    d) Timmy is misnamed; he is a risk lover.
    e) none of the above

Difficulty: 2
Correct: D

3. There are two events, 1 and 2. The probability of event 1 is p and the probability of event 2 is 1-p. Sally Kink is an expected utility maximizer with a utility function $pu(c1) + (1-p)u(c2)$ where for any number, x, $u(x) = 2x$ if $x < 1000$ and $u(x) = 2000 + x$ if x is greater than or equal to 1000.
    a) Sally is a risk lover.
    b) Sally will be risk averse if she is poor but will be a risk lover if she is rich.
    c) Sally will be a risk lover if she is poor but a risk averter if she is rich.
    d) If there is no chance of her wealth being greater than 1000, Sally will take any bet that has a positive expected value of net winnings.
    e) none of the above

Difficulty: 2
Correct: E

4. Socrates owns just one ship. The ship is worth $200 million dollars. If the ship sinks, Socrates loses $200 million. The probability that it will sink is .02. Socrates' total wealth is $225 million. He is an expected utility maximizer with von Neuman Morgenstern utility U(W) equal to the square root of W. What is the maximum amount that Socrates would be willing to pay for full-coverage insurance on his ship?
   a) $4 million.
   b) $2 million.
   c) $3.84 million.
   d) $4.82 million.
   e) $5.96 million.

Difficulty: 2
Correct: C

5. Buck Columbus is thinking of starting a pinball palace near a large midwestern university. Buck is an expected utility maximizer with a von Neuman Morgenstern utility function, $U(W) = 1000 + W - .01W^2$ where W is the number of thousands of dollars of wealth he has. Buck's total wealth is $20,000 and he would have to invest it all to start the palace. With probability 2/3 the palace will be a failure and he'll lose his investment. With probability 1/3 it will succeed and his wealth will grow to $x. Ignoring interest, what is the smallest x for which the investment is worthwhile?
   a) $60,000
   b) $54,000
   c) $80,000
   d) $73,487
   e) $72,000

Difficulty: 2
Correct: C

6. Oskar's preferences over gambles in which the probability of events 1 and 2 are both 1/2 can be represented by the von Neuman Morgenstern utility function $.5v(y1) + .5v(y2)$ where y1 is his consumption if event 1 happens and y2 is his consumption if event 2 happens and where the function v(x) is the square root of x for any x. A gamble that allows him a consumption of 9 if event 1 happens and 25 if event 2 happens is exactly as good for Oskar as being sure to have an income of
   a) 12.5.
   b) 9.
   c) 16.
   d) 17.
   e) none of the above

Difficulty: 2
Correct: A

7. Mabel and Emil were contemplating marriage. They got to talking. Mabel said that she always acted according to the expected utility hypothesis where she tried to maximize the expected value of the log of her income. Emil said that he too was an expected utility maximizer, but he tried to maximize the expected value of the square of his income. Mabel said, "I fear we must part. Our attitudes toward risk are too different." Emil said, "Never fear, my dear, the square of income is a monotonic increasing function of the log of income, so we really have the same preferences." Who is right about whether their preferences toward risk are different?
a) Mabel
b) Emil
c) neither one
d) both

Difficulty: 1
Correct: E

8. Ronald has $18,000. But he is forced to bet it on the flip of a fair coin. If he wins he has $36,000. If he loses he has nothing. Ronald's expected utility function is $.5\sqrt{x}+.5\sqrt{y}$ where x is his wealth if heads come up and y is his wealth if tails come up. Since he must make this bet he is exactly as well off as if he had a perfectly safe income of
a) $16,000.
b) $15,000.
c) $12,000.
d) $11,000.
e) $9,000.

Difficulty: 1
Correct: A

9. Gary likes to gamble. Donna offers to bet him $70 on the outcome of a boat race. If Gary's boat wins, Donna would give him $70. If Gary's boat does not win, Gary would give her $70. Gary's utility function is $U(c1,c2,p1,p2)=p1c1^2+p2c2^2$ where p1 and p2 are the probabilities of events 1 and 2 and where c1 and c2 are his consumption if events 1 and 2 occur respectively. Gary's total wealth is currently only $80 and he believes that the probability that he will win the race is .3. Will he increase his expected utility by taking the bet?
a) yes
b) no
c) He is indifferent between taking it and not taking it.

Difficulty: 3
Correct: A

10. Clancy has $1200. He is thinking of betting on a boxing match. For $4, he can buy a coupon that will pay $10 if Boxer A wins and nothing otherwise. For $6 he can buy a coupon that will pay $10 if Boxer B wins and nothing otherwise. Clancy doesn't agree with these odds. He thinks that the two fighters each have a probability of 1/2 of winning. If he is an expected utility maximizer who tries to maximize the expected value of the ln W where ln W is the natural log of his wealth, it would be rational for him to buy
a) 50 "A coupons" and no "B coupons".
b) 100 "A coupons" and no "B coupons".
c) 50 "B coupons" and no "A coupons".
d) 100 "B coupons" and no "A coupons".
e) 100 of each kind of coupon. ·

Difficulty: 3
Correct: E

11. Diego has $6400. He plans to bet on a soccer game. Team A is a favorite to win. Assume no ties can occur. For $.80 one can buy a ticket that will pay $1 if team A wins and nothing if B wins. For $.20 one can buy a ticket that pays $1 if team B wins and nothing if A wins. Diego thinks the two teams are equally likely to win. He buys tickets so as to maximize the expected value of ln W (the natural log of his wealth). After he buys his tickets, team A loses a star player and the ticket prices move to $.50 for either team. Diego buys some new tickets and sells some of his old ones. The game is then played and team A wins. How much wealth does he end up with?
a) $5000
b) $15000
c) $6400
d) $8400
e) $10000

True or False Questions

Difficulty: 1
Correct: F

1. Of any two gambles, no matter what their expected returns, a risk averter will choose the one with the smaller variance.

Difficulty: 2
Correct: T

2. An expected utility maximizer's preferences between two bundles contingent on event 1 happening must be independent of what he will get if event 2 happens.

Difficulty: 1
Correct: T

3. If someone has convex preferences between all contingent commodity bundles, then he or she must be risk averse.

Short-Answer Questions

Difficulty: 2   1.   Gaston Gourmand loves good food. Due to an unusual ailment, he has a probability of 1/4 of losing his sense of smell, which would greatly reduce his enjoyment of food. Gaston finds an insurance company that will sell him "insurance" where he gets \$3x if he loses his smell and gets \$x if he doesn't. He can also buy "negative insurance" where he pays \$3x if he loses his sense of smell and gets x dollars if he doesn't. Gaston says, "Money will be only half as important to me if I lose my sense of smell." If we look at his expected utility function, we see what he means. Where c1 is his consumption if he retains his sense of smell and c2 is his income if he loses his sense of smell, Gaston has the expected utility function $U(c1,c2)=3/4\sqrt{c1}+1/4(1/2\sqrt{c2})$. What insurance should he buy?

Negative insurance so that his wealth is 4 times as large if he doesn't lose his smell than if he does.

Difficulty: 2   2.   Oliver takes his wealth of \$1000 to a casino. He can bet as much as he likes on the toss of a coin, but the "house" takes a cut. If Oliver bets \$x on heads, then if heads come up, he gets \$.8x and if tails come up he pays \$x. Similarly if he bets \$x on tails and if tails comes up he wins \$.8x and if heads come up he pays \$x. Draw a graph with dollars contingent on heads and dollars contingent on tails on the two axes. Show Oliver's budget constraint. Oliver is an expected utility maximizer with the utility function $U(h,t)=1/2h^2+1/2t^2$ where h is his wealth if heads come up and t is his wealth if tails come up. Draw the highest indifference curve that Oliver can reach with his budget. What bets if any does he make?

Budget kinks at (1000,1000), it meets the axes at (1800,0) and (0,1800). Indifference curves are quarter circles. Oliver will gamble his entire wealth, either betting it all on heads or all on tails.

Difficulty: 3

3. Linus Piecewise is an expected utility maximizer. There are two events, H and T, which each have probability 1/2. Linus has preferences over lotteries in which his wealth is h if H happens and t if T happens that are representable by the utility function $U(h,t) = u(h)/2 + u(t)/2$. The function u() takes the following form. For any x, $u(x) = x$ if $x < 100$ and $u(x) = 100 + x/2$ if x is greater than or equal to 100. Draw a graph showing the indifference curves for Linus that pass through a) the point (50,0) b) the point (50,100) c) the point (100,100) d) the point (150,100).

Curve a is a line with slope -1. Curve b has 3 linear segments: A line from (100,50) to (50,100), a line with slope -2 to the left of (50,100), and a line with slope -1/2 to the right of (100,50). Curve c has two segments, a line with slope -2 going to the left and a line with slope -1/2 to the right of (100,100). Curve d has 3 segments, a line from (150,100) to (100,150), and lines from (150,100) to (200,0) and from (0,200) to (100,150).

Difficulty: 2

4. The "certainty equivalent" of a gamble is defined to be the amount of money for which, if you were promised it with certainty, would be indifferent to the gamble. a) If an expected utility maximizer has a von Neuman Morgenstern utility function $U(W) = \sqrt{W}$ and if the probability of events 1 and 2 are both 1/2, write a formula for the certainty equivalent of a gamble that gives you x if event 1 happens and y if event 2 happens. b) Generalize your formula in part a) to the case where the probability of event 1 is p and the probability of event 2 is 1-p. c) Generalize the formula in part a) to the case where $U(W) = W^a$ for $a > 0$.

a) certainty equivalent is $(1/\sqrt{2x} + 1/\sqrt{2y})^2$
b) $(p\sqrt{x} + (1-p)\sqrt{y})^2$ c) $1/2x^a + 1/2y^a)^{(1/a)}$

Chapter 14
RISKY ASSETS

Multiple-Choice Questions

Difficulty: 2
Correct: D

1. Firm A sells lemonade and firm B sells hot chocolate. If you invest $100 in Firm A, in one year you will get back $(30 + T)$ where T is the average temperature (Fahrenheit) during the summer. If you invest $100 in firm B, in one year you will get back $(150-T)$ where T is the average temperature during the summer. The expected value of T is 70 and the standard deviation of T is 10. If you invest $50 in Firm A and $50 in Firm B, what is the standard deviation of your return on your investment?
   a) 10
   b) 20
   c) 5
   d) 0
   e) none of the above

Difficulty: 2
Correct: A

2. A risk-free asset is available at 5% interest. Another asset is available with a mean rate of return of 15%, but with a standard deviation of 5%. An investor is considering an investment portfolio consisting of some of each stock. On a graph with standard deviation on the horizontal axis and mean on the vertical axis, the budget line that expresses the alternative combinations of mean return and standard deviation possible with portfolios of these assets is
   a) a straight line with slope 2.
   b) a straight line with slope -3.
   c) a straight line with increasing slope as you move left.
   d) a straight line with slope -1.
   e) a straight line with slope -1/3.

Difficulty: 2
Correct: A

3. Marvin is an expected utility maximizer. He chooses his portfolio so as to maximize the expected value of $2,000,000x-x^2$. If m is the mean of Marvin's income and s is the standard deviation, we can write Marvin's income as a function of mean and standard deviation in the following way:
   a) $U=2,000,000m-s^2$
   b) $U=2,000,000m-s$
   c) $U=m-s/2,000,000$
   d) $U=2,000,000+s$
   e) none of the above

Difficulty: 1
Correct: E

4. You have been hired as a portfolio manager for a stock brokerage. Your first job is to invest $100,000 in a portfolio of two assets. The first asset is a "safe asset" with a sure return of 4% interest. The second asset is a risky asset with a 26% expected rate of return but the standard deviation of this return is 10%. Your client wants a portfolio with as high a rate of return as possible consistent with a standard deviation no larger than 4%. How much of her money do you invest in the safe asset?
   a) $22,000
   b) $40,000
   c) $64,000
   d) $36,000
   e) $60,000

Difficulty: 1
Correct: B

5. Bill owns an export business. The expected profit from his business is $100,000 a year. For every 1% increase in the value of the Japanese yen relative to the dollar, its profits increase by $20,000. Bill plans to buy one of two firms. One is an import business which returns an expected profit of $70,000. For every 1% increase in the value of the Japanese yen relative to the dollar, the profits of this firm shrink by $5,000. The second is a safe domestic firm which is certain to yield him $70,000 a year. The two firms cost the same. If Bill is risk averse, which should he buy?
   a) the domestic firm
   b) the import firm
   c) He is indifferent between them.
   d) not enough information to tell

True or False Questions

Difficulty: 1
Correct: F

1. If two assets have the same expected rate of return but different variances, a risk-averse investor should always choose the one with the smaller variance, no matter what other assets she holds.

Difficulty: 1
Correct: T

2. If the returns on two assets are negatively correlated, then a portfolio that contains some of each will have less variance in its return per dollar invested than either asset has by itself.

Short-Answer Questions

Difficulty: 3

1. If you invest $100 now in firm A, in one year you will get back $(30+T) where T is the average temperature during the next summer. If you invest $100 now in firm B, in one year you will get back $(180-T). The expected value of T is 70 and the standard deviation of T is 10. a) Draw a graph showing the combinations of expected return and standard deviation that you can have by dividing $100 between stock in A and stock in B. (Hint: Expected value has the property that $E(ax+b) = aE(x)+b$ and standard deviation has the property that $SD(ax+b) = [(\text{absolute value of } a) \text{ times } SD(x)]+b$.) b) What is the expected value and standard deviation of the safest investment strategy you can make by this means? c) What is the highest expected value you can achieve?

    a) The locus includes the line segment from (S,E) = (0,105) to (S,E) = (10,110) as well as the line segment from (0,105) to (10,100). b) 105 and 0 c) 110.

Chapter 15
Consumer's Surplus

Multiple-Choice Questions

Difficulty: 1
Correct: C

1. Ella's utility function is min{3x,y}. If the price of x is 10 and the price of y is 5, how much money would she need to be able to purchase a bundle that she likes as well as the bundle (x,y) = (25,12)?
   a) 310
   b) 245
   c) 100
   d) 140
   e) none of the above

Difficulty: 2
Correct: E

2. Reginald is fond of cigars. His utility function is $U(x,c) = x + 10c - .5c^2$ where c is the number of cigars he smokes per week and x is his consumption of other goods. Reginald has $200 a week to spend. Cigars used to cost him $1 each, but their price went up to $2 each. This price increase was as bad for him as a loss of how much income?
   a) $5
   b) $7.25
   c) $9
   d) $8
   e) $8.5

Difficulty: 2
Correct: B

3. Sam's utility function is $U(x,y) = 2x + y$ where x is the number of x's he consumes per week and y is the number of y's he consumes per week. Sam has $200 a week to spend. The price of x is 4. Sam currently doesn't consume any y. Sam has received an invitation to join a club devoted to consumption of y. If he joins the club, Sam can get a discount on the purchase of y. If he belonged to the club he could buy y for $1 a unit. How much is the most Sam would be willing to pay to join this club?
   a) nothing
   b) $100 a week
   c) $50 a week
   d) $40 a week
   e) none of the above

Difficulty: 2
Correct: A

4. Yoram's utility function is $U(x,y) = 2x + 5y$. The price of x is $4 and the price of y is $15. Yoram has $150 a week to spend on x and y. Yoram is offered a chance to join a club of y-consumers. If he joins, he can get y at a price of $10. What is the most that Yoram would be willing to pay to join the club?
    a) nothing
    b) $30 a week
    c) $50 a week
    d) $75 a week
    e) none of the above

Difficulty: 2
Correct: E

5. Minnie gets 4 tapes for her birthday, but they are currently useless to her because she doesn't have a tape recorder and she cannot return them for a refund. Her utility function is $U(x,y,z) = x + f(y)\sqrt{z}$ where z is the number of tapes she has, y is the number of tape recorders she has and x is the money she has to spend on other stuff. Let $f(y) = 0$ if $y < 1$ and $f(y) = 7$ otherwise. The price of tapes is $7.99. What is her reservation price for a tape recorder?
    a) 20
    b) 7
    c) 24
    d) 0
    e) none of the above

Difficulty: 1
Correct: A

6. Izaak likes to eat pizza and to fish. The more fishing he does the happier he is, up to 8 hours a day. If he fishes longer than 8 hours he gets a sore back and is less happy than if he hadn't fished at all. His utility function is $U(x,y) = x + 4y$ where x is money spent on pizza and y is hours per day spent fishing. His income is $47 a day and he has no expenses other than pizza. The Bureau of Fisheries has just decided to allow people without fishing licenses to fish only 4 hours a day. But if you buy a fishing license, you can fish as many hours as you wish. How much is Izaak willing to pay for a license?
    a) 16
    b) 13
    c) 18
    d) 9
    e) none of the above

Difficulty: 1
Correct: D

7.   Ellsworth's utility function is $U(x,y) = \min\{x,y\}$. Ellsworth has \$150 and the price of x and the price of y are both 1. Ellsworth's boss is thinking of sending him to another town where the price of x is 1 and the price of y is 2. The boss offers no raise in pay. Ellsworth, who understands compensating and equivalent variation perfectly, complains bitterly. He says that although he doesn't mind moving for its own sake and the new town is just as pleasant as the old, having to move is as bad as a cut in pay of \$A. He also says he wouldn't mind moving if when he moved he got a raise of \$B. What are A and B?
a)   A=50, B=50
b)   A=75, B=75
c)   A=75, B=100
d)   A=50, B=75
e)   none of the above

Difficulty: 1
Correct: B

8.   Doug's money metric utility function is $m(p1,p2,x1,x2) = 1/2(\sqrt{p1p2x1x2})$. If he has an income of 100 and is offered the choice of living in two towns which are otherwise the same but where the prices in town A are p1=4, p2=9 and the prices in town B are p1=5, p2=7, which town will he prefer?
a)   town A
b)   town B
c)   He will be indifferent.
d)   Town A if his income is less than 500 and town B if his income exceeds 500.
e)   none of the above

Difficulty: 2
Correct: D

9.   Poindexter's utility function is $U(x,y) = \text{Min}\{x+2y, 3x+y\}$ where x is butter and y is guns. If the price of butter is 4 and the price of guns is 5, how much would it cost Poindexter to have a bundle that he likes as well as 4 units of butter and 3 units of guns?
a)   31
b)   32
c)   29
d)   28
e)   none of the above

True or False Questions

Difficulty: 1
Correct: F

1.   Consumer's surplus is another name for excess demand.

Difficulty: 1
Correct: T

2.   If the price of x is 3 and the price of y is 2, then the money metric utility of the bundle (3,2) at these prices is no greater than 13 but might be smaller.

Difficulty: 1
Correct: T

3. The key idea in the theory of consumer surplus is that the total amount you pay for something is usually less than the amount you would be willing to pay rather than do without it altogether.

Difficulty: 2
Correct: F

4. The equivalent variation in income from a tax is the amount of extra income that a consumer would need to be as well off after the tax is imposed as he was originally.

Difficulty: 2
Correct: T

5. With quasilinear preferences, the equivalent variation and the compensating variation in income due to a tax are the same.

Difficulty: 1
Correct: F

6. Producer's surplus at price p is the vertical distance between the supply curve and the demand curve at price p.

Difficulty: 1
Correct: T

7. The compensating and equivalent variations of a specified change in taxes can always be determined if the money metric utility function is known.

Difficulty: 1
Correct: T

8. An individual's money metric utility function will determine his or her indifference curves.

Difficulty: 1
Correct: T

9. If somebody is buying 10 units of x and the price of x falls by \$1, then that person's consumer surplus must increase by at least \$1.

Short-Answer Questions

Difficulty: 3

1. The "indirect utility function" for a consumer with a utility function $U(x1,x2)$ is defined to be a function $V(p1,p2,M)$ such that $V(p1,p2,M)$ is the maximum of $U(x1,x2)$ subject to the constraint that the consumer can afford $(x1,x2)$ at the prices $(p1,p2)$ with income M. a) Find the indirect utility function for someone with the utility function $U(x,y)=2x+y$. b) Find the indirect utility function for someone with the utility function $U(x,y)=\min\{2x,y\}$. Explain how you got your answers.

a) $M/(\min\{p1/2,p2\}$. b) $M/(2p1+p2)$.

Chapter 16
MARKET DEMAND

Multiple-Choice Questions

Difficulty: 1
Correct: E

1. A peck is 1/4 of a bushel. If the price elasticity of demand for wheat is -.8 when wheat is measured in bushels, then when wheat is measured in pecks, the price elasticity of demand for wheat will be
   a)   -.2
   b)   -.4
   c)   -.32
   d)   -3.2
   e)   none of the above

Difficulty: 1
Correct: B

2. The demand curve is q=250-.5p. The inverse demand curve is:
   a)   q=250-2p
   b)   p=500-2q
   c)   q=1/(250-p)
   d)   p=1/(250-q)
   e)   p=250-.5q

Difficulty: 3
Correct: A

3. If the demand function is q=m-2 (ln p) over some range of values of p, then at all such values of p, the absolute value of the elasticity of demand
   a)   increases as p increases.
   b)   decreases as p increases.
   c)   is constant as p changes.
   d)   increases with p at small values and decreases with p at large values.
   e)   decreases with p at large values and increases with p at small values.

Difficulty: 1
Correct: C

4. If the demand function for tickets to a play is Q=500-20p, at what price will total revenue be maximized?
   a)   5
   b)   25
   c)   12.5
   d)   10
   e)   none of the above

Difficulty: 2
Correct: D

5. Rollo would love to have a Mercedes. His preferences for consumption in the next year are represented by a utility function $U(x,y)$ where $x=0$ if he has no Mercedes and $x=1$ if he has a Mercedes for the year and where y is the amount of income he has left to spend on other stuff. If $U(0,y)=\sqrt{y}$ and $U(1,y)=(10/9)\sqrt{y}$, and if Rollo's income is $50,000 a year, how much would he be willing to pay per year to have a Mercedes?
   a) $5555.55
   b) $5,000
   c) $12,200
   d) $9,500
   e) $10,000

Difficulty: 2
Correct: C

6. In Ozone, California, people all have the same tastes and they all like hot tubs. Nobody wants more than one hot tub but a person with wealth $M will be willing to pay up to .01M for a hot tub. The distribution of wealth in Ozone is as follows. The number of people with a wealth greater than $W for any given W is approximately 1,000,000/W. The price elasticity of demand for hot tubs in Ozone, California is
   a) -.1
   b) -.01
   c) -1
   d) -.4
   e) none of the above

Difficulty: 2
Correct: B

7. In Manifold, Missouri (pop, 1,000), people all have the same tastes and they all like Buicks. Nobody wants more than one Buick, but a person with income $M is willing to pay about .10M per year to have a Buick. Nobody in Manifold has an income greater than $50,000 and nobody has an income less than $10,000. For incomes, M, between $10,000 and $50,000, the number of people with incomes greater than M is about 1250-.025M. If it costs $2000 a year to have a Buick, how many people in Manifold will demand Buicks?
   a) 500
   b) 750
   c) 100
   d) 600
   e) 800

Difficulty: 2
Correct: C

8.   Rod cares about the number of cars he has and the amount of money he has to spend on other stuff. The only possibilities of interest for Rod are having 0, 1, or 2 cars. Where x is the number of cars he has and y is the money he has per year for other stuff, Rod's utility is $U(0,y)=\sqrt{y}$, $U(1,y)=(15/14)\sqrt{y}$ and $U(2,y)=(10/9)\sqrt{y}$. Rod's income is $25,000 a year. It would cost Rod $2500 a year to have 1 car and $3500 a year to have 2 cars. How many cars will he choose?
a)   0
b)   1
c)   2
d)   There is not enough information to tell.

Difficulty: 2
Correct: B

9.   Dr. Social Science has recently figured out how to clone consumers. His first effort was done on the population of Walla, Washington. Each original citizen got a clone who had exactly the same income and preferences. Which of the following statements describes what happened to the demand function for tunafish casseroles in Walla?
a)   The elasticity doubled and the slope remained constant.
b)   The elasticity did not change at any price.
c)   The elasticity of demand doubled and the slope doubled.
d)   The elasticity halved and the slope remained constant.
e)   none of the above

Difficulty: 2
Correct: A

10.   At the price of 3, tourists demand 976 airplane tickets. At the same price, business travelers demand 464. At the price 7, tourists demand 168 tickets and business travelers demand 444. Assuming that the demand curves of businessmen and tourists are both linear in price, what is the slope of market demand at the price 5?
a)   -1/207
b)   -1/42
c)   -1/198
d)   -1/329
e)   none of the above

True or False Questions

Difficulty: 1
Correct: T

1.   The inverse demand curve, P(x), for a good x measures the price at which the quantity x would be demanded.

Difficulty: 2
Correct: F

2.   In general, aggregate demand depends only on prices and total income and not on income distribution.

Difficulty: 2
Correct: T

3. If consumer 1 has the demand function x1 = 1000-2p and consumer 2 has the demand function x2 = 500-p, then the aggregate demand function for an economy with just these two consumers would be x = 1500-3p.

Difficulty: 1
Correct: T

4. If a consumer has to pay his reservation price for a good, then he gets no consumer surplus from purchasing it.

Difficulty: 1
Correct: T

5. If a price changes, then changes in consumption at the intensive margin are changes that happen because consumers change the amounts that they consume but do not either stop consuming or start consuming the good.

Difficulty: 1
Correct: F

6. If the demand curve is linear, then the elasticity of demand is the same at all prices.

Difficulty: 1
Correct: F

7. If the demand function is q = 3m/p, then the elasticity of demand decreases as price increases.

Difficulty: 1
Correct: F

8. If the demand curve for soybeans is price inelastic, then we would expect that when bad weather reduces the size of the soybean crop, total revenue of soybean producers will fall.

Difficulty: 2
Correct: F

9. If the demand curve is linear, then the ratio of marginal revenue to price is constant.

Difficulty: 2
Correct: T

10. If a rational consumer must consume either zero or one unit of a good, then an increase in the price of that good with no change in income or in other prices can never lead to an increase in the consumer's demand for it.

Difficulty: 1
Correct: F

11. In the reservation price model, either aggregate demand is zero or everyone demands one unit of the good.

Difficulty: 1
Correct: F

12. The Laffer effect occurs only if there is a backward-bending labor supply curve.

Difficulty: 2
Correct: T

13. If the demand curve were plotted on graph paper with logarithmic scales on both axes, then its slope would be the elasticity of demand.

Difficulty: 1
Correct: T

14. The market demand curve is simply the horizontal sum of the individual demand curves.

Difficulty: 1
Correct: F

15. The demand curve is inelastic for inferior goods and elastic for normal goods.

Short-Answer Questions

Difficulty: 2

1. Suppose that the inverse demand function for wool is $p = A/q$ for some constant A. Suppose that 1/4 of the world's wool is produced in Australia. a) If Australian wool production increases by 1% and the rest of the world holds its output constant, what will be the effect on the world price of wool? b) How is the marginal revenue to Australia from an extra unit of wool related to the price of wool?

a) Price will fall by about .25%. b) Marginal revenue is 3/4 of price.

Difficulty: 2

2. Bart Wurst runs the only hotdog stand in a large park in a large boring town. On Sundays people in this town all sit in the park and sunbathe. For any t between 0 and 30, the number of people who are sitting within t minutes of Bart's stand is $10t^2$. People in Bart's town are lazy and hate to walk. They think that every minute of walking they do is as bad as spending $.10. Everybody in the park has a reservation price of $1 for a hot dog where the cost of a hot dog includes the subjective cost of walking as well as the money price they have to pay when they get there. (Nobody has ever thought of fetching a hot dog for someone else.) Find a formula for the demand curve for Bart's hot dogs. Explain how you got it.

If Bart charges p where $0 < p < 1$, his extensive margin is the customers who are at distance t* from Bart where $p + .10t* = 1$. Then $t* = 10 - p$ and the demand for hot dogs at prices p is the number, $(10-p)^2$, of people within t* of Bart.

Difficulty: 3   3.   In Tassel, Illinois (pop, 20,000), there are two kinds of families, those who like swimming pools and those who don't. Half of the population is of each type. Families who like swimming pools are willing to spend up to 5% of their income each year on a swimming pool. Families who don't like them would pay nothing for a swimming pool. Nobody wants more than one swimming pool and nobody has thought of sharing a swimming pool. Incomes in Tassel range between $10,000 and $110,000. For incomes, M, in this range, the number of families in Tassel with income greater than M is about 22,000-.2M. (The two types of families have the same income distribution.) Find the aggregate demand function for swimming pools in Tassel (demand for swimming pools as a function of annual cost of having one).

The number of people willing to pay at least p is half of the number who have income at least 20p. Therefore the aggregate demand function is 11,000-2p.

Difficulty: 3   4.   This problem concerns the demand for swimming pools in Tassel, Illinois as described in the previous problem. Suppose that every family income in town increases by $1,000. Where price is on the vertical axis and quantity on the horizontal, what happens to the demand curve for swimming pools? Describe the shift in the demand curve both geometrically and numerically.

Everybody's willingness to pay rises by $50. If price is on the vertical axis and quantity on the horizontal axis, the demand curve shifts upwards by $50.

Difficulty: 3   5.   Ethel is trying to decide whether to have 0 cars, 1 car, or 2 cars. If x is the number of cars she has and y is the amount of money she has per year to spend on other stuff, Ethel's utility function is $U(x,y)$ where $U(0,y)=\sqrt{y}$, $U(1,y)=(15/14)\sqrt{y}$, and $U(2,y)=(10/9)\sqrt{y}$. Suppose that it costs $2000 a year to have 1 car and $4000 a year to have 2 cars. Ethel finds that the right thing to do depends on her income. What is her willingness to pay for 1 car if her income is M? What is the lowest income at which she would have 1 car? What is the lowest income at which she would have 2 cars?

Her willingness to pay for 1 car is about .129M where M is her income. The lowest income at which she would get 1 car is $15,504. If we solve the equation $U(1,y-2000)=U(2,y-4000)$ we find $55,143. At incomes above that she prefers 2 cars. At incomes below that she would be better off to have 1 car.

Chapter 17
EQUILIBRIUM

Multiple-Choice Questions

Difficulty: 1
Correct: B

1. The inverse demand function for pickles is p=780-7q and the inverse supply function is p=300+q. What is the equilibrium price?
    a) 480
    b) 360
    c) 640
    d) 240
    e) none of the above

Difficulty: 1
Correct: B

2. The demand function for fresh strawberries is q=200-5p and the supply function is q=60+2p. What is the equilibrium price?
    a) 10
    b) 20
    c) 40
    d) 50
    e) none of the above

Difficulty: 1
Correct: D

3. The inverse demand function for melons is p=240-3q where q is the number of crates that are sold. The inverse supply function is p=28+q. In the past there was no tax on melons but now a tax of $12 per crate has been imposed. What are the quantities produced before and after the tax was imposed?
    a) 24 crates before and 6 crates after.
    b) 5 crates before and 96 crates after.
    c) 75 crates before and 44 crates after.
    d) 53 crates before and 50 crates after.
    e) none of the above

Difficulty: 1
Correct: B

4. The inverse demand function for eggs is p=200-4q where q is the number of cases of eggs. The inverse supply function is p=2+2q. In the past, eggs were not taxed, but now a tax of $18 per case has been introduced. What is the effect of the tax on the quantity of eggs supplied?
    a) quantity drops by 2 cases
    b) quantity drops by 3 cases
    c) quantity drops by 6 cases
    d) quantity drops by 4 cases
    e) none of the above

Difficulty: 1
Correct: C

5. The inverse demand function for cases of whisky is p=300-5q and the inverse supply function is p=6+2q. If the tax on whisky is increased from zero to $14 a case, how much does the price paid by consumers rise?
   a) $15
   b) $12
   c) $10
   d) $6
   e) none of the above

Difficulty: 1
Correct: A

6. The inverse demand function for cigars is p=240-2q and the inverse supply function is p=3+q. Cigars are taxed at $4 per box. Who pays the larger share of the tax?
   a) consumers
   b) suppliers
   c) They share it equally.
   d) There is not enough information to tell.

Difficulty: 2
Correct: D

7. Xaquane and Yullare are obscure, but talented, 18th century painters. The world's stock of Xaquanes is 100 and the world's stock of Yullares is 70. The demand for each painter's work depends on its own price and the price of the other painter's work. If Px is the price of Xaquanes and Py is the price of Yullares, the demand function for Xaquanes is 101-3Px+2Py and the demand function for Yullares is 72+Px-Py. What is the equilibrium price for Yullare's paintings?
   a) 5
   b) 11
   c) 12
   d) 7
   e) none of the above

Difficulty: 1
Correct: C

8. In a certain kingdom, the demand function for rye bread was q=480-6p and the supply function was q=120+3p where p is the price in zlotys and q is loaves of bread. The king made it illegal to sell rye bread for a price above 30 zlotys per loaf. To avoid shortages, he agreed to pay bakers enough of a subsidy for each loaf of bread so as to make supply equal demand. How much would the subsidy per loaf have to be?
   a) 21 zlotys
   b) 14 zlotys
   c) 30 zlotys
   d) 20 zlotys
   e) none of the above

Difficulty: 1
Correct: A

9. The demand function for butter is q=600-5p and the supply function is q=120+3p. The government decides to support the price of butter at a price floor of 86 by buying butter and destroying it. How many units of butter must the government destroy?
    a) 208
    b) 300
    c) 150
    d) 12
    e) none of the above

Difficulty: 1
Correct: B

10. The demand function for rental apartments is q=960-7p and the supply function is q=160+3p. The government makes it illegal to charge a rent higher than 35. How much excess demand will there be?
    a) 149
    b) 450
    c) 364
    d) 726
    e) None of the above.

Difficulty: 1
Correct: D

11. The demand function for abalone is q=30-9p and the supply function is q=51+6p. Suddenly the yuppies discover abalone. The quantity demanded at every price doubles. The supply function, however, remains the same as before. What is the effect on the equilibrium price and quantity?
    a) The price doubles and the quantity remains constant.
    b) The quantity doubles and the price remains constant.
    c) Both price and quantity double.
    d) Both price and quantity increase, but neither doubles.
    e) none of the above

True or False Questions

Difficulty: 1
Correct: T

1. If the supply curve is vertical, then the amount supplied is independent of price.

Difficulty: 1
Correct: F

2. If the supply curve is horizontal, then an upward shift in the demand function will lead to a higher price and quantity in equilibrium.

Difficulty: 1
Correct: T

3. If the supply curve slopes up and to the right, then if the demand curve shifts upward and the supply curve does not shift, the equilibrium price and quantity must necessarily increase.

Difficulty: 1
Correct: F

4. Supply and demand theory shows us that the burden of a sales tax is shared equally by suppliers and demanders whether the tax is collected from the sellers or collected from the buyers.

Difficulty: 1
Correct: F

5. An economic situation is Pareto optimal if there is no way to make someone better off.

Difficulty: 1
Correct: T

6. If the amount of a good supplied is independent of the price, then if a sales tax is imposed on the good, the price paid by consumers will not change at all.

Short-Answer Questions

Difficulty: 1

1. Use supply and demand analysis to examine the following statement: "The practice of giving food stamps is self-defeating. Food stamps effectively lower the price of food. When food becomes available at lower prices, demand will increase thereby forcing the price up to its initial level." Is this reasoning correct? Draw supply and demand curves to illustrate your answer.

   The subsidy would shift the demand curve to the right, much as the quotation says, but if the supply curve slopes up, then the new equilibrium should take place with a greater supply and a lower net price for those who use food stamps. The market price will rise, but not by the full amount of the discount one gets with food stamps.

Difficulty: 2

2. Long ago, a kindly prince noticed the misery of his subjects. His subjects all had the same preferences and the same low incomes. The demand function of each subject for bread was $q = 26 - p$ where p is the price of bread and q is the number of loaves per week. The supply of bread per capita per week was given by the function $q = .3p$. The king declared since his subjects did not even get a loaf of bread per day, he would help them by making it illegal to sell bread for more than 10 groschens per loaf. Unhappily, a bread shortage arose and people waited in long lines to get bread. a) Draw a graph to show why. Put numerical labels on the important points on your graph. b) If the citizens could earn 4 groschens per hour at work that was exactly as unpleasant as waiting in line, what would be the equilibrium waiting time for a loaf of bread?

   b) 3.25 hours.

Chapter 18
TECHNOLOGY

Multiple-Choice Questions

Difficulty: 1
Correct: B

1. In any production process, the marginal product of labor equals
    a) the value of total output minus the cost of the fixed capital stock.
    b) the change in output that occurs when a one-unit change is made in the amount of labor input.
    c) total output divided by total labor inputs.
    d) total output produced with the given labor inputs.
    e) the average output of the least skilled workers employed by the firm.

Difficulty: 1
Correct: A

2. If a firm moves from one point on a production isoquant to another point on the same isoquant, which of the following will certainly not happen?
    a) The level of output will change.
    b) The ratio in which the inputs are combined will change.
    c) The marginal products of the inputs will change.
    d) The rate of technical substitution will change.
    e) Profitability will change.

Difficulty: 2
Correct: A

3. A firm has the production function $f(x,y) = \sqrt{x} + y$ where x is the amount of factor x it uses and y is the amount of factor y. On a diagram we put x on the horizontal axis and y on the vertical axis. We draw some isoquants. Now we draw a straight line on the graph and we notice that where this line meets any isoquant, the isoquants all have the same slope. The straight line we drew was
    a) vertical.
    b) horizontal.
    c) diagonal through the origin with slope .5.
    d) diagonal with slope 2.
    e) diagonal with slope greater than 2.

True or False Questions

Difficulty: 1
Correct: F

1. The production set of a firm is the set of all products the firm can produce.

Difficulty: 1
Correct: F

2. A production isoquant is a locus of combinations of inputs that are equally profitable.

Difficulty: 1
Correct: F

3. If there are constant returns to scale, then doubling the amount of any input will exactly double the amount of output.

Difficulty: 1
Correct: T

4. The economist's distinction between long and short run is that the quantities of some factor inputs can be varied in the short run but not in the long run.

Difficulty: 2
Correct: T

5. If the production function is $f(x,y) = \min\{2x+y, x+2y\}$, then there are constant returns to scale.

Difficulty: 2
Correct: T

6. If the production function is $f(x,y) = x + \min\{x,y\}$, there are constant returns.

Difficulty: 2
Correct: T

7. If the production function is $f(x,y) = \min\{12x, 3y\}$, there is convexity in production.

Difficulty: 1
Correct: F

8. If the production function is $f(x,y) = xy$, then there are constant returns to scale.

Difficulty: 2
Correct: T

9. It is possible to have decreasing marginal products for all inputs and yet to have increasing returns to scale.

Difficulty: 1
Correct: T

10. If factor x is on the horizontal axis and factor y is on the vertical axis, the slope of the isoquant through a point (x^*, y^*) is the negative of the ratio of the marginal product of x to the marginal product of y.

Short-Answer Questions

Difficulty: 2

1. On separate axes, draw typical production isoquants for each of the following production functions. a) $f(x,y) = \min\{2x, x+y\}$ b) $f(x,y) = xy$ c) $f(x,y) = x + \min\{x,y\}$ d) $f(x,y) = x + (\text{square root of } y)$.

For a), the isoquants have a kink at the line x=y. At a typical point on this line, say x=y=3, the isoquant has a vertical segment going all the way to the sky and another segment running from (3,3) to (6,0). b) These are rectangular hyperbolas. c) If x is on the horizontal axis and y on the vertical axis, an isoquant has a kink on the line x=y. To the left of this line, an isoquant is vertical, to the right of this line, an isoquant has slope -1. d) The isoquants are convex to the origin. If you draw a horizontal line through across two or more isoquants, they will all have the same slope where they meet this line.

Chapter 19
PROFIT MAXIMIZATION

Multiple-Choice Questions

Difficulty: 2
Correct: D

1. A competitive firm produces output using 3 fixed factors and one variable factor. The firm's short run production function is $Q = 400x - 2x^2$, where x is the amount of variable factor used. The price of output is $2 per unit and the price of the variable factor is $40 per unit. In the short run, how many units of x should the firm use?
    a) 31.66
    b) 80
    c) 200
    d) 95
    e) none of the above

Difficulty: 2
Correct: A

2. A competitive firm produces a single output using several inputs. The price of output rises by $2 per unit. The price of one of the inputs increases by $3 and its quantity increases by 2 units. The prices of all other inputs stayed unchanged. From the weak axiom of profit maximization we can tell that
    a) the output of the good must have increased by at least 3 units.
    b) the inputs of the other factors must have stayed constant.
    c) the production function is convex.
    d) the output of the good must have decreased.
    e) the inputs of the other factors must have increased by at least 2 units.

Difficulty: 2
Correct: E

3. If there is perfect certainty, a competitive firm will
    a) seek to maximize its immediate profits because otherwise it will go broke.
    b) maximize the ratio of the present value of its sales to the present value of its costs.
    c) equalize its profits in all periods.
    d) equalize its sales in all periods.
    e) none of the above

Difficulty: 1
Correct: A

4. A firm produces one output using one input. When the cost of the input was 3 and the price of the output was 3, the firm used 6 units of input to produce 18 units of output. Later when the cost of the input was 7 and the price of the output was 4, the firm used 5 units of input to produce 20 units of output. Is this behavior consistent with WAPM?
   a) Yes
   b) No
   c) There is not enough information to determine the answer.

Difficulty: 2
Correct: C

5. A firm uses just one input, x. Its production function is $q = 2\sqrt{x}$. The price of output is p and the factor price is w. The amount of the factor that the firm demands is
   a) p/w.
   b) $\sqrt{p/w}$.
   c) $(p/w)^2$.
   d) p-w.
   e) $p - 2\sqrt{w}$.

True or False Questions

Difficulty: 1
Correct: F

1. The weak axiom of profit maximizing behavior states that in a modern mixed economy, firms have only a weak incentive to maximize profits.

Difficulty: 1
Correct: F

2. A fixed factor is a factor of production that is used in fixed proportion to the level of output.

Difficulty: 1
Correct: T

3. The marginal product of a factor is just the derivative of the production function with respect to the amount of this factor, holding the amounts of other factor inputs constant.

Difficulty: 1
Correct: F

4. If the value of the marginal product of factor x increases as the quantity of x increases and the value of the marginal product of x is equal to the wage rate, then the profit maximizing amount of x is being used.

Difficulty: 2
Correct: T

5. If the price of the output of a profit maximizing, competitive firm rises and all other prices stay constant, then it cannot happen that the quantity of output falls.

Difficulty: 1
Correct: T

6. If a firm has constant returns to scale, then its long-run maximum profits must be zero.

Difficulty: 2
Correct: F

7. Just as in the theory of utility maximizing consumers, the theory of profit maximizing firms allows the possibility of "Giffen factors." These are factors for which a fall in price leads to a fall in demand.

Short-Answer Questions

Difficulty: 3

1. A competitive firm has a production function described as follows. "Weekly Output is the square root of the minimum of the number of units of capital and the number of units of labor employed per week." Suppose that in the short run this firm must use 16 units of capital but can vary its amount of labor freely. a) Write down a formula that describes the marginal product of labor in the short run as a function of the amount of labor used. (Be careful at the boundaries.) b) If $w=1$ and $p=4$, how much labor will the firm demand in the short run? c) What if $w=1$ and $p=10$? d) Write down an equation for the firm's short run demand for labor as function of w and p.

    a) $MP = 1/2\sqrt{L}$ if $L<16$, $MP=0$ if $L>16$. b) 4 c) 16 d) $L=(p/2w)^2$

Chapter 20
COST MINIMIZATION

Multiple-Choice Questions

Difficulty: 1
Correct: C

1. George runs a cookie factory. His cookies are made with sugar, peanut oil, and soybean oil. The number of boxes of cookies that he produces is $f(su,po,so)=\min\{su,po+so)\}$ where su is the number of bags of sugar, po the number of canisters of peanut oil, and so the number of canisters of soybean oil that he uses. The price of a bag of sugar is 10. The price of a canister of peanut oil is 12. The price of a canister of soybean oil is 10. If George makes 220 boxes of cookies in the cheapest way possible, how many canisters of soybean oil will he use?
   a) 100
   b) 120
   c) 220
   d) 300
   e) 90

Difficulty: 1
Correct: D

2. A firm has the production function $Q=11\sqrt{x}\sqrt{y}$ where x and y are the amounts of factors x and y that the firm uses as inputs. If the firm is minimizing unit costs, and if the price of factor x is 3 times the price of factor y, then in what ratio will the firm use factors x and y?
   a) $x/y=3$.
   b) $x/y=4/11$.
   c) $x/y=1/2$.
   d) $x/y=1/3$.
   e) We can't tell without more information.

Difficulty: 1
Correct: D

3. A firm has fixed costs of $10,000. Its short run production function is $Q=\sqrt{x}$ where x is the amount of variable factor it used. The price of the variable factor is $1000 per unit. Where y is the amount of output, the short run total cost function is:
   a) $1000\sqrt{y}$-$10,000.
   b) $\sqrt{y}$ + $10,000.
   c) $(1000y-10,000)^2$.
   d) $1000y^2+$10,000.
   e) $(1000y+10,000)^2$.

Difficulty: 2
Correct: C

4. A firm has two factories, one with the cost function c(y)=2(y squared)+90 and the other with the cost function c(y)=6(y squared)+40. If they wish to produce a total of 32 units, how many units will be produced by the second factory?
   a) 7
   b) 2
   c) 8
   d) 14
   e) none of the above

Difficulty: 1
Correct: A

5. A company can rent one of two copying machines. The first costs $34 a month to rent and costs an additional 2 cents per copy to use. The second costs $107 a month to rent and an additional 1 cent per copy to use. How many copies would the company need to make per month in order for it to be worthwhile to rent the second machine?
   a) 7300
   b) 13300
   c) 12400
   d) 6900
   e) none of the above

Difficulty: 2
Correct: A

6. A firm produces ping pong balls using two inputs. When input prices are (15,7) the firm uses the input bundle (17,71). When the input prices are (12,24) the firm uses the bundle (77,4). The amount of output is the same in both cases. Is this behavior consistent with WACM?
   a) Yes.
   b) No.
   c) It depends on the level of fixed costs.
   d) We have to know the price of output before we can test WACM.

Difficulty: 1
Correct: B

7. As assistant vice-president in charge of production for a computer firm, you are asked to calculate the cost of producing 170 computers. The production function is $Q=\min\{x,y\}$ where x and y are the amounts of two factors used. The price of x is 18 and the price of y is 10. What is your answer?
   a) 2580
   b) 4760
   c) 8460
   d) 6180
   e) none of the above

Difficulty: 3
Correct: B

8. As head of the planning commission of Eastern Motors, your job is to determine where to locate a new plant. The only inputs used in your cars are steel and labor and the production function is Cobb-Douglas where $F(S,L) = (S^{.8})$ times $(L^{.2})$ where S is tons of steel and L is units of labor. You can locate your plant either in country A or country B. In country A, steel costs 7 per ton and labor costs 7 per unit. In country B, steel costs 8 per ton and labor costs 5 per unit. In which country should you locate your factory so as to minimize costs per unit of output?
   a) Country A.
   b) Country B.
   c) The two locations are equally costly.

Difficulty: 2
Correct: D

9. A competitive firm uses two inputs, x and y. Total output is the square root of x times the square root of y. The price of x is 17 and the price of y is 11. The company minimizes its costs per unit of output and spends $517 on x. How much does it spend on y?
   a) 766
   b) 480
   c) 655
   d) 517
   e) none of the above

True or False Questions

Difficulty: 2
Correct: T

1. Quasi-fixed costs are those costs that can be avoided if and only if a firm produces zero output.

Difficulty: 1
Correct: T

2. Increasing returns to scale imply that average costs are a decreasing function of output.

Short-Answer Questions

Difficulty: 1

1. A firm has a production function described as follows: "Weekly output is equal to the square root of the minimum of the amount of capital and the number of hours of labor used per per week." Suppose that the cost of a unit of capital is r and the price of a unit of labor is w and the level of output is y. Write down the long run total cost as a function of w, r, and y.

$c(w,r,y) = (w+r)y^2.$

Difficulty: 2

2.   The production function for good y is y=max{10x1,4x2} where x1 and x2 are the amounts of factors 1 and 2. Find the cost function for good y.

The cost function is min{p1y/10,p2y/4}.

Difficulty: 2

3.   The production function for tuna casseroles is min{x,y^2}, where x is the amount of factor 1 and y is the amount of factor y. Find the cost function for tuna casseroles. The price of x is p1 and the price of y is p2.

c(w1,w2)=p1x+p2$\sqrt{y}$.

Difficulty: 2

4.   The cost function, c(w1,w2,y), of a firm gives the cost of producing y units of output when the wage of factor 1 is w1 and the wage of factor 2 is w2. Find the cost functions for the following firms: a) a firm with production function f(x1,x2)=min{2x1,3x2} b) a firm with production function f(x1,x2)=2x1+3x2 c) f(x1,x2)=max{2x1,3x2}

a)w1/2+w2/3 b)min{w1/2,w2/3} c)min{w1/2,w2/3}

Chapter 21
COST CURVES

Multiple-Choice Questions

Difficulty: 1
Correct: B

1. The marginal cost curve of a firm is MC=2y. The variable costs to produce 10 units of output are
   a) 50.
   b) 100.
   c) 150.
   d) 200.
   e) 20.

Difficulty: 1
Correct: D

2. The following relationship must hold between the average total cost (ATC) curve and the marginal cost curve (MC):
   a) If MC is rising, ATC must be rising.
   b) If MC is rising, ATC must be greater than MC.
   c) If MC is rising, ATC must be less than MC.
   d) If MC is rising, MC must be greater than ATC.
   e) If ATC is rising, MC must be less than ATC.

Difficulty: 1
Correct: C

3. A goatherd has the cost function $c(y)=2y^2$ where y is the number of tubs of goat cheese she sells per month. She receives $40 a tub for her goat cheese. How many tubs should she produce per month?
   a) $\sqrt{20}$.
   b) 400
   c) 10
   d) 100
   e) 20

Difficulty: 2
Correct: C

4. A firm has a short run cost function $c(y)=3y+24$ for $y>0$ and $c(0)=13$. The firm's quasi-fixed costs are:
   a) 13
   b) 24
   c) 11
   d) 37
   e) impossible to determine from this information.

Difficulty: 3
Correct: C

5. A competitive firm has the short run cost function $c(y)=3y^3-6y^2+15y+30$. The firm will produce a positive amount in the short run if and only if the price is greater than
   a) 10.
   b) 24.
   c) 12.
   d) 16.
   e) 8.

True or False Questions

Difficulty: 1
Correct: F

1. The average variable cost curve must always be U shaped.

Difficulty: 1
Correct: F

2. The marginal cost curve passes through the minimum point of the average fixed cost curve.

Difficulty: 1
Correct: T

3. If the average cost curve is U shaped, then the marginal cost curve must cross the average cost curve at the bottom of the U.

Short-Answer Questions

Difficulty: 1

1. Not long ago, the Canadian edition of a famous textbook on principals of economics had a diagram depicting a U-shaped average fixed cost curve. This occasioned great mirth around the campfires of some economists in the Great White North and did much to shorten a long hard winter. Explain what is wrong with drawing a U-shaped average fixed cost curve.

Average fixed cost must decline monotonically with output and would asymptotically approach zero. Remember that average fixed cost is just a constant divided by output.

Difficulty: 3

2. Hildegard, an intelligent and charming Holstein cow, grazes in a very large, mostly barren pasture with a few lush patches of grass. When she finds a new grassy area, the amount of grass she gets from it is equal to the square root of the number of hours, h, that she spends grazing there. Finding a new patch of grass on which to graze takes her one hour. Since Hildegard does not have pockets, the currency in which her costs are measured is time. a) What is the total cost to Hildegard of finding a new plot of grass and getting y units of grass from it? b) Find an expression for her marginal costs and her average cost per patch of grass as a function of the amount of grass she gets from each patch. c) How much time would she spend in each plot if she wants to maximize her food intake? (Hint: Minimize average costs per unit of grass eaten.)

a) $1+y^2$ b) $2y$, $1/y+y$ c) 1 hour.

Difficulty: 2

3. A competitive firm has the short run cost function $c(y) = y^3 - 2y^2 + 5y + 6$. Write down equations for a) the firm's average variable cost function, b) the firm's marginal cost function. c) At what level of output is average variable cost minimized? d) Graph the short-run supply function for this firm, being careful to label the key points on the graph with the numbers specifying the exact prices and quantities at these points.

a) $y^2 - 2y + 5$ b) $3y^2 - 4y + 5$ c) $y = 1$ d) The AVC curve is U-shaped with its bottom at $y = 1$, $c = 2$. The marginal cost curve is also U-shaped. It bottoms out at $y = 2/3$ and crosses the AVC curve from below at $y = 1$.

Chapter 22
FIRM SUPPLY

Multiple-Choice Questions

Difficulty: 1
Correct: D

1. A profit-maximizing firm continues to operate even though it is losing money. It sells its product at a price of $100. From these facts we deduce that
    a) average total cost is less than $100.
    b) average fixed cost is less than $100.
    c) marginal cost is increasing.
    d) average variable cost is less than $100.
    e) marginal cost is decreasing.

Difficulty: 1
Correct: C

2. A profit maximizing dairy farm is currently producing 10,000 gallons of milk per day. The government is considering two alternative policies. One is to give the farm a lump sum subsidy of $500 per month. The other policy is to give the firm a subsidy of $.05 per unit of output.
    a) Production will be increased by either kind of subsidy.
    b) Production will not change.
    c) Production will be increased only by the per unit subsidy.
    d) Which subsidy will have the greater effect on production depends on whether fixed costs are greater than variable costs.
    e) Production will be increased by either kind of subsidy if and only if there are not decreasing returns to scale.

Difficulty: 1
Correct: E

3. Marge Costa produces plastic dog dishes using a process that requires only labor and plastic as inputs and has constant returns to scale. With the process she is currently using, a laborer can turn out 30 dog dishes an hour. The plastic in a dog dish costs Marge $.10. She has no fixed costs. Marge faces a perfectly competitive market for plastic dog dishes, and she decides that she is maximizing profits when she makes 300 dog dishes an hour. What is the market price of dog dishes?
    a) $.21
    b) $.12
    c) $.40
    d) $.20
    e) There is not enough information to determine this.

Difficulty: 1
Correct: E

4. A competitive firm has the following production function: $Q = \min\{x1, x2\}$. The price of x1 is 5 and the price of x2 is 9. Due to a lack of warehouse space, the company cannot use more than 18 units of x1. The firm must pay an electricity bill of 3 regardless of how much it produces unless it shuts down altogether. What is the smallest integer price that would lead the firm to produce a positive amount?
   a) 9
   b) 20
   c) 14
   d) 24
   e) 15

Difficulty: 1
Correct: A

5. A competitive firm has a single factory with the cost function $c(y) = 4y^2 + 89$ and produces 28 units in order to maximize profits. Although the price of output does not change, the firm decides to build a second factory with the cost function $c(y) = 8y^2 + 39$. To maximize its profits, how many units should it produce in the second factory?
   a) 14
   b) 21
   c) 9
   d) 13
   e) none of the above

True or False Questions

Difficulty: 1
Correct: F

1. A competitive firm realizes that the demand curve it confronts has a significant negative slope.

Difficulty: 1
Correct: T

2. In a perfectly competitive industry, the industry demand curve may be downward sloping.

Difficulty: 1
Correct: F

3. Price equals marginal cost is a sufficient condition for profit maximization.

Difficulty: 2
Correct: T

4. If the long run supply curve of a competitive firm is $q = 3p$, then it can not have constant returns to scale.

Short-Answer Questions

Difficulty: 3

1. The Lost Mountains of northern Iowa are inhabited by the rare Marshallian deer. Patches of grass are far apart in this rugged land. If a deer finds a fresh patch of grass and spends h hours grazing it, it gets $\sqrt{h}$ units of grass. The deer compete for grass. When there are n deer, it takes a deer n^2 minutes to find a fresh patch. A deer can survive if it gets 1 unit of grass every 200 minutes. a) Find the average cost in time of a unit of grass if a deer gets y units of grass from each patch. b) How much time will an efficient deer spend in each patch when there are n deer? (Hint: Min. Avg. Cost) c) Since there is free entry into the deer business, the equilibrium population is the maximum number of efficient deer who can survive. How many is this?

a) $y + n^2/y$ b) n minutes c) 100

Chapter 23
INDUSTRY SUPPLY

Multiple-Choice Questions

Difficulty: 2
Correct: C

1. In East Icicle, Minnesota, on the northern edge of the corn belt, the growing season is short and the soil is poor. Corn yields are meager unless a great deal of expensive fertilizer is used. In Corncrib, Illinois the land is fertile and flat and the growing season is 20 days longer. For any given expenditure per acre, corn yields are far greater than in East Icicle. Farmers in both places are profit maximizers who grow corn. We deduce that
   a) marginal costs are higher in E. Icicle than in Corncrib.
   b) more fertilizer is used per acre in E. Icicle than in Corncrib.
   c) marginal costs are the same in both places.
   d) yields per acre are higher in Corncrib.
   e) more than one of the above

Difficulty: 3
Correct: C

2. A competitive industry has 10,000 identical firms. For each firm in the industry, the long run cost of producing y units of output is $c(y) = \$100 + y^2$ if $y > 0$ and $c(0) = 0$. The government imposes a lump sum tax of $300 on each firm in the industry. Firms can avoid this tax only by going out of business. There is free entry and exit into this industry. In the long run
   a) the number of firms stays constant and the price of output rises by $30.
   b) the number of firms doubles and the price of output doubles.
   c) the number of firms is halved and the price of output is doubled.
   d) the number of firms stays constant and the price of output rises by less than $30.
   e) none of the above.

Difficulty: 2
Correct: B

3. The bicycle industry is made up of 100 firms with the long run cost curve $c(y) = 2 + y^2/2$ and 100 firms with the long run cost curve $c(y) = 3 + y^2/3$. No new firms can enter the industry. What is the long run industry supply curve at prices greater than 2?
   a) $y = 30p$
   b) $y = 250p$
   c) $y = 200p$
   d) $y = 170p$
   e) none of the above

Difficulty: 2
Correct: B

4. Two firms constitute the entire doghouse industry. One has a long run cost curve of $3 + 4y^2/3$ and the other has a long run cost curve of $10 + y^2/10$. If no new firms enter the industry, at which of the following prices will exactly one firm operate?
   a) 1
   b) 3
   c) 5
   d) 7
   e) none of the above

Difficulty: 1
Correct: B

5. On a small island, papayas can only be sold in the market in the center of the island. Although papayas only cost 1 to raise, they can be sold in the market for 3. But it costs .1 per kilometer to transport them to market. If an acre of land grows 200 papayas, how much rent does an acre of land 4 kilometers from the market command?
   a) 302
   b) 320
   c) 240
   d) 262
   e) none of the above

Difficulty: 2
Correct: A

6. On a tropical island there are 100 boat builders, numbered 1 through 100. Each can build up to 12 boats a year. Where y denotes the number of boats built per year, boat builder 1 has a cost function $c(y) = 11 + y$. Boat builder 2 has a cost function $c(y) = 11 + 2y$ and, more generally, for each i, from 1 to 100, boat builder i has a cost function $c(y) = 11 + iy$. If the price of boats is 25, how many boats will be built per year?
   a) 288
   b) 112
   c) 200
   d) 156
   e) none of the above

True or False Questions

Difficulty: 1
Correct: T

1. The short run industry supply curve can be found by horizontally summing the supply curves of all the individual firms in the industry.

Difficulty: 2
Correct: T

2. It is possible to have an industry in which all firms make zero economic profits in long run equilibrium.

Difficulty: 1
Correct: T

3. The possibility of more firms entering an industry in the long run tends to make long run industry supply more price elastic than short run industry supply.

Short-Answer Questions

Difficulty: 2   1.   The cost per bushel of growing corn on a given acre of land depends partly on how intensely the land is farmed and partly on the quality of the soil, the amount of rainfall and the length of the growing season. Suppose that the last three factors are summarized by a single index "f" for fertility. Suppose that the long run total cost of producing y hundred bushels of corn on an acre of land of fertility f is $c(y,f)$ where $c(y,f)=(1+y^2)/f$ for $y>0$ and $c(0,f)=0$. a) Write down a formula for the long run average cost function per hundred bushels of corn from an acre of land of quality f. b) At what level of output is long run average cost minimized on an acre of land of quality f? c) What is the lowest price per hundred bushels at which an acre of land of quality f will be used to produce corn?

a) $LRAC=(y+1/y)/f$ b)1 hundred bushels c) $2/f$.

Difficulty: 2   2.   This question is an extension of the previous question on corn production. Suppose that in the entire economy, the total number of acres with fertility greater than f is given by the formula $N(f)$ where for all $f>.001$, $N(f)=A/f$ and where $N(f)=1000f$ for all $f<.001$. a) At a price of \$100 per bushel, what would be the fertility level of the least fertile land that is devoted to corn production? b) What would be the total supply of corn at a price of \$100? c) Write an equation for aggregate supply of corn as a function of the price per hundred bushels.

a).02 b) 50A. c)$pA/2$.

Difficulty: 3   3.   This question continues the analysis of corn production discussed in the previous two problems, using the cost functions described in these problems. a) If the price of corn is \$100 per hundred bushels, how much rent will be earned per year on an acre of land for which $f=.1$? b) More generally, write down a function relating annual rent on an acre of land to its fertility, f, and the price of corn, p. c) If the interest rate is 5%, corn prices are expected to remain at \$100 per hundred bushels, and cost functions are not expected to change, what would be the market value of an acre of land of fertility, f?

a)\$80 b) $p-2/f$ c) $2000-40/f$.

Chapter 24
MARKETS

Short-Answer Questions

Difficulty: 3

1. This comes from an actual newspaper story. "The average price of a home in W. county rose more than 12% last year...but the number of sales fell nearly 15%. 'It's the old law of supply and demand', said a spokesman for the Board of Realtors. 'The number of sales is down because there's a higher demand for properties but there isn't a corresponding number to sell.'" a) What does the "old law of supply and demand" predict would happen to price and quantity if the demand curve shifts outward and the supply curve does not change? b) Draw a diagram to illustrate the case of a shift in demand and or supply curves that is consistent with the observed change in prices and quantities.

   a) The price would rise and the quantity would rise. Even if the supply were very inelastic, the number of sales would not fall if the supply curve did not shift. b) One simple case would be a leftward shift in the supply curve and no change in the demand curve.

Multiple-Choice Questions

Difficulty: 2
Correct: C

1. A monopolist faces the inverse demand function $p=100-2q$ where q is the firm's output. The monopolist has no fixed cost and his average variable cost is 10 at all levels of output. Which of the following expresses the monopolist's profits as a function of his output?
   a) $100-2q+10$
   b) $100-8q$
   c) $90q-2q^2$
   d) $100q-2q^2-10$
   e) none of the above

Difficulty: 1
Correct: E

2. A monopolist faces the inverse demand curve $p=320-4q$. At what level of output is his total revenue maximized?
   a) 20
   b) 320
   c) 160
   d) 80
   e) 40

Difficulty: 2
Correct: B

3. The demand for a monopolist's output is 7000 divided by the square of the price in dollars that it charges per unit. The firm has constant marginal costs equal to 1 dollar per unit. To maximize its profits it should charge a price of:
   a) 1
   b) 2
   c) 3
   d) 1.5
   e) 2.5

Difficulty: 2
Correct: A

4. A profit-maximizing monopolist faces the demand curve, $q=100-3p$. It produces at a constant marginal cost of $20 per unit. A sales tax of $10 per unit is imposed on the monopolist's product. The price of the monopolist's product
   a) rises by $5.
   b) rises by $10
   c) rises by $20
   d) rises by $12
   e) stays constant.

Difficulty: 2
Correct: C

5. The demand for a monopolist's output is 10,000 divided by the square of the price he charges. The monopolist produces at a constant marginal cost of $5. If the government imposes a sales tax of $10 per unit on the monopolist's output, the monopolists price will rise by
    a) $5
    b) $10
    c) $20
    d) $12
    e) none of the above

Difficulty: 3
Correct: C

6. The demand for a monopolist's output is 1000 divided by the square of $(p+1)$ where p is the price the monopolist charges. At a price of 3, what is the absolute value of the elasticity of demand for the monopolist's output?
    a) 1
    b) 2
    c) 1.5
    d) 2.5
    e) 3

Difficulty: 3
Correct: D

7. The demand for a monopolist's output is 10,000 divided by the square of $(p+1)$. The monopolist has constant marginal costs equal to $2 per unit. What price will it charge to maximize its profits?
    a) 2
    b) 3
    c) 4
    d) 5
    e) none of the above

Difficulty: 2
Correct: D

8. A monopolist faces a constant marginal cost of $1 per unit. If at the price he is charging, the price elasticity of demand for the monopolist's output is -.5, then
    a) the price he is charging must be 2.
    b) the price he is charging must exceed 2.
    c) the price he is charging must be less than 2.
    d) the monopolist cannot be maximizing profits.
    e) the monopolist must use price discrimination.

Difficulty: 1
Correct: E

9. A profit-maximizing monopolist sets
    a) price equal to average cost.
    b) price equal to marginal cost.
    c) price equal to marginal cost plus a pro-rated share of overhead.
    d) price equal to marginal revenue.
    e) marginal revenue equal to marginal cost.

Difficulty: 1
Correct: C

10. If a natural monopolist sets price equal to average cost, it will
    a) produce too much output from the standpoint of efficiency.
    b) lose money.
    c) produce too little output from the standpoint of efficiency.
    d) maximize its profits.
    e) face excess demand.

Difficulty: 1
Correct: D

11. A profit maximizing monopolist faces a downward sloping demand curve that has a constant elasticity of -3. The firm charges a price of 12 for its output. What is its marginal cost at this level of output?
    a) 6
    b) 4
    c) 12
    d) 8
    e) 10

Difficulty: 1
Correct: D

12. A monopolist has constant marginal costs of $1 per unit. The demand for his output is $1000/p$ if p is less than or equal to 50. The demand is 0 if p>50. What is his profit maximizing level of output?
    a) 5
    b) 10
    c) 15
    d) 20
    e) 25

Difficulty: 2
Correct: B

13. The demand curve for the output of a certain industry is linear, $q=A-Bp$. There are constant marginal costs of C. For all values of A, B, and C such that A>0, B>0, and 0<C<A:
    a) If the industry is monopolized, the prices will be exactly twice as high as if the industry is competitive.
    b) If the industry is competitive, output will be exactly twice as great as if the industry is monopolized.
    c) If the industry is monopolized, prices will be more than twice as high as if the industry is competitive.
    d) If the industry is monopolized, output will be more than half as large as if the industry is competitive.
    e) none of the above

Difficulty: 3
Correct: B

14. A monopolist receives a subsidy from the government for every unit of output that is consumed. He has constant marginal costs and the subsidy that he gets per unit of output is greater than his marginal cost of production. But to get the subsidy on a unit of output, somebody has to consume it. From these facts we can conclude that
    a) he will pay consumers to consume his product.
    b) if he sells at a positive price, demand must be elastic at that price.
    c) he will sell at a price where demand is elastic.
    d) he will give the good away.
    e) none of the above

Difficulty: 2
Correct: C

15. A monopolist faces the demand curve $q = 50 - p/2$ where q is the number of units sold and p is the price in dollars. He has quasifixed costs, C, and constant marginal costs of $20 per unit of output. Therefore his total costs are $C + 20q$ if $q > 0$ and 0 if $q = 0$. What is the largest value of C for which he would choose to produce positive output?
    a) $20
    b) $1000
    c) $800
    d) $600
    e) $50

Difficulty: 2
Correct: C

16. A natural monopolist has the a total cost function $c(q) = 350 + q$ where q is its output. The inverse demand function for the monopolist's product is $p = 100 - 2q$. Government regulations require this firm to produce a positive amount and to set price equal to average cost. To comply with these requirements
    a) is impossible for this firm.
    b) the firm must produce 40 units.
    c) the firm could produce either 5 units or 35 units.
    d) the firm must charge a price of 70.
    e) the firm must produce 20 units.

Difficulty: 2
Correct: D

17. A monopolist has the total cost function, $c(q) = 500 + 7q$. The inverse demand function for this monopolist's output is $130 - 3q$. If the firm is required by law to meet demand at a price equal to its marginal cost, how much money will the firm lose?
    a) 1288
    b) 240
    c) 290
    d) 500
    e) 700

Difficulty: 2
Correct: B

18. A monopolist enjoys a monopoly over the right to sell automobiles on a certain island. He imports automobiles from abroad at a cost of $10,000 each and sells them at the price that maximizes profits. One day, the island's government annexes a neighboring island and extends the monopolist monopoly rights to this island. People on the annexed island have the same tastes and incomes and there are just as many people as on the first.
   a) The monopolist doubles his price and his sales stay constant.
   b) The monopolist keeps his price constant and his sales double.
   c) The economist raises his price but does not necessarily double it.
   d) The monopolist's profits more than double.
   e) none of the above

Difficulty: 2
Correct: C

19. A monopolist is able to practice third degree price discrimination between two markets. The demand function in the first market is 500-2q and the demand function in the second market is 1500-6q. To maximize his profits, he should
   a) charge a higher price in the second market than in the first.
   b) charge a higher price in the first market than in the second.
   c) charge the same price in both markets.
   d) sell only in one of the two markets.
   e) none of the above

Difficulty: 2
Correct: B

20. A monopolist finds that a person's demand for its product depends on his or her age. The inverse demand function of a person of age y, can be written $p=A(y)-q$ where $A(y)$ is an increasing function of y. The product cannot be resold from one buyer to another and the monopolist knows the ages of its consumers. If the monopolist maximizes its profits
   a) older people will pay higher prices and purchase less of this product.
   b) older people will pay higher prices and purchase more of this product.
   c) older people will pay lower prices and purchase more of this product.
   d) everyone pays the same price but old people consume more.
   e) none of the above

Difficulty: 3
Correct: A

21. A monopolist has discovered that the inverse demand function of a person with income M for the monopolist's product is $p = .002M - q$. The monopolist is able to observe the incomes of its consumers and to practice second degree price discrimination according to income. The monopolist has a total cost function, $c(q) = 100q$. The price it will charge a consumer depends on the consumer's income, M, according to the formula:
   a) $p = .001M + 50$
   b) $p = .002M - 100$
   c) $p = M^2$
   d) $p = .01 M^2 + 100$
   e)   none of the above

Difficulty: 2
Correct: D

22. An airline has exclusive landing rights at the local airport. The airline flies one flight per day to New York with a plane that has a seating capacity of 100. The cost of flying the plane per day is $\$4,000 + 10q$ where q is the number of passengers. The number of flights to New York demanded is $q = 165.5p$. If the airline maximizes its monopoly profits, the difference between the marginal cost of flying an extra passenger and the amount the marginal passenger is willing to pay to fly to New York is
   a)   \$10.
   b)   \$100.
   c)   \$140.
   d)   \$170.
   e)   none of the above

Difficulty: 2
Correct: C

23. A computer software company has developed a new and better spreadsheet program. Its discovery is protected by copyrights so it can act as a monopolist for this product. The demand function for this software is $Q = 51,000 - 100p$. Any one consumer will want only one copy. The marginal cost consists of the cost of producing another copy and its documentation for a consumer and is just \$10. If the company sells this software at the profit maximizing monopoly price, the number of consumers who would not buy the software at the monopoly price but would pay more than the marginal cost is
   a)   12,000.
   b)   14,000.
   c)   25,000.
   d)   50,000.
   e)   none of the above

Difficulty: 2
Correct: D

24. A monopoly has the demand curve q = 10,000-100p. Its total cost function is c(q) = 1000+10q. The government plans to tax the monopoly's profits at a rate of 50%. If it does so
   a) the monopoly will increase its price by 50%.
   b) the monopoly will increase its price by more than 50%.
   c) the monopoly will recover some, but not all, of the tax it pays by increasing its price.
   d) the monopoly will not change its price or the quantity it sells.
   e) none of the above

Difficulty: 2
Correct: E

25. A profit maximizing monopolist ends up earning exactly zero profit. For this firm at its profit maximizing output, it must be that:
   a) there are large fixed costs.
   b) demand is price inelastic.
   c) marginal revenue is greater than marginal cost.
   d) price equals marginal cost.
   e) average total cost is greater than marginal cost.

True or False Questions

Difficulty: 1
Correct: T

1. Since a monopoly charges a price higher than marginal cost, it will produce an inefficient amount of output.

Difficulty: 1
Correct: F

2. If the interest rate is 10%, the monopolist will choose a markup of price over marginal cost of at least 10%.

Difficulty: 1
Correct: F

3. A natural monopoly occurs when a firm gains ownership of the entire stock of some natural resource and thus is able to exclude other producers.

Difficulty: 1
Correct: F

4. A monopsony occurs when two previously competing firms reach an agreement to collude on price.

Difficulty: 2
Correct: T

5. Third degree price discrimination occurs when a monopolist sells output to different people at different prices, but every unit that an individual buys costs him or her the same amount.

Difficulty: 1
Correct: F

6. A monopolist who is able to practice third degree price discrimination will make greater profits than a monopolist who is able to practice first degree price discrimination.

Difficulty: 2
Correct: F

7. A monopolist who is able to charge different prices in different markets will charge a higher price in the market where demand is greater at any given price.

Difficulty: 2
Correct: T

8. In a monopolistically competitive industry with zero profits, each firm will produce a smaller amount than the amount that minimizes average costs.

Short-Answer Questions

Difficulty: 3

1. A baseball team's attendance depends on the number of games it wins per season and on the price of its tickets. The demand function it faces is $Q = N(20-p)$ where Q is the number of tickets (in hundred thousands) sold per year, p is the price per ticket and N is the fraction of its games that the team wins. The team can increase the number of games it wins by hiring better players. If the team spends C million dollars on players it will win the fraction $.7-1/C$ of its games. Over the relevant range, marginal cost of selling an extra ticket is zero. a) Write an expression for the firm's profits as a function of ticket price and expenditure on players. b) Find the ticket price that maximizes revenue. c) Find the profit maximizing expenditure on players and the profit maximizing fraction of games to win.

a) $(.7-1/C)(20-p)p-C$ b) $p=10$ c) $C=10$

Multiple-Choice Questions

Difficulty: 3
Correct: D

1. An industry has two firms each of which produce output at a constant unit cost of $10 per unit. The demand function for the industry is q=1,000,000/p. The Cournot equilibrium price for this industry is:
   a) 5.
   b) 10.
   c) 15.
   d) 20.
   e) 25.

Difficulty: 2
Correct: C

2. An industry has two firms. The inverse demand function for this industry is p=200-4q. Both firms produce at a constant unit cost of $8 per unit. What is the Cournot equilibrium price for this industry?
   a) 24
   b) 30
   c) 40
   d) 42
   e) 50

Difficulty: 3
Correct: C

3. One unit of zinc and one unit of copper are needed to produce a unit of brass. The world's supply of zinc and the world's supply of copper are owned by two different monopolists. For simplicity assume that it costs nothing to mine zinc and copper, that no inputs are needed to produce brass and that the brass industry operates competitively. Then the price of a unit of brass equals the cost of the inputs used to make it. The demand function for brass is q=900-2p where p is the price of brass. The zinc and copper monopolists each set a price, believing that the other monopolist will not change his price. What is the equilibrium price of brass?
   a) 100
   b) 200
   c) 300
   d) 50
   e) 25

Difficulty: 2
Correct: C

4. A duopoly faces the inverse demand curve p=160-2q. Both firms in the industry have constant costs of $10 per unit of output. In Cournot equilibrium how much output will each duopolist sell?
   a) 75
   b) 54
   c) 25
   d) 35
   e) 48

Difficulty: 2
Correct: B

5. Suppose that the price elasticity of demand for airline flights between two cities is constant and equal to -1.5. If 4 airlines with equal costs are in Cournot equilibrium for this industry, then the ratio of price to marginal cost in the industry is:
    a) 8/7
    b) 9/8
    c) 7/6
    d) 3/2
    e) none of the above

Difficulty: 2
Correct: C

6. A city has two major league baseball teams, A and B. The number of tickets sold by either team depends on the price of the team's own tickets and the price of the other team's ticket. Ticket sales, measured in hundreds of thousands per season, by the two teams are 21-2Pa+Pb for team A and 21+Pa-2Pb for team B. The marginal cost of having an extra spectator is zero for both teams. Each team believes the other's price is independent of its own choice of price and each team sets its own price so as to maximize its revenue. What price do they charge per ticket?
    a) Both charge $5.
    b) Both charge $6.
    c) Both charge $7.
    d) Both charge $4.
    e) none of the above

Difficulty: 3
Correct: D

7. A city has two newspapers. Demand for either paper depends on its own price and the price of its rival. Demand functions for papers A and B respectively, measured in tens of thousands of subscriptions, are 21-2Pa+Pb and 21-Pb-2Pa. The marginal cost of printing and distributing an extra paper just equals the extra advertising revenue one gets from another reader, so each paper treats marginal costs as zero. Each paper maximizes its revenue assuming that the other's price is independent of its own choice of price. If the papers enter a joint operating agreement where they set prices to maximize total revenue, by how much will newspaper prices rise?
    a) 3
    b) 2
    c) 0
    d) 3.5
    e) 2.5

Difficulty: 1
Correct: C

8. There are two major producers of corncob pipes in the world, both located in Herman, Missouri. Suppose that the inverse demand function for corncob pipes is q=100-2p where q is measured in thousands of pipes. What is the Cournot reaction function of firm 1 to the output of firm 2?
   a) 100-2y1
   b) 100-2y2
   c) 25-.5y1
   d) 50-4y1
   e) 50-2y1

Difficulty: 2
Correct: D

9. An industry has two firms. They produce at constant unit cost of $10 per unit. The demand curve for the industry is q=220-.5p. If firm 1 is a Stackleberg leader, how much output will it produce?
   a) 10
   b) 15
   c) 20
   d) 25
   e) 30

True or False Questions

Difficulty: 1
Correct: F

1. In Cournot equilibrium each firm chooses the quantity that maximizes its own profits assuming that the firm's rival will keep his price constant.

Difficulty: 1
Correct: F

2. In Bertrand competition between two firms, each firm believes that if he changes his output, the rival firm will change his output by the same amount.

Difficulty: 1
Correct: T

3. The larger the number of identical firms in Cournot equilibrium, the closer the industry price approaches to the competitive price.

Difficulty: 2
Correct: T

4. A Staeckleberg leader chooses his actions on the assumption that his rival or rivals will adjust to the leader's actions in such a way as to maximize their own profits.

Difficulty: 1
Correct: F

5. Conjectural variation refers to the fact that in a single market there is variation among firms in their estimates of the demand function in future periods.

Difficulty: 1
Correct: T

6. A duopoly in which two identical firms are engaged in Bertrand competition will not distort prices from their competitive levels.

Difficulty: 2
Correct: T

7. A Stackelberg leader will necessarily make at least as much profit as he would if he acted as a Cournot oligopolist.

Chapter 27
GAME THEORY

Multiple-Choice Questions

Difficulty: 2
Correct: C

1. A game has two players. Each player has two possible strategies. One strategy is called "cooperate", the other is called "defect". Each player writes on a piece of paper either a C for cooperate or a D for defect. If both players write C, they both get a payoff of $100. If both players defect they each get a payoff of 0. If one player cooperates and the other player defects, the cooperating player gets a payoff of S and the defecting player gets a payoff of T. To defect will be a dominant strategy for both players
   a) if $S + T > 100$.
   b) if $T > 2S$.
   c) if $S < 0$ and $T > 100$.
   d) if $S < T$ and $T > 100$.
   e) for all S and T.

True or False Questions

Difficulty: 2
Correct: T

1. A situation where everyone is playing a dominant strategy must be a Nash equilibrium.

Difficulty: 2
Correct: F

2. In a Nash equilibrium, everyone must be playing a dominant strategy.

Difficulty: 2
Correct: F

3. In the prisoners' dilemma game, if each prisoner believed that the other prisoner would deny the crime, then both would deny the crime.

Difficulty: 1
Correct: F

4. A general has the two possible pure strategies--sending all of his troops by land or all of his troops by sea. An example of a mixed strategy is where he sends 1/4 of his troops by land and 3/4 of his troops by sea.

Difficulty: 1
Correct: F

5. While game theory predicts noncooperative behavior for a single play of prisoners' dilemma, it would predict cooperative tit-for-tat behavior if the same people play prisoners' dilemma together for, say, 20 rounds.

Difficulty: 1
Correct: F

6. A Nash equilibrium strategy for a cartel made up of n identical firms with constant unit costs is for each firm to produce one nth of the amount a profit maximizing monopoly would produce.

Short-Answer Questions

Difficulty: 2

1. The coach of the offensive football team has two options on the next play. He can run the ball or he can pass. His rival can defend either against the run or against the pass. Suppose that the offense passes. Then if the defense defends against the pass, it will make zero yards and if the defense defends against the run, it will make 25 yards. Suppose that the offense runs. If the defense defends against the pass, the offense will make 10 yards and if the defense defends against a run, the offense will gain 2 yards. a) Write down a payoff matrix for this game. b) Is there a Nash equilibrium in pure strategies for this game? If so, what is it? If not, demonstrate that there is none.

This game does not have a Nash equilibrium in pure strategies. The best response to a pass (run) is a defense against the pass (run). But the best response to a defense against the pass (run) is to run (pass).

Chapter 28
EXCHANGE

Multiple-Choice Questions

Difficulty: 2
Correct: E

1. In a pure exchange economy with two persons and two goods one person always prefers more to less of both goods and one person likes one of the goods and hates the other so much that she would have to be paid to consume it. Both are endowed with positive amounts of both good. The competitive equilibrium price of the good that one person hates must be
    a) negative.
    b) smaller than the price of the good both people like.
    c) less than 1.
    d) could be positive or negative, depending on details of tastes and technology.
    e) at least zero.

True or False Questions

Difficulty: 1
Correct: F

1. Partial equilibrium analysis concerns only supply or only demand while general equilibrium analysis deals with supply and demand at the same time.

Difficulty: 1
Correct: T

2. A pure exchange economy is an economy where goods are traded but there is no production.

Difficulty: 1
Correct: F

3. In general equilibrium analysis, an allocation is a feasible allocation if every consumer is consuming a bundle that costs no more than his or her income.

Difficulty: 2
Correct: T

4. From Walras' law it follows that in a market with two goods, if demand equals supply in one market, then demand must equal supply in the other market.

Difficulty: 2
Correct: T

5. If the assumptions of the first theorem of welfare economics apply, then if the economy is in a competitive equilibrium, then any reallocation that benefits someone must harm someone else.

Difficulty: 2
Correct: T

6. If there are consumption externalities, then a competitive equilibrium is not necessarily Pareto optimal.

Difficulty: 1
Correct: T

7. A competitive equilibrium allocation must be a feasible allocation.

Difficulty: 2
Correct: T

8. The second welfare theorem states that if preferences are convex, then any Pareto optimal allocation could be achieved as a competitive equilibrium after some reallocation of initial endowments.

Difficulty: 1
Correct: T

9. In a competitive pure exchange economy, if the total value of excess demand for all types of food is zero, then the total value of excess demand for all nonfood commodities must be zero.

Difficulty: 1
Correct: T

10. Every allocation on the contract curve is Pareto optimal.

Difficulty: 1
Correct: T

11. If the price vector (12,27) is a competitive equilibrium price vector, then so is the price vector (24,54).

Difficulty: 2
Correct: T

12. If demand varies continuously with price, then even if there are thousands of goods there will be at least one set of prices such that demand equals supply in every market.

Difficulty: 3
Correct: T

13. If allocation x is a competitive equilibrium at prices p and everybody likes his bundle in allocation y better than his bundle in allocation x, then allocation y is worth more than allocation x at prices p.

Short-Answer Questions

Difficulty: 2

1. In a pure exchange economy, Ollie's utility function is $U(x,y) = 3x + y$ and Fawn's utility function is $U(x,y) = xy$. Ollie's initial allocation is 1 x and no y's. Fawn's initial allocation is no x's and 2 y's. Draw an Edgeworth box for Fawn and Ollie. Put x's on the horizontal axis and y's on the vertical axis. Measure goods for Ollie from the lower left and goods for Fawn from the upper right. Mark the initial allocation with the letter W. The locus of Pareto optimal points consists of two line segments. Describe these line segments in words or formulas and show them on your graph.

    The Edgeworth box is 1 unit wide and 2 units high. Along the contract curve, Fawn consumes 3 times as much y as x. The contract curve consists of a line running from the upper right corner of the box to the point on the bottom of the box where Fawn consumes all of the y and 2/3 units of x and a line from this point to the lower left of the box.

Difficulty: 3

2. An economy has 2000 people. 1000 of them have utility functions $U(x,y) = x+y$ and 1000 of them have utility functions $U(x,y) = \min\{2x,y\}$. Everybody has an initial allocation of 1 unit of x and 1 unit of y. Find the competitive equilibrium prices and consumptions for each type of person.

Prices are 1 and 1. The first type of person will consume 2/3 units of y and 4/3 units of x and the second type of person will consume 4/3 units of y and 2/3 units of x.

Difficulty: 2

3. Will likes apples and hates bananas. Wanda likes both apples and bananas. Both of them have convex preferences. Will's initial endowment is 10 apples and 5 bananas. Wanda's initial endowment is 5 bananas and 10 apples. a) Draw an Edgeworth box with apples on the horizontal axis. Label the initial endowment point, W. b) Show two indifference curves for each person. c) Show where on your diagram the Pareto optimal allocations are.

The Pareto optimal allocations include all of the allocations where Will has no bananas. If stuff for Will is measured from the lower left corner, then these allocations are all along the bottom of the box.

Chapter 29
PRODUCTION

True or False Questions

Difficulty: 2
Correct: T

1. If there are constant returns to scale in an industry, then in competitive equilibrium, profits in that industry must necessarily be zero.

Difficulty: 1
Correct: F

2. When there is production, a competitive equilibrium is not Pareto optimal unless there are increasing returns to scale.

Difficulty: 1
Correct: T

3. The marginal rate of substitution between two goods indicates the rate at which an efficient economy would have to give up one good to obtain more of the other.

Difficulty: 1
Correct: F

4. If there are two people and two goods, person A has comparative advantage in the production of good 1 if person A can produce good 1 more cheaply than person B can.

Short-Answer Questions

Difficulty: 2

1. On a certain small island, there are 100 units of labor and 200 units of capital. Two goods can be produced. Good A is produced with fixed coefficients, using 1 unit of labor and 3 units of capital per unit of output. Good B is produced with fixed coefficients, using 1 unit of labor and 1 unit of capital per unit of ouput. Let Xa denote the quantity of good A and Xb be the quantity of good B that is produced. The set of feasible outputs combinations for this economy is restricted by the fact that it cannot use more than 100 units of labor or 200 units of capital. a) Write down two inequalities expressed in terms of Xa and Xb that must be satisfied at feasible output combinations. b) Draw a graph showing the economy's production possibility set. Put numerical labels on your graph so that this graph is precisely described.

a) Xa + Xb < = 100, 3Xa + Xb < = 200 b) Production possibility set is the area in the intersection of the halfspaces from a.

Chapter 30
WELFARE

True or False Questions

Difficulty: 1
Correct: F

1. According to Arrow's impossibility theorem, it is impossible to find a social ordering that is complete, reflexive and transitive.

Difficulty: 2
Correct: T

2. If a social welfare function is an increasing function of each person's utility, then every allocation that maximizes this social welfare function subject to feasibility constraints must be Pareto optimal.

Difficulty: 1
Correct: F

3. An allocation is fair if whenever one person envies another, the envied person does not envy the envier.

Difficulty: 2
Correct: F

4. In a pure exchange economy if the initial allocation is Pareto optimal, then competitive equilibrium is fair.

Difficulty: 2
Correct: T

5. In a competitive equilibrium, no matter how different their preferences may be, no two people with the same income will envy each other's consumption bundles.

Difficulty: 1
Correct: F

6. An allocation which leaves somebody worse off than he was in the initial allocation can not be Pareto optimal.

Difficulty: 2
Correct: F

7. If allocation x is Pareto optimal and allocation y is not, then everyone is at least as well off with x as with y and someone is better off with x than with y.

Difficulty: 1
Correct: F

8. The utility possibilities frontier is the boundary of the production possibility set.

Difficulty: 1
Correct: T

9. In a pure exchange economy, if an allocation is Pareto efficient it is impossible to have two people who prefer each other's consumption bundles to their own.

Short-Answer Questions

Difficulty: 2

1. No one is meaner and uglier than Gladys. Someone is meaner and uglier than Harold. Therefore Gladys is meaner and uglier than Harold. Is this reasoning correct? If so, explain why. If not, explain why not. (Assume that people can be ranked from ugliest to least ugly by a complete transitive ordering and that there are no ties. Likewise assume that people can be ranked from meanest to least mean by a complete transitive ordering and that there are no ties.)

    The reasoning is incorrect. Consider the following example. There are 3 people: Fred, Gladys and Harold. The rankings for ugly are Gladys is ugliest, Fred is second ugliest and Harold is least ugly. The rankings for mean are Fred is meanest, Harold is second meanest and Gladys is least mean. Then nobody is meaner and uglier than Gladys. Fred is meaner and uglier than Harold, but Gladys is not meaner and uglier than Harold.

Difficulty: 2

2. Lucy loves Schroeder, but Schroeder does not love Lucy. Both consume only one good. Where L is the amount of the good that Lucy consumes, and S is the amount that Schroeder consumes, Lucy's utility is $U(L,S)=L-16/S$. Schroeder cares only about his own consumption. We write his utility as $U(S)=S$. There are 12 units of the good to be divided between Lucy and Schroeder. a) Find all of the Pareto optimal allocations. (Hint: there is some positive number such that any allocation of the 12 units that gives Schroeder at least that much is Pareto optimal) b) Draw a utility possibility frontier for Lucy and Schroeder.

    All divisions of the 12 units such that Schroeder gets at least 4 are Pareto optimal.

Chapter 31
EXTERNALITIES

True or False Questions

Difficulty: 1
Correct: F

1. A trade between two people is an example of an externality.

Difficulty: 1
Correct: F

2. The only known way to eliminate externalities is through taxes or subsidies.

Difficulty: 1
Correct: F

3. The efficient amount of air pollution is in general independent of whether polluters or pollutees pay to reduce pollution.

Difficulty: 1
Correct: F

4. A Pigouvian tax on pollution is designed to collect enough revenue to pay for pollution detection by the government.

Difficulty: 2
Correct: F

5. If there are negative externalities in production or consumption, competitive equilibrium is unlikely to be Pareto efficient, but positive externalities enhance the efficiency of the market.

Difficulty: 1
Correct: T

6. The tragedy of the commons refers to the tendency for common property to be overused.

Difficulty: 1
Correct: F

7. If preferences are quasilinear, then the delineation of property rights has no distributional consequences.

Short-Answer Questions

Difficulty: 3

1. Two firms in a grimy Ohio town produce the same product in a competitive industry. Each has an old factory using an old technology. It still pays to operate these factories but it would not pay to expand them. The only variable factor used by either firm is labor. Each firm pollutes the other and thus reduces the output of the other firm. The production functions of firms A and B respectively are $Qa = \sqrt{La} - (2/3)Qb$ and $Qb = \sqrt{Lb} - (1/3)Qa$ where La and Lb are the amounts of labor used by firms A and B. The wage rate of labor is 1 and the price of the firms' output is 12. a)If the two firms each maximize profits independently, what is their total output and how much quasi-rents do their factories earn? b) If someone buys them both and maximizes joint profits, how much quasi-rents are earned in total?

Each produces 48 and quasirents are 12 for each. Each produces 36 and quasirents total 40.

Chapter 32
PUBLIC GOODS

Multiple-Choice Questions

Difficulty: 2
Correct: E

1. A quiet town in Kansas has 2000 people, all of whom have the same preferences. There is one private good and one public good. Each person, i, in town has the utility function $U(x_i, y) = x_i + \sqrt{y}$ where x_i is the amount of private good that individual i gets and y is the amount of public good that the town provides. If the private good costs \$1 per unit and the public good costs \$10 per unit, what is the Pareto optimal amount of public good for the town to provide?
    a) 100 units
    b) 500 units
    c) 2000 units
    d) 8000 units
    e) 10,000 units

Difficulty: 2
Correct: C

2. The Sons of Knute had a hunting lodge up on Loon Lake which burned down last winter. They plan to rebuild it this summer and are trying to decide how large the new lodge should be. The organization has 50 members. The marginal rate of substitution of each of them between square feet of hunting lodge and money to spend on other goods is 1.2-.0004 Y where Y is the size of the hunting lodge in square feet. What is the efficient size for the new hunting lodge?
    a) 1000 square feet
    b) 1200 square feet
    c) 2000 square feet
    d) 2400 square feet
    e) none of the above

True or False Questions

Difficulty: 1
Correct: F

1. To say that preferences are single-peaked means that everybody either prefers more public goods to less or everybody prefers less public goods to more.

Difficulty: 1
Correct: T

2. If preferences are single-peaked, then pairwise majority voting among alternative options will not lead to voting cycles.

Difficulty: 1
Correct: F

3. A tax imposed on polluters to give them an incentive to make an efficient reduction in pollution is called a Clarke tax.

Difficulty: 1
Correct: T

4. If a pure public good is provided by voluntary contributions, economic theory predicts that in general too little will be supplied.

Difficulty: 2
Correct: F

5. A Pareto optimal amount of public goods is shown on a graph with quantities of public goods on the x axis by the point at which the horizontal sum of the marginal rate of substitution curves meets the marginal cost curve.

Difficulty: 2
Correct: F

6. One of the problems with the Clarke tax mechanism is that when it is used, people have an incentive to lie about their preferences.

Short-Answer Questions

Difficulty: 3

1. An otherwise charming island is inhabited by two religious groups who hate each other. The island is presided over by a benevolent monarch who is extremely concerned about envy between groups. He chooses the distribution of income on the island so as to maximize the social welfare function, $W(x,y) = \min\{2x-y, 2y-x\}$ where x is the utility of the average member of group X and y is the utility of the average member of group Y. a) If the monarch can accomplish any distribution of utility such that $x+3y=24$, diagram the utility possibility frontier and the monarch's isowelfare lines. b) What income distribution maximizes W? c) Show that an equal increase in both groups income will always please the monarch. d) If the initial incomes are equal, when do increases in both groups' utility reduce W?

    a) see prob 99 b) 6,6 c) adding a constant to both x and y increases 2x-y and 2y-x. d) when either's income increases by more than twice the increase in the other's.

Part III

ANSWERS TO *WORKOUTS*
IN INTERMEDIATE MICROECONOMICS

Chapter 1

NAME_____

The Market

Introduction. The problems in this chapter examine some variations on the apartment market described in the text. In most of the problems we work with the true demand curve constructed from the reservation prices of the consumers rather than the "smoothed" demand curve that we used in the text.

Remember that the reservation price of a consumer is that price where he is just indifferent between renting or not renting the apartment. At any price below the reservation price the consumer will demand one apartment, at any price above the reservation price the consumer will demand zero apartments, and exactly at the reservation price the consumer will be indifferent between having zero or one apartments.

1.1 (30) Suppose that we have 8 people who want to rent an apartment. Their reservation prices are given below. (To keep the numbers small, think of these numbers as being daily rent payments.)

Person = A B C D E F G H
Price = 40 25 30 35 10 18 15 5

(a) Plot the market demand curve in the following graph. Hint: when the market price is equal to some consumer i's reservation price there will be two different quantities of apartments demanded since consumer i will be indifferent between having or not having an apartment.

NAME _____ 3

(a) Suppose that person A decides to buy the condominium. What will be the highest price at which demand will equal supply? What will be the lowest price? Enter your answers in the table below under Person A. Then do the same thing for persons B, C, etc.

Person	A	B	C	D	E	F	G	H
High price	18	18	18	18	25	25	25	25
Low price	15	15	15	15	18	15	15	18

(b) Suppose that there were two people at each reservation price and 10 apartments and that one of the apartments was turned into a condominium. What would happen to the equilibrium price? __Nothing.__

1.3 (20) Suppose now that a monopolist owns all the apartments and that he is trying to determine which price and quantity maximize his revenues.

(a) Fill in the box with the maximum price and revenue that the monopolist can make if he rents 1, 2, ..., 8 apartments. (Assume that he must charge one price for all apartments.)

Number	1	2	3	4	5	6	7	8
Price	40	35	30	25	18	15	10	5
Revenue	40	70	90	100	90	90	70	40

(b) Which of the people A–F would get apartments? __A, B, C, D.__

(c) If the monopolist were required by law to rent exactly 5 apartments, what price would he charge to maximize his revenue? __$18__

(d) Who would get apartments? __A, B, C, D, F.__

(e) If this landlord could charge each individual a different price, and he knew the reservation prices of all the individuals, what is the maximum revenue he could make if he rented all 5 apartments? __$148__

(f) If 5 apartments were rented, which individuals would get the apartments?__

__A, B, C, D, F.__

1.4 (20) Suppose that there are 5 apartments to be rented and that the city rent control board sets a maximum rent of $9. Further suppose that people A, B, C, D, and E manage to get an apartment, while F, G, and H are frozen out.

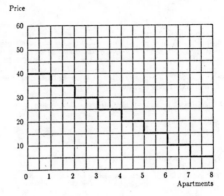

Price

(b) Suppose the supply of apartments is fixed at 5 units. In this case there is a whole range of prices that will be equilibrium prices. What is the highest price that would make the demand for apartments equal to 5 units? __$18.__

(c) What is the lowest price that would make the market demand equal to 5 units? __$15.__

(d) With a supply of 4 apartments, which of the people A–H end up getting apartments? __A, B, C, D.__

(e) What if the supply of apartments increases to 6 units. What is the range of equilibrium prices? __$10-$15.__

1.2 (30) Suppose that there are originally 5 units in the market, and that 1 of them is turned into a condominium.

(a) If subletting is legal—or, at least, practiced– who will sublet to whom in equilibrium? __E, who is willing to pay only $10 for an apartment would sublet to F, who is willing to pay $18.__

(Assume that people who sublet can evade the city rent control restrictions.)

(b) What will be the maximum amount that can be charged for the sublet payment? __$18__

(c) If you have rent control with unlimited subletting allowed, which of the consumers described above will end up in the 5 apartments? __A, B, C, D, F__

(d) How does this compare to the market outcome? __It's the same.__

1.5 (20) In the text we argued that a tax on landlords would not get passed along to the renters. What would happen if instead the tax was imposed on renters?

(a) To answer this question, consider the group of people in Problem 1. What is the maximum that they would be willing to pay to the landlord if they each had to pay a $5 tax on apartments to the city? Fill in the box below with these reservation prices.

Person	A	B	C	D	E	F	G	H
Reservation Price	35	20	25	30	5	13	10	0

(b) Using this information determine the equilibrium price if there are 5 apartments to be rented. It is __$13.__

(c) Of course, the total price a renter pays consists of his or her rent plus the tax. This amount is __$18.__

(d) How does this compare to what happens if the tax is levied on the landlords? __It's the same.__

Chapter 2

The Budget Set

Introduction. The budget set represents the set of consumption bundles that the consumer can afford to purchase. The best way to construct the budget set is to first find the equation characterizing the bundles that are exactly affordable (the budget line) and draw that. If the budget line is a straight line, it is helpful to ask how much the consumer would be able to consume if she spent all of her money on one good or the other, and then connect those two points with a straight line.

2.1 (20) Draw budget lines to illustrate each of the following cases.

(a) $p_1 = 1$, $p_2 = 1$, $m = 10$.

(b) $p_1 = 2$, $p_2 = 1$, $m = 20$.

(c) $p_1 = 1$, $p_2 = 0$, $m = 10$.

(d) $p_1 = p_2$, $m = 15p_1$. (Hint: How much good 1 could you afford if you spend your entire budget on good 1?)

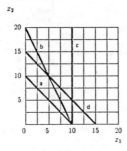

2.2 (20) You have $40 to spend on two commodities. Commodity 1 costs $10 per unit and commodity 2 costs $5 per unit.

(a) Write down your budget equation. $10x_1 + 5x_2 = 40$.

(g) Now suppose that the amount you are allowed to spend increases to $60 while the price of commodity 1 remains at $20 and the price of commodity 2 remains at $5. Write down your budget equation.____

$20x_1 + 5x_2 = 60$. ___ Put this budget line on your graph in black ink.

(h) On your diagram, use black ink to shade in the area representing commodity bundles that you can afford after the increase in price and income but could not afford in part (a). Use blue ink to shade in the area representing commodity bundles that you could afford initially but can not afford after the changes.

(i) Solve algebraically for the intersection of the black and the blue budget lines. (Hint: Remember how to solve two linear equations in two unknowns?) At the intersection of these lines, there are 2 _____

_____units of x_1 and 4 _____units of x_2.

2.3 (10) Illustrate in the diagram below how the budget line changes when money income and the price of bread remain fixed but the price of chocolate goes down.

chocolate

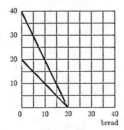

bread

2.4 (20) Your budget is such that if you spend your entire income, you could afford either 3 units of good x and 8 units of good y or 8 units of x and 3 units of y.

(b) If you spent all of your income on commodity 1, how much could you buy? 4._____

(c) If you spent all of your income on commodity 2, how much could you buy? 8._____

(d) Use blue ink to draw your budget line in the graph below.

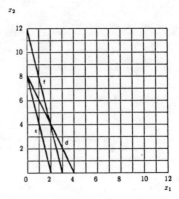

(e) Suppose that the price of commodity 1 is increased to $20 while everything else stays the same. Write down your new budget equation.____

$20x_1 + 5x_2 = 40$ _____

(f) How much of commodity 1 could you now buy if you spent all of your income on commodity 1? 2 units._____On the diagram you drew above, use red ink to draw your new budget line.

(j) Illustrate these two consumption bundles and draw the budget line in the graph below.

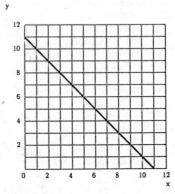

(k) What is the ratio of the price of x to the price of y? 1._____

(l) If you spent all of your income on x, how much x could you buy?___ 11._____

(m) If you like both goods and have nothing else to spend your income on, argue that you definitely would not choose to buy 5 units of x and 5 units of y at these prices and this income.

Given the budget constraint you could obtain 5.5 units

of each good, which would make you better off.

2.5 (40) On the planet Mungo, they have two kinds of money, blue money and red money. Every commodity has two prices— a red money price and a blue money price. Every Mungoan likewise has two incomes. One is its red money income and the other is its blue money income. (There is no need for awkwardness about sex-neutral pronouns, since although Mungo has two sexes, neither of them is remotely like either of ours—but that is another story.)

In order to buy an object, one has to pay that object's red money price in red money and its blue money price in blue money. (The shops simply have two cash registers and you have to pay at both registers to buy an object.) It is forbidden to trade one kind of money for the other and this prohibition is strictly enforced by Mungo's ruthless and efficient monetary police. (Columbus, Ohio, is rumored to be a penal colony for Mungoans who have violated this restriction.)

- There are just two consumer goods on Mungo, ambrosia and bubblegum. All Mungoans prefer more of each good to less.
- The blue prices are 1 bcu (bcu stands for blue currency unit) per unit of ambrosia and 1 bcu per unit of bubble gum.
- The red prices are 2 rcus (red currency units) per unit of ambrosia and 4 rcus per unit of bubblegum.

(a) On the graph below, draw the red budget (with a red ink) and the blue budget (with blue ink) for a Mungoan named Harold whose blue income is 9 and whose red income is 24. Shade in the "budget set" containing all of the commodity bundles that Harold can afford, given his two budget constraints. Remember, Harold has to have enough blue money and enough red money to purchase a bundle of goods.

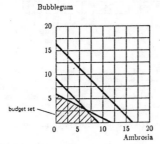

(b) Another Mungoan, Gladys, faces the same prices that Harold does and has the same red income as Harold, but Gladys has a blue income of 16. Explain how it is that Gladys will not spend its entire blue income

_____

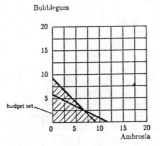

2.6 (20) Jonathan Livingstone Yuppie is a prosperous young lawyer. Although he lives in an intermediate price theory workbook, he has in his own words, "outgrown those confining two-commodity limits". Jonathan consumes three goods, unblended Scotch whiskey, designer tennis shoes, and meals in French gourmet restaurants. The price of Jonathan's brand of whiskey is $20 per bottle, the price of designer tennis shoes is $80 per pair and the price of gourmet restaurant meals is $50 per meal. After he has paid his taxes and alimony, Jonathan has $400 a week to spend.

(a) Write down a budget equation for Jonathan, where W stands for the number of bottles of whiskey, T stands for the number of pairs of tennis shoes and M for the number of gourmet restaurant meals that he

consumes. $20W + 80T + 50M = 400.$

(b) Draw a three dimensional diagram to show his budget set. Label the intersections of the budget set with each axis.

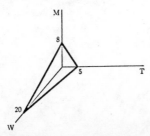

no matter what its tastes may be. (Hint: draw a picture of Gladys's blue budget line.)

If Gladys satisfies its red constraint, then it cannot

spend all of its blue income.

_____

(c) (This part is a little trickier. You may find it helpful to take some scratch paper and fiddle around with drawing some budget lines on it.) Harold's cousin, Irene, works in an ambrosia brewery. Irene is allowed a discount on the blue price of ambrosia. For Irene the blue price of ambrosia is only 1/2 bcu per unit of ambrosia, but Irene must pay the same red prices for everything and the same blue price for bubblegum that Harold and Gladys pay. Irene's red income is 24. What is the largest its blue income could be if it spends all of its blue income *and* all of its red

income? $\underline{6}$

(d) There is a group of radical economic reformers on Mungo who believe that the currency rules on Mungo are unfair. "Why should everyone have to pay two prices for everything," they say. They propose the following scheme. Mungo will continue to have two currencies, every good will continue to have a blue price and a red price, and every Mungoan will continue to have a blue income and a red income. But nobody needs to pay both prices.

Instead, everyone on Mungo must declare itself to be either a Blue Money Purchaser (a "Blue") or a Red Money Purchaser (a "Red") before it buys anything at all. Blue money purchasers must make all of their purchases in blue money at the blue prices, spending only their blue incomes. Red money purchasers must make all of their purchases in red money, spending only their red incomes. Suppose that Harold, whom we met above, continues to have the same income after this reform and that prices do not change. Before declaring which kind of Purchaser it will be, Harold contemplates the set of commodity bundles that it could possibly attain. Some of these it could reach by declaring itself to be a "Blue" and some it could attain by declaring itself to be a "Red". On the diagram below, shade in the entire set of commodity bundles that Harold could obtain by making one declaration or the other.

(c) Suppose that he determines that he will buy one pair of designer tennis shoes per week. What equation must be satisfied by the combinations of restaurant meals and whiskey that he could afford?

$20W + 50M = 320.$

2.7 (20) On the planet Spuddo there are only three commodities: potatoes, meatballs, and jam. Prices have been remarkably stable for the last 50 years or so. Potatoes cost 3 crowns per sack, meatballs cost 9 crowns per crock, and jam costs 6 crowns per jar.

(a) Write down a budget equation for a citizen named Gunnar who has an income of 360 crowns per year. Let P stand for the number of sacks of potatoes, M for the number of crocks of meatballs and J for the number

of jars of jam consumed by Gunnar in a year. $3P + 9M + 6J = 360.$

(b) The citizens of Spuddo are in general very clever people, but they are not good at multiplying by 3. This made shopping for potatoes excruciatingly difficult for many citizens. Therefore it was decided to make potatoes the numeraire while retaining the same relative prices as in the past. A new unit of currency (called the potato chip) was introduced.

What would be the price in terms of the new currency, of potatoes _____

$\underline{1}$ _____ of meatballs $\underline{3}$ _____, and

of jam $\underline{2}$ _____? What would Gunnar's income in the new currency have to be for him to be exactly able to afford the same

commodity bundles that he could afford before the change? $\underline{120}$

_____Write down Gunnar's new budget equation. How can you tell that this is the same budget as he had before?

$P + 3M + 2J = 120.$ The new budget equation is

obtained from the old one by dividing both sides of

the old one by 3. According to elementary mathematics,

$x = y$ if and only if $x/3 = y/3$

2.8 (20) Edmund Stench consumes two commodities, namely garbage and punk rock video cassettes. He doesn't actually eat the former but keeps it in his back yard where it is eaten by billy goats and assorted vermin. The reason that he accepts the garbage is that people pay him $2 per sack for taking it. He has no other source of income. Video cassettes cost him $6 each.

(a) If Edmund gets zero sacks of garbage, how many video cassettes can he buy? __0.__

(b) If he gets 15 sacks of garbage, how many video cassettes can he buy? __5.__

(c) Write down an equation for his budget line. $\underline{6C - 2G = 0}$ or equivalently, $6C = 2G$.

Garbage

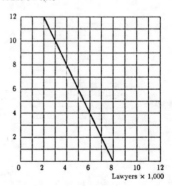

(d) Draw Edmund's budget line and shade in his budget set.

2.9 (20) If you think Edmund is odd, consider his brother Emmett. Emmett consumes speeches by politicians and university administrators. He is paid $1 per hour for listening to politicians and $2 per hour for listening to university administrators. (Emmett is in great demand to help fill empty chairs in public lectures because of his distinguished appearance and his ability to refrain from making rude noises.) Emmett consumes one good for which he must pay. We have agreed not to disclose what that good is, but we can tell you that it costs $10 per unit and we shall here call it simply good X. In addition to what he is paid for consuming speeches, Emmett receives a pension of $20 per week.

(a) Write down a budget equation stating those combinations of the three commodities, good X, speeches by politicians, and speeches by university administrators that Emmett could afford to consume per week. $\underline{10X}$ $-1P - 2A = 20$ or equivalently, $10X = 1P + 2A + 20.$

(b) On the graph below, draw a two dimensional diagram showing the locus of consumptions of the two kinds of speeches that would be possible for Emmett if he consumed 10 units of X per week.

Administrator speeches

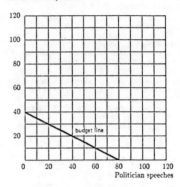

2.10 (20) Harry Hype of Hollywood, California, has $5,000 to spend to advertise a new kind of dehydrated sushi. Market research shows that the people most likely to buy this new product are recent recipients of M.B.A. degrees and lawyers who own hot tubs. Harry is considering advertising in two publications, a boring business magazine and a trendy consumer publication for people who wish they lived in California.

Fact 1: Ads in the boring business magazine cost $500 each and ads in the consumer magazine costs $250 each.

Fact 2: Each ad in the business magazine will be read by 1,000 recent M.B.A.'s and 300 lawyers with hot tubs.

Fact 3: Each ad in the consumer publication will be read by 300 recent M.B.A.'s and 250 lawyers who own hot tubs.

Fact 4: Nobody who reads one magazine reads the other.

(a) If Harry spends his entire advertising budget on the business publication, explain how it is that there will be 10,000 instances of former M.B.A.'s reading his ads and there will be 3,000 instances of his ads being read by lawyers with hot tubs.

He can buy $5000/500 = 10$ ads. Each ad is read by 1,000 MBA's and by 300 lawyers. Therefore the number of readings by MBA's is $10 \cdot 1,000 = 10,000$ and the number of readings by lawyers is $10 \cdot 300 = 3,000.$

(b) If he spent his entire advertising budget on the consumer publication, how many times will an ad of his be read by a recent M.B.A.? _____ 6,000; ____by a lawyer with hot tub? 5,000.

(c) Suppose he spent half of his advertising budget on each publication. How many readings of his ads by recent M.B.A.'s would he get __8,000;__ _____and how many readings of his ads by lawyers with hot tubs? __4,000.__

(d) Draw a budget line showing the combinations of number of readings by recent M.B.A.'s and by lawyers with hot tubs that he can obtain with his advertising budget. (Hint: You have found three points on this line already.) Does your budget extend in a straight line all the way to the axes? __No.__ ____Write an equation for this budget line? ____ $M + 2L = 16,000.$ With a fixed advertising budget, how many instances of an ad being read by an MBA must you sacrifice to have an additional instance of an ad being read by a lawyer with a hot tub? __2.__

M.B.A.'s × 1,000

Chapter 3
Preferences

Introduction. Most of the problems in this section ask you to draw indifference curves for a consumer with certain peculiar tastes. Don't be surprised or disappointed if you can not immediately see the answer when you look at the problem and don't expect that you will find the answers hiding somewhere in your textbook. You will best find the answers by thinking and doodling on scratch paper. A good way to start is to draw some axes on scratch paper and label them, then mark a point on your graph and ask yourself, "what other points on the graph would the consumer find indifferent to this point?" If it is possible, draw a line connecting such points, making sure that the shape of the line you have drawn reflect the features required by the problem. This gives you one indifference curve. Now pick another point that is preferred to the first one you drew and draw an indifference curve through it.

3.1 (30) Freddy Blodger loves money but hates to work. He has strictly convex preferences between income per week and hours of work per week.

(a) Draw some indifference curves for Freddy in the graph below.

Income per week

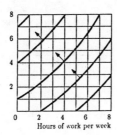

(b) Put your pencil on the graph at (4, 4). Which directions do you have to move to make Freddy indifferent to this point? <u>Northeast.</u>

NAME _____   19

(b) On the axes below, draw a few of Flossy's indifference curves and use your diagram to illustrate which of the two time allocations discussed above Flossy would prefer.

Hours dating

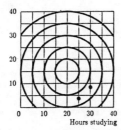

Hours studying

3.4 (20) It turns out that our friends from Mungo have three feet: two left feet and one right foot. If Mungoites always wear shoes on all feet, illustrate a typical set of indifference curves in the graph below.

Assume that if you have two left shoes and two right shoes, the extra right shoe is useless. Similarly if you have three left shoes and one right shoe, the extra left shoe is useless. Draw lines connecting the combinations of shoes that are indifferent to having 2 left shoes and 1 right shoe. Now sketch another indifference curve through the point 4 left shoes, 2 right shoes.

Left shoes

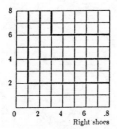

Right shoes

---

18 PREFERENCES (Ch. 3)

(c) Which direction do you have to move to make Freddy better off than at (4, 4)? <u>Northwest—the direction involving less work and more money.</u>

(d) What does convexity imply about the slope of the indifference curve as the hours of work increase? <u>The slope must get steeper in order to make the weakly preferred set convex.</u>

3.2 (20) Randy Ratpack hates studying both economics and history. The more time he spends studying either the less happy he is. But Randy has strictly convex preferences.

(a) Sketch an indifference curve for Randy where the two commodities are hours per week spent studying economics and hours per week spent studying history. Will the slope of an indifference curve be positive or negative? <u>Negative.</u>

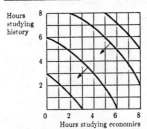

Hours studying economics

3.3 (10) Flossy Toothsome likes to spend some time studying and some time dating. In fact her indifference curves between hours per week spent studying and hours per week spent dating are concentric circles around her favorite combination which is 20 hours of studying and 15 hours of dating per week. The closer she is to her favorite combination, the happier she is.

(a) Suppose that Flossy is currently studying 25 hours a week and dating 3 hours a week. Would she prefer to be studying 30 hours a week and dating 8 hours a week? <u>Yes.</u> (Hint: Remember the formula for the distance between two points in the plane?)

---

20 PREFERENCES (Ch. 3)

3.5 (20) Shirley Sixpack is in the habit of drinking three 16 ounce cans of beer each evening while watching "The Best of Bowlerama" on TV. She has a strong thumb and a big refrigerator, so that she doesn't care about the size of the cans that beer comes in, so long as she gets her 48 ounces of beer per night.

(a) On the graph below, draw some of Shirley's indifference curves between 16 ounce cans and 8 ounce cans of beer. Use blue ink to draw these indifference curves.

8 ounce cans

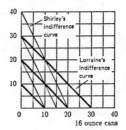

16 ounce cans

(b) Lorraine Quiche likes to have a beer while she watches Masterpiece Theatre. She only allows herself an 8 ounce glass of beer at any one time. Since her cat doesn't like beer and she hates stale beer, if there is more than 8 ounces in the can she just pours the excess into the sink. On the graph above, use red ink to draw some of Lorraine's indifference curves.

3.6 (30) Joan likes chocolate cake and ice cream, but after 10 slices of cake, she gets tired of cake and eating more cake makes her less happy. Joan always prefers more ice cream to less. Joan's parents require her to eat everything put on her plate. In the axes below use blue ink to draw a set of indifference curves that depict her preferences between plates with different amounts of cake and ice cream. Be sure to label the axes.

(a) Suppose that Joan's preferences are as before, but that her parents allow her to leave anything on her plate that she doesn't want. On the graph below, use red ink to draw some indifference curves depicting her preferences between plates with different amounts of cake and ice cream.

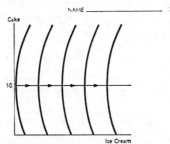

Cake

Ice Cream

3.7 (20) Mary Granola consumes two goods. grapefruits and avocados. If she has more grapefruits than avocados, her marginal rate of substitution is 2: for every avocado she gives up, she has to get two more grapefruits. However, if she has fewer grapefruits than avocados, then each grapefruit she consumes is just worth 2 avocados to her; i.e., her MRS is 1/2.

(a) In the graph below, draw an indifference curve for Mary through the bundle $(10G, 10A)$. Draw another indifference curve through $(20G, 20A)$.

Grapefruits

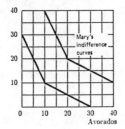

Mary's indifference curves

Avocados

(b) Does Mary have convex preferences? **Yes.**

3.8 (30) The Bear family is trying to decide what to have for dinner. Baby Bear says that his ranking of the possibilities is (honey, grubs, Goldilocks). Mama Bear ranks the choices (grubs, Goldilocks, honey) while Papa Bear's ranking is: (Goldilocks, honey, grubs). They decide to take each pair of alternatives and let a majority vote determine the family rankings.

Money

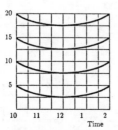

Time

3.10 (20) Henry Hanover is currently consuming 20 cheeseburgers and 20 Cherry Cokes a week. A typical indifference curve for Henry is depicted below.

Cherry Coke

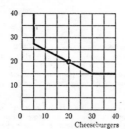

Cheeseburgers

(a) If someone offered to trade Henry one extra cheeseburger for every Coke he gave up, would Henry want to do this? **No.**

(b) What if it were the other way around: for every cheeseburger Henry gave up, he would get an extra Coke. Would he accept this offer? **Yes.**

(a) Papa suggests that they first consider honey vs. grubs, and then the winner of that contest vs. Goldilocks. Which alternative will be chosen?__ **Goldilocks.**

(b) Mama suggests instead that they consider honey vs. Goldilocks and then the winner vs. grubs. Which gets chosen? **Grubs.**

(c) What order should Baby Bear suggest if he wants to get his favorite food for dinner? **Grubs versus Goldilocks, then Honey versus the winner.**

(d) What is wrong with the Bear family's "collective preferences" as determined by voting?

They are not transitive.

3.9 (20) Ralph Rigid likes to eat lunch at 12 noon. However, he also likes to save money so he can buy other consumption goods by attending the "early bird specials" and "late lunchers" promoted by his local diner. This means that he is willing to eat earlier or later than his preferred times if he is sufficiently compensated for it. In the graph below, draw a few of Ralph's indifference curves for money to spend on "all other goods" and dining time.

(c) What is the maximum number of cheeseburgers he would give up at an exchange rate of 2 cheeseburgers for 1 Coke? **15.**

(d) At what rate of exchange would Henry be willing to stay put at his current consumption level? **2 cheeseburgers for 1 Coke.**

3.11 (20) Tommy Twit is happiest when he has 8 cookies and 4 glasses of milk per day. Whenever he has more than his favorite amount of either food. giving him still more makes him worse off. Whenever he has less than his favorite amount of either food. giving him more makes him better off. His mother makes him drink 6 glasses of milk and only allows him 4 cookies per day. One day when his mother was gone. Tommy's sadistic sister made him eat 13 cookies and only gave him 1 glass of milk, despite the fact that Tommy complained bitterly about the last 5 cookies that she made him eat and he begged for more milk. Although Tommy complained later to his mother. he had to admit that he liked the diet that his sister forced on him better than what his mother demanded.

(a) Use black ink to draw some indifference curves for Tommy that are consistent with this story.

Milk

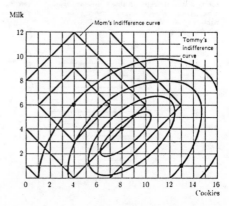

Mom's indifference curve

Tommy's indifference curve

Cookies

(b) Tommy's mother believes that the optimal amount for him to consume is 6 glasses of milk and 4 cookies. She measures deviations by absolute values. If Tommy consumes some other bundle, say, (c, m), she measures his departure from the optimal bundle by $D = |6 - m| + |4 - c|$. The larger D is, the worse off she thinks Tommy is. Use blue ink in the graph above to sketch a few of Mrs. Twit's indifference curves for Tommy's consumption.

Chapter 4

Utility

Introduction. This chapter contains problems to familiarize you with various utility functions. Given a utility function $u(x, y)$, the indifference curves are determined by the equation $u(x, y) = k$ for each different value of the constant k. If you are asked to graph an indifference curve you can simply pick a value of k, solve this equation for y in terms of x, and then graph that function.

4.1 (30) Hy Perbola's utility function is $U(X, Y) = XY$.

(a) Suppose that Hy originally consumed 4 units of X and 12 units of Y. If his consumption of Y is reduced to 8, how much X must he have to be well off as he was to begin with? <u>6 units.</u> On the graph below indicate Hy's original consumption and draw an indifference curve through this point.

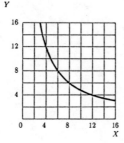

Y

(b) Which bundle would Hy like better, 3 units of X and 10 units of Y or 4 units of X and 8 units of Y? <u>He would prefer (4,8).</u>

(c) As you can verify, Hy is indifferent between the two commodity bundles (4,6) and (8,3). Consider the bundles (8,12) and (16,6), each of which contains exactly twice as much of each good as the first two bundles. Is Hy also indifferent between these two bundles? <u>Yes.</u>

(c) Foster's utility function represents a special form of preferences described in the text. What is the name for this kind of preferences? ____
<u>Quasilinear preferences.</u>

4.3 (20) Recall that Mungoites have 2 left feet and 1 right foot. We want to derive a utility function for a Mungoite who has L left shoes and R right shoes. (Don't worry about fractional shoes—half a shoe is better than none.)

(a) First draw some indifference curves in the graph below.

Left shoes

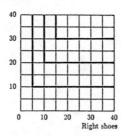

Right shoes

(b) We'll assign a utility to the bundle (L, R) that consists of the *minimum* number of left shoes the Mungoite could have, and still be as well off as it is at (L, R). Label your indifference curves with this utility function. Does this result in higher indifference curves getting labels with higher numbers? <u>Yes.</u>

(c) If $L > 2R$, what label does an indifference curve get? <u>2R.</u>

(d) If $L < 2R$ what label does an indifference curve get? <u>L.</u>

(d) Can you show that it is always true that if two bundles are regarded as indifferent for someone with Hy's utility function, then if you doubled the amount of each good in each bundle, the new bundles will also be regarded as indifferent?

If (X, Y) is indifferent to (W, Z), then the utilities must be the same, which means $XY = WZ$. It follows that $2X2Y = 2W2Z$, which means that the bundles $(2X, 2Y)$ and $(2W, 2Z)$ are indifferent.

4.2 (20) Foster Interface has the following utility function: $U(X, Y) = 2\sqrt{X} + Y$.

(a) If Foster originally consumed 9 units of X and 10 units of Y, and if his consumption of X is reduced to 4 units, how much Y would he have to be given so that he would be exactly as well off as he was originally? <u>12.</u>

(b) On the graph below, indicate Foster's original consumption and draw an indifference curve passing through this point. As you can verify, Foster is indifferent between the bundle, (9,10) and the bundle (25,6). If you doubled the amount of each good in each bundle, you would have bundles (18,20) and (50,12). Are these two bundles on the same indifference curve? <u>No.</u> (Hint: How do you check whether two bundles are indifferent when you know the utility function?)

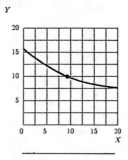

Y

X

(e) What is a utility function that represents Mungoite preferences for shoes? <u>min $\{L, 2R\}$.</u>

(f) If $L > 2R$, what does an extra left shoe add to utility? <u>0.</u>

(g) If $L < 2R$ what does an extra left shoe add to utility? <u>1.</u>

4.4 (20) Remember Shirley Sixpack and Lorraine Quiche from the last chapter? Shirley thinks a 16 ounce can of beer is just as good as two 8 ounce cans since she drinks 48 ounces at a sitting. Lorraine only drinks 8 ounces at a time and hates stale beer, so she thinks a 16 ounce can is no better or worse than an 8 ounce can.

(a) Write a utility function that represents Shirley's preferences between commodity bundles comprised of 8 ounce cans and 16 ounce cans of beer. Let X stand for the number of 8 ounce cans and Y stand for the number of 16 ounce cans. <u>$u(X, Y) = X + 2Y$, or a monotonic transformation of this.</u>

(b) Now write a utility function that represents Lorraine's preferences. <u>$u(X, Y) = X + Y$, or a monotonic transformation.</u>

(c) Write down a different utility function from the first one you wrote that would also represent Shirley's preferences. <u>$u(X, Y) = 2X + 4Y$ would be one example. Any other monotonic transformation would do.</u>

(d) Give an example of two commodity bundles such that Shirley likes the first bundle better than the second bundle while Lorraine likes the second bundle better than the first bundle. <u>An example is the following. Shirley would prefer two 16 ounce cans and no 8 ounce cans to three 8 ounce cans and no 16 ounce cans. Lorraine would prefer three 8 ounce cans and no 16 ounce cans to two 16 ounce cans. Of course there are many other possible examples.</u>

4.5 (30) Which of the following are positive monotonic transformations? Circle your answers.

(a) $v = 3.141592u$

(e) $v = -e^{-u}$

(b) $v = -17u$

(f) $v = 1/u$

(c) $v = 2u - 10,000$

(g) $v = -1/u$

(d) $v = \log u$

_A,C,D,E,G._

4.6 (20) Martha Modest has preferences represented by the utility function $U(a,b) = ab/100$ where a is the number of ounces of animal crackers that she consumes and b is the number of ounces of beans that she consumes.

(a) On the graph below, sketch the locus of points that Martha finds indifferent to having 8 ounces of animal crackers and 2 ounces of beans. Also sketch the locus of points that she finds indifferent to having 6 ounces of animal crackers and 4 ounces of beans.

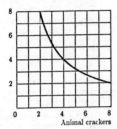

Beans

Animal crackers

(b) Bertha Brassy has preferences represented by the utility function $V(a,b) = 1,000a^2b^2$ where a is the number of ounces of animal crackers that she consumes and b is the number of ounces of beans that she consumes. On the graph below, sketch the locus of points that Bertha finds indifferent to having 8 ounces of animal crackers and 2 ounces of beans. Also sketch the locus of points that she finds indifferent to having 6 ounces of animal crackers and 4 ounces of beans.

(c) Does Willy have convex preferences? _No._

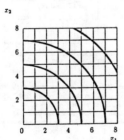

x_2

x_1

4.8 (20) Harry Mazzola has the utility function $u(x_1, x_2) = \min\{x_1 + 2x_2, x_2 + 2x_1\}$ where x_1 is his consumption of corn chips and x_2 is his consumption of French fries.

(a) On the graph below, use blue ink to show the locus of points for which $x_1 + 2x_2 = 12$ and also use blue ink to draw the locus of points for which $x_2 + 2x_1 = 12$. Shade in the region where both $x_1 + 2x_2 \geq 12$ and $x_2 + 2x_1 \geq 12$.

(b) What value does Harry's utility function take along the lower boundary of this region? _12._ Use black ink to sketch in the indifference curve along which Harry's utility is 12. Also use black ink to sketch in the indifference curve along which Harry's utility is 6. Is there anything about Harry Mazzola that reminds you of Mary Granola?

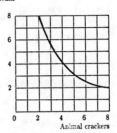

Beans

Animal crackers

(c) Are Martha's preferences convex? _Yes._

(d) Are Bertha's? _Yes._

(e) What can you say about the difference between the indifference curves you drew for Bertha and those you drew for Martha? _There is no difference between their indifference curves._

(f) How could you tell this was going to happen without having to draw the curves? _Their utility functions only differ by a monotonic transformation._

4.7 (20) Willy Wheeler has preferences represented by the utility function $U(x, y) = x_1^2 + x_2^2$.

(a) Draw a few of his indifference curves.

(b) What kind of geometric figure are they? _Quarter circles._

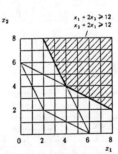

x_2

$x_1 + 2x_2 \geq 12$
$x_2 + 2x_1 \geq 12$

x_1

4.9 (20) Joe Bob has a utility function given by $u(x_1, x_2) = x_1^2 + 2x_1x_2 + x_2^2$.

(c) Compute Joe Bob's marginal rate of substitution of good 2 for good 1. _1._

(d) Joe Bob's straight cousin, Ernie, has a utility function $v(x_1, x_2) = x_2 + x_1$. Compute Ernie's marginal rate of substitution. _1._

(e) Do $u(x_1, x_2)$ and $v(x_1, x_2)$ represent the same preferences? _Yes._

(f) Can you show that Joe Bob's utility function is a monotonic transformation of Ernie's? (Hint: Some have said that Joe Bob is square.) _Yes, by observing that $u(x_1, x_2) = [v(x_1, x_2)]^2$._

Chapter 5

Choice

Introduction. Here we use what we know about budget lines. preferences, and utility functions to determine the optimal choices of consumers. Most of the exercises here are graphical: you draw the budget lines and the indifference curves and then pick out the most preferred point on each indifference curve.

5.1 (20) Clara's utility function is $U(X,Y) = X(Y + 2)$.

(a) In the table below, fill in the quantity of Y which together with the corresponding quantity of X gives Clara a utility of 36.

X	Y
1	34
2	16
3	10
4	7
6	4

(b) On the axes below mark each of these points and sketch Clara's indifference curve for $U = 36$. Suppose that the price of each good is 1 and that Clara has an income of 10. Draw in her budget line.

(c) How much X will she choose to consume?   6 units of X.

(d) How much Y will she choose to consume?   4 units of Y.

(e) Now suppose that the prices are as before. but Flem's income is 29. Draw his new budget line. How much X will he choose? 1 unit of X How much Y? 14 units of Y.

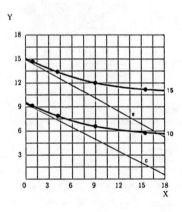

5.3 (20) Remember our friend Ralph Rigid from Chapter 3? His favorite diner, Food for Thought, has adopted the following policy to reduce the crowds at lunch time: if you show up for lunch t hours before or after 12 noon. you get to deduct t dollars from your bill. (This holds for any fraction of an hour as well.)

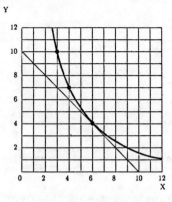

(e) Using calculus, you will find that Clara's marginal rate of substitution equals the price ratio when $(Y + 2)/X = p_X/p_Y$. Using this fact and the budget equation, solve for Clara's demand for Y as a function of prices and her income. $Y = m/2P_y - 1.$

5.2 ((20) Flem Snopes's utility function is $U(X,Y) = \sqrt{X} + Y$.

(a) On the axes below, find and label the point on the indifference curve that give Flem a utility of 10 and where he consumes 1 unit of X. Also find and label the points on this curve where he consumes 4 units of X, 9 units of X, and 16 units of X.

(b) Now label points on the indifference curve that give him a utility of 15 where he consumes respectively, 1, 4, 9, and 16 units of X. Sketch in indifference curves corresponding to utilities of 10 and 15.

(c) Suppose that the price of X is 1 and the price of Y is 2. Suppose that Flem's income is 19. Draw Flem's budget line.

(d) How much X does he choose to buy? 1 unit of X How much Y? 9 units of Y.

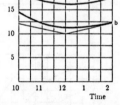

(a) Using blue ink, illustrate Ralph's budget set in the above graph, where the horizontal axis measures the time of day that he eats lunch and the vertical axis measures the amount of money that he will have to spend on things other than lunch. Assume that he has $15 total to spend and that lunch at noon costs $5. (Hint: How much money would he have left if he ate at noon? at 1 p.m.? at 11 a.m.?)

(b) Recall that Ralph's preferred lunch time is 12 noon, but that he is willing to eat at other time if the food is sufficiently cheap. Using black ink, draw in some indifference curves for Ralph that will lead to 2 P.M. as being his optimal choice of dining time.

5.4 (20) The market price for peanut butter is $2 a jar, and the market price for jam is $4 a jar.

(a) If John Laitner consumes only peanut butter, what can we say about how many jars of peanut butter John would be willing to give up to get one jar of jam? Answer: it is (greater, less) than Less than 2.

(b) Suppose that John has an income of $80. Draw a picture that illustrates John's budget set, an indifference curve consistent with the above description, and his optimal consumption point.

(c) Is it necessary for John's indifference curve to have the same slope as his budget line at his optimal consumption point? No.

Jam

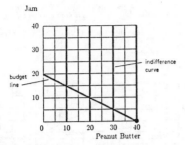

5.5 (40) Norm and Sheila consume only meat pies and beer. Meat pies used to cost $2 each and beer was $1 per can. Their income used to be $60 per week but they had to pay an income tax of $10. Use red ink to sketch their old budget line for meat pies and beer.

Beer

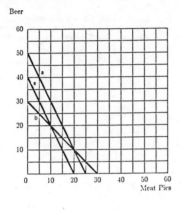

Food

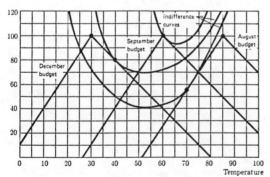

(a) When Joe first arrives in September, the temperature of his apartment is 60 degrees. Use black ink to draw Joe's budget constraint. (Hint: answering the following questions may help you to draw the graph.)

(b) What would the temperature in his room be and how much would he have left to spend on food if he spends nothing on heating or cooling?_

60 degrees, $100.

(c) How much food could he buy if he heated the room to 70 degrees?

$80.

(d) How much food could he buy if he cooled the room to 50 degrees?

$70.

(e) In December, the outside temperature is 30 degrees and in August poor Joe is trying to understand macroeconomics while the temperature outside is 85 degrees. On the same graph you used above, draw Joe's budget constraints for the months of December (in blue ink) and August (in red ink.)

(a) They used to buy 30 cans of beer per week and spent the rest of their income on meat pies. How many meat pies did they buy? 10.

_____

(b) The government decided to eliminate the income tax and to put a sales tax of $1 per can on beer, raising its price to $2 per can. Assuming that Norm and Sheila's pre-tax income and the price of meat pies did not change, draw their new budget line in blue ink.

(c) The sales tax on beer induced Norm and Sheila to reduce their consumption of it to 20 cans per week. What happened to their consumption of meat pies? It stayed the same: 10.

(d) How much revenue did this tax raise from Norm and Sheila? $20.

(e) Suppose that instead of just taxing beer, the government had decided to tax both beer and meat pies at the same percentage rate in such a way that it would raise the same revenue from Norm and Sheila as the tax on beer alone described above. Assuming that the price of beer and meat pies goes up by the full amount of the tax, use black ink to draw the new budget line on the graph.

(f) Are Norm and Sheila better off having just beer taxed or having both beer and meat pies taxed, if both sets of taxes raise the same revenue?

Both.

5.6 (40) Joe Grad has just arrived at the big U. He has a fellowship that covers his tuition and the rent on an apartment. In order to get by, Joe has become a grader in intermediate price theory, earning $100 a month. Out of this $100 he must pay for his food and utilities in his apartment. His utilities expenses consist of heating costs when he heats his apartment and air-conditioning costs when he cools it. To raise the temperature of his apartment by a degree, it costs $2 per month (or $20 per month to raise it ten degrees). To use air-conditioning to cool his apartment by a degree, it costs $3 per month. Whatever is left over after paying the utilities, he uses to buy food at $1 per unit.

(f) Draw a plausible set of indifference curves for Joe in such a way that the following are true. (i) His favorite temperature for his apartment would be 65 degrees if it cost him nothing to heat it or cool it. (ii) Joe chooses to use the furnace in December, air-conditioning in August, and neither in September. (iii) Joe is better off in December than in August.

(g) In what months is the slope of Joe's budget constraint equal to the slope of his indifference curve? August and December.

(h) In December Joe's marginal rate of substitution between food and degrees Fahrenheit is 2.

(i) In August it is 3.

(j) In September, Joe's marginal rate of substitution between food and degrees Fahrenheit in his apartment is between 2 and 3.

5.7 (30) The State Education Commission wants to encourage "computer literacy" in the high schools under its jurisdictions. Currently the average high school in the state devotes approximately $20,000 of its $60,000 instruction budget to this subject, and the State Education Board would like to see this amount increased. However, opinions differ on how much they would like to see it increased, and what the most effective way is to do this. The following have been proposed.

Plan A: Some members of the Commission want to see a straight grant of $10,000 to each high school in the state to spend in whatever way they see fit. These people feel that given the high importance now attached to computer literacy, most school districts would devote a significant proportion of these funds to computer education.

Plan B: Some other members of the Commission are in favor of the plan to make a $10,000 grant to each high school, but they want to require each school to spend at least $10,000 on computer instruction as a condition of receiving the grant.

Plan C: Another group of the Commission wants to make the $10,000 grant to high schools, but they want to require each high school receiving the grant to spend at least $10,000 more than they are currently spending on computer instruction.

Plan D: A fourth faction favors a matching grant program, where the State agrees to share the costs of computers with the high schools. For each dollar spent on computer education, a high school will receive a half a dollar from the state to add to its operating budget.

Plan E: The fifth group likes a modified version of the above plan: they want a matching grant, as above, but the maximum amount that each high school would get would be limited to $10,000.

We want to analyze the effect of these 5 plans on the budget possibilities of a typical high school. The graphs below have the amount of money devoted to computers on the horizontal axis, and the amount of money devoted to other instruction on the vertical axis.

(a) Show how plans A, B, C, D, and E affect the budget set of a typical high school in the graph below. Use black ink to draw the budget line without any of these plans and use colored ink for the other plans. Label the budget lines with A, B, C, and D.

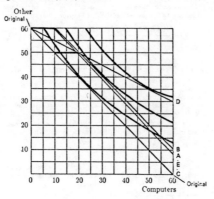

(b) Of the 5 plans, which plan would probably lead to the largest increase in money spent on computers? D. Draw some indifference curves to illustrate your answer.

5.8 (30) The telephone company allows one to choose between two different pricing plans. For a fee of $12 per month you can make as many local phone calls as you want, at no additional charge per call. Alternatively, you can pay $8 per month and be charged 5 cents for each local phone call that you make. Suppose that you have a total of $20 per month to spend.

(a) On the graph below, use black ink to sketch a budget line for someone who chooses the first plan. Use red ink to draw a budget line for someone who chooses the second plan. Where do the two budget lines cross?____

(80, 8).

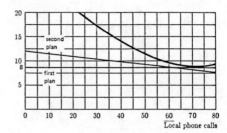

(b) On the graph above, use yellow ink to draw indifference curves for someone who prefers the second plan to the first. Use blue ink to draw an indifference curve for someone who prefers the first plan to the second.

Chapter 6

Demand

NAME_____

Introduction. Many of the exercises in this chapter ask you to find a demand function for an individual when we know his preferences. In some of these problems, there is a "corner" solution where only one good is consumed. In other cases equilibrium is at a kink. (For example, this happens in the case of perfect complements.) In problems of either of these two kinds, it is usually easy to solve for the quantities demanded at given prices simply by looking at diagrams and doing a little algebra.

When the consumer is choosing positive amounts of all commodities and indifference curves have no kinks, the consumer chooses a point of tangency between his budget line and the highest indifference curve that it touches. In these cases the way to solve for the demand function is to solve two equations for two unknowns. The unknowns are the quantities of the two goods demanded. One of your two equations says the ratio of marginal utility of good 1 to the marginal utility of good 2 is equal to the ratio of the price of good 1 to the price of good 2. The other equation is just the budget constraint. Now when you have these equations, you want to solve for the quantity of good 1 demanded as a function of the prices and of income. This is the demand function for good 1. Likewise you solve for the demand for good 2 as a function of prices and income. Notice that in a demand function you should express the demand for each good only as a function of prices and income and not as a function of the quantity of the other good. Typically these problems require a little bit of calculus (to calculate the marginal utilities) and a little bit of algebra (to solve the two equations.) We have deliberately chosen examples where this calculation requires only taking very easy derivatives and solving very simple equations.

Some of the problems ask you to calculate price and or income elasticities either from demand functions that are given to you or from demand functions that you have found. These problems are especially easy if you know a little calculus. For example, if the demand function for good 1, is $x_1(p_1, p_2, m)$, and you want to calculate the income elasticity of demand when prices are (p_1, p_2) and income is m, you need only to calculate $\partial x_1(p_1, p_2, m)/\partial m$ and multiply it by $m/x_1(p_1, p_2, m)$ to find the income elasticity.

6.1 (20) Remember Shirley Sixpack, who thinks that two 8 ounce cans of beer are exactly as good as one 16 ounce can of beer. Suppose that these are the only sizes of beer available to her and that she has $20 to spend on beer. Suppose that an 8 ounce beer costs $.80 and a 16 ounce beer costs $1. On the graph below, draw Shirley's budget line in blue ink and draw some of her indifference curves in red.

NAME _____ 47

(a) How much curds will Miss Muffet demand in this situation?_____

8 curds.

(b) How much whey?__16 whey._____(Hint: Have you noticed something kinky about Miss Muffet?)

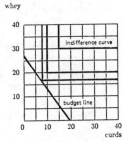

6.3 (20) Linus has a demand function with the equation $q = 10 - 2p$.

(a) What is his elasticity of demand when the price is 3? __−1.5.__

(b) At what price is his elasticity of demand equal to −1? __2.5__

(c) Suppose that his demand function takes the general linear form. $q = a - bp$. Write down an algebraic expression for his elasticity of demand at an arbitrary price p. __$\epsilon = -b(a/p - b)$__

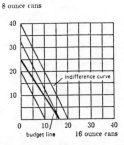

(a) At these prices, which size can will she buy, or will she buy some of each?

16 oz. cans.

(b) Suppose that the price of 16 ounce beers remains $1 and the price of 8 ounce beers falls to $.60. Will she buy more 8 ounce beers? No.

(c) What if the price of 8 ounce beers falls to $ .40? How many 8 ounce beers will she buy then? 50 cans.

(d) Write a general formula for Shirley's demand for 16 ounce beers as a function of prices p_8, p_{16}, and her income, m?

$$D_{16} = \begin{cases} m/p_{16} & \text{if } p_{16} < 2p_8 \\ 0 & \text{if } p_{16} > 2p_8 \\ \text{any affordable amount} & \text{if } p_{16} = p_8 \end{cases}$$

6.2 (15) Miss Muffet always likes to have things "just so". In fact the only way she will consume her curds and whey is in the ratio of 2 units of whey per unit of curds. She has an income of $20. Whey costs $.75 per unit. Curds cost $1 per unit. She has an income of $20. On the graph below, draw Miss Muffet's budget line and plot some of her indifference curves.

(d) (10) In this problem and in some of the earlier problems, we have been a bit careless in describing linear demand functions. It would have been more accurate to say that $q = \max\{0, a - bp\}$ Explain why.

It doesn't make sense to demand a negative quantity. When we draw linear demand curves we suppose that demand is zero whenever $a - bp < 0$

6.4 (30) Richard and Mary Stout have fallen on hard times, but remain rational consumers. They are making do on $80 a week, spending $40 on food and $40 on all other goods. On the graph below, use black ink to draw a budget line. Label their consumption bundle, A.

(a) The Stouts suddenly become eligible for food stamps. This means that they can go to the agency and buy coupons that can be exchanged for $2 worth of food, and they only have to pay $1 for such coupons. However, the maximum number of coupons they can buy per week is 10. On the graph, draw their new budget line with red ink.

$ Worth of Other things

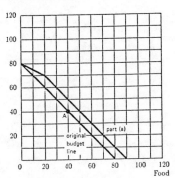

(b) If the Stouts have homothetic preferences, how much more food will

they buy once they enter the food stamp program? __5 units.__

6.5 Donald Fribble is a stamp collector. The only things other than stamps that Fribble consumes are Hostess Twinkies. It turns out that Fribble's preferences are represented by the utility function $u(s,t) = s + \ln t$ where s is the number of stamps he collects and t is the number of Twinkies he consumes.

(a) Write an expression that says that the ratio of Fribble's marginal utility for Twinkies to his marginal utility for stamps is equal to the ratio

of the price of Twinkies to the price of stamps. __$MRS = t$.__

_____(Hint: The derivative of $\ln t$ with respect to t is $1/t$ and the derivative of s with respect to s is 1.)

(b) Use the budget equation and the equation that you found in the last part to solve the demand function for Twinkies when income is m, the prices are p_s for stamps and p_T for Twinkies and when $m > p_s$. The

demand function for Twinkies is __$t = p_s/p_t$__

(c) In general, the demand for any good may depend on its own price, income, and the prices of all other goods. Which of these variables have

no effect on Donald's demand for Twinkies? __Income will have__

__no effect.__

(d) What is Donald's price elasticity of demand for Twinkies when $m >$

p_s? __$\epsilon = -1$.__

(e) What is his income elasticity of demand for Twinkies when $m > p_s$?

__His income elasticity of demand is zero.__

(f) Donald's wife complains that whenever Donald gets an extra dollar,

he always spends it all on stamps. Is she right when $m > p_s$? __Yes.__

(g) Write down Fribble's demand function for postage stamps when $m > p_s$. (Hint: Use his budget constraint and his demand function for Twinkies to find out how his demand for stamps depends on his income and the

prices of each good.) __$s = \dfrac{m}{p_s} - 1$.__

(d) Write down an equation that states that the consumption bundle

(x,y) is exactly on Doug's budget line. __$5x + 20y = 1,000$.__

(e) Solve these two simultaneous equations to show how much of x Doug will buy and how much of y he will buy.

$$10x + 40y = 2,000$$

$$15x - 40y = 0,$$

therefore, adding the two equations yields

$$25x = 2,000,$$

or $x = 80$, which implies $y = 30$.

6.7 Following the same procedure you used in the previous problem to find Douglas Cornfield's demand at particular prices and incomes, derive general formulas for Doug's demand function for good x and good y as a function of prices and of his income. The answer is $x(p_x, p_y, m) =$

__$x = 2m/5P_x$,__ and $y(p_x, p_y, m) =$ __$y = 3m/5P_y$.__

(a) What is the numeric value of Cornfield's income elasticity for x? ___

__1__

(b) What is the numeric value of his price elasticity of demand for x?

__-1__

(c) In the graph below, draw Cornfield's Engel curve for x in red ink and his Engel curve for y in blue ink.

(h) Suppose that the price of Twinkies is $2 and the price of stamps is $1. On the graph below, for incomes greater than $1, draw Fribble's Engel curve for Twinkies in red ink and his Engel curve for stamps in blue ink. Label the axes.

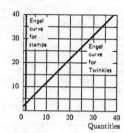

(i) If $m < p_s$, what would Fribble's demand for postage stamps be? ___

__If $m < p_s$, $s = 0$__ _____What would his demand for

Twinkies be? __$t = m/p_t$.__ (Hint: On what part of the envelope do you stick a postage stamp?)

Calculus **6.6** (20) Douglas Cornfield, of Hogsholm, Iowa has preferences which can be represented by the utility function, $u(x,y) = x^2 y^3$.

(a) Write down a function expressing his marginal rate of substitution

between x and y. __$MRS = -2y/3x$.__

(b) If Douglas is consuming 20 units of x and 10 units of y, how much x

would he be willing to give up for an extra unit of y? __$-1/3$.__

(c) Suppose that Douglas has $1,000 to spend, the price of x is $5 per unit and the price of y is $20 per unit. Write down an equation that states that the slope of Doug's budget line is equal to the slope of his indifference

curve at the consumption bundle (x,y). __$p_x/p_y = 5/20 = 2y/3x$.__

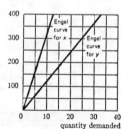

(d) In the graph below, draw Cornfield's income offer curve.

Calculus **6.8** (20) Douglas has a cousin named Gary Stone. Gary's preferences were just the same as Douglas's until the day he fell into a cement mixer. Gary was rescued, physically unharmed, but somehow the ordeal shifted his indifference curves. Gary's new preferences are representable by the utility function $U(x,y) = (x+1)^2 (y+2)^3$.

(a) Write down an expression for Gary's marginal rate of substitution as

a function of his consumption of x and y. __$MRS = -2(y+2)/$__

__$3(x+1)$__

(b) At the optimum consumption point, Gary's MRS will equal the price ratio. Use this equation and Gary's budget constraint to find Gary's demand function for x and his demand function for y. Where there is not a corner solution, the demand functions are $x_d = \underline{x_d = 1/5P_x}$ $(2I - 3P_x + 4P_y)$, and $y_d = 1/5P_y(3I - 4P_y + 3P_x)$.

6.9 A sharp-eyed neighbor girl, Suzy Optimum, first noticed the difference in preferences between Douglas and Gary. She observed that they responded differently to changes in income.

(a) If Douglas's income doubles will his demand for x double, more than double, or less than double? __Double__

(b) If Gary's income doubles, will his demand for x double, more than double, or less than double? __Less than double.__

(c) She also noticed that for only one of the cousins is demand for x affected by the price of y. Which cousin is that? __Gary.__

(d) After close examination, Suzy Optimum noticed that Gary's indifference curves can be found by drawing Douglas's indifference curves and then translating the graph so that its origin is moved to $(-1, -2)$. Illustrate this on the two graphs below and draw a few indifference curves. On your graphs, draw an income offer curve for each of the two cousins for the case where the price of x equals the price of y.

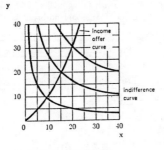

specific point in time who has income Y, which he or she wants to spend on consumption, C, I.R.A. savings, S_1, or ordinary savings S_2. Suppose that the utility function is taken to be:

$$U(C, S_1, S_2) = S_1^a S_2^\beta C^\gamma.$$

The budget constraint of the consumer is given by:

$$C + S_1 + S_2 = Y$$

and the limit that he or she can contribute to the IRA is denoted by L.

(a) Derive the demand function for S_1 and S_2 for a consumer for whom the limit L *is* binding. __The consumer wants to maximize the utility function__ $U(C, S_1, S_2) = L^a S_2^\beta C^\gamma$ __with respect to__ S^2 __and__ C. __This is a monotonic transformation of an ordinary Cobb-Douglas utility function.__ __The budget constraint is__ $C + S_2 = Y - L$. __The demands therefore take the form__ $S_1 = L$, $S_2 = \frac{\beta}{\beta + \gamma}$ $(Y - L)$, __and__ $C = \frac{\gamma}{\beta + \gamma}(Y - L)$. (Hint: Since the consumer is at his limit I.R.A. savings, you already know the answer for how much S_1 is. Now you are left with the problem of how the consumer allocates his remaining budget between consumption and ordinary savings. But this reduces to a problem of the kind you know how to solve: a problem with two goods and a Cobb-Douglas demand function.)

(b) Derive the demand functions for S_1 and S_2 for a consumer for whom the limit L is *not* binding. __This is a straight Cobb-Douglas__ __demand problem.__ __The answers are__ $S_1 = \frac{a}{a+\beta+\gamma}Y$, $S_2 = \frac{\beta}{a+\beta+\gamma}Y$, $C = \frac{\gamma}{a+\beta+\gamma}Y$. Hint: Try the general method you used to solve for Dorothy's demand in an earlier problem.

6.12 (20) Percy consumes cakes and ale. His demand function for cakes is $q_c = m - 30p_c + 20p_a$ where m is his income, p_a is the price of ale, p_c is the price of cakes, and q_c is his consumption of cakes. Percy's income is $100 and the price of ale is $1 per unit.

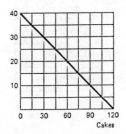

6.10 (20) Douglas has an urbane sister, Dorothy, who lives in Cedar Rapids and has much broader interests than Douglas. She consumes 4 different commodities, a, b, c, and d. (She disdains both y and z.) Her utility function is $u(a, b, c, d) = abc^2 d$.

(a) Find the ratio of Dorothy's marginal utility for b to her marginal utility for a. __a/b__ the ratio of Dorothy's marginal utility for c to her marginal utility for a __$a/2c$__ the ratio of her marginal utility for d to her marginal utility for a __a/d__

(b) The price of good a is 1, and the price of each of the other goods is 2. Write down equations that state the price of each of the other goods relative to the price of a equals the ratio of Dorothy's marginal utility for that good to her marginal utility for a. __$b/a = 1/2$; $c/2a = 1/2$; $d/a = 1/2$.__

(c) Use these equations and the budget constraint to solve for Dorothy's demand functions for goods a, b, c, and d. __$a = m/5p_a$,__ $b = m/5p_b$, $c = 2m/5p_c$, and $d = m/5p_d$.

6.11 (40) Under current tax law certain individuals can save up to $2,000 a year in an Individual Retirement Account (IRA), a savings vehicle that has an especially favorable tax treatment. Consider an individual at a

(a) Is ale a substitute for cakes or a complement? __Ale is a substitute for cakes.__ Explain. __An increase in the price of ale reduces demand for cakes.__

(b) Write down an equation for Percy's demand function for cakes where income and the price of ale are held fixed at $100 and $1. __$q_c = 120 - 30p_c$__

(c) Write an equation for Percy's inverse demand function for cakes where income and the price of ale are held fixed as above. __$p_c = 4 - q_c/30$__

(d) At what price would Percy buy 30 cakes? __$3__

_____ Use blue ink to sketch Percy's inverse demand curve for cakes on the axes below. Be sure to label the axes.

(e) Suppose that the price of ale rises to $2 per unit. On the graph you just drew, use red ink to draw in Percy's new inverse demand curve for cakes.

Chapter 7
Revealed Preference

Introduction. In the previous exercises you were given the consumer's preferences and then solved for his or her demand behavior. In this chapter we will turn this process around: you are given information about a consumer's demand behavior and want to use that information to infer something about preferences. The main tool is the principle of revealed preference: if a bundle X was purchased when Y was affordable, then X must be preferred to Y.

7.1 (20) Freddy Frolic consumes only asparagus and tomatoes, which are highly seasonal crops in Freddy's part of the world. He sells umbrellas for a living, which provides a fluctuating income depending on the weather. But Freddy doesn't mind: he never thinks of tomorrow, so each week he spends as much as he earns. One week, when the prices of asparagus and tomatoes were each $1 a pound, Freddy consumed 10 pounds of each. Use blue ink to show the budget line in the diagram below. Label Freddy's consumption bundle, with the letter A.

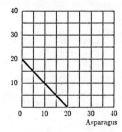

Tomatoes / Asparagus

(a) What is Freddy's income? $20.

(b) The next week the price of tomatoes rose to $2 a pound, but the price of asparagus remained at $1 a pound. By chance, Freddy's income had changed so that his old consumption bundle of (10,10) was just affordable at the new prices. Use red ink to draw this new budget line on the graph

7.3 (20) Here is a table of prices and the demands of a consumer named Ronald whose behavior was observed in 5 different price-income situations.

Obs	p_1	p_2	x_1	x_2
A	1	1	5	35
B	1	2	35	10
C	1	1	10	15
D	3	1	5	15
E	1	2	10	10

(a) Sketch each of his budget lines and label the point chosen in each case by the letters A, B, C, D, and E.

(b) Is Ronald's behavior consistent with the Weak Axiom of Revealed Preference? Yes.

(c) Shade lightly in red ink, all of the points that you are certain are worse for Ronald than the bundle C.

(d) Suppose that you are told that Ronald has convex and monotonic preferences and that he obeys the strong axiom of revealed preference. Shade lightly in blue ink all of the points that you are certain are *at least as good as* the bundle C.

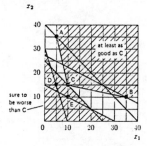

x_2 / x_1

7.4 Felicia, a hard-working economics major, spent the entire term observing undergraduate behavior in the local cafeteria. She found that the typical undergraduate's demand function for weekly consumption of

above. Does your new budget line go through the point A? Yes.

(c) What is the slope of this line?. $-1/2$.

(d) How much asparagus can he afford now if he spent all of his income on asparagus? 30 pounds.

(e) What is Freddy's income now? $30.

(f) Use yellow marker to highlight the bundles of goods on Freddy's new red budget line that he definitely will *not* purchase with this budget. Is it possible that he would increase his consumption of tomatoes when his budget changes from the blue line to the red one? No.

7.2 (10) Pierre consumes bread and wine. For Pierre, the price of bread is 4 francs per loaf and the price of wine is 4 francs per liter. Pierre has an income of 40 francs per day. Pierre consumes 6 units of wine and 4 units of bread.

Bob also consumes bread and wine. For Bob, the price of bread is 1/2 dollar per loaf and the price of wine is 2 dollars per liter. Bob has an income of $15 per day.

(a) If Bob and Pierre have the same tastes, can you tell whether Bob is better off than Pierre or vice versa? Bob is better off. Explain
He can afford Pierre's bundle and would still have income left to buy more bread or wine.

(b) Suppose prices and incomes for Pierre and Bob are as above and that Pierre's consumption is as before. Suppose that Bob spends all of his income. Give an example of a consumption bundle of wine and bread. 7.5 units of wine and no bread is one example.
This is a bundle that Pierre can afford but does not choose. If Pierre and Bob had the same preferences, we would have a violation of the weak axiom of revealed preference because each can afford, but rejects, the other person's bundle.

hamburgers and hot dogs is described by the demand functions:

$$h = \frac{m}{p_h + p_d}$$
$$d = \frac{m}{p_h + p_d}$$

In these demand functions m stands for money income, and h and d refer to hamburgers and hot dogs respectively. Felicia is interested in determining whether the behavior exhibited by the undergraduates can be viewed as utility maximization subject to a budget constraint. Having studied revealed preference theory, she decides to check these demand functions to see if they satisfy the Weak Axiom of Revealed Preference.

(a) Suppose that you have 2 different sets of prices (p_h, p_d) and (q_h, q_d) and that income is constant at 1. Write down a mathematical expression that says that the demanded bundle at the prices (p_h, p_d) is directly revealed preferred to the demanded bundle at the prices (q_h, q_d). (Use the algebraic form for the demand function given above.) Show that your expression can be simplified to $p_h + p_d \leq q_h + q_d$.

$$p_h \frac{m}{q_h + q_d} + p_d \frac{m}{q_h + q_d} \leq m.$$

(b) Now write down a mathematical expression that says that the demand at the prices (q_h, q_d) is revealed preferred to demand at the prices (p_h, p_d).

$$q_h \frac{m}{p_h + p_d} + q_d \frac{m}{p_h + p_d} \leq m.$$

(c) When are both of these expressions satisfied at once? Only when $p_h + p_d = q_h + q_d$.

(d) If both expressions are satisfied at once, could different bundles be bought at the two different price situations? No.

(e) Do the demand functions given above satisfy the Weak Axiom of Revealed Preference? (Look closely at the statement of the Weak Axiom.) Yes.

7.5 (30) Here is a table that illustrates some observed prices and choices for three different goods at three different prices.

Obs	p_1	p_2	p_3	x_1	x_2	x_3
1	2	2	2	2	2	2
2	1	3	2	3	1	2
3	2	3/2	5	4	1	3/2

(a) Fill in the entry in row i and column j of the matrix below with the value of the jth bundle at the ith prices. We'll do one to get you started. The value of the bundle 1 at prices 1 is $2 \times 2 + 2 \times 2 + 2 \times 2 = 12$, so we put a 12 in row 1, column 1. The value of bundle two at prices one is $2 \times 3 + 2 \times 1 + 2 \times 2 = 12$, so we also put a 12 in row 1, column 2. Verify the entries that are already in the table, and then fill in the missing entries.

Obs	1	2	3
1	12	12	13
2	12	10	10
3	17	17.5	17

(b) Fill in the entry in row i and column j of the table below with a D if observation i is directly revealed preferred to observation j. For example, at the first observation, the consumer's expenditure is \$12; however, we have seen that it would also have cost him \$12 to buy bundle 2. Since he could have bought bundle 2, but chose instead to buy bundle 1, bundle 1 is revealed preferred to bundle 2. Thus we put a D in row 1, column 2. Formally, there is a D in row i column j if the number in the ij entry of the table in part *(a)* is (less than or equal to, greater than) the entry in row i, column i. Do these observation satisfy the Weak Axiom of Revealed Preference? __Less than. Yes.__

Obs	1	2	3
1	D	D	I
2	I	D	D
3	D	I	D

(c) Now fill in row i, column j with an I if observation i is *indirectly* revealed preferred to j. Do these observations satisfy the Strong Axiom of Revealed Preference? __No.__

7.6 (20) It is January and Joe Grad, whom we met in Chapter 5, is shivering in his apartment when the phone rings. It is Mandy Manana, one of the students whose price theory problems he graded last term. Mandy asks if Joe would be interested in spending the month of February in her apartment. Mandy, who has switched majors from economics to political science, plans to go to Aspen for the month and so her apartment

(c) Joe calls Mandy and tells her his decision. Mandy offers to pay half the service charge. Draw Joe's budget line if he accepts Mandy's new offer. Joe now accepts Mandy's offer. From the fact that Joe accepted this offer we can tell that he plans to keep the temperature in Mandy's apartment above __40 degrees.__

7.7 (20) Lord Peter Pommy is a distinguished criminologist, schooled in the latest techniques of forensic revealed preference. Lord Peter is investigating the disappearance of Sir Cedric Pinchbottom who abandoned his aging mother on a street corner in Liverpool and has not been seen since. Tireless research has revealed that Sir Cedric has left England and is living under an assumed name somewhere in the Empire. Lord Peter has three possibilities. These are R. Preston McAfee of Brass Monkey, Ontario, Canada, Richard Manning of North Shag, New Zealand, and Richard Stevenson of Gooey Shoes, Falkland Islands. Which of these is Sir Cedric? Lord Peter has obtained Sir Cedric's diary in which were recorded his consumption habits in minute detail. By careful observation, he has also been able to determine the consumption behavior of McAfee, Manning, and Stevenson. All three of these worthies, like Sir Cedric, spend their entire incomes on beer and sausage. Their dossiers reveal the following:

- **Sir Cedric Pinchbottom** — In the year before his departure, Sir Cedric consumed 10 kilograms of sausage and 20 liters of beer per week. At that time, beer cost 1 English pound per liter and sausage cost 1 English pound per kilogram.

- **R. Preston McAfee** — McAfee is known to consume 5 liters of beer and 20 kilograms of sausage. In Brass Monkey, Ontario beer costs 1 Canadian dollar per liter and sausage costs 2 Canadian dollars per kilogram.

- **Richard Manning** — Manning consumes 5 kilograms of sausage and 10 liters of beer per week. In North Shag, a liter of beer costs 2 New Zealand dollars and sausage costs 2 New Zealand dollars per kilogram.

- **Richard Stevenson** — Stevenson consumes 5 kilograms of sausage and 30 liters of beer per week. In Gooey Shoes, a liter of beer costs 10 Falkland Island pounds and sausage costs 20 Falkland Island pounds per kilogram.

(a) For each of the three fugitives, use a different color of ink to draw his budget line and label the consumption bundle he chooses. On this graph, superimpose Sir Cedric's budget line and his choice.

will be empty (alas). All Mandy asks is that Joe pay the monthly service charge of \$40 charged by her landlord and the heating bill for the month of February. Since her apartment is much better insulated than Joe's, it only costs \$1 per month to raise the temperature by 1 degree. Joe thanks her and says he will let her know tomorrow. Joe puts his earmuffs back on and muses. If he accepts Mandy's offer, he will still have to pay rent on his current apartment but he won't have to heat it. If he moved, heating would be cheaper, but he would have the \$40 service charge. The outdoor temperature averages 20 degrees Fahrenheit in February and it costs him \$2 per month to raise his apartment temperature by 1 degree. Joe is still grading homework and has \$100 a month left to spend on food and utilities after he has paid the rent on his apartment. The price of food is still \$1 per unit.

(a) Draw Joe's budget line for February if he moves to Mandy's apartment and on the same graph, draw his budget line if he doesn't move.

(b) After drawing these lines himself, Joe decides that he would be better off not moving. From this, we can tell, using the principle of revealed preference that Joe must plan to keep his apartment at a temperature of less than __60 degrees.__

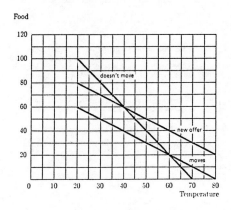

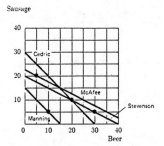

(b) After pondering the dossiers for a few moments, Lord Peter announced, "Unless Sir Cedric has changed his tastes, I can eliminate one of the suspects. Revealed preference tells me that one of the suspects is innocent." Which one? __McAfee.__

(c) After thinking a bit longer, Lord Peter announced. "If Sir Cedric left voluntarily, then he would have to be better off than he was before. Therefore if Sir Cedric left voluntarily and if he has not changed his tastes, he must be living in __Falklands.__ "

7.8 The McCawber family is having a tough time making ends meet. They spend \$100 a week on food and \$50 on other things. A new welfare program has been introduced which gives them a choice between receiving a grant of \$50 per week that they can spend any way they want, or buying any number of \$2 food coupons for \$1 apiece. (They naturally are not allowed to resell these coupons.) Food is a normal good for the McCawbers. As a family friend, you have been asked to help them decide on which option to choose. Drawing on your growing fund of economic knowledge, you proceed as follows.

(a) On the graph below, draw their old budget line in red ink and label their current choice C. Now use black ink to draw the budget line that they would have with the grant. If they chose the coupon option, how much food could they buy if they spent all their money on food coupons? ____ __\$300;__ ____ How much could they spend on other things if they

bought no food? <u>$150.</u> _____ Use blue ink to draw their budget line if they choose the coupon option.

Other things

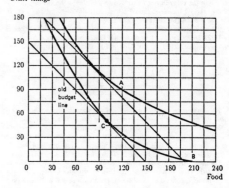

(b) Using the fact that food is a normal good for the McCawbers. and knowing what they purchased before, darken the portion of the black budget line where their consumption bundle could possibly be if they chose the lump sum grant option. Label the ends of this line segment A and B.

(c) After studying the graph you have drawn. you report to the McCawbers. "I have enough information to be able to tell you which choice to make. You should choose the _____ coupon _____ because <u>you can get more food even when other expenditure</u> <u>is constant.</u>

(c) How. if at all. would your answer to Part *a* change if the CPI were a Paasche index?
In this case you can't tell.

(d) Mr. McCawber thanks you for your help and then asks, "Would you have been able to tell me what to do if you hadn't known whether food was a normal good for us? " On the axes below, draw the same budget lines you drew on the diagram above, but draw indifference curves for which food is not a normal good and for which the McCawbers would be better off with the program you advised them not to take.

Other things

7.9 In 1984, Bruce Springsteen tried to figure out if he was making more money then than he had in 1975. In 1975, he made $2.5 million and he earned $5.4 million in 1984. The Consumer Price Index, which we will assume is a Laspeyres index with base year 1975 was 100 in 1975 and 180 in 1984. (Note: The scale of the Consumer Price Index is expressed as $100 \times I_p$ where I_p is the Laspeyres index as defined in your text.)

(a) Assuming that Bruce spent all of his income in 1975, was Bruce's 1984 income big enough to buy his 1975 bundle at 1984 prices or can't you tell? <u>Yes, it was big enough.</u>

(b) What is the smallest amount of money that Bruce could have made in 1984 without changing your answer to Part *a*? <u>$4.5 million.</u>

Chapter 8

Slutsky Equation

Introduction. The Slutsky equation breaks down the effect of a price change into two pieces, the substitution effect and the income effect. The substitution effect measures how the consumer's demand for a good would change if its price was changed but, at the same time, income was adjusted so as to keep the original consumption bundle affordable. The income effect measures how the consumer's demand would change if the prices were kept constant and only income was allowed to change.

8.1 (20 Neville's passion is fine wine. When the prices of all other goods are fixed at current levels, Neville's demand function for high quality claret is $q = .02m - 2p$, where p is the price of claret (in British pounds) and q is the number of bottles of claret that he demands. Neville's income is 5000 pounds and the price of a bottle of suitable claret is 25 pounds.

(a) How many bottles of claret will Neville buy. **50**

(b) If the price of claret rose to 30 pounds, how much income would Neville have to have in order to be exactly able to afford the amount of claret and the amount of other goods that he bought before the price change. **5250 pounds.** At this income, and a price of 30 pounds, how many bottles would Neville buy? **45 bottles**

(c) At his original income of 5000 and a price of 30, how much claret would Neville demand? **40 bottles.**

(d) When the price of claret rose from 25 to 30, the number of bottles that Neville demanded decreased by **10.** The substitution effect **reduced** his demand by **5** bottles and the income effect **reduced** his demand by **5** bottles.

8.2 (10) Consider the figure below which shows the budget constraint and the indifference curves of good King Zog. Zog is in equilibrium with an income of $300, facing prices $p_x = \$4$ and $p_y = \$10$.

(g) On the axes below, sketch an Engel curve and a demand curve that would be reasonable given the information in the figure above. Be sure to label the axes on both your graphs.

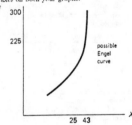

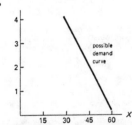

8.3 (5) Maude spends all of her income on delphiniums and hollyhocks. She thinks that delphiniums and hollyhocks are perfect substitutes. Delphiniums cost $2.00 a unit and hollyhocks cost $3.00 a unit.

(a) If the price of delphiniums decreases to $1.00 a unit, will Maud necessarily buy more of them? **Yes.** What part of the change in consumption is due to the income effect and what part is due to the substitution effect?
All due to income effect.

(b) Continue to suppose that delphiniums and hollyhocks are perfect substitutes for Maud and $p_d = \$2.00$ and $p_h = \$3.00$. If Maud has $40 to spend, draw her budget line in blue ink. Draw the highest indifference curve that she can attain in red ink, and label the point that she chooses as *A.*

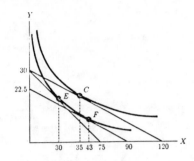

(a) How much x does Zog consume? **30**

(b) If the price of x falls to $2.50 while income and the price of y stay constant, how much x will Zog consume? **35**

(c) How much income must be taken away from Zog to isolate the Hicksian income and substitution effects. (i.e., to make him just able to reach his old indifference curve at the new prices)? **$75**

(d) The total effect of the price change is to change consumption from the point **E,** to the point **C**

(e) The income effect corresponds to the movement from the point **F,** to the point **C,** while the substitution effect corresponds to the movement from the point **E,** to the point **F.**

(f) Is x a normal good or an inferior good? **An inferior good.**

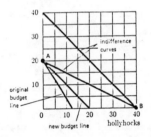

(c) Now let the price of hollyhocks fall to $1.00 a unit while the price of delphiniums does not change. Draw her new budget line in black ink. Draw the highest indifference curve that she can now reach with red ink. Label the point she chooses now as *B.*

(d) How much would Maud's income have to be after the price of hollyhocks fell, so that she could just exactly afford her old commodity bundle *A*? **$40**

(e) What part of the change in Maud's demand when the price of hollyhocks fell to $1.00 is due to the income effect and what part due to the substitution effect?
All substitution effect.

8.4 (5) Suppose now that we have two goods that are perfect complements. Let the price of one good change. What part of the change in demand is due to the substitution effect and what part is due to the income effect?
All income effect.

8.5 (20) Douglas Cornfield's demand function for good x is $x(p_x, p_y, m) = 2m/5p_x$. If his income is $1000, if the price of x is $5 and the price of y is $20, then if the price of x falls to $4, then his demand for x will change from **80** to **100.**

(a) If his income were to change at the same time so that he could exactly afford his old commodity bundle at $p_x = 4$, what would his new income be? __920;__ What would be his demand for x at this new level of income? __92.__

(b) The substitution effect is a change in demand from __80__ to __92;__ The income effect of the price change is a change in demand from __92__ to __100.__

(c) On the axes below, use blue ink to draw Douglas Cornfield's budget line before the price change. Locate the bundle he chooses at these prices on your graph and label this point *A*. Use black ink to draw Douglas Cornfield's budget line after the price change. Label his consumption bundle after the change by *B*.

money for other goods

(d) On the graph above, use yellow ink to draw a budget line with the new prices but with an income that just allows Douglas to buy his old bundle, *A*. Find the bundle that he would choose with this budget line and label this bundle *C*.

(b) Tim loses $30 he was sure he had a moment ago. He decides to sell the rest of his bottle of wine to a 'friend' and spend the money on cigars.

Cigars are an inferior good; wine is a normal good.

(c) The price of wine goes up and Tim decides to cut back his purchases of cigars.

Cigars are a normal good.

(d) The price of wine and cigars both rise by 20%. Tim cuts his expenditures on both items by the same proportion.

Both goods are normal goods.

(e) The price of cigars falls by 50%. Tim lowers his consumption of cigars by 5% and uses all the extra money to buy more wine.

Cigars are a Giffen good and therefore and inferior good. Wine is a normal good.

(e) On your graph, draw a red mark over the part of the horizontal axis that represents the change in consumption of x due to the substitution effect. Draw a yellow mark over the part of the horizontal axis that represents the change in consumption of x due to the income effect.

8.6 (10) Illustrate in the diagram below indifference curves that will result in a zero substitution effect. Draw in two budget lines that illustrate this zero substitution effect.

other

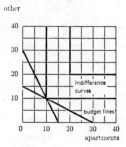

indifference curves

budget lines

apartments

8.7 (30) Tim spends all of his income on 'Sneaky Pete' wine and 'Old Stogie' cigars. In each of the following cases, you observe an event and then try to figure out what it has told you about Tim's income elasticity of demand for each good (*i.e.*, is it a normal, inferior, or luxury good, or can you not tell anything from the event you have observed. Point it out if a good is shown to be Giffen as well. Note: these categories are not mutually exclusive). By the way, Tim has convex preferences and likes both goods.

(a) Tim finds a $10 bill on the street while looking for half-smoked cigarettes. He immediately goes out and buys $10 worth of 'Old Stogies'.

Cigars are a normal good; the income elasticity of wine is zero.

(f) While looking for the $30 he lost earlier, Tim finds an only slightly used bottle of Sneaky Pete. He drinks it down and does not change his purchases of wine or cigars.

Does not tell us anything about income elasticities.

8.8 We observe that Mr. Consumer allows himself to spend $100 per month on cigarettes and ice cream. The price of cigarettes in $1 per pack while ice cream costs $2 per pint. Faced with these prices, Mr. C buys 30 pints of ice cream and 40 packs of cigarettes in January. Being from Minnesota, Mr. C's preferences for cigarettes and ice cream are unaffected by the season of the year.

(a) In February, Mr. C again has $100 for his 'vices', but now cigarettes cost $1.25 per pack. Mr. C now consumes 30 pints of ice cream and 32 packs of cigarettes. Does this tell us anything about the income elasticity of demand for cigarettes? __No.__ __of demand for ice cream?__ Must be greater than or equal to zero.

(b) In March, Mr. C again has $100 to spend and ice cream is on sale for $1 per pint. Cigarettes, meanwhile, have increased to $1.50 per pack. Is he better off than in January, worse off, or can you not make such a comparison? __He can afford January bundle in March, so he must be better off in March.__

(c) How does your answer to the last question change if cigarettes have instead increased in March to $2 per pack? __Now can't tell anything.__

(d) In April cigarettes have in fact risen to $2 per pack and ice cream is still on sale for $1 per pint. Mr. Consumer buys 34 packs of cigarettes and 32 pints of ice cream. Is he better off or worse off than in January? __Worse off in April than January.__ __Can you compare his utility to the February level?__ Better off in April than in February.

(e) In May cigarettes stay at $2/pack and the sale on ice cream ends, the price returns to $2/pint. On the way to the store, however, Mr. C finds Tim's $30. He now has $130 to spend on 'vices.' Without knowing what he purchased, can you compare his utility to any of the previous months? __Yes.__ _____ Which ones and how do they compare?

He is better off in May than in February.

Chapter 9

Buy and Sell

Introduction. This chapter examines demand theory when consumers receive their income from selling their endowment of goods. Remember the endowment will always be on the budget line, since the consumer always has the option of choosing not to purchase or sell anything.

9.1 (15) Abishag Appleby owns 20 quinces and 10 kumquats. She has no income from any other source, but she can buy or sell either quinces or kumquats at their market prices. The price of kumquats is two times the price of quinces. There are no other commodities of interest.

(a) How many quinces could she have if she was willing to do without

kumquats? _40._

(b) Draw Abishag's budget set, using blue ink, and label the endowment bundle with the letter E.

Kumquats

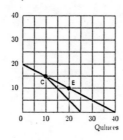

(c) Write down an equation for her budget line. $2K + Q = 40$ or,

equivalently, $2(K - 10) + (Q - 20) = 0$.

(e) What would be Mario's consumption bundle if the price of tomatoes were $15 and his money income were fixed at the original level given

in part (a)? He will consume _7.5_ pounds of tomatoes and

_7.5_ pounds of eggplant.

(f) The change in the demand for tomatoes due to the substitution ef-

fect is _0._ The change in the demand for tomatoes due to

the ordinary income effect is _−7.5._ The change in the demand

for tomatoes due to the endowment income effect is _+2.5._ The

total change in the demand for tomatoes is _−5._

(g) Illustrate the bundles described above and label them with the letter indicating the part they are from.

Eggplant

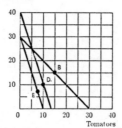

9.4 (20) Priscilla finds it optimal not to engage in trade at the going prices and just consumes her endowment. Draw a budget line and an indifference curve that illustrate Priscilla's situation. Use a revealed preference argument to show that when the price of good 1 falls, she must choose to consume at least as much of good 1 as before, regardless of the shape of her indifference curves.

(d) Suppose that the price of both goods were to double, what would

happen to Abishag's budget set? Nothing.

9.2 (15) Suppose that in the previous problem, Abishag decides to sell 10 quinces. Label her final consumption bundle in your graph with the letter C.

(a) Now suppose that the price of kumquats falls so that they cost the same as quinces. On the diagram above, draw Abishag's new budget line, using red ink.

(b) On the graph, use yellow marker to denote the portion of Abishag's new budget line where the principle of revealed preference tells us that her new demand might possibly be.

9.3 (20) Mario has a small garden where he raises eggplant and tomatoes to consume and to sell in the market. He always consumes eggplant and tomatoes together in a 1:1 ratio. One week his garden yielded 25 pounds of eggplant and 5 pounds of tomatoes. At that time the price of each vegetable was $5 per pound.

(a) What is the monetary value of Mario's endowment of vegetables?___

$150.

(b) Mario ends up consuming _15_ pounds of tomatoes and

_15_ pounds of eggplant.

(c) Mario will find it optimal to sell _10_ pounds of _____

eggplant; and to buy _10_ pounds of tomatoes.

(d) Suppose that the price of tomatoes rises to $15 a pound. What is

the value of Mario's endowment now? _$200;_ His new consump-

tion bundle consists of _10_ tomatoes and _10_

_____ eggplants.

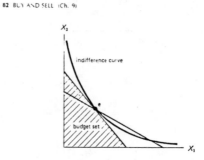

Indifference curve must be tangent at endowment, so

tilting indifference curve gives pure substitution effect.

9.5 (30) Potatoes are a Giffen good for Paddy, who has a small potato farm. The price of potatoes fell but Paddy increased his potato consumption. At first this astonished the village economist, who thought that a decrease in the price of a Giffen good was supposed to reduce demand. But then he remembered that Paddy was a net supplier of potatoes. With the help of a graph, he was able to explain Paddy's behavior. In the axes below, show how this could have happened. Put "potatoes" on the horizontal axis and "all other goods" on the vertical axis. Label the old equilibrium A and the new equilibrium B. Draw a point C so that the Slutsky substitution effect is the movement from A to C and the Slutsky income effect is the movement from C to B. On this same graph, you are also going to have to show that potatoes are a Giffen good. To do this, draw a budget line showing the effect of a fall in the price of potatoes if Paddy didn't own any potatoes, but only had money income. Label the new consumption point under these circumstances by D. (Warning: You probably will need to make a few dry runs on some scratch paper to get the whole story straight.)

all
other
goods

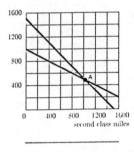

D
A
C
B
endowment

potatoes

9.6 Agatha must travel on the Orient Express from Istanbul to Paris. The distance is 1500 miles. You can choose to travel as many of the 1500 miles as you wish in first class coach or in second class coach. You have to pay 10 cents a mile for every mile that you travel second class and 20 cents a mile for every mile that you travel first class. Agatha much prefers first class to second class travel, but because of a misadventure in an Istanbul bazaar, Agatha has only $200 left with which to buy her tickets. Luckily, she still has her toothbrush and a suitcase full of provisions which she plans to eat on the way. Agatha therefore plans to spend her entire $200 on her tickets for her trip. She will travel as far as she can afford to on first class with her $200 but she must travel all the way to Paris.

(a) On the graph below, use red ink to show the locus of combinations of first and second class tickets that Agatha can just afford to purchase with her $200. Use blue ink to show the locus of combinations of first and second class tickets that are sufficient to carry her the entire distance from Istanbul to Paris. Locate the combination of first and second class miles that Agatha will choose on your graph and label it A.

first class miles

1600

1200

800

400

A

0   400   800 1200 1600
second class miles

_____

_____ None _____ How much of a change was due to an income

effect? _____ −166.66 _____

9.7 Suppose that Agatha from the previous problem had spent her $200 to buy first and second class tickets on the Orient Express when the price of first class tickets was $.20 and the price of second class tickets was $.10. After she boarded the train, she discovered to her amazement that the price of second hand tickets has fallen to $.05 while the price of first class tickets remains at $.20. She also learned that it is possible when you are on the train to buy or sell first class tickets for $.20 a mile and to buy or sell second class tickets for $.05 a mile. Agatha has no money left to buy either kind of ticket, but she does have the tickets that she has already bought.

(a) On the graph below, use pencil to show the combinations of tickets that she could afford at the old prices. Use blue ink to show the combinations of tickets that will take her exactly 1500 miles. Mark the point that she chooses with the letter A.

first class miles

1600

1200

800

400

A

0   400   800 1200 1600
second class miles

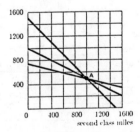

(b) Use red ink to draw a line showing all of the combinations of first class and second class travel that she can afford by trading her endowment of first and second class tickets at the new prices on board the train.

(c) On your graph, show the point that she chooses after finding out about the price change. Does she choose more less or the same amount of second class tickets? _____ The same. _____

(b) Let m_1 be the number of miles she travels by first class coach and m_2 be the number of miles she travels by second class coach. Write down two equations that you can solve to find the number of miles she chooses to travel by first class coach and the number of miles she chooses to travel by second class coach.

$$.2m_1 + .1m_2 = 200, \quad m_1 + m_2 = 1500$$

(c) The number of miles that she travels by second class coach is _____

1,000

(d) Suppose that just before she was ready to buy her tickets, the price of second class tickets fell to $.05 while the price of first class tickets remained at $.20. On the graph that you drew above, use pencil to show the combinations of first and second class tickets that she can afford with her $200 at these prices. On your graph, locate the combination of first and second class tickets that she would now choose. (Remember, she is going to travel as much first class as she can afford to and still make the 1,500 mile trip on $200). Label this point C. How many miles does she travel by second class now? $33.33. _____ (Hint: For an exact solution you will have to solve two linear equations in two unknowns.) Is second class travel a normal good for Agatha? _____ No _____ Is it a Giffen good for her? _____ Yes

(e) Suppose that just after the price change, Agatha misplaced her handbag. Although she kept most of her money in her sock, the money she lost was just enough so that she could exactly afford the combination of first and second class tickets that she bought before the price change. How much money did she lose? $50. _____ Use black ink to draw the locus of combinations of first and second class tickets that she can just afford after discovering her loss. Label the point that she chooses with a B. How many miles will she travel by second class now?

1,000

(f) Suppose that Agatha finds her handbag again. How many miles will she travel by second class now (assuming she didn't buy any tickets before she found her lost handbag)? $33.33. _____ When the price of second class tickets fell from $.10 to $.05, how much of a change in Agatha's demand for second class tickets was due to a substitution effect?

_____

Chapter 10

Labor Supply

Introduction. Here we examine some labor supply functions. It is convenient to consider the demand for leisure, and to let labor supply be the difference between the endowment of leisure and the demand for leisure.

10.1 (30) Fred has just arrived at college and is trying to figure out how to supplement the meager checks that he gets from home. "How can anyone live on $50 a week for spending money?" he asks. But he asks to no avail. "If you want more money, get a job," say his parents.

So Fred glumly investigates the possibilities. The amount of leisure time that he has left after allowing for necessary activities like sleeping, brushing teeth, and studying for his economics classes is 50 hours a week. He can get a part-time job at a local fast food establishment cleaning tables at $5.00 an hour. Given that Fred's utility function for leisure and money to spend on consumption is $U(C, L) = CL$, we want to determine how many hours he will end up working per week.

Let's try to solve Fred's problem algebraically. A utility function of the form $u(x_1, x_2) = x_1 x_2$ is a special case of a Cobb-Douglas utility function. It turns out that the demand functions for this utility have the form:

$$x_1 = \frac{m}{2p_1}$$
$$x_2 = \frac{m}{2p_2}$$

(a) The two goods that Fred is concerned with are money to spend on consumption, which has a price of 1, and leisure which has a price of ___$5/hr___

(b) Fred has an endowment that consists of $50 of money to spend on consumption and ___50___ hours of leisure, some of which he might "sell" for money.

(c) The money value of his endowment bundle, including both his money allowance and the market value of his leisure time is therefore ___$300.___

_____The amount of money that he will find optimal to spend on consumption is given by the Cobb-Douglas demand function. It is ___$150.___

(g) Given that Fred's parents send him $50 a week, what is Fred's supply function of labor as a function of the wage rate? $L^s(w) = 25 -$ ___25/w___ hours. What would his supply function of labor be if his parents didn't send him any money? $L^s(w) = 25$ ___hours.

10.2 (20 Fred's cousin Norman is in the same situation. He has the same tastes for consumption and leisure, the same job opportunities, and the same amount of free time. But there are two differences between Fred and Norman. The first one is that Norman's parents send him a $100 check each week. The second one is that Norman lives across town and would have to take a taxi cab to the fast food place, which he estimates would cost him $50 a week. He doesn't mind riding the cab, since he can study on it, but the $50 fare seems a bit steep. How much money would Norman have left to spend on consumption if he took the cab to work each week? ___$wL + 50.___ On the graph below, draw Norman's budget set and illustrate his optimal consumption and labor supply if he decides to work. (Use the information from the last problem.)

(a) What utility does he get from this choice? ___4,500.___

(b) What if Norman decided not to work at all? What utility would he get? ___5,000.___

(c) What is Norman's utility maximizing supply of labor? ___0___

_____hours.

(d) Illustrate Norman's budget set and indifference curves in the graph below, along with his optimal supply of labor.

(d) The amount of leisure that Fred will choose to consume is _____ ___30___ hours. This means that his optimal labor supply will be ___20___ hours.

(e) Illustrate Fred's optimal consumption and labor supply in the graph below and draw a few indifference curves. The indifference curves should be consistent with the utility function given above.

Consumption

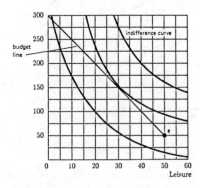

(f) Can you write down the algebraic formula for Fred's demand for leisure, where the price of other goods is 1, the wage rate is w, where $\bar{C}$ is his income sent from home and where $\bar{L} = 50$ is his total endowment of leisure time? To give you a clue, lets find his demand function for consumption. The total value of Fred's endowment is $m = \bar{C} + 50w$. Using the Cobb-Douglas demand function for consumption demand and recalling that the price of consumption goods is 1, we have

$$C = m/2$$
$$= \frac{(\bar{C} + 50w)}{2} = \bar{C}/2 + 25w$$

Now to find the supply function for labor, you need to find his demand function for leisure and subtract his leisure demand from his endowment of leisure. The answer is ___$L = 25 - \bar{C}/2w$___

Consumption

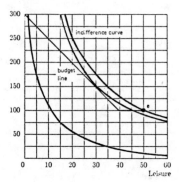

10.3 (5) If leisure is an inferior good, must the slope of the labor supply function necessarily be positive? Explain.

Use Slutsky's equation to write: $\frac{\Delta L}{\Delta w} = \frac{\Delta L^s}{\Delta w} + (\bar{L} - L)\frac{\Delta L}{\Delta m}$. Now note that the substitution effect is always negative, $(\bar{L} - L)$ is always positive, and hence if labor is inferior, $\frac{\Delta L}{\Delta w}$ is necessarily negative. Thus the slope of the labor supply curve is positive.

10.4 (20) Wally Piper is a plumber. He charges $10 per hour for his work and he can work as many hours as he likes. Wally has no source of income other than his labor. On the graph below, draw Wally's budget set, showing the various combinations of weekly leisure and income that Wally can afford.

Income

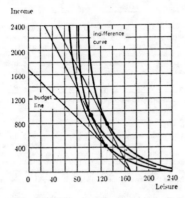

(a) Write down an equation that describes Wally's budget constraint.

$I + 10R = 1,680.$

(b) While self employed, Wally chose to work 40 hours per week. The construction firm, Glitz and Drywall, had a rush job to complete. They offered Wally $20 an hour and said that he could work as many hours as he liked. Wally still chose to work only 40 hours per week. On the graph you drew above, draw in Wally's new budget line and draw indifference curves that are consistent with his choice of working hours when he was self-employed and when he worked for Glitz and Drywall.

(c) Glitz and Drywall were in a great hurry to complete their project and wanted Wally to work more than 40 hours. They decided that instead of paying him $20 per hour, they would pay him only $10 an hour for the first 40 hours that he worked per week and $20 an hour for every hour of "overtime" that he worked beyond 40 hours per week. On the graph that you drew above, use red ink to sketch in Wally's budget line with this pay schedule. Draw the indifference curve through the point that Wally chooses with this pay schedule. Will Wally work more than 40 hours or

less than 40 hours per week with this pay schedule? _More._

(b) All individuals receive a lump sum payment of $100 per week from the government. There is no tax on the first $100 per week of labor income. But all labor income above $100 per week is subject to a 50% income tax.

Consumption

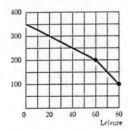

(c) If an individual is not working, he receives a payment of $100. If he works he does not receive the $100 and all wages are subject to a 50% income tax.

Consumption

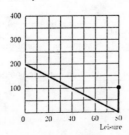

10.5 Mr. I. M. Cog works in a machine factory. In each of the following situations write down Mr. Cog's budget constraint. Let C be the number of consumer goods he consumes and let R be the number of hours of leisure that he chooses.

(a) Mr. Cog earns $5.00 an hour, has 18 hours to devote to labor or leisure, and consumer goods cost $1.00 each. He has no non-labor income.

$C + 5R = 90.$

(b) Mr. Cog faces the identical circumstances as above, but he also receives $10.00 in interest from his meager savings. $C + 5R = 100.$

(c) Mr. Cog faces the same conditions as in part (a), but decides that he can live on only 4 hours of sleep per night, and therefore devotes 20 hours a day to either labor of leisure. $C + 5R = 100.$

(d) After vehemently complaining to the management that he "just feels like a Cog in a machine factory," Mr. Cog gets a raise from $5.00 an hour to $10.00 an hour. He continues to devote 20 hours a day to either labor or leisure. $C + 10R = 200.$

10.6 (20) George Johnson earns $5 per hour in his job as a truffle sniffer. After allowing time for all of the activities necessary for bodily upkeep, George has 80 hours per week to allocate between leisure and labor. Sketch the budget constraints for George resulting from the following government programs.

(a) There is no government subsidy or taxation of labor income.

Consumption

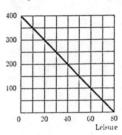

(d) The same conditions as in part (c) apply, with the exception that the first 20 hours of labor are exempt from the tax.

Consumption

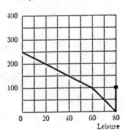

(e) All wages are taxed at 50%, but as an incentive to encourage work, the government gives a payment of $100 to anyone who works more than 20 hours a week.

Consumption

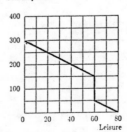

Chapter 11

Intertemporal Choice

Introduction. Here we examine some applications of present value. Remember: the present value of a stream of payments indicates the value of the endowment. Thus a stream of payments that has a higher present value than another stream must be preferred to one with a lower present value.

11.1 (30) Chillingsworth owns a large, poorly insulated home. His annual fuel bill for home heating averages $500 per year. An insulation contractor suggests to him the following options.

Plan A. Insulate just the attic. If he does this, he will permanently reduce his fuel consumption by 15%. Total cost of insulating the attic is $500.

Plan B. Insulate the attic and the walls. If he does this, he will permanently reduce his fuel consumption by 20%. Total cost of insulating the attic and the walls is $900.

Plan C. Insulate the attic and the walls and install a solar heating unit. If he does this, he will permanently reduce his fuel costs to zero. Total cost of this option is $10,000 for the solar heater and $900 for the insulating.

(a) Assume for simplicity of calculations that the house and the insulation will last forever. Calculate the present value of the dollars saved on fuel from each of the three options if the interest rate is 10%. The present values are: Plan A? $750; Plan B? $1000; Plan C? $5000.

(b) Each plan requires an expenditure of money to undertake. The difference between the present value and the present cost of each plan is: Plan A? $750 - 500 = 250$; Plan B? $1000 - 900 = 100$; Plan C? $5000 - 10900 = -5900$.

(c) If the price of fuel is expected to remain constant which option should he choose if he can borrow and lend at an annual interest rate of 10%? A.

(d) Which option should he choose if he can borrow and lend at an annual rate of 5%? B.

(d) What is the slope of his intertemporal budget constraint? $-(1+r)$.

11.4 (20) Becky Sharp has a utility function $U(c_1, c_2) = c_1^a c_2^{1-a}$ where $0 < a < 1$ and where c_1 and c_2 are her consumptions in periods 1 and 2 respectively.

Recall that preferences of this type are known as Cobb-Douglas preferences. We saw earlier that if utility has the form $u(x_1, x_2) = x_1^a x_2^{1-a}$ and the budget constraint has the standard form, then the demand functions for the goods have the form $x_1 = am/p_1$ and $x_2 = (1-a)m/p_2$.

(a) Suppose that Becky's income is m_1 in period 1 and m_2 in period 2. Write down her budget constraint in terms of present values.
$$c_1 + c_2/(1+r) = m_1 + m_2/(1+r).$$

(b) We want to compare this budget constraint to one of the "standard" form. In terms of Becky's budget constraint, what is p_1? 1 _____ What is p_2? $1/(1+r)$ What is m? $m_1 + m_2/(1+r)$

(c) Suppose that $a = .2$. Solve for Becky's demand functions for consumption in each period as a function of m_1, m_2, and r. Her demand function for consumption in period 1 is:
$$c_1 = .2m_1 + .2m_2/(1+r).$$

(d) Her demand function for consumption in period 2 is:
$$c_2 = .8(1+r)m_1 + .8m_2.$$

(e) Suppose that the government offers to pay half of the cost of any insulation or solar heating device. Which option would he now choose at interest rates 10%? B; 5%? C.

(f) Suppose that there is no government subsidy but suppose that fuel prices are expected to rise by 5% per year. What is the present value of fuel savings from each of the three proposals if interest rates are 10%? (Hint: If a stream of income is growing at x% and being discounted at y%, its present value should be the same as that of a constant stream of income discounted at what percent? You may use an approximation.)

Plan A? $1500; Plan B? $2000; Plan C? $10000; _____ Which proposal should Chillingsworth choose if interest rates are 10%? B; 5%? C.

11.2 (10) You are considering investing in a project with the following features. If you undertake the project, then right now you would have to buy a machine that costs $100. One year from now you would have to spend $55 more to maintain the machine. There are no other costs or expenses. Two years from now the machine would produce output that is worth $x and then the machine would fall apart and have no resale value.

(a) If the interest rate is 10%, write an equation that can be solved for the smallest amount that $x could be for this to be a worthwhile investment.
$$x/(1.1)^2 = 100 + 55/1.1 \text{ or } x = 181.5$$

11.3 (10) Peregrine Pickle purchases (c_1, c_2) and earns (m_1, m_2) in periods 1 and 2 respectively. Suppose the interest rate is r.

(a) Write down Peregrine's intertemporal budget constraint in present value terms $c_1 + \frac{c_2}{(1+r)} = m_1 + \frac{m_2}{(1+r)}$.

(b) If Peregrine does not consume anything in period 1, what is the most $m_1(1+r) + m_2$. This is equivalent to the future value of his income.

(c) If Peregrine does not consume anything in period 2, what is the most $m_1 + \frac{m_2}{(1+r)}$. This is equivalent to the present value of his income.

(e) An increase in the interest rate will _____ decrease _____ her period 1 consumption. It will _____ increase _____ her period 2 consumption and _____ increase _____ her savings in period 1.

11.5 (20) Decide whether each of the following statements is True or False. Then explain why your answer is correct. Draw a graph to illustrate your argument concerning each of the statements. (Hint: You need to use the Slutsky decomposition into income and substitution effects.)

(a) "If both current and future consumption are normal goods, an increase in the interest rate will necessarily make a saver save more."

False. The substitution effect would tend to make him consume less in the first period and save more. But for a saver, the income effect on demand for current consumption operates in the opposite direction. In general, either effect could dominate the other.

(b) "If both current and future consumption are normal goods, an increase in the interest rate will necessarily make a saver choose more consumption in the second period."

True. The income and substitution effect both lead to more consumption in the second period.

11.6 (20) Suppose that a consumer has an endowment of $20 each period.

He can borrow money at an interest rate of 200%, and he can lend money at a rate of 0%.

(a) Use blue ink to illustrate his budget set in the graph below. (Hint: The boundary of the budget set is not a single straight line.)

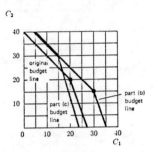

C_2

(b) The consumer is offered an investment that will change his endowment to $m_1 = 30$ and $m_2 = 15$. Would the consumer be **Better off.** by taking this new endowment? Use red ink to draw the new budget set in the graph above.

(c) Now use pencil or black ink to draw the budget set for $m_1 = 15$, $m_2 = 30$. Is the consumer **Can't tell.** with this endowment than with the original endowment?

11.7 (40) Nickleby has an income of $2,000 this year and he expects an income of $1,100 next year. He can borrow and lend money at an interest rate of 10%. Consumption goods cost $1 per unit this year and there is no inflation.

(a) What is the present value of Nickleby's endowment? **$3,000.**

(b) What is the future value of Nickleby's endowment? **$3,300.**

(i) Will he borrow or save in the first period? **Save** How much? **500**

(j) On your graph use red ink to show what Nickleby's budget line would be if the interest rate rose to 20%. Knowing that Nickleby chose the point A at a 10% interest rate, even without knowing his utility function, you can determine that his new choice can not be on certain parts of his new budget line. Use yellow marker to darken the part of his new budget line where that choice can not be.

(k) What are the two equations that one must solve to find Nickleby's optimal choice when the interest rate is 20%. $1.2 = C_2/C_1$
$C_1 + C_2/1.2 = M_1 + M_2/1.2$

(l) Solve for Nickleby's optimal choice when the interest rate is 20%. Nickleby will consume **1458.3** units in period 1 and **1750** units in period 2.

(m) Will he borrow or save in the first period? **Save** How much? **541.7**

11.8 (20) We return to the planet Mungo. On Mungo, macroeconomists and bankers are jolly, clever creatures, and there are two kinds of money, yellow money and blue money. Recall that to buy something in Mungo you have to pay for it twice, once with blue money and once with yellow money. Everything has a blue money price and a yellow money price and nobody is ever allowed to trade one kind of money for the other. There is a blue money bank where you can borrow and lend blue money at a 50% annual interest rate. There is a yellow money bank where you can borrow and lend yellow money at a 25% annual interest rate.

A Mungoan named Jane consumes only one commodity, ambrosia, but it must decide how to allocate its consumption between this year and next year. Jane's income this year is 100 blue currency units and no yellow currency units. Next year, its income will be 100 yellow currency units and no blue currency units. The blue currency price of ambrosia is one b.c.u. per flagon this year and will be two b.c.u.'s per flagon next year. The yellow currency price of ambrosia is one b.c.u. per flagon this year and will be the same next year.

(c) With blue ink, show the combinations of consumption this year and consumption next year that he can afford. Label Nickleby's endowment with the letter E.

Consumption next year

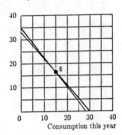

Consumption this year

(d) Suppose that Nickleby has the utility function $U(C_1, C_2) = C_1 C_2$. Write down Nickleby's marginal rate of substitution between consumption this year and consumption next year. (Your answer will be a function of the variables C_1, C_2.)

$$MRS = -C_2/C_1.$$

(e) What is the slope of Nickleby's budget line? **-1.1**

(f) Write down an equation that states that the slope of Nickleby's indifference curve between consumption in the two years is equal to the slope of his budget line when the interest rate is 10%. $1.1 = C_2/C_1$.

(g) What is the second equation that one must solve to find the optimal C_1 and C_2? $C_1 + C_2/1.1 = 2000 + 1100/1.1$.

(h) Solve these two equations. Nickleby will consume **1500** units in period 1 and **1650** units in period 2. Label this point A on your diagram.

(a) If Jane spent all of its blue income in the first period, it would be enough to pay the blue price for **100** flagons of ambrosia. If Jane saved all of this year's blue income at the blue money bank, it would have **150** b.c.u.'s next year. This would give it enough blue currency to pay the blue price for **75** flagons of ambrosia. On the graph below, draw Jane's blue budget line, depicting all of those combinations of current and next period's consumption that it has enough blue income to buy.

Ambrosia next period

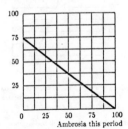

Ambrosia this period

(b) If Jane planned to spend no yellow income in the next period and to borrow as much yellow currency as it can pay back with interest with next period's yellow income, how much yellow currency could it borrow? **80.**

(c) The (exact) real rate of interest on blue money is **-25%**. The real rate of interest on yellow money is **25%**.

(d) On the axes below, draw Jane's blue budget line and its yellow budget line. Shade in all of those combinations of current and future ambrosia that Jane can afford given that she has to pay with both currencies.

Ambrosia next period

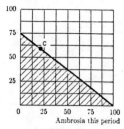

(e) It turns out that Jane finds it optimal to operate *on* its blue budget line and *beneath* its yellow budget line. Find such a point on your graph and mark it with a *C*.

(f) On the following graph, show what happens to Jane's original budget set if the blue interest rate rises and the yellow interest rate does not change. On your graph shade in the part of the new budget line where Jane's new demand could possibly be. (Hint: Apply the principle of revealed preference. Think about what bundles were available but rejected when Jane chose to consume at *C* before the change in blue interest rates.)

Ambrosia next period

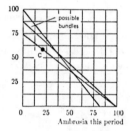

_____ This is the case where the consumer considers consumption in each of the two periods as perfect complements and where the vertex of the indifference curve occurs at (m_1, m_2).

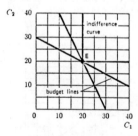

11.12 (40) Consider a two period model where the consumer has income (m_1, m_2) and consumption (c_1, c_2). He has to pay income tax at rate t in each period, and the interest rate is constant at r.

(a) Suppose that the interest income is tax exempt. Write down the
$$c_1 + c_2/(1 + r) = (1 - t)[m_1 + m_2/(1 + r)].$$

(b) Suppose that the consumer now has to pay income tax on his interest income, and gets to deduct his interest expenses. What is the form of his
$$c_1 + c_2/(1 + (1 - t)r) = (1 - t)[m_1 + m_2/(1 + (1 - t)r].$$

Now suppose that the consumer can invest some amount X in a pension plan in period 1. He does not have to pay taxes on the amount put in the pension plan in period 1. The money in the pension plan will earn interest at rate r, and the consumer does not have to pay tax on this interest income. However, when the consumer withdraws his money, $X(1 + r)$, in period 2, he has to pay tax on it as income.

(c) If the consumer consumes c_1 in period 1, how much will he be able to
_____ If he saves X, he will have $c_1 = (1 - t)(m_1 - X)$
left to consume. Solving for X gives: $X = m_1 - c_1/(1 - t)$.

11.9 (20) Dr. No owns a bond, serial number 007, issued by the James Company. The bond pays $100 for each of the next three years, at which time the bond is retired and pays its face value of $1000.

(a) How much is the James bond 007 worth to Dr. No at an interest rate of 10%? $\underline{100/1.1 + 100/1.1^2 + 100/1.1^3 + 1000/1.1^3 = 1000}$

(b) How valuable is James bond 007 at an interest rate of 5%? _____
$$100/1.05 + 100/1.05^2 + 100/1.05^3 + 1000/1.05^3 =$$

(c) Ms. Yes offers Dr. No $1,100 for the James bond 007. Should Dr. No say yes or no to Ms. Yes if the interest rate is 10%? $\underline{\text{Yes}}$.
What if the interest rate is 5%? $\underline{\text{no.}}$

(d) In order to destroy the world, Dr. No hires Professor Know to develop a nasty zap beam. In order to lure Professor Know from his cushy-soft university position, Dr. No will have to pay the professor $100 a year. The nasty zap beam will take three years to develop, at the end of which it can be built for $1000. If the interest rate is 5% how much money will Dr. No need today to finance this dastardly program? $\underline{\$1136.16, \text{which}}$ is the present value calculated in the first part of the problem. _____ If the interest rate was at 10% would the world be in more or less danger from Dr. No? $\underline{\text{More danger, since the dastardly}}$ plan is now cheaper.

11.10 (10) If a consumer is a borrower and the interest rate falls will she remain a borrower or become a lender? $\underline{\text{She will remain a}}$ borrower, _____ Will she be better or worse off after the change? $\underline{\text{better off}}$

11.11 (10) Illustrate preferences for which the consumer is neither a borrower nor a lender regardless of the interest rate. Label the endowment with the letter E and draw a couple of budget lines. _____

(d) What is the consumer's intertemporal budget constraint?
$$c_1 + c_2/(1 + r) = (1 - t)[m_1 + m_2/(1 + r)].$$

Chapter 12

Asset Markets

Introduction. The fundamental equilibrium condition for asset markets is that in equilibrium the rate of return on all assets must be the same. This simple condition has many important implications that we will investigate in this chapter.

12.1 (10) You are thinking about buying two plots of land. The first one is a plot in a good neighborhood. You are certain you can sell this land in a year's time for $121,000. The second plot is in a slightly shabby neighborhood, but you are sure that this plot will be worth $110,000 in a year. (Both of these amounts are net of sales costs, etc.) Because of other obligations, you can only hold each property for a year, and due to strict zoning regulations no one can use the property for any purpose during that year. The market interest rate is 10% per year.

(a) At what price would you just be willing to purchase the first plot?__

$110,000

(b) At what price would you just be willing to purchase the second plot?__

$100,000

(c) What will be the rate of appreciation of value on the lot in the good neighborhood? _____10%._____What about the lot in the shabby neighborhood? _10%._

12.2 (30) Publicity agents for the Detroit Felines announce the signing of a phenomenal new quarterback, Archie Parabola. They say that the contract is worth $1,000,000 and will be paid in installments of $50,000 per year for the next 20 years. The contract contains a clause that guarantees he will get all of the money even if he is injured and can not play a single game. Sports writers declare that Archie has become an "instant millionaire."

(g) Use the answer to the above question to calculate the present value of Archie's contract? $8.50 \times 50,000 = \$425,000.$

Calculus 12.3 (20) You are the business manager of P. Bunyan Forests, Inc. and are trying to decide when you should cut your trees. The market value of the lumber that you will get if you let your trees reach the age of t years is given by the function $W(t) = e^{20t - .001t^2}$. Mr. Bunyan can earn an interest rate of 5% per year on money in the bank. (Hint: It follows from elementary calculus that if $F(t) = e^{g(t)}$, then $F'(t)/F(t) = g'(t)$.)

(a) How old should Mr. Bunyan let the trees get? 75 years.

(b) At what age do the trees have the greatest market value?_____ 100 years.

12.4 (20) You expect the price of a certain painting to rise by 8% per year forever. The market interest rate for borrowing and lending is 10%. Assume there are no brokerage costs in purchasing and selling.

(a) If you pay $z for the painting now and sell it in a year, how much has it cost you to hold the painting rather than to have loaned the $z at the market interest rate? It has cost .02z.

(b) You would be willing to pay $100 a year to have the painting on your walls. Write an equation that you can solve for the price at which you would be just willing to buy the painting _____The equation is .02x = 100.

(c) How much should you be willing to pay to buy the painting? _____ $5,000.

(d) Does the amount you would be willing to pay to buy the painting now depend on whether you would get tired of the painting after a while and decide to sell it? No.

12.5 (20) J. Cousteau owns a catfish farm, and has calculated that if he buys $10 of catfish he can expect the amounts of money given in the following table from harvesting the fish at various times in the future. If Mr. Cousteau puts money in the bank he can receive 10% interest.

(a) Archie's brother, Fenwick, who majored in economics, explains to Archie that he is not a millionaire. In fact, his contract is worth less than half a million dollars. Explain in words why this is so.

The present value of $50,000 a year for 20 years will be less than a million dollars, since sums of money delivered later will be worth less than if they were delivered now.

Archie wasn't too good at math; in fact, he thought that the next number after 50 was "Hike!" So his brother tried to reason out the calculation for him. Here is how it goes:

(b) Suppose that the interest rate is 10% and is expected to remain at 10% forever. How much would it cost the team to buy Archie a perpetuity that would pay him and his heirs $1 per year *forever*? $10.

(c) How much would it cost to buy a perpetuity that paid $50,000 a year for ever? $500,000.

(d) If the interest rate is 10%, what is the present value of $1 to be received in 20 years? $0.15. (Use a calculator or the table in the text to find a numerical answer.)

(e) If the interest rate is and will remain at 10%, how much is the present value of a stream of income of $1 per year starting 20 years from now and going on forever? $1.50. (Hint: Since the interest rate is assumed never to change, in 20 years perpetuities will cost the same in the money of that time as they cost now in current dollars. But the cost of buying that perpetuity is deferred for 20 years.)

(f) What is the present value of a stream of $1 per year for 20 years?_____ $8.50. (Hint: All you have to do is subtract the value of a perpetuity paying $1 per year, starting in 20 years from the value of such a perpetuity starting now.)

Harvest Time	1	2	3	4	5
Value of Fish	12	13.8	15.18	16.4	17.37
Rate of Return	20	15	10	8	6
Total Value	12	13.80	15.18	16.69	18.36

(a) Fill in the third line of the table with the rate of return that M. Cousteau earned in the previous period.

(b) When should he harvest those "little suckers"? The fish should be harvested in the third year.

(c) Fill in the last line of the table with the value of M. Cousteau's initial $10 investment if he follows the optimal harvesting rule.

12.6 (20) Fisher Brown is taxed at 40% on his income from ordinary bonds. Ordinary bonds pay 10% interest. Interest on municipal bonds is not taxed at all.

(a) If the interest rate on municipal bonds is 7%, should he buy municipal bonds or ordinary bonds? Brown should buy municipal bonds.

(b) Hunter Black makes less money than Fisher Brown and is taxed at only 25% on his income from ordinary bonds. Which kind of bonds should he buy? Black should buy ordinary bonds.

(c) If Fisher has $1,000,000 in bonds and Hunter has $10,000 in bonds, how much taxes does Fisher pay on his interest from bonds? 0,
_____ How much taxes does Hunter pay on his interest from bonds? $250

(d) The government is considering a new tax plan under which no interest income will be taxed. If the interest rates on the two types of bonds do not change, and Fisher and Hunter are allowed to adjust their portfolios, how much will Fisher's after-tax income be increased? $30,000,
_____ How much will Hunter's after-tax income be increased?_ $250

(e) What would the change in the tax law do to the demand for municipal
It would reduce it to zero.

(f) What interest rate will new issues of municipal bonds have to pay in
order to attract purchasers? They will have to pay 10%.

(g) What do you think will happen to the market price of the old municipal bonds, which had a 7% yield originally? The price of the
old bonds will fall until their yield equals 10%.

12.7 (20) In the text we discussed the market for oil assuming zero production costs, but now suppose that it is costly to get the oil out of the
ground. Suppose that it costs $5 dollars per barrel to extract oil from
the ground. Let the price in period t be denoted by p_t and let r be the
interest rate.

(a) If a firm extracts a barrel of oil in period t, how much profit does it
make in period t? $p_t - 5$

(b) If a firm extracts a barrel of oil in period $t + 1$, how much profit does
it make in period $t + 1$? $p_{t+1} - 5$

(c) What is the present value of the profits from extracting a barrel of
The present values are $(p_{t+1} - 5)/(1 + r)^{t+1}$ and
$(p_t - 5)/(1 + r)^t$, respectively.

(d) If the firm is willing to supply oil in each of the two periods, what
must be true about the relation between the present value of profits from
The present values must be equal. The equation
expressing this is $\dfrac{p_{t+1} - 5}{(1 + r)^{t+1}} = \dfrac{p_t - 5}{(1 + r)^t}$.

(e) Solve the equation in the above part for p_{t+1} as a function of p_t and
r. The expression is $p_{t+1} = (1 + r)p_t - 5r$.

(f) Is the percentage rate of price increase between periods larger or
The percent change in price is smaller.

12.8 (20) On the planet Stinko, the principle industry is turnip growing.
The turnips are processed in Ole Factories to produce food and drink
for the residents. For centuries the turnip fields have been fertilized by
guano which was deposited by the now-extinct giant scissor-billed kiki-
bird. It costs $5 per ton to mine kiki-bird guano and deliver it to the
fields. Unfortunately, the country's stock of kiki-bird guano is about to
be exhausted. Fortunately the scientists on Stinko have devised a way
of synthesizing kiki-guano from political science textbooks and swamp
water. This method of production makes it possible to produce a product
indistinguishable from kiki-guano and to deliver it to the turnip fields at
a cost of $30 per ton. The interest rate on Stinko is 10%. There are
perfectly competitive markets for all commodities.

(a) Given the current price and the demand function for kiki guano, the
The price of guano delivered to the field must be
the present value of $30. This is $27.27 = 30/1.1.

(Hint: In equilibrium, sellers must be indifferent between selling their
kiki guano right now or at any other time before the total supply is
exhausted. But we know that they must be willing to sell it right up until
the day, one year from now, when the supply will be exhausted and the
price will be $30, the cost of synthetic guano.)

(b) Suppose that everything is as we have said previously except that
the deposits of kiki-guano will be exhausted 10 years from now. What
must be the current price of kiki-guano? $30/(1.1)^{10} = 11.57$ (Hint:
$1.1^{10} = 2.59$.)

12.9 (30) In the text we considered a competitive market for oil. Here
let us consider what would happen if there were one firm that owned all
the oil and charged a price that would maximize the present value of its
stream of profits. (That is, the single firm behaved as a monopolist.)
Suppose that the demand for oil is constant at D barrels per year, the
total supply of oil is S barrels, and there is an alternative technology
widely available that will provide synthetic oil at C dollars per barrel.

(a) The monopolist would charge what the market would
bear every period, which would be C (minus a penny).

(b) The price would be constant and therefore would
not rise at the rate of interest.

Chapter 13

Uncertainty

13.1 (20) Clarence Bunsen is an expected utility maximizer. His preferences among contingent commodity bundles are represented by the expected utility function

$$u(c_1, c_2, \pi_1, \pi_2) = \pi_1 \sqrt{c_1} + \pi_2 \sqrt{c_2}.$$

Clarence's friend, Hjalmer Ingqvist, has offered to bet him $1,000 on the outcome of the toss of a coin. That is, if the coin comes up heads, Clarence must pay Hjalmer $1,000 and if the coin comes up tails, Hjalmer must pay Clarence $1,000. The coin is a fair coin, so that the probability of heads and the probability of tails are both 1/2. If he doesn't accept the bet, Clarence will have $10,000 with certainty. In the privacy of his car dealership office over at Bunsen Motors, Clarence is making his decision. (Clarence uses the pocket calculator that his son, Elmer, gave him last Christmas. You will find that it will be helpful for you to use a calculator too.) Let Event 1 be "coin comes up heads" and let Event 2 be "coin comes up tails".

(a) If Clarence accepts the bet, then in Event 1, he will have _____ **$9,000** _____dollars and in Event 2, he will have _____ **$11,000** _____dollars.

(b) Since the probability of each event is 1/2, Clarence's expected utility for a gamble in which he gets c_1 in Event 1 and c_2 in Event 2 can be described by the formula $\frac{1}{2}\sqrt{c_1} + \frac{1}{2}\sqrt{c_2}$

(c) Therefore, Clarence's expected utility if he accepts the bet with Hjalmer will be ____ **99.8746** ____(Use that calculator.)

(d) If Clarence decides not to bet, then in Event 1, he will have _____ **$10,000** _____dollars and in Event 2, he will have _____ **$10,000** _____dollars.

of your equation you would write down Clarence's utility if he doesn't bet. On the right side of the equation, you write down an expression for Clarence's utility if he makes a bet so that his consumption will be zero in Event 1 and x in Event 2. Then you can solve this equation for x, which will allow you to easily compute the answer to Clarence's question. The equation that you write when you do this is **The equation is** $100 = \frac{1}{2}\sqrt{x}.$ The solution for x is $x = 40,000.$

(d) Your answer to the last part gives you two points on Clarence's indifference curve between the contingent commodities, money in Event 1 and money in Event 2. (Poor Clarence has never heard of indifference curves or of contingent commodities, so you will have to work this part for him, while he heads down to the Chatterbox Cafe for morning coffee.) One of these points is where money in both events is $10,000. On the graph below, label this point, *A*. The other is where money in Event 1 is zero and money in Event 2 is ____ **40,000.** ____On the graph below, label this point *B*.

Money in Event 2 (×1,000)

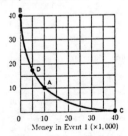

Money in Event 1 (×1,000)

(e) You can very quickly find a third point on this indifference curve. The coin is a fair coin and the only reason that Clarence cares whether heads or tails turn up, is because that determines his prize. Therefore Clarence will be indifferent between two gambles that are the same except that the assignment of prizes to outcomes are reversed. In this example, Clarence will be indifferent between point *B* on the graph and a point in which he gets zero if Event 2 happens and ____ **40,000** ____if Event 1 happens. Find this point on the Figure above and label it *C*.

(e) If Clarence decides not to bet, his expected utility will be ____ **100** ____

(f) Having calculated his expected utility if he bets and if he does not bet, Clarence determines which is higher and makes his decision accordingly.

Does Clarence take the bet? **No**

13.2 (30) It is a slow day at Bunsen Motors, so since he has his calculator warmed up, Clarence Bunsen (whose preferences toward risk were described in the last problem) decides to study his expected utility function more closely.

(a) Clarence first thinks about really *big* gambles. What if he bet his entire $10,000 on the toss of a coin, where he loses if heads and wins if tails? Then if the coin came up heads, he would have ____ **0** ____dollars and if it came up tails, he would have ____ **$20,000** ____dollars. His expected utility if he took the bet would be ____ **70.71,** ____while his expected utility if he didn't take the bet would be ____ **100** ____Therefore, he concludes that he would not take such a bet.

(b) Clarence then thinks "Well, of course I wouldn't want to take a chance on losing all of my money on just an ordinary bet. But, what if somebody offered me a really good deal. Suppose I had a chance to bet where if a fair coin came up heads, I lost my $10,000, but if it came up tails, I would win $50,000. Would I take the bet? If I took the bet, my expected utility would be ____ **122.5,** ____while if I didn't take the bet, my expected utility would be ____ **100.** ____Therefore, I should ____ **take** ____the bet."

(c) Clarence later asks himself, "If I make a bet where I lose my $10,000 if the coin comes up heads, what is the smallest amount that I would have to win in the event of tails in order to make the bet a good one for me to take?" After some trial and error, Clarence finds that the answer is ____ **$30,000.** ____

You might want to find the answer by trial and error too, but it is easier to find the answer by solving down an equation. On the left side

(f) Another gamble that is on the same indifference curve for Clarence as not gambling at all is the gamble where he loses $5,000 if heads turn up and where he wins ____ **$6,715.73** ____dollars if tails turn up. (Hint: To solve this problem, put the utility of not betting on the left side of an equation and on the right side of the equation, put the utility of having $10,000 − $5,000 in Event 1 and $10,000 + x in Event 2. Then solve the resulting equation for x. On the axes above, plot this point and label it *D*. Now sketch in the entire indifference curve through the points that you have labelled.)

13.3 (30) Hjalmer Ingkvist's son-in-law, Earl, has not worked out very well. It turns out that Earl likes to gamble. His preferences over contingent commodity bundles are represented by the expected utility function $u(c_1, c_2, \pi_1, \pi_2) = \pi_1 c_1^2 + \pi_2 c_2^2.$

(a) Just the other day, some of the boys were down at Skoog's tavern when Earl stopped in. They got to talking about just how bad a bet they could get him to take. At the time, Earl had $100. Kenny Olson shuffled a deck of cards and offered to bet Earl $20 that Earl would not cut a spade from the deck. Assuming that Earl believed that Kenny wouldn't cheat, the probability that Earl would win the bet was 1/4 and the probability that Earl would lose the bet was 3/4. If he won the bet, Earl would have ____ **120** ____dollars and if he lost the bet, he would have ____ **80** ____dollars. Earl's expected utility if he took the bet would be ____ **8,400** ____and his expected utility if he did not take the bet would be ____ **10,000.** ____Therefore he refused the bet.

(b) Just when they started to think Earl might have changed his ways, Kenny offered to make the same bet with Earl except that they would bet $100 instead of $20. What is Earl's expected utility if he takes that bet? ____ **10,000.** ____Would Earl be willing to take this bet? **He is just indifferent about taking it or not.**

(c) Let Event 1 be the event that a card drawn from a fair deck of cards is a spade. Let Event 2 be the event that the card is not a spade. Earl's preferences between income contingent on Event 1, c_1, and income contingent on Event 2, c_2, can be represented by the equation. $u = \frac{1}{4}c_1^2 + \frac{3}{4}c_2^2.$ ____Use blue ink on the graph below to sketch Earl's indifference curve passing through the point (100, 100).

Money in Event 2

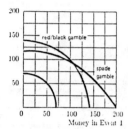

below, mark Sam's "endowment" of contingent consumption if he makes no bets with the casino, and label it E.

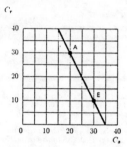

(d) On the same graph, let us draw Hjalmer's son-in-law Earl's indifference curves between contingent commodities where the probabilities are different. Suppose that a card is drawn from a fair deck of cards. Let Event 1 be the event that the card is black. Let event 2 be the event that the card drawn is red. Suppose each event has probability 1/2. Then Earl's preferences between income contingent on event 1 and

income contingent on event 2 are represented by the formula _____

$u = \frac{1}{2}c_1^2 + \frac{1}{2}c_2^2$.

_____ On the graph, use red ink to show two of Earl's indifference curves, including the one that passes through (100, 100).

13.4 (20) Sidewalk Sam makes his living selling sunglasses at the boardwalk in Atlantic City. If the sun shines, Sam makes $30 and if it rains Sam only makes $10. For simplicity, we will suppose that there are only two kinds of days, sunny ones and rainy ones.

(a) One of the casinos in Atlantic City has a new gimmick. They are accepting bets on whether or not it will be sunny or rainy the next day. The way it works is, the casino sells dated "rain coupons" for $1 each. If it rains the next day, the casino will give you $2 for every rain coupon you bought on the previous day. If it doesn't rain, your rain coupon is worthless. Sam buys these coupons on credit from the casino. At the end of any day, he takes his earnings from sunglasses sales and the coupons that he bought the previous day. He first goes to the credit window at the casino and pays $1 for each of the coupons that he bought the day before. If it was a rainy day, he then walks over to the pay out window and gets $2 for each of the rain coupons he bought the day before. If it has not been rainy, he just throws away his rain coupons. In the graph

(b) On the same graph, mark the combination of consumption contingent on rain and consumption contingent on sun that he could achieve by buying 10 rain coupons from the casino. Label it A.

(c) On the same graph, use blue ink to draw the budget line representing all of the other patterns of consumption that Sam can achieve by buying rain coupons. (Assume that he can buy fractional coupons, but not negative amounts of them.) What is the slope of Sam's budget line at points above and to the left of his initial endowment? **The slope is -2.**

(d) Suppose that the casino also sells sunshine coupons. These tickets cost $2. With these tickets, the casino gives you $1 if it doesn't rain and nothing if it does. Sam can get the same credit arrangement as for rain coupons. On the graph above, use red ink to sketch in the budget line of contingent consumption bundles that Sam can achieve by buying sunshine tickets.

(e) If the price of a dollar's worth of consumption when it rains is set equal to 1, what is the price of a dollar's worth of consumption if it shines? **The price is 2.**

13.5 (30) Suppose that Sidewalk Sam from the previous problem has the following utility function for consumption in the two states of nature:

$$u(c_s, c_r, \pi) = c_s^{1-\pi} c_r^{\pi}.$$

where c_s is the dollar value of his consumption if it shines, c_r is the dollar value of his consumption if it rains, and π is the probability that it will rain.

(a) Suppose now that the probability that it will rain is $\pi = .5$. Recall that if a utility function has the form Cobb Douglas form, $u(x_1, x_2) = x_1^a x_2^{1-a}$, then demand functions take the form $x_1 = am/p_1$ and $x_2 = (1-a)m/p_2$, where m is the monetary value of the endowment. Using the prices derived above, the value of Sam's endowment is **70.**

(b) Using this fact, what is Sam's optimal amount of consumption when it rains? **35.**

(c) How many rain coupons will Sam buy? **25** How many sunshine coupons will he buy? **12.5**

13.6 (20) Sidewalk Sam's brother Morgan von Neumanstern is an expected utility maximizer. His von Neumann-Morgenstern utility function for wealth is $u(c) = \ln c$. Sam's brother also sells sunglasses on another beach in Atlantic City and makes exactly the same income that Sam does. He can make exactly the same deal with the casino that Sam can. If Morgan believes that there is a 50% chance of rain and a 50% chance of sun every day, what would his expected utility of consuming (c_r, c_s) be? $u = \frac{1}{2}\ln c_r + \frac{1}{2}\ln c_r$.

(a) **Morgan's utility function is just the natural log of Sam's, so the answer is yes.**

(b) What will Morgan's optimal pattern of consumption be? Answer: Morgan will consume **17.5** on the sunny days and **35** _____ on the rainy days. How does this compare to Sam's consumption? **This is the same as Sam's consumption.**

13.7 (20) Billy John Pigskin, of Mule Shoe, Texas has a von Neumann-Morgenstern utility function of the form $u(c) = \sqrt{c}$. Billy John also weighs about 300 pounds and can outrun jackrabbits and pizza delivery trucks. Billy John is beginning his senior year of college football. If he is not seriously injured, he will receive a $1,000,000 contract for playing professional football. If an injury ends his football career, he will receive a $40,000 contract as a refuse removal facilitator in his home town. There is a 10% chance that Billy John will be injured badly enough to end his career.

(a) What is Billy John's expected utility? **We calculate** $.1\sqrt{40,000} + .9\sqrt{1,000,000} = 920.$

(b) If Billy John pays p for an insurance policy that would give him $1,000,000 if he suffered a career ending injury while in college, then he would be sure to have an income of $1,000,000 - p$ no matter what happened to him. Write an equation that can be solved to find the largest price that Billy John would be willing to pay for such an insurance policy. **The equation is** $920 = \sqrt{1,000,000 - p}.$

(c) Solve this equation for p. $p = 153,600.$

13.8 (30) You have $200 and are thinking about betting on the Big Game next Saturday. Your team, the Golden Boars, are scheduled to play their traditional rivals the Robber Barons. It appears that the going odds are 2 to 1 against the Golden Boars. That is to say if you want to bet $10 on the Boars you can find someone who will agree to pay you $20 if the Boars win in return for your promise to pay him $10 if the Robber Barons win. Similarly if you want to bet $10 on the Robber Barons, you can find someone who will pay you $10 if the Robber Barons win, in return for your promise to pay him $20 if the Robber Barons lose. Suppose that you are able to make as large a bet as you like, either on the Boars or on the Robber Barons so long as your gambling losses do not exceed $200. (To avoid tedium, let us ignore the possibility of ties.)

(a) If you do not bet at all, you will have $200 whether or not the Boars win. If you bet $50 on the Boars then after all gambling obligations are settled, you will have a total of **$300** _____ dollars if the Boars win and **$150** _____ dollars if they lose. On the graph below, use blue ink to draw a line that represents all of the combinations of "money if the Boars win" and "money if the Robber Barons win" that you could have by betting from your initial $200 at these odds.

Money if the Boars Lose

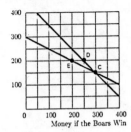

(b) Label the point on this graph where you would be if you did not bet at all with an *E*.

(c) After careful thought you decide to bet $50 on the Boars. Label the point you have chosen on the graph with a *C*. Suppose that after you have made this bet, it is announced that the star Robber Baron quarterback suffered a sprained thumb during a tough economics midterm examination and will miss the game. The market odds shift from 2 to 1 against the Boars to "even money" or 1 to 1. That is, you can now bet on either team and the amount you would win if you bet on the winning team is the same as the amount that you would lose if you bet on the losing team. You can not cancel your original bet, but you can make new bets at the new odds. Suppose that you keep your first bet, but you now also bet $50 on the Robber Barons at the new odds. If the Boars win, then after you collect your winnings from one bet and your losses from the other, how much

money will you have left? _____250_____ If the Robber Barons win, how much money will you have left after collecting your winnings

and paying off your losses? _____200_____

(d) Use red ink to draw a line on the diagram you made above, showing the combinations of "money if the Boars win" and "money if the Robber Barons win" that you could arrange for yourself by adding possible bets at the new odds to the bet you made before the news of the quarterback's misfortune. On this graph, label the point *D* that you reached by making the two bets discussed above.

Chapter 14

NAME_____

Asset Markets with Uncertainty

14.1 (30) Ms. Lynch has a choice of two assets: the first is a risk free asset which offers a rate of return of r_f, and the second is a risky asset (a china shop which caters to large mammals) which has an expected rate of return of r_m and a standard deviation of σ_m.

(a) If x is the percent of wealth Ms. Lynch invests in the risky asset what is the equation for the expected rate of return on the portfolio?___

$r_x = xr_m + (1-x)r_f$,_____What is the equation for

the standard deviation of the portfolio?___$\sigma_x = x\sigma_m$.___

(b) By solving the second equation above for x and substituting the result into the first equation, derive an expression for the rate of return on the portfolio in terms of the portfolio's riskiness.___$r_x = \frac{r_m - r_f}{\sigma_m}\sigma_x + r_f$.

(c) Suppose that Ms. Lynch can borrow money at the interest rate r_f and invest it in the risky asset. If $r_m = 20$, $r_f = 10$ and $\sigma_m = 10$, what will be Ms. Lynch's expected return if she borrows an amount equal to 100% of her initial wealth and invests it in the risky asset? **Apply the formula** $r_x = xr_m + (1-x)r_f$ **with** $x = 2$ **to get** $r_x = 2 \times 20 - 1 \times 10 = 30.$

_____(Hint: This is just like investing 200% of her wealth in the risky asset.)

(d) Suppose that Ms. Lynch can borrow or lend at the risk free rate. If r_f is 10%, r_m is 20%, and σ_m is 10% what is the formula for the "budget line" Ms. Lynch faces?___$r_x = \sigma_x + 10.$___Plot this budget line in the graph below.

_____

NAME _____ **125**

(b) If Mr. Smith invests x percent of his wealth in the risky asset what will be the standard deviation of his wealth?___$\sigma_x = 10x$.___

(c) Solve the above two equations for the expected return on Mr. Smith's wealth as a function of the standard deviation he accepts._____ The budget line is $r_x = 2\sigma_x + 10$.

(d) Plot this "budget line" on the graph.

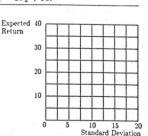

Expected Return

(e) If Mr. Smith's utility function is $u(r_x, \sigma_x) = \min\{r_x, 30 - 2\sigma_x\}$, then Since the utility function has the perfect complements form, the optimal solution must involve setting $r_x = 30 - 2\sigma_x$. The budget line requires that $2\sigma_x + 10 = r_x$. Solving these two equations in two unknowns yields $r_x = 20$ and $\sigma_x = 5.$

(f) Plot Mr. Smith's optimal choice and an indifference curve through it in the graph.

(g) What fraction of his wealth should Mr. Smith invest in the risky Using the answer to part *(a)*, we want to find an x that solves $20 = r_x = 30x + 10(1-x)$. The answer is $x = .5.$

14.3 (20) Assuming that the Capital Asset Pricing Model is valid complete the following table. In this table p_0 is the current price of asset i and Ep_1 is expected price of asset i next period.

Expected Return

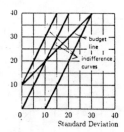

Standard Deviation

(e) Which of the following risky assets would Ms. Lynch prefer to her present risky asset, assuming she can only invest in one risky asset at a time, and that she can invest a fraction of her wealth in whichever risky asset she chooses. Write the words "better", "worse", or "same" after each of the assets.

Asset A with $r_a = 17\%$, and $\sigma_a = 5\%$ **A: better**

Asset B with $r_b = 30\%$, and $\sigma_b = 25\%$ **B: worse**

Asset C with $r_c = 11\%$, and $\sigma_c = 1\%$ **C: same**

Asset D with $r_d = 25\%$, and $\sigma_d = 14\%$ **D: better.**

(f) Suppose Ms. Lynch's utility function has the form $u(r_x, \sigma_x) = r_x - 2\sigma_x$.

How much of her portfolio will she invest in the original risky asset? ___**nothing**___(You might want to graph a few of Ms. Lynch's indifference curves before answering, e.g., graph the combinations of r_x and σ_x which imply $u(r_x, \sigma_x) = 0, 1, \dots$ etc.)

14.2 (30) Fenner Smith is contemplating dividing his portfolio between two assets, a risky asset that has an expected return of 30% and a standard deviation of 10%, and a safe asset that has an expected return of 10% and a standard deviation of 0%.

(a) If Mr. Smith invests x percent of his wealth in the risky asset, what will be his expected return?___$r_x = 30x + 10(1-x)$.___

---

r_f	r_m	r_i	β_i	p_0	Ep_1
10	20	10	0	100	110
10	20	25	1.5	100	125
10	15	20	2	200	240
0	30	20	2/3	40	48
10	22	10	0	80	88

14.4 (20) Farmer Alf Alpha has a pasture located on a sandy hill. The return to him from this pasture is a random variable depending on how much rain there is. In rainy years the yield is good, in dry years the yield is poor. The market value of this pasture is $5,000. The expected return from this pasture is $500 with a standard deviation of $100. Every inch of rain above average means an extra $100 in profit and every inch of rain below average means another $100 less profit than average. Farmer Alf has another $5,000 that he wants to invest in a second pasture. There are two possible pastures that he could buy.

(a) One is located on low land that never floods. This pasture yields an expected return of $500 per year no matter what the weather is like. What is Alf Alpha's expected rate of return on his *total* investment if he buys this pasture for his second pasture?___**10%.**___What is the standard deviation of his rate of return in this case?___$\frac{1}{2}\%$.

(b) Another pasture that he could buy is located on the very edge of the river. This gives very good yields in dry years but in wet years it floods. This pasture also costs $5,000. The expected return from this pasture is $500 and the standard deviation is $100. Every inch of rain *below* average means an extra $100 in profit and every inch of rain above average means another $100 less profit than average. If Alf buys this pasture and keeps his original pasture on the sandy hill, what is his expected rate of return on his total investment.___**10%.**___What is the standard deviation of the rate of return on his total investment in this case?___zero percent.

(c) If Alf is a risk averter, which of these two pastures should he buy and why? He should choose the second pasture since it has the same expected return and lower risk.

Chapter 15

Consumer's Surplus

15.1 (20) In the graph below. you see a representation of Sarah Gamp's indifference curves between cucumbers and other goods. Suppose that the references prices of cucumbers and the reference price of "other goods" are both 1.

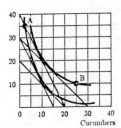

Other goods / Cucumbers

(a) What is the money metric utility for the bundle A? $\underline{20}$

(b) What is the money metric utility for the bundle B? $\underline{30}$

(c) Suppose now that the reference price for cucumbers is 2 and the reference price for other goods is 1. Now what is the money metric utility of bundle A? $\underline{30}$

(d) What is the money metric utility of bundle B using these new reference prices? $\underline{45}$

(e) What level of money metric utility would be assigned to the bundle (20.5) when prices are ($2. $.50)? $\underline{\$20}$ _____What about the bundle (4.25)? $\underline{\$20}$

15.4 (20) F. Flintstone has quasilinear preferences and his inverse demand function for Brontosaurus Burgers is $P(b) = 30 - 2b$. Mr. Flintstone is currently consuming 10 burgers at a price of 10 dollars.

(a) How much money would he be willing to pay to have this amount rather than no Burgers at all? $\underline{\$200}$ What is his level of (net) consumer's surplus? $\underline{100}$

(b) The town of Bedrock, the only supplier of Brontosaurus Burgers, decides to raise the price from $10 a burger to $14 a burger. What is Mr. Flintstone's change in consumer's surplus? $\underline{-36}$

15.5 (10) Karl Kapitalist is willing to produce $p/2 - 5$ widgets at every price. p. If the price of widgets is $100, what is Karl's producer's surplus if he is producing 45 widgets? $\underline{2,025}$

15.6 (20) Ms. Q. Moto loves to ring the church bells for up to 10 hours a day. Where m is income, and x is hours of bell ringing, her utility function is: $u(m, x) = m + 3x$ so long as $x \leq 10$. If $x > 10$ she develops painful blisters and is worse off than if she didn't ring the bells. Her income, m, is equal to $100 and the sexton allows her to ring the bell for 10 hours.

(a) Due to complaints from the villagers, the sexton has decided to restrict Ms. Moto to 5 hours of bell ringing per day. This is bad news for Ms. Moto. In fact she regards it as just as bad as losing $\underline{\$15}$ _____dollars of income.

(b) The sexton relents and offers to let her ring the bells as much as she likes so long as she pays $2 per hour for the privilege. How much ringing does she do now? $\underline{10 \text{ hours}}$ This tax on her activities is as bad as a loss of how much income? $\underline{\$20}$

(e) No matter what the reference prices. the money metric utility of bundle A must be (higher. lower) than the money metric utility for bundle B. $\underline{\text{Lower.}}$

15.2 (20) Suppose a consumer considers goods x and y to be perfect complements. that is $u(x, y) = \min\{x, y\}$.

(a) What level of utility does the consumer achieve with the bundle (4.4)? $\underline{\text{The utility level under the perfect complements utility function is 4.}}$

(b) If the prices are $2 and $2 per unit of x and y respectively. what is the money metric utility level for this bundle? $\underline{4 \times 2 + 4 \times 2 = 16.}$

(c) What is the level of money metric utility if the prices are (2.3)? $\underline{\text{the money metric utility is } 4 \times 2 + 4 \times 3 = 20.}$

(d) What level of utility does the consumer obtain with the bundle (5.8)? $\underline{\text{The utility level of bundle } (5, 8) \text{ is } 5.}$

(e) What are the levels of money metric utility for this bundle with prices (2.2) and (2.3) respectively? $\underline{\$20}$ and $\underline{\$25}$

15.3 (20) The Consumer was in the store the other day in order to pick up some more x's and y's (of which, as you know, The Consumer is peculiarly fond). The Consumer's utility function is: $u(x, y) = x^{1/2}y^{1/2}$. Her income is $20.

(a) When the prices of goods x and y are $2 and $.50 respectively. her demand for x is $\underline{x = 5,}$ and for y is $\underline{y = 20.}$

(b) What level of utility would The Consumer's money metric utility function assign to the x, y bundle (5.20). if the prices are ($2. $.50). $\underline{\text{the money metric utility level must be equal to } \$20.}$

(c) The villagers continue to complain. The sexton raises the price of bell ringing to $4 an hour. How much ringing does she do now? $\underline{0 \text{ ringing.}}$

_____This tax. as compared to the situation in which she could ring the bells for free is as bad as a loss of how much income? $\underline{\$30}$

15.7 (30) A clever and charming economics graduate student named John. is interested in only two things (besides economics). dating beautiful and intelligent women and eating chocolate chip cookies. His utility function is $u(x, y) = x_1^{1/2} x_2^{1/2}$ where x_1 is the number of hours per week spent dating beautiful women and x_2 is the number of bags of chocolate chip cookies that he consumes. He finds that he spends $1 an hour on dates and $1 per bag on chocolate chip cookies. He has only $20 per month to spend.

(a) What is John's optimal level of consumption at these prices and income? $\underline{\text{He consumes } x_1 = x_2 = 10.}$

(b) Write an expression for $m(1.1. x_1. x_2)$. the minimum cost at prices (1.1) of purchasing a bundle that John likes as well as $(x_1. x_2)$. $\underline{2x_1^{1/2} x_2^{1/2} = 2\sqrt{x_1 x_2}.}$ (Hint: Note that the formula for the money metric utility function for the Cobb-Douglas case in your textbook simplifies greatly for this special case.)

(c) One day, John was shocked to discover that the government had put a tax of $1 per bag on chocolate chip cookies so that the price was now $2. How much of each good did John buy then? $x_1 = \underline{10,}$ $x_2 = \underline{5.}$

(d) How much revenue did the government collect from John by means of its tax on cookies? $\underline{\text{The revenue collected was } \$5.}$

(e) How much income would John have needed at the pre-tax prices to be as well off as he was after the tax was imposed? $\underline{2\sqrt{50} = 10\sqrt{2}.}$

(f) How much would John have been willing to pay to avoid the tax? ____

$20 - 2\sqrt{50}.$ _____ This amount is known as the _____

equivalent _____ variation.

(g) Which is larger, this amount or the amount of revenue collected from John by the tax? The equivalent variation is larger. _____

(h) Write an expression for $m(1, 2, x_1, x_2)$, the minimum cost at prices

$(1, 2)$ of purchasing a bundle that John likes as well as (x_1, x_2). ____

$2\sqrt{2} x_1^{1/2} x_2^{1/2},$ _____ After the tax was imposed, how much would you

have to pay John to make him as well off as he was before the tax? ____

$20\sqrt{2} - 20,$ _____ This amount is known as the _____

compensating _____ variation.

(i) Which is bigger, the compensating or the equivalent variation, or are

they the same? The compensating variation is larger. _____

15.8 (30) At time t the prices are (p_1^t, p_2^t) and The Consumer optimally chooses (x_1^t, x_2^t). At time s the prices are (p_1^s, p_2^s) and The Consumer optimally chooses (x_1^s, x_2^s). The total expenditures in periods s and t are therefore $e^t = p_1^t x_1^t + p_2^t x_2^t$ and $e^s = p_1^s x_1^s + p_2^s x_2^s$.

(a) Using the money metric utility function $m(p_1, p_2, x_1, x_2)$ write an expression for how much money The Consumer would need at time t to

be as well off as he was at time s. $m(p_1^t, p_2^t, x_1^s, x_2^s).$ _____

(b) The true cost of living index, I, is the amount of money The Consumer would need at time t to be as well off as he was at time s divided by his expenditure at time s. Using the answer to the above question, write

down an expression for I. $I = m(p_1^t, p_2^t, x_1^s, x_2^s)/e^s.$ _____

(c) One way that The Consumer could be as well off at time t as he was at time s is by consuming the *same* bundle at time t as he consumed at

time s. How much would this cost him? $p_1^t x_1^s + p_2^t x_2^s.$ _____

(d) This means that $m(p_1^t, p_2^t, x_1^s, x_2^s)$ must be (greater than or equal to, exactly equal to, less than or equal to) $p_1^t x_1^s + p_2^t x_2^s.$
Less than or equal to. _____

(b) If the price of cow feed is p and her income is m, how much cow

feed does Lolita choose? $1 - p$ _____ How much hay does she

choose? $m - p(1 - p)$ _____ (Hint: The money that she doesn't spend on feed is used to buy hay.)

(c) Plug these numbers into her utility function to find out the utility level

that she enjoys at this price and this income. $u = m + (1 - p)^2/2$

(d) Recall that the money metric utility, $m(1, p, x, y)$ is defined to be the amount of income one would need when the price of hay is $1, and the price of feed is p, to be as well off as she was with the bundle (x, y). Write an equation that says that Lolita is exactly as well off with income m and

price p as she would be with bundle (x, y). The equation is $\dfrac{(1-p)^2}{2}$

$+ m = x - x^2/2 + y.$

(e) Use the above expression to derive the result that $m(1, p, x, y) = x - x^2/2 + y - (1 - p)^2/2$. Write a sentence explaining what you did. Just solve the equation given in the last part for m.

(f) Suppose that Lolita's daily income is $3 and that the price of feed is

$.50. What bundle does she buy? $(1/2, 11/4)$ _____ What bundle

would she buy if the price of cow feed rose to $1? $(0, 3)$ _____

(g) How much money would Lolita be willing to pay to avoid having the

price of hay rise to $1? $1/8$ _____ This amount is known as

the equivalent _____ variation.

(h) Suppose that the price of cow feed rose to $1. How much extra money would you have to pay Lolita to make her as well off as she was at the old

prices? $1/8$ _____ This amount is known as the _____

compensating, _____ variation. Which is bigger, the compensating or

the equivalent variation, or are they the same? same _____

(e) The Laspeyres price index is defined by:

$$L_P = \frac{p_1^t x_1^s + p_2^t x_2^s}{e^s}.$$

The Laspeyres price index must be (greater than or equal to, exactly equal to, less than or equal to) the true cost of living index I.
Greater than or equal to. _____

15.9 (30) Suppose The Consumer's preferences can be represented by the utility function $u(x_1, x_2) = \min\{x_1, x_2\}$.

(a) What is the form of his money metric utility function? $(p_1 + p_2)$

$\min\{x_1, x_2\},$ _____ Write an expression for his true cost of living index, using the simplification gained from the fact that he would have bought

the same amount of both goods in period s. ? $I = \dfrac{p_1^t + p_2^t}{p_1^s + p_2^s}$

(b) If The Consumer's preferences can be represented by the utility function $u(x_1, x_2) = x_1 + x_2$ what is the form of his money metric utility

function? $m(p_1, p_2, x_1, x_2) = (x_1 + x_2) \min\{p_1, p_2\}.$

His true cost of living index? $I = \min\{p_1^t, p_2^t\}/\min\{p_1^s, p_2^s\}.$

Calculus **15.10 (40)** Lolita, an intelligent and charming Holstein cow, consumes only two goods, cow feed (made of ground corn and oats) and hay. Her preferences are represented by the utility function $U(x, y) = x - x^2/2 + y$ where x is her consumption of cow feed and y is her consumption of hay. Lolita has been instructed in the mysteries of budgets and optimization and always maximizes her utility subject to her budget constraint. Lolita has an income of $m which she is allowed to spend as she wishes on cow feed and hay. The price of hay is always $1, and the price of cow feed will be denoted by p where $0 < p \le 1$.

(a) Write Lolita's inverse demand function for cow feed. $p = 1 - x,$

_____ (Hint: Lolita's utility function is quasilinear. When y is the numeraire and the price of x is p, the inverse demand function for someone with quasilinear utility $f(x) + y$ is found by simply by setting

$p = f'(x)$.) Write Lolita's demand function for cow feed. $x = 1 - p$

_____

(i) At the price $.50 and income $3, how much (net) consumer's surplus

is Lolita getting? $1/8$

Chapter 16

Market

16.1 (30) In Gas Pump. South Dakota. there are two kinds of consumers. Buick owners and Dodge owners. Every Buick owner has a demand function for gasoline: $D_B(p) = 20 - 5p$ for $p \le 4$ and $D_B(p) = 0$ if $p > 4$. Every Dodge owner has a demand function $D_D(p) = 15 - 3p$ for $p \le 5$ and $D_D(p) = 0$ for $p > 5$. (Quantities are measured in gallons per week and price is measured in dollars.) Suppose that Gas Pump has 150 consumers. 100 Buick owners and 50 Dodge owners.

(a) If the price is $3, what is the total amount demanded by each individual Buick Owner? _____5_____ and by each individual Dodge owner? _____6._____

(b) What is the total amount demanded by all Buick owners?_____ _____500_____ What is the total amount demanded by all Dodge owners? _____300._____

(c) What is the total amount demanded by all consumers in Gas Pump at a price of 3? _____800._____

(d) On the graph below. use blue ink to draw the demand curve representing the total demand by Buick owners. Use black ink to draw the demand curve representing total demand by Dodge owners. Use red ink to draw the market demand curve for the whole town.

(e) What is the slope of the market demand curve for the whole town when the price of gasoline is $1 per gallon? Slope is $-1/650$.

(f) What is the slope of the market demand curve for the town when the price of gasoline is $4.50 per gallon? Slope is $-1/150$.

(g) What is the slope of the market demand curve when the price of gasoline is $10 per gallon The demand at this price is zero; the slope is infinite.

(a) Does Ms. Child have convex preferences? No.

(b) If Ms. Child pays $20 for one bottle of wine. how much will she have to spend on other goods? $80, What will be her utility level? 139

(c) Write down an equation that determines Ms. Child's reservation price for a bottle of wine. $75 + \dfrac{(100 - R)^2}{100} = \dfrac{(100)^2}{100}$

(d) What is Ms. Child's reservation price for a bottle of wine? $50.

16.4 (20) Ken's utility function is $u_K(x_1. x_2) = x_1 + x_2$ and Barbie's utility function is $u_B(x_1. x_2) = (x_1 + 1)(x_2 + 1)$. Good 1 can only be provided in discrete amounts: we will always have either $x_1 = 0$ or $x_1 = 1$. The price of the two goods are $p_1 = 1$ and $p_2 = 1$, and Ken and Barbie each have wealth $m > 1$.

(a) What is Ken's reservation price for good 1? $1.

(b) Write an equation that can be solved to find Barbie's reservation price for good 1. $(m - p + 1)2 = m + 1$ What is Barbie's reservation price for good 1? $p = (m + 1)/2$

(c) If Ken and Barbie each have a wealth of 3. plot the market demand curve for good 1.

Quantity

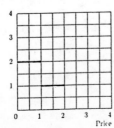

Price

(h) At what prices does the market demand curve have kinks? _____ At $p = 4$ and $p = 5$.

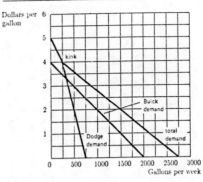

16.2 (20) For each of the following demand curves. compute the inverse demand curve.

(a) $D(p) = \max\{10 - 2p. 0\}$ $p(q) = 5 - q/2$ if $q < 10$. There is no non-negative price that would get buyers to buy more than 10.

(b) $D(p) = 100p^{-3}$ $p(q) = 10,000/q^2$

(c) $\ln D(p) = \ln 20 - 2\ln p$ $p(q) = 20^{.5}q^{-.5}$

(d) $\ln D(p) = 10 - 4p$ $p(q) = (10 - \ln q)/4$

16.3 (20) Ms. Child is considering purchasing a nice bottle of wine. Her utility function for bottles of wine, b, and money to be spent on other things. y. is given by $u(b. y) = 75b^2 + y^2/100$. Wine comes only in discrete units of bottles and costs p dollars per bottle. and she has exactly $100 to spend.

16.5 (20) The demand function for yo-yos is $D(p) = 4 - 2p + \frac{1}{100}M$ where p is the price of yo-yos and M is income. If M is 100 and p is 1:

(a) What is the income elasticity of demand for yo-yos? $1/3$

(b) What is the price elasticity of demand for yo-yos? $-2/3$

16.6 (10) If the demand function for zarfs is $P = 10 - Q$.

(a) At what price will total revenue realized from their sale be at a maximum? $P = 5$

(b) How many widgets will be sold at that price? $Q = 5$

16.7 (30) The demand function for football tickets for a typical game at a large midwestern university is $D(p) = 200,000 - 10,000p$. The university has a clever and avaricious athletic director who sets his ticket prices so as to maximize revenue. The university's football stadium holds 110,000 spectators.

(a) Write down the inverse demand function $p(q) = 20 - q/10,000$

(b) Write an expression for total revenue as a function of the number of tickets sold $R(q) = 20q - q^2/10,000$

(c) Write down an expression for marginal revenue as a function of the number of tickets sold. $MR = 20 - q/5,000$

(d) On the graph below, use blue ink to draw the inverse demand function and use red ink to draw the marginal revenue function. On your graph, also draw a vertical blue line representing the capacity of the stadium.

Price

(e) What price will generate the maximum revenue? $10 _____ What quantity will be sold at this price? 100,000.

(f) At this quantity, what is marginal revenue? 0 _____ At this quantity, what is the price elasticity of demand? -1 _____ Will the stadium be full? it will not be full.

(g) A series of winning seasons caused the demand curve function for football tickets to shift upwards. The new demand function is $q(p) =$ 300,000 − 10,000p. What is the new inverse demand function? $p(q) = 30 - q/10,000.$

(h) Write an expression for marginal revenue as a function of output. MR $= 30q - q^2/10,000.$ Use red ink to draw the new demand function and use black ink to draw the new marginal revenue function.

Calculus **16.8** (30) The demand function for drangles is $q(p) = (p+1)^{-2}$.

(a) What is the price elasticity of demand at price p? $2p/(p+1)$

(b) At what price is the price elasticity of demand for drangles equal to minus one? At $p = 1$.

(c) Write an expression for total revenue from the sale of drangles as a function of their price. $R(p) = pq = p/(p+1)^2.$ Use calculus to find the revenue maximizing price. Don't forget to check the second order condition. Differentiating and solving gives $p = 1.$

(d) Suppose that the demand function for drangles takes the more general form $q(p) = (p+a)^b$ where $a > 0$ and $b < -1$. Calculate an expression for the price elasticity of demand at price p. $\epsilon = bp/(p+a);$ At what price is the price elasticity of demand equal to −1? $p = -a/(1+b).$

(i) Ignoring stadium capacity, what price would generate maximum revenue? $15 _____ What quantity would be sold at this price? 150,000 _____ Does the stadium hold this many people? no.

(j) As you noticed above, the quantity that would maximize total revenue given the new higher demand curve is greater than the capacity of the stadium. Clever though the athletic director is, he can not sell seats he hasn't got. He notices that if he moves along his new demand function, his total revenue is an increasing function of the number of seats sold until the number of seats is 150,000, _____ which is bigger than his stadium capacity. Therefore he should sell 110,000 _____ tickets at a price of $p = \$19.$

(k) When he does this, his marginal revenue from selling an extra seat is 8. _____ The elasticity of demand for tickets at this price quantity combination is $8 = (1 + 1/\epsilon)19$ to get $\epsilon = -19/11$.

(l) How much could the athletic director increase the revenue per game by adding 1,000 new seats to his stadium's capacity and adjusting the ticket price to maximize his revenue? 7,900

(m) How much could he increase the revenue per game by adding 40,000 new seats? $160,000 _____ 60,000 new seats? $120,000

(n) Why is the extra revenue gained from adding 40,000 seats not given by 40 times the extra revenue gained from adding 1,000 seats? Because the amount the market is willing to pay for an additional seat decreases the more seats are sold; that is, the demand curve slopes down.

Chapter 17

NAME_____

Supply and Demand

Introduction. Supply and demand problems are bread and butter for economists. In the problems below, you will typically want to solve for equilibrium prices and quantities by writing an equation that sets supply equal to demand. Where the price received by suppliers is the same as the price paid by demanders, one writes supply and demand as functions of the same price variable, p, and solves for the price that equalizes supply and demand. But if, as happens with taxes and subsidies, suppliers face different prices from demanders, it is a good idea to denote these two prices by separate variables, p_s and p_d. Then one can solve for equilibrium by solving a system of two equations in the two unknowns p_s and p_d. The two equations are the equation that sets supply equal to demand and the equation that relates the price paid by demanders to the net price received by suppliers. For example if demanders must pay a tax or t for every unit they purchase, then $p_d = p_s + t$.

17.1 (30) The demand for yak butter is $q = 120 - 4p$ and the supply is $2p - 30$ where p is the price measured in dollars per hundred pounds and q is the quantity measured in hundred pound units.

(a) On the axes below, use blue ink to draw the demand curve and the supply curve for yak butter.

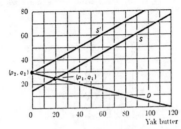

Price

(b) Write down the equation that you would solve to find the equilibrium price. $120 - 4p = 2p - 30$.

────────────

NAME _____ 145

17.2 (20) Here are the supply and demand equations for throstles, where p is the price in dollars:

$$D(p) = 200 - p$$
$$S(p) = 150 + p.$$

On the axes below, draw the demand and supply curves for throstles, using blue ink.

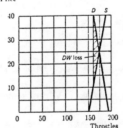

Price

Throstles

(a) What is the equilibrium price __25__ and quantity __175__ of throstles.

(b) Suppose that the government decides to restrict the industry to selling only 160 throstles. What will be the equilibrium demand price for 160 units? __40__ How many throstles would suppliers supply at that price? __190__ What price would the suppliers need to get in order to supply just 160 units? __10.__

(c) The government wants to make sure that only 160 throstles are bought, but it doesn't want the firms in the industry to receive more than the minimum price that it would take to have them supply 160 units of the good. One way to do this is for the government to issue 160 ration coupons. Then in order to buy a throstle, a consumer would need to present a ration coupon along with the necessary amount of money to pay for the good. If the ration coupons were freely bought and sold on the open market, what would be the equilibrium price of these coupons.?

The price should be 30.

────────────

(c) What is the equilibrium price of yak butter? __25__

_____What is the equilibrium quantity? __20.__

_____Locate the equilibrium price and quantity on the graph and label them p_1 and q_1.

(d) A terrible drought strikes the central Ohio steppes, traditional homeland of the yaks. The supply schedule shifts to $2p - 60$. The demand schedule remains as before. Draw the new supply schedule. Write down the equation that you would solve to find the new equilibrium price of yak butter. __$120 - 4p = 2p - 60$.__

(e) The new equilibrium price is __30,__ and the quantity is __zero.__ Locate the new equilibrium price and quantity on the graph and label them p_2 and q_2.

(f) The government decides to relieve stricken yak butter consumers and producers by paying a subsidy of $5 per hundred pounds of yak butter to producers. If p is the price paid by consumers for yak butter, what is the total amount received by producers for each unit they produce? __$p + 5$__ When the price paid by consumers is p, how much yak butter is produced? __$2p - 50$__

(g) Write down an equation that can be solved for the equilibrium price paid by consumers, given the subsidy program. __$2p - 50 = 120 - 4p$__ What are the equilibrium price paid by consumers and quantity of yak butter now? __$p = 170/6$ and the equilibrium quantity is $170/3 - 50 = 20/3$.__

(h) Suppose the government had paid the subsidy to consumers rather than producers. What would be the equilibrium net price paid by consumers? __$p = 170/6$__ The equilibrium quantity would be __$q = 20/3$.__

────────────

(d) On the graph above, shade in the area that represents the deadweight loss from restricting the supply of throstles to 160. How much is this expressed in dollars? __$225 = 15 \times 30/2.$__
(Hint: What is the formula for the area of a triangle?)

17.3 (20) The demand curve for salted codfish is $D(P) = 100 - 5P$ and the supply curve $S(P) = 5P$.

(a) The equilibrium market price is __$10__ and the equilibrium quantity sold is __50.__

(b) A quantity tax of $2 per unit sold is placed on salted codfish. The new price paid by the demanders will be __$11,__ and the new price received by the suppliers will be __$9__ The equilibrium quantity sold will be __45.__

(c) The deadweight loss due to this tax will be __$5 = 2 \times 5/2$__

17.4 (20) The demand function for merino ewes is $D(P) = 100/P$ and the supply function is $S(P) = P$.

(a) What is the equilibrium price? __$10.__

(b) What is the equilibrium quantity? __10.__

(c) An ad valorem tax of 300% is imposed on merino ewes so that the price paid by demanders is four times the price received by suppliers. What is the equilibrium price paid by the demanders for merino ewes now? __$20__ What is the equilibrium price received by the suppliers for merino ewes? __5__ What is the equilibrium quantity? __20.__

17.5 (20) King Kanuta rules over a small tropical island, Nutting Atoll, whose primary crop is coconuts. The main currency of Nutting Atoll is dollars. The demand function, expressing total demand for coconuts per week by King Kanuta's subjects is given by $D(P) = 1,200 - 100P$ and the supply curve for coconuts per week is given by $S(p) = 100P$.

(a) What will be the equilibrium price of coconuts and the equilibrium

quantity sold? _$6 and 600._

(b) One day the King decided to impose a tax on his subjects in order to collect coconuts for the Royal Larder. The King required that every consumer who consumed a coconut would have to pay a coconut to the King as a tax. Thus, if a consumer wanted 5 coconuts for himself, he would have to purchase 10 coconuts in order to give 5 to the King. If

$p_D = 2p_S$

(c) When the price paid to suppliers is p_S, how many coconuts will be demanded as a function of p_S for purposes of consumption? (Hint: Express p_D in terms of p_S and substitute into the _We have $p_D = 2p_S$,_ so that the quantity demanded will be $1200 - 200p_S$.

(d) Recalling that for every coconut demanded by the King's subjects, the King gets a coconut, write an equation relating the demand function $D(p_D)$ and the supply function $S(p_S)$ that must hold in equilibrium. _$2D(p_d) = S(p_S)$._

(e) Solve this equation for the equilibrium value of p_S and the equilibrium total number of coconuts produced. _$p_s = 24/5,\ 480$_

(f) King Kanuta's subjects resented paying the extra coconuts to the King, and whispers of revolution started spreading throughout the palace. Worried by the hostile atmosphere, the King changed the coconut tax.

This is equivalent to the above arrangement since it doesn't matter who pays the tax. The equilibrium supply price is 24/5 and the quantity sold to the consumers is 480/2 = 240. The consumers paid 48/5 per coconut consumed.

17.6 (20) Schrecklich and LaMerde are two justifiably obscure 19th century impressionist painters. The world's total stock of paintings by Schrecklich is 100 and the world's stock of paintings by LaMerde is 150. The two painters are regarded by connoisseurs as being very similar in style. Therefore the demand for either painter's work depends both on its own

was _$P_S = 23,$_ and the equilibrium price of LaMerdes was _$P_S = 9.$_

(e) On the diagram you drew above, use red ink to draw a line that shows the locus of price combinations at which the demand for Schrecklichs equals the supply of Schrecklichs after the fire. On your diagram, label the new equilibrium combination of prices E'.

17.7 (20) The demand function for a commodity has a constant price elasticity equal to -1. When the price of the good is $10 per unit, the total amount demanded is 6,000 units.

(a) Write down an equation for the demand function _$q = 60,000p^{-1} = 60,000/p$._ Graph this demand function below with blue ink. (Hint: If the demand curve has a constant price elasticity equal to ϵ, then $D(p) = ap^\epsilon$ for some constant a. You have to use the data of the problem to solve for the constants a and ϵ that apply in this particular case.)

price

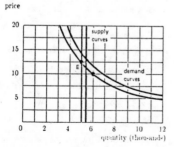

(b) If the supply is perfectly inelastic at 5,000 units, what is the equilibrium price? _$12._ Show the supply curve on your graph and label the equilibrium with an E.

price and the price of the other painter's work. The demand function for Schrecklich is $D_S(P) = 200 - 4P_S - 2P_L$ and the demand function for LaMerdes is $D_L(P) = 200 - 3P_L - P_S$, where P_S and P_L are respectively the price in dollars of a Schrecklich painting and a LaMerde painting.

(a) Write down two simultaneous equations that state the equilibrium condition that the demand for each painter's work equals supply.

The equations are $200 - 4P_S - 2P_L = 100$ and $200 - 3P_L - P_S = 150$.

(b) Solving these two equations, one finds that the equilibrium price of Schrecklichs is _$P_S = 20,$_ and the equilibrium price of LaMerdes is _$P_L = 10.$_

(c) On the diagram below draw a line that represents all of combinations of prices for Schrecklichs and LaMerdes such that the supply of Schrecklichs equals the demand for Schrecklichs. Draw a second line that represents those price combinations at which the demand for LaMerdes equals the supply of LaMerdes. Label the unique price combination at which both markets clear with the letter E.

P_L

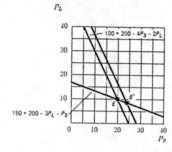

(d) A fire in a bowling alley in Hamtramck, Michigan, destroyed one of the world's largest collections of works by Schrecklich. The fire destroyed a total of 10 Schrecklichs. After the fire the equilibrium price of Schrecklichs

(c) Suppose that the demand curve shifts outward by 10%. Write down the new equation for the demand function. _$q = 66,000/p.$_ Suppose that the supply curve remains vertical but shifts to the right by 5%. Solve for the new equilibrium price _12.51_ and quantity _5,250._

(d) By what percentage approximately did the equilibrium price rise? _about 5 percent._ Use red ink to draw the new demand curve and the new supply curve on your graph.

(e) Suppose that in the above problem the demand curve shifts outward by $x\%$ and the supply curve shifts right by $y\%$. By approximately what percentage will the equilibrium price rise? _By around $(y - x)\%$._

17.8 (30) An economic historian[*] reports that econometric studies indicate for the pre-civil war period, 1820–1860, the price elasticity of demand for cotton from the American South was approximately one. Due to the rapid expansion of the British textile industry, the demand curve for American cotton is estimated to have shifted outwards by about 5% per year during this entire period.

(a) If during this period, cotton production in the U.S. grew by 3% per year, what (approximately) must be the rate of change of the price of cotton during this period. _It would rise by about 2% a year._

(b) Graph the demand for cotton through the point where the price is 20 and the quantity is 20. What is the total revenue when the price is 20? _400_ What is the total revenue when the price is 10? _400._

* Gavin Wright, *The Political Economy of the Cotton South*, W. W. Norton, 1978.

price of cotton

quantity of cotton

(c) If the change in the quantity of cotton supplied by the U.S. is to be interpreted as a movement along an upward sloping long run supply curve, what would the elasticity of supply have to be? __1.5 percent__

_____(Hint: From 1820 to 1860 quantity rose by about 3% per year and price rose by __2 percent__ per year. [See your earlier answer.] If the quantity change is a movement along the long run supply curve, then the long run price elasticity must be what?)

(d) The American Civil War, beginning in 1861, had a devastating effect on cotton production in the American South. Production fell by about 50% and remained at that level throughout the war. What would you predict would be the effect on the price of cotton? __It would double if demand didn't change.__

(e) What would be the effect on total revenue of cotton farmers in the American South? __Since the demand has elasticity of −1, the revenue would stay the same.__

(f) The expansion of the British textile industry ended in the 1860's and for the remainder of the 19th century the demand curve for American cotton remained approximately unchanged. By about 1900, the American South approximately regained its prewar output level. What do you think happened to cotton prices then? __They would recover to their old levels.__

(e) What is the new equilibrium price paid by demanders? __It is $7.5.__

(f) What is the change in the price paid by the demanders caused by the subsidy, expressed as a percentage of the old price? __The percent change is −1.5/9 ≈ −17%.__

(g) If the cross-elasticity of demand between bananas and apples is +.5, what will happen to the quantity of apples demanded as a consequence of the banana subsidy, if the price of apples stays constant? (State your answer in terms of percentage change.) __It will go down by about 8 percent.__

17.11 (20) The demand curve for ski lessons is given by $D(p_D) = 100 - 2p_D$ and the supply curve is given by $S(p_S) = 2p_S$.

(a) What is the equilibrium price? __$25.__

(b) What is the equilibrium quantity? __50.__

(c) A tax of $10 per ski lesson is imposed on consumers. Write down an equation that relates the price paid by demanders to the price received by suppliers. __$p_D = p_S + 10$__ Write down an equation that states that supply equals demand. __$100 - 2p_D = 2p_S$.__

(d) Solve these two equations for the two unknowns p_S and p_D. What is the equilibrium price p_D facing demanders of the good? __$p_D = \$30$.__

(e) How much of the good will be supplied if the $10 tax is imposed? __40 units.__

17.9 (10) The number of bottles of chardonnay demanded per year is $1,000,000 - 90,000P$, where P is the price per bottle (in U.S. dollars). The number of bottles supplied is $10,000P$.

(a) What is the equilibrium price? __The price is $10__ What is the equilibrium quantity? __The quantity is 100,000.__

(b) Suppose that the government introduces a new tax such that the wine maker must pay a tax of $5 per bottle for every bottle that he produces. What is the new equilibrium price paid by consumers? __$10.50__

_____What is the new price received by suppliers? __$5.50__

_____What is the new equilibrium quantity? __55,000.__

17.10 (20) The inverse demand function for bananas is $P_d = 18 - 3Q_d$ and the inverse supply function is $P_s = 6 + Q_s$ where prices are measured in cents. In equilibrium it must be that the quantity demanded equals the quantity supplied, so that $Q_s = Q_d$. If there are no taxes or subsidies, it must also be that in equilibrium, the demand price equals the supply price, $P_s = P_d$. Therefore you can solve for the equilibrium quantity by setting $6 + Q = 18 - 3Q$ where $Q = Q_s = Q_d$.

(a) If there are no taxes or subsidies, what is the equilibrium quantity? __The quantity is 3__ What is the equilibrium market price? __The price is $9.__

(b) If a subsidy of 2 cents per pound is paid to banana growers, then in equilibrium it still must be that the quantity demanded equals the quantity supplied, but now the price received by sellers is 2 cents higher than the price paid by consumers. What equation involving the inverse demand and supply curves can we solve to find the new equilibrium quantity? __$18 - 3Q_D = 6 + Q_S - 2$.__

(c) What is the new equilibrium quantity? __The quantity is 3.5.__

(d) What is the new equilibrium price received by suppliers? __The equilibrium supply price is $9.5.__

(f) A senator from a mountainous state suggests that although ski lesson consumers are rich and deserve to be taxed, ski instructors are poor and deserve a subsidy. He proposes a $6 subsidy on production while maintaining the $10 tax on consumption of ski lessons. This policy would be equivalent to __It is equivalent to a tax of $4.__

17.12 (20) Suppose that in Ham Harbor there are two kinds of renters: short-term and long-term. The demand of the long-term renters for apartments is given by $D_L = 100 - 4p$ and the demand of the short-term renters is given by $D_S = 200 - 6p$. The total supply of apartments in Ann Arbor is 100.

(a) What is the market clearing price? __20.__

(b) What is the equilibrium demand by the long-term people? __20__ The short-term people? __80.__

(c) Now suppose that all of the apartments rented by the long-term people are converted to condominiums and bought by their current residents. Write the equation for the new supply of *rental* housing. __$S = 80$__

(d) Write the equation that determines the new equilibrium price for rental housing. __The equation is $200 - 6p = 80$.__ What will the new equilibrium rental price for apartments be? __$p = 20$.__

(e) In nearby Yipsilanti there are similar short-term and long-term renters but with different demand curves and different tastes than the Ann Arbor renters. The current price of apartments in Yipsilanti is $30. Then the same sort of condo conversion occurs. What will happen to the equilibrium price of apartments? __It will remain constant at $30.__

Chapter 18

Technology

18.1 (20) Prunella raises peaches. Her production function is $f(L,T) = L^{\frac{1}{2}}T^{\frac{1}{2}}$, where L is the amount of labor she uses and T is the amount of land she uses.

(a) This production function exhibits (constant, increasing, decreasing) returns to scale. __Constant returns to scale.__

On the graph below, use blue ink to draw a curve showing Prunella's output as a function of labor input if she has 1 unit of land. Locate the points on your graph at which the amount of labor is 0, 1, 4, 9, and 16 and label them.

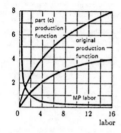

output

(b) Assuming she has 1 unit of land, how much extra output does she get from adding an extra unit of labor when she uses 1 unit of labor? $\sqrt{2} - 1 \approx .41$ 4 units of labor? $\sqrt{5} - 2 \approx .24$. If you know calculus, compute the marginal product of labor at these input levels and compare it with the result from the unit increase in labor output found above. __The derivative is $1/2\sqrt{L}$, which gives answers of .5 and .25 for $L = 1$ and $L = 4$.__

(b) Suppose that $f(x_1, x_2) = \min\{x_1, x_2\}$ and $x_1 = x_2 = 10$. What is the marginal product of a small increase in x_1? __0__ What is the marginal product of a small increase in x_2? __0__ What is the effect of a small increase in x_1 on the marginal product of a small increase in x_2? __Makes it larger.__

Calculus **18.4 (20)** Suppose the production function is Cobb-Douglas and $f(x_1, x_2) = x_1^{1/2} x_2^{3/2}$.

(a) Write an expression for the marginal product of x_1 at the point (x_1, x_2). __$\frac{1}{2}x_1^{-1/2} x_2^{3/2}$__

(b) The marginal product of x_1 (increases, decreases, remains constant) __Decreases__ for small increases in x_1, holding x_2 fixed.

(c) The marginal product of good 2 is __$3/2 x_1^{1/2} x_2^{1/2}$, increases.__ and it (increases, remains constant, decreases) for small increases in x_2.

(d) An increase in the amount of x_2, (increases, leaves unchanged, increases) the marginal product of x_1. __Increases.__

(e) The technical rate of substitution between x_2 and x_1 is __$-x_2/3x_1$__

(f) This technology demonstrates (increasing, constant, decreasing) returns to scale. __Increasing.__

18.5 (20) You manage a crew of 100 workers who could be assigned to make either of two products. Product A requires 2 workers per unit of output. Product B requires 8 workers per unit of output.

(c) Suppose that Prunella increases the size of her orchard to 4 units of land. Use red ink to draw a new curve on the graph above showing output as a function of labor input. Also use red ink to draw a curve showing marginal product of labor as a function of labor input when the amount of land is fixed at 4.

18.2 (20) Suppose that the production function is given by $f(x_1, x_2) = x_1 + x_2$.

(a) The marginal product for x_1 is __1, remains constant__ and (increases, remains constant, decreases) as x_1 increases. The marginal product of x_2 is __1, remains constant__ and (increases, remains constant, decreases) as x_1 increases. The technical rate of substitution between x_2 and x_1 is __-1, constant.__ This technology demonstrates (increasing, constant, decreasing) returns to scale.

(b) Suppose that the production function is given by $f(x_1, x_2) = x_1 + 3x_2$. The marginal product for x_1 is __1, remains constant__ and (increases, remains constant, decreases) as x_1 increases. The marginal product of x_2 is __3, remains constant__ and (increases, remains constant, decreases) as x_2 increases. The technical rate of substitution between x_2 and x_1 is __$-1/3$, constant.__ This technology demonstrates (increasing, constant, decreasing) returns to scale.

18.3 (20) Suppose x_1 and x_2 are used in fixed proportions and $f(x_1, x_2) = \min\{x_1, x_2\}$.

(a) Suppose that $x_1 < x_2$. The marginal product for x_1 is __1, remains constant__ and (increases, remains constant, decreases) for small increases in x_1. For x_2 the marginal product is __0, remains constant__ and (increases, remains constant, decreases) for small increases in x_2. The technical rate of substitution between x_2 and x_1 is __0, constant.__ This technology demonstrates (increasing, constant, decreasing) returns to scale.

(a) Write down an equation to express the combinations of products A and B that could be produced using exactly 100 workers. __$B = 12.5 - A/4$.__ On the diagram below, shade in the area depicting the combinations of A and B that could be produced with 100 workers. (Assume that it is possible for some workers to do nothing at all and that there are no other limitations on production possibilities.)

B

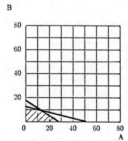

(b) Suppose now that every unit of product A that is produced requires the use of 2 shovels as well as 2 workers and that every unit of product B produced requires 4 shovels and 8 workers. On the graph you have just drawn, use a different color ink to shade in the area depicting combinations of A and B that could be produced with 60 shovels if there were no worries about the labor supply. Write down an equation for the set of combinations of A and B that require exactly 60 shovels. __$B = 15 - A/2$.__

(c) On the diagram you have just drawn, show the area that represents possible output combinations when one takes into account both the limited supply of labor and the limited supply of shovels.

(d) On your diagram locate the feasible combinations of inputs that use up all of the labor and all of the shovels. If you didn't have the graph, what equations would you solve to determine this point? __Solve the equations $B = 12.5 - A/4$ and $B = 15 - A/2$.__

18.6 (20) Timothy Alsike of Baraboo, Wisconsin, has just purchased 80 acres of pasture land. He is thinking about what kind of cows to put on his new pasture. Holsteins (the black and white ones) are bigger than Guernseys (the sweet looking reddish brown ones) and produce more milk than Guernseys, but this milk has a lower percentage butterfat content than Guernsey milk.

(a) The pasture will support 1 Guernsey cow for every 4 acres or 1 Holstein cow for every 5 acres. Timothy plans to have a mixed herd, some Guernseys some Holsteins. Write an expression to describe the set of combinations of Guernseys and Holsteins that he could support on his pasture. Illustrate this set on the graph below. (Don't worry about the anatomical implausibility of fractional cows. Having a cow for half the time is for this example the equivalent of having half of a cow.) _____

$H = 16 - 4G/5.$

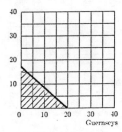

Holsteins

(b) Suppose that Holsteins each produce 60 pounds of milk and 2 pounds of butterfat per day and Guernseys produce 40 pounds of milk and 2 pounds of butterfat per day. Show on a graph the various combinations of milk and butterfat that could be produced on the pasture. (Hint: What combination of milk and butterfat would he produce if all of his cows were Holsteins? What if they were all Guernseys? What if they were half and half?)

(a) For what values of *a*, *b*, and *c*, would this production function exhibit decreasing returns to scale? When $a + b + c < 1$ constant returns to scale? When $a + b + c = 1$.

18.9 (20) The production function for fragles is $f(K, L) = L/2 + \sqrt{K}$, where L is the amount of labor used and K the amount of capital used.

(a) There are (constant, increasing, decreasing) returns to scale. The marginal product of labor is (constant, increasing, decreasing).

Decreasing; constant.

(b) In the short run, capital is fixed at 4 units. Labor is variable. On the graph below, use blue ink to draw output as a function of labor input in the short run. Use red ink to draw the marginal product of labor as a function of labor input in the short run and use black ink to draw the average product of labor as a function of labor input in the short run.

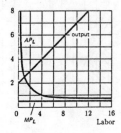

Fragles

Butterfat

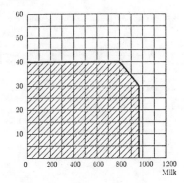

18.7 (10) Give an example of a Cobb-Douglas production function that has increasing returns to scale but diminishing marginal returns to each factor.

$x_1^a x_2^b$ for $a < 1$, $b < 1$, but $a + b > 1$.

18.8 (30) Suppose the production function has the form:

$$f(x_1, x_2, x_3) = A x_1^a x_2^b x_3^c$$

where $a + b + c > 1$. Prove that this production function exhibits increasing returns to scale.

$$f(t x_1, t x_2, t x_3) = A(t x_1)^a (t x_2)^b (t x_3)^c \, t^{a+b+c}$$

$f(x_1, x_2, x_3)$, which implies increasing returns to scale

since $a + b + c > 1$.

Chapter 19

NAME_____

Profit Maximization

19.1 (20) Brother Jed takes heathens and reforms them into righteous individuals. There are two inputs needed in this process: heathens (which are widely available), and preaching. The production function has the following form: $r_p = \min\{h, p\}$, where r_p is the number of righteous persons produced, h is the number of heathens who attend Jed's sermons, and p is the number of hours of preaching. For every person converted, Jed receives a payment of s from the grateful convert. Sad to say. heathens do not flock to Jed's sermons of their own accord. Jed must offer heathens a payment of w to attract them to his sermons. Suppose the amount of preaching is fixed at $\bar{p}$ and that Jed operates as a prophet maximizer ... that is, a *profit* maximizer.

(a) Sketch the shape of this production function in the graph below. Label the axes and indicate the amount of the input where $h = \bar{p}$.

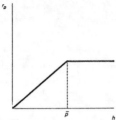

(b) If $h < \bar{p}$, what is the marginal product of heathens?____**1,**____

_____What is the value marginal product of an additional

heathen?__**s**____

(c) If $h > \bar{p}$, what is the marginal product of heathens?____**0,**____

_____What is the value marginal product in this case? ____**0.**____

_____

(c) In the diagram below, draw the appropriate isoprofit line for each of the three periods. Utilizing the theory of revealed profitability. shade in a possible technology for the observed production behavior.

The three isoprofit lines are given by $y = x$, $y = 1 + .5x$, and $y = 2 + .25x$, the region which is bounded above by each of these three lines is the possible technology.

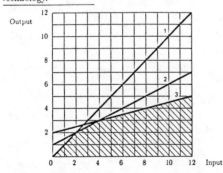

19.4 (20) Allie's Apples, Inc. purchases apples in bulk and sells two products, boxes of apples and jugs of cider. Allie's has capacity limitations of three kinds: warehouse space. pressing facilities, and crating facilities. A box of apples requires 6 units of warehouse space, 2 units of crating facilities, and no pressing facilities. A jug of cider requires 3 units of warehouse space, 2 units of crating facilities, and 1 unit of pressing facilities. The total amounts available each day are: 1200 units of warehouse space, 600 units of crating facilities, and 250 units of pressing facilities.

(a) If the only capacity limitations were on warehouse facilities, and if all warehouse space were used for the production of apples, how many

boxes of apples could be produced in one day? ____**200;**____

_____How many jugs of cider could be produced each day if. instead, all warehouse space were used in the production of cider and there were

no other capacity constraints? ____**400.**____Draw a blue line in the following graph to represent the warehouse space constraint on production combinations.

(d) If $w < s$. how many heathens will be converted?____$\bar{p}$,____

_____If $w > s$. how many heathens will be converted? ____**0.**____

_____

19.2 (10) Is it possible for a competitive profit maximizing firm in long-run equilibrium to be earning positive profits *and* have a production function which exhibits increasing returns to scale? Why or why not?

No, it is not possible. Suppose a firm is earning positive profits at some level of input. By doubling the amount of inputs it can more than double its profits. But then it couldn't be profit maximizing in the first place.

19.3 (20) A profit maximizing firm produces one output. y, and uses one input, x, to produce it. The price per unit of the factor is denoted by w and the price of the output is denoted by p. You observe the firm's behavior over three periods and find the following:

Period	y	x	w	p
1	1	1	1	1
2	2.5	3	.5	1
3	4	8	.25	1

Table 1. Observations on a profit maximizing firm.

(a) Write down an equation which gives the firm's profits, π, as a function of the amount of input x it uses, the amount of output y it uses, and the

per unit cost of the input w. ____$\pi = y - wx$____

(b) Rearrange this expression so that it expresses the level of output. $f(x)$,

in terms of profits, inputs, and factor price. ____$y = \pi + wx.$____

_____

(b) Following the same reasoning. draw a red line to represent the constraints on output to limitations on crating capacity. How many boxes of apples could Allie produce if he only had to worry about crating capacity?

____**300,**____How many jugs of cider? ____**300.**____

(c) Finally draw a black line to represent constraints on output combinations due to limitations on pressing facilities. How many boxes of apples could Allie produce if he only had to worry about the pressing capac-

ity and no other constraints? _____How many jugs of cider?

An infinite number of apples, and 250 jugs of cider.

(d) Now shade the area which represents feasible combinations of daily production of apples and cider for Allie's Apples.

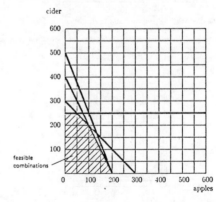

(e) Allie's can sell apples for $5.00 per box of apples and cider for $2.00 per jug. Draw a black line to show the combinations of sales of apples and cider that would generate a revenue of $1000 per day. Draw a black isoprofit line for $5.000 per day. Draw a black isoprofit line that maximizes

profits. At the profit maximizing production plan, Allie's is producing ____

____**200**____boxes of apples and ____**0**____

_____jugs of cider and total revenues are _____ $1,000.

Calculus **19.5 (20)** The short-run production function of a competitive firm is given by $f(L) = 6L^{2/3}$. If $w = 6$ and $p = 3$, how many units of labor will the firm hire? _____ 8 units of labor _____ How much output will it produce? 24 units of output.

Calculus **19.6 (20)** A Los Angeles firm uses a single input to produce a recreational commodity according to a production function $f(x) = 4\sqrt{x}$, where x is the number of units of input. The commodity sells for $100 per unit. The input costs $50 per unit.

(a) Write down a function that states the firm's profit as a function of the amount of input. _____ $\pi = 400\sqrt{x} - 50x$. _____

(b) What is the profit maximizing amount of input? _____ 16 units of the input _____ of output? _____ 16 units of the output.

(c) Suppose that the firm is taxed $20 per unit of its output and the price of its input is subsidized by $10. What is its new output level? _____ 16. _____ What is its new input level? _____ 16.

(d) Suppose that instead of these taxes and subsidies, the firm is taxed at 50% of its profits. Write down its after-tax profits as a function of the amount of input. _____ $\pi = .50 \times (400\sqrt{x} - 50x)$. _____ What is the profit maximizing amount of output? _____ amount doesn't change.

19.7 (30) T-bone Pickens is a corporate raider. This means that he looks for companies that are not maximizing profits, buys them, and then tries to operate them at higher profits. T-bone claims that he learned his methods from studying agricultural economics in the School of Animal Husbandry where they taught him to "buy sheep and sell deer."

In any event T-bone is examining the records for a couple of refineries that he might buy, the Shill Oil Company, and the Golf Oil Company. Each of these companies buys oil and produces gasoline. During the time period that T-bone is examining, the price of gasoline fluctuated significantly, while the cost of oil remained constant at $10 a barrel. For simplicity, we assume that oil is the only input to gasoline production.

(c) Is there any evidence that Golf Oil is not maximizing profits? Explain?

Yes. When the price of gasoline was $40, Golf could have made more money by doing the same thing that it did when the price of gasoline was $20.

(d) How much profits could Golf Oil have made when the price of gasoline was $40 a barrel if they had chosen to produce the same amount that they did when the price was $20 a barrel? _____ $8 million _____ What profits did Golf actually make when the price of gasoline was $40? _____ $6 million

19.8 (10) After carefully studying Shill Oil, T-bone Pickens decides that it has probably been maximizing its profits. But he still is very interested in buying Shill Oil. He wants to use the gasoline they produce to fuel his delivery fleet for his chicken farms, Capon Truckin'. In order to do this Shill Oil would have to be able to produce 5 million barrels of gasoline from 8 million barrels of oil. Mark this point on your graph. Assuming that Shill always maximizes profits, would it be technologically feasible for it to produce this input-output combination? Why or why not?

No, it could not produce this combination. If it could, then it would have made more profits by choosing that combination than what it actually did when the price of oil was $40.

19.9 Suppose that firms operate in a competitive market, attempt to maximize profits, and only use one factor of production. Then we know that for any changes in the input and output price, the input choice and the output choice must obey the Weak Axiom of Profit Maximization. $\Delta p \Delta y - \Delta w \Delta x \geq 0$.

Which of the following propositions can be proven by the Weak Axiom of Profit Maximizing Behavior (WAPM)? Respond yes or no and give a short argument.

Shill Oil produced 1 million barrels of gasoline using 1 million barrels of oil when the price of gasoline was $10 a barrel. When the price of gasoline was $20 a barrel, Shill produced 3 million barrels of gasoline using 4 million barrels of oil. Finally, when the price of gasoline was $40 a barrel, Shill used 10 million barrels of oil to produce 5 million barrels of gasoline.

Golf Oil (which is managed by Martin E. Lunch III) did exactly the same when the price of gasoline was $10 and $20, but when the price of gasoline hit $40, Golf produced 3.5 million barrels of gasoline using 8 million barrels of oil.

(a) Using black ink plot Shill Oil's isoprofit lines and choices for the three different periods. Label them 10, 20, and 40. Using red ink draw Golf Oil's isoprofit line and production choice. Label it with a 40 in red ink.

Million barrels of gasoline

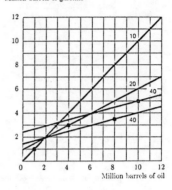

Million barrels of oil

(b) Is there any evidence that Shill Oil is not maximizing profits? Explain?

No. The Shill Oil data satisfy the Weak Axiom of Profit Maximization.

(a) If the price of the input does not change, then a decrease in the price of the output will imply that the firm will produce the same amount or less output.

Yes. If the price of the input doesn't change, we have $\Delta w = 0$, so WAPM says $\Delta p \Delta y \geq 0$.

(b) If the price of the output remains constant, then a decrease in the input price will imply that the firm will use the same amount or more of the input.

Yes. If the price of the output doesn't change, we have $\Delta p = 0$, so WAPM says $-\Delta w \Delta x \geq 0$.

(c) If both the price of the output and the input increase and the firm uses more of the input, then the firm will produce more output.

Yes. In this case the signs of the terms are: $(+)\Delta y - (+)\Delta x \geq 0$ which implies $\Delta y \geq 0$.

(d) If both the price of the output and the input increase and the firm produces less output, then the firm will use more of the input.

No, WAPM implies this can not happen. In this case the sign pattern is $(+)(-) - (+)(+) \geq 0$, which cannot happen.

Chapter 20

NAME_____

Cost Functions

20.1 (20) Nadine sells user-friendly software. Her firm's production function is: $f(x_1, x_2) = x_1 + 2x_2$, where x_1 is the amount of unskilled labor and x_2 is the amount of skilled labor that she employs.

(a) In the graph below, draw a production isoquant representing input combinations that will produce 20 units of output. Draw another isoquant representing input combinations that will produce 40 units of output.

x_2

(graph with axes x_1 from 0 to 40 and x_2 from 0 to 40, two lines labeled 40 and 20)

(b) Does this production function exhibit increasing, decreasing or constant returns to scale? __Constant.__

(c) If Nadine uses only unskilled labor, how much unskilled labor would she need in order to produce y units of output? __y.__

(d) If Nadine uses only skilled labor to produce output, how much skilled labor would she need in order to produce y units of output? __$\frac{y}{2}$.__

(c) If the firm wanted to produce 10 effronteries, how much copper would it need? __10 units__ How much zinc would it need? __5 units__

(d) If the firm faces factor prices (1,1) what is the cheapest way for it to produce 10 effronteries? __using bundle $(10, 5)$__ How much will this cost? __\$15.__

(e) If the firm faces factor prices (w_1, w_2), what is the cheapest cost to produce 10 effronteries? __$c(w_1, w_2, 10) = 10w_1 + 5w_2$.__

(f) If the firm faces factor prices (w_1, w_2), what will be the minimal cost of producing y effronteries? __$(w_1 + w_2/2)y$.__

20.3 (20) Joe Grow, an avid indoor gardener, has found that the number of happy plants, h, depends on the amount of light, l, and water, w. In fact, Joe noticed that plants require two parts light for every one part water, and any more or less will be wasted. Thus, Joe's production function is as follows: $h = \min\{l, 2w\}$.

(a) Suppose Joe is using 1 unit of light, what is the least amount of water he can use and still produce a happy plant? __$1/2$ unit of water.__

(b) Suppose Joe wants to produce 2 happy plants, what are the minimum amounts of light and water required? __$(2, 1)$__

(c) If each unit of light costs w_1 and each unit of water costs w_2, what does Joe's cost function look like as a function of w_1, w_2, and h? _____
$c(w_1, w_2, h) = w_1 h + \frac{w_2}{2}h.$

(d) What is Joe's conditional factor demand for light?
$l(w_1, w_2, h) = h.$

(e) If Nadine faces factor prices (1,1) what is the cheapest way for her to produce 20 units of output? $x_1 = $ __$x_1 = 0$,__ $x_2 = $ __$x_2 = 10$__

(f) If Nadine faces factor prices (1,3), what is the cheapest way for her to produce 20 units of output? $x_1 = $ __$x_1 = 20$,__ $x_2 = $ __$x_2 = 0$__

(g) If Nadine faces factor prices (w_1, w_2), what will be the minimal cost
$c = \min\{20w_1, 10w_2\} = 10\min\{2w_1, w_2\}.$

(h) If Nadine faces factor prices (w_1, w_2), what will be the minimal cost of producing y units of output? __$c(w_1, w_2, y) = \min\{w_1, w_2/2\}y.$__

20.2 (20) The Ontario Brassworks produces brazen effronteries. As you know brass is an alloy of copper and zinc, used in fixed proportions. The production function is given by: $f(x_1, x_2) = \min\{x_1, 2x_2\}$, where x_1 is the amount of copper it uses and x_2 is the amount of zinc that it uses in production.

(a) Illustrate a typical isoquant for this production function in the graph below.

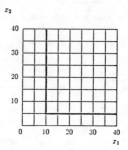

(b) Does this production function exhibit increasing, decreasing or constant returns to scale? __Constant.__

(e) What about for water? __$w(w_1, w_2, h) = h/2.$__

20.4 (20) Joe's sister, Flo Grow, is a university administrator. She uses an alternative method of gardening. Flo has found that happy plants only need fertilizer, and talk. (*Warning:* Any frivolous observations about university administrators' talk being a perfect substitute for fertilizer is regarded by the authors of this workbook as being in extremely poor taste.) Where f is the number of bags of fertilizer used and t is the number of hours she talks to her plants, the number of happy plants produced is exactly $h = t + 2f$. Suppose fertilizer costs w_1 per bag and talk costs w_2 per hour.

(a) If Flo uses no fertilizer, how many hours of talk must she devote if she wants one happy plant? __1 hour.__

(b) If she doesn't talk to her plants at all, how many bags will she need for one happy plant? __$1/2$ bag.__

(c) If $w_2 < w_1/2$, would it be cheaper for Flo to use fertilizer or talk to raise one happy plant? __It would be cheaper to talk.__

(d) Write down an expression for Flo's cost function.
$c(w_1, w_2, h) = \min\{\frac{w_1}{2}, w_2\}h.$

(e) What is Flo's conditional factor demand for talk?
$t(w_1, w_2, h) = h$ if $w_2 < w_1/2$ and 0 otherwise

(f) What is her conditional factor demand for fertilizer?
$f(w_1, w_2, h) = h/2$ if $w_2 > w_1/2$ and 0 otherwise

(If $w_2 = w_1/2$ then a variety of possibilities result).

20.5 (30) Remember T-bone Pickens, the corporate raider? Now he's concerned about his chicken farms, Pickens' Chickens. He feeds his chickens on a mixture of soybeans and corn. depending on the prices of each. According to the data submitted by his managers, when the price of soybeans was $10 a bushel and the price of corn was $10 a bushel, they used 50 bushels of corn and 150 bushels of soybeans for each coop of chickens. When the price of soybeans was $20 a bushel and the price of corn was $10 a bushel, they used 300 bushels of corn and no soybeans. When the price of corn was $20 a bushel and the price of soybeans was $10 a bushel, they used 250 bushels of soybeans and no corn. During each of these periods, the number of chickens produced was the same.

(a) Graph these three input combinations and isocost lines in the following diagram.

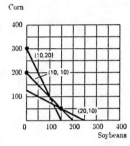

(b) How much money did Pickens' managers spend when the prices were (10, 10)? __$2,000__ When the prices were (10, 20)? __$2,500__ When the prices were (20, 10)? __$3,000.__

(c) Is there any evidence that Pickens' managers were not minimizing costs? Why or why not?

There is no evidence that they were not minimizing costs since the data satisfy the Weak Axiom of Cost Minimization.

(d) If the input costs w per unit, what is the average cost of producing y units? $AC(w, y) =$ ___yw___

20.7 (10) A university cafeteria produces square meals, using only one input and a rather remarkable production process. We are not allowed to say what that ingredient is, but an authoritative kitchen source says that "fungus is involved". The cafeteria's production function is $f(x) = x^2$. where x is the amount of input and $f(x)$ is the number of square meals produced.

(a) Does the cafeteria have increasing, constant, or decreasing returns to scale? ___increasing___

(b) How many units of input does it take to produce 100 square meals? ___10___ If the input costs w per unit, what does it cost to produce 100 square meals? ___10w___

(c) How many units of input does it take to produce y square meals? ___$\sqrt{y}$___ If the input costs w per unit, what does it cost to produce y square meals? ___$w\sqrt{y}$___

(d) If the input costs w per unit, what is the average cost of producing y square meals? $AC(w, y) =$ ___$\frac{w}{\sqrt{y}}$___

20.8 (10) A cost-minimizing firm finds that its marginal product of capital is 6 and its marginal product of labor is 2. It must be that w/r equals ___$\frac{1}{3}$.___

Calculus **20.9** (10) If the production function is given by $f(K, L) = 2\ln K + 3\ln L$ and the wage rate of labor and the rental rate of capital are both 1, then the cost minimizing ratio K/L must be ___$\frac{2}{3}$___

20.10 (20) Irma's Handicrafts produces plastic deer for lawn ornaments. "It's hard work", says Irma, "but anything to make a buck." Her production function is given by: $f(x_1, x_2) = (\min\{x_1, 2x_2\})^{1/2}$, where x_1 is the amount of plastic used, x_2 is the amount of labor used, and $f(x_1, x_2)$ is the number of deer produced.

(d) Pickens wonders whether there are any prices of corn and soybeans at which his managers will use 50 bushels of soybeans and 150 bushels of corn to produce the same number of chickens. How much would this production plan cost when the prices were $p_s = 10$ and $p_c = 10$? __$2,000__ When the prices were $p_s = 10, p_c = 20$? __$3,500__ When the prices were $p_s = 20, p_c = 10$? __$2,500.__

(e) If Pickens' managers were always minimizing costs, could 50 bushels of soybeans and 150 bushels of corn ever be a cost minimizing bundle at any prices which produced the same level of output as the other input choices? Why?

No. This bundle costs less than each observed choice at each set of prices; if it were capable of producing the same amount of output, it would have been chosen.

20.6 (10) A geneological firm called Roots produces its output using only one input. Its production function is $f(x) = \sqrt{x}$.

(a) Does the firm have increasing, constant, or decreasing returns to scale? ___Decreasing.___

(b) How many units of input does it take to produce 10 units of output? ___100 units;___ If the input costs w per unit, what does it cost to produce 10 units of output? ___100w.___

(c) How many units of input does it take to produce y units of output? ___y^2,___ If the input costs w per unit, what does it cost to produce y units of output? ___$y^2 w$___

(a) In the graph below, draw a production isoquant representing input combinations that will produce 4 deer. Draw another production isoquant representing input combinations that will produce 5 deer.

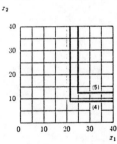

(b) Does this production function exhibit increasing, decreasing, or constant returns to scale? ___Decreasing.___

(c) If Irma faces factor prices $(1, 1)$, what is the cheapest way for her to produce 4 deer? ___Use $(16, 8)$___ How much does this cost? ___$24___

(d) At the factor prices $(1, 1)$, what is the cheapest way to produce 5 deer? ___Use $(25, 12.5)$___ How much does this cost? ___$37.50___

(e) At the factor prices $(1, 1)$, the cost of producing y deer with this technology is $c(1, 1, y) =$ ___$3y^2/2$___

(f) At the factor prices, (w_1, w_2), the cost of producing y deer with this technology is $c(w_1, w_2, y) =$ ___$(w_1 + w_2/2)y^2$___

20.11 (20) Al Deardwarf is another lawn ornament manufacturer. Al has found a way to automate the production of lawn ornaments completely. He doesn't use any labor, only wood and plastic. Al says he likes the business "because I needs the dough." Al's production function is given by: $f(x_1, x_2) = (x_1 + 2x_2)^{1/2}$, where x_1 is the amount of plastic used, x_2 is the amount of wood used, and $f(x_1, x_2)$ is the number of deer produced.

(a) In the graph below, draw a production isoquant representing input combinations that will produce 4 deer. Draw another production isoquant representing input combinations that will produce 5 deer.

(b) Does this production function exhibit increasing, decreasing, or constant returns to scale? __Decreasing returns to scale.__

(c) If Al faces factor prices $(1,1)$, what is the cheapest way for him to produce 4 deer? __(0, 8)__ How much does this cost? __$8.__

(d) At the factor prices $(1,1)$, what is the cheapest way to produce 6 deer? __(0, 18),__ How much does this cost? __$18__

(e) At the factor prices $(1,1)$, the cost of producing y deer with this technology is $c(1,1,y) =$ __$y^2/2$__

(f) At the factor prices, $(1,3)$, the cost of producing y deer with this technology is $c(1,3,y) =$ __y^2__

20.12 (10) Suppose that Al Deardwarf from the last problem can not vary the amount of wood that he uses in the short run and is stuck with using 20 units of wood. Suppose also that he can change the amount of plastic that he uses even in the short run.

(a) If the cost of plastic is $1 per unit and the cost of wood is $1 per unit, how much would it cost Al to make 100 deer? __$9,980__

(b) Write down Al's short run cost function at these factor prices. __$c(1,1,y) = y^2 - 20.$__

Chapter 21
Cost Curves

21.1 (20) Mr. Otto Carr, owner of Otto's Autos, sells cars. Otto buys autos for $c each and has no other costs.

(a) What is his total cost if he sells 5 cars?_____ $5c$ _____What if he sells 10 cars?_____ $10c$ _____Write down the equation for Otto's total costs assuming he sells y cars: $TC(y) = $ _____ $TC(y) = cy.$

_____

(b) What is Otto's average cost function? $AC(y) = $ _____ $AC(y) = c$ _____For every additional auto Otto sells his costs increase by? _____ c _____Write down Otto's marginal cost function _____ $MC(y) = c.$

_____

(c) In the graph below draw Otto's average and marginal cost curves if $c = 20$.

AC, MC

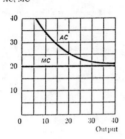

(b) The first method has an average cost function _____ $AC_1(y) = 1 + 200/y,$ _____and a marginal cost function _____ $MC_1(y) = 1.$ _____. For the second method these costs are _____ $AC_2(y) = 5 + 10/y,$ _____and _____ $MC_2(y) = 5.$

_____

(c) If Rex wrecks 40 cars per year, which method should he use? _____ Method 2 _____If Rex wrecks 50 cars per year, which method should he use? _____ Method 1 _____What is the smallest number of cars per year for which it would pay him to buy the hydraulic smasher?_____ 48 cars per year. _____

21.4 (20) Mary Magnolia wants to open a flower shop, the Petal Pusher, in a new mall. She has her choice of three different floor sizes, 200 square feet, 500 square feet, or 1,000 square feet. The monthly rent will be $1 a square foot. Mary estimates that if she has F square feet of floor space and sells y bouquets a month, her variable costs will be $c_v(y) = y^2/F$ per month.

(a) If she has 200 square feet of floor space, write down her marginal cost function: _____ $MC = \frac{y}{100},$ _____and her average cost function: _____ $AC = \frac{200}{y} + \frac{y}{200}.$ _____At what amount of output is average cost minimized?_____ $y = 200$ _____At this level of output, how much is average cost?_____ $AC = 2.$

(b) If she has 500 square feet, write down her marginal cost function: _____ $MC = y/250,$ _____and her average cost function: _____ $AC = (500/y) + y/500.$ _____. At what amount of output is average cost minimized?_____ 500 _____At this level of output, how much is average cost?_____ 2.

(d) Suppose Otto has to pay $b a year to produce obnoxious television commercials. Otto's total cost curve is now: $TC(y) = $ _____ $TC(y) = cy + b,$ _____, his average cost curve is now: $AC(y) = $ _____ $AC(y) = c + b/y,$ _____, and his marginal cost curve is: $MC(y) = $ _____ $MC(y) = c.$

(e) If $b = $ 100, use red ink to draw Otto's average cost curve on the graph above.

21.2 (10) Otto's brother, Dent Carr, is in the auto repair business. Dent recently had little else to do, and decided to calculate his cost conditions. He found that the total cost of repairing s cars is $TC(s) = 2s^2 + 10$. But Dent's attention was diverted to other things ... and that's where you come in. Please complete the following:

Dent's Total Variable Costs: _____ $2s^2$ _____

Total Fixed Costs: _____ 10 _____

Average Variable Costs: _____ $2s$ _____

Average Fixed Costs: _____ $10/s$ _____

Average Total Costs: _____ $2s + 10/s$ _____

Marginal Costs: _____ $4s.$

21.3 (20) A third brother, Rex Carr, owns a junk yard. Rex can use one of two methods to destroy cars. The first involves purchasing a hydraulic car smasher which costs $200 a year to own and then spending $1 for every car smashed into oblivion; the second method involves purchasing a shovel that will last one year and costs $10 and paying the last Carr brother, Scoop, to bury the cars at a cost of $5 each.

(a) Write down the total cost functions for the two methods where y is output per year: $TC_1(y) = $ _____ $TC_1(y) = y + 200$ _____, $TC_2(y) = $ _____ $TC_2(y) = 5y + 10$

_____

(c) If she has 1,000 square feet of floor space, write down her marginal cost function: _____ $MC = y/500,$ _____and her average cost function: _____ $AC = (1,000/y) + y/1,000.$ _____At what amount of output is average cost minimized?_____ 1,000 _____At this level of output, how much is average cost?_____ 2

(d) Use red ink to show Mary's average cost curve and her marginal cost curves if she has 200 square feet. Use blue ink to show her average cost curve and her marginal cost curve if she has 500 square feet. Use black ink to show her average cost curve and her marginal cost curve if she has 1,000 square feet. Label the average cost curves AC and the marginal cost curves MC.

Dollars

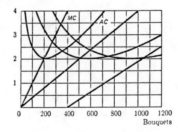

(e) Use yellow marker to show Mary's long run average cost curve and her long run marginal cost curve in your graph. Label them LRAC and LRMC.

Calculus **21.5** (20) Touchie MacFeelie publishes comic books. The only inputs he needs are old jokes and cartoonists. His production function is

$$Q = .1J^{\frac{1}{2}}L^{\frac{3}{4}}$$

where J is the number of old jokes used, L the number of hours of cartoonists' labor used as inputs, and Q is the number of comic books produced.

(a) Does this production process exhibit increasing. decreasing. or constant returns to scale? __increasing__ Explain your answer.

since $f(tJ, tL) = t^{5/4} f(J, L) > t f(J, L)$.

(b) If the number of old jokes used is 100. write an expression for the marginal product of cartoonists' labor as a function of L. $MP = \frac{3}{4L^{1/4}}$

_____ Is the marginal product of labor decreasing or increasing as the amount of labor increases? __decreasing.__

Calculus 21.6 (20) Touchie MacFeelie's irascible business manager. Gander Mac-Grope. announces that old jokes can be purchased for $1 each and that the wage rate of cartoonists' labor is $2.

(a) Suppose that in the short run, Touchie is stuck with exactly 100 old jokes (for which he paid $1 each) but is able to hire as much labor as he wishes. How much labor would he have to hire in order produce Q comic books? $Q^{4/3}$.

(b) Write down Touchie's short run total cost as a function of his output

$2Q^{4/3} + 100$.

(c) His short run marginal cost function is $\frac{8}{3} Q^{1/3}$

(d) His short run average cost function is $2Q^{1/3} + 100/Q$.

Calculus 21.7 (40) Touchie asks his brother. Sir Francis MacFeelie. to study the long run picture. Sir Francis. who has carefully studied the appendix to Chapter 20 in your text. prepared the following report.

(a) If all inputs are variable. and if old jokes cost $1 each and cartoonist labor costs $2 per hour. the cheapest way to produce exactly one comic

$10^{\frac{4}{5}} \left(\frac{4}{3}\right)^{\frac{3}{5}} \approx 7.4$ jokes and $10^{\frac{4}{5}} \left(\frac{3}{4}\right)^{\frac{2}{5}} \approx 5.6$ hours of labor.

(b) This would cost $3 \times 10^{\frac{4}{5}} \left(\frac{4}{3}\right)^{\frac{3}{5}} \approx 18.7$ dollars.

(c) Given our production function. the cheapest proportions in which to use jokes and labor are the same no matter how many comic books we print. But when we double the amount of both inputs. the number of comic books produced is multiplied by $2^{5/4}$

Calculus 21.8 If the cost function of a firm is $c(y) = 4y^2 + 16$. then the output level that minimizes average cost is $y^* = 2$

(a) For the above cost function. average variable cost is minimized when output is equal to $y^* = 0$

Calculus 21.9 Consider the cost function $c(y) = y^2 + 4$.

(a) The average cost function is $AC = y + \frac{4}{y}$

(b) The marginal cost function is $MC = 2y$.

(c) The level of output that yields the minimum average cost of production is $y = 2$.

(d) The average variable cost function is $AVC = y$.

(e) At what level of output does average variable cost equal marginal cost? At $y = 0$.

21.10 (10) A competitive firm has a production function of the form: $Y = 2L + 5K$. If $w = \$2$ and $r = \$3$. what will be the minimum cost of producing 10 units of output? $6.

Chapter 22

Firm Supply

22.1 (5) A profit maximizing perfectly competitive firm will always operate where market price is equal to __Marginal cost__ Furthermore, it must be true that at the given output level marginal cost is (rising, falling) __rising__ and that the price is (greater than. less than)_____ __greater than__ the firm's average variable costs.

Calculus **22.2** (20) A competitive firm has the following short run cost function: $c(y) = y^3 - 8y^2 + 30y + 5$. The firm will operate in the short run if and only if the price is greater than or equal to __$14.__

22.3 (20) Remember Otto's brother. Dent Carr, who is in the auto repair business? Dent found that the total cost of repairing s cars is $c(s) = 2s^2 + 100$.

(a) This implies that Dent's average cost is equal to __$2s + 100/s$,__ _____average variable cost is equal to __$2s$,__ and his marginal cost is equal to __$4s$.__ On the graph below plot the above curves, and also plot Dent's supply curve.

$

(b) If the only way that Mr. McGregor can vary his output is by varying the amount of fertilizer applied to his cabbage patch, write an expression for his marginal cost curve. __$MC = y/50$__

(c) If the price of a cabbage is $2 per cabbage, how many cabbages will Mr. McGregor produce? __$y = 100$__ How many sacks of fertilizer will he buy? __100__

(d) The price of fertilizer and of cabbages remain as before, but Mr. McGregor learns that he could find summer jobs for Flopsy and Peter in a local sweatshop. Flopsy and Peter would together earn $300 for the __$c(y) = 300 + (y/10)^2$__

(e) Should he continue to grow cabbages or should he put Flopsy and Peter to work in the sweatshop? __Sweatshop.__ How high would the total __Suppose he requires Flopsy and Peter to work for him. The he wants to maximize profits $= py - (y/10)^2$. This yields a demand function of $y = 5p$, and with $p = 2$, McGregor would supply 10 cabbages. He would then have a profit of $19 = 2 \times 10 - 1$. Thus if Flopsy and Peter can earn more that $19 elsewhere, it would be unprofitable to run the cabbage patch.__

22.6 (30) Severin. the herbalist, is famous for his hepatica. His total cost function is $c(y) = y^2 + 10$ for $y > 0$ and $c(0) = 0$. (That is, his cost of producing zero units of output is zero.)

(a) What is his marginal cost function? __$2y$__ What is his average cost function? __$y + 10/y$.__

(b) At what quantity is his marginal cost equal to his average cost?_____ __$\sqrt{10}$__ At what quantity is his average cost minimized? __$\sqrt{10}$__

(c) In a competitive market, what is the lowest price at which he will supply a positive quantity? __$2\sqrt{10}$__ How much would he supply at that price? __$\sqrt{10}$__

(b) If the market price is $20. how many cars will Dent be willing to repair? __5__ If the market price is $40. how many cars will Dent repair? __10.__

(c) Suppose the market price is $40 and Dent maximizes his profits. On the above graph. shade in and label the following areas: total costs, total revenue. and total profits.

22.4 (20) Suppose that a firm produces with a constant returns to scale technology, and that the minimum cost of producing one unit of output is $\bar{c}$ dollars.

(a) What is the minimum cost of producing y units of output? __$y\bar{c}$__ _____If this firm operates in a competitive market and the market price is greater than $\bar{c}$. how many units of output will the firm be willing to produce? __infinite__ What if the market price is less than $\bar{c}$? __0__ What if the market price is equal to $\bar{c}$? __any number__

(b) If a large number of the above firms operate in a given market, what do you think the equilibrium market price will be? __price would be $\bar{c}$.__ Can you tell how much each of the firms will produce in equilibrium? __output produced can not be determined.__

Calculus **22.5** (20) Mr. McGregor owns a 5-acre cabbage patch. He forces his wife, Flopsy, and his son, Peter, to work in the cabbage patch without wages. Assume for the time being that the land can be used for nothing other than cabbages and that Flopsy and Peter can find no alternative employment. The only input that Mr. McGregor pays for is fertilizer. If he uses x sacks of fertilizer, the amount of cabbages that he gets is $10\sqrt{x}$. Fertilizer costs $1 per sack.

(a) What is the total cost of the fertilizer needed to produce 100 cabbages? __$100__ What is the total cost of the amount of fertilizer needed to produce y cabbages? __$y^2/100$__

22.7 (30) Stanley Ford makes mountains out of molehills. He can do this with almost no effort, so for the purposes of this problem, let us assume that molehills are the only input used in the production of mountains. Suppose mountains are produced at constant returns to scale and that it takes 100 molehills to make 1 mountain. The current market price of molehills is $20 each. A few years ago, Stan bought an "option" that permits him to buy up to 2,000 molehills at $10 each. His option contract explicitly says that he can buy fewer than 2,000 molehills if he wishes, but he can not resell the molehills that he buys under this contract. In order to get governmental permission to produce mountains from molehills, Stanley would have to pay $10,000 for a molehill-masher's license.

(a) The marginal cost of producing a mountain for Stanley is __$1,000__ if he produces fewer than 20 mountains. The marginal cost of producing a mountain is __$2,000__ if he produces more than 20 mountains.

(b) On the graph below, show Stanley Ford's marginal cost curve (in blue ink) and his average cost curve (in red ink).

$

(c) If the price of mountains is $1,600. how many mountains will Stanley produce? __20 mountains.__

(d) The government is considering raising the price of a molehill masher's license to $11,000. Stanley claims that if it does so he will have to go out of business. Is Stanley telling the truth? __No.__ What

They maximum they could charge is the
amount of his profits excluding the license fee, $12,000.

(e) Stanley's lawyer. Eliot Sleaze, has discovered a clause in Stanley's option contract that allows him to resell the molehills that he purchased under the option contract at the market price. On the graph above.

He will sell all of his molehills and produce zero
mountains.

22.8 (30) Lady Wellesleigh makes silk purses out of sows ears. She is the only person in the world who knows how to do so. It takes one sow's ear and 1 hour of her labor to make a silk purse. She can buy as many sows ears as she likes for $1 each. Lady Wellesleigh has no other source of income than her labor. Her utility function is a Cobb-Douglas function $U(c,r) = c^{1/3}r^{2/3}$, where c is the amount of money per day that she has to spend on consumption goods and r is the amount of leisure that she has. Lady Wellesleigh has 24 hours a day that she can devote either to leisure or to working.

(a) Lady Wellesleigh can either make silk purses or she can earn $5 an hour as a seamstress in a sweat shop. If she worked in the sweat shop, how

many hours would she work?____8____(Hint: To solve for this amount, write down Lady Wellesleigh's budget constraint and recall how to find the demand function for someone with a Cobb-Douglas utility function.)

(b) If she could earn a wage of $w an hour as a seamstress. how much would she work?____$24 - 80/w$.____

(c) If the price of silk purses is $p. how much money will Lady Wellesleigh earn per purse after she pays for the sows' ears that she uses as inputs.

$p - 1$.

(d) If she can earn $5 an hour as a seamstress. what is the lowest price at which she will make any silk purses? ____$6.____

(e) What is the supply function for silk purses? $S(p) = 24 - \frac{80}{p-1}$.

_____(Hint: The price of silk purses determines the "wage rate" that Lady W. can earn by making silk purses. This determines the number of hours she will choose to work and hence the supply of silk purses.)

Chapter 23
Industry Supply

NAME_____

23.1 (30) Al Deardwarf's cousin. Zwerg. makes plaster garden gnomes. The technology in the garden gnome business is as follows. You need a gnome mold. plaster and labor. A gnome mold is a piece of equipment that costs $1000 and will last exactly one year. After a year. a gnome mold is completely worn out and has no scrap value. With a gnome mold. you can make 500 gnomes per year. For every gnome that you make. you also have to use a total of $7 worth of plaster and labor. In the short run. you can change your employment of plaster and labor as you wish. If you want to produce only 100 gnomes a year with a gnome mold. you spend only $700 a year on plaster and labor. and so on. The number of gnome molds in the industry can not be changed in the short run. To get a newly built one. you have to special-order it from the mold-making factory. The gnome-mold making factory only takes orders on January 1 of any given year. and it takes one whole year from the time a gnome mold is ordered until it is delivered on the next January 1. When a gnome mold is installed in your plant, it is stuck there. To move it would destroy it. Gnome molds are useless for anything other than making garden gnomes.

For many years, the demand function facing the garden gnome industry has been $D(p) = 60,000 - 5,000p$, where $D(p)$ is the total number of garden gnomes sold per year and p is the price. Prices of inputs have been constant for many years and the technology has not changed. Nobody expects any changes in the future and the industry is in long run equilibrium. The interest rate is 10%. When you buy a new gnome mold. you have to pay for it when it is delivered. For simplicity of calculations. we will assume that all of the gnomes that you build during the one year life of the gnome mold are sold at Christmas and that the employees and plaster suppliers are paid only at Christmas for the work they have done during the past year. Also for simplicity of calculations. let us approximate the date of Christmas by December 31.

(a) If you invested $1.000 in the bank on January 1. how much money could you expect to get out of the bank one year later? **$1,100**

_____If you received delivery on a gnome making mold on January 1 and paid for it at that time. how much return net of variable costs would you have to have during the year to make it worthwhile to buy the machine? **$100** Remember that the machine will be worn out and worthless at the end of the year.

NAME _____ **195**

invention of a new kind of plaster was announced. This new plaster made it possible to produce garden gnomes using the same molds. but it reduced the cost of the plaster and labor needed to produce a gnome from $7 to $5 per gnome. Assume that consumers' demand function for gnomes in 1988 was not changed by this news. The announcement came early enough in the day for everybody to change his order for gnome molds to be delivered on January 1. 1989. but of course, the number of molds available to be used in 1988 is already determined from orders made one year ago. The manufacturer of garden gnome molds contracted to sell them for $1000 a year ago, so he can't change the price he charges on delivery.

(a) In 1988, what will be the equilibrium total output of garden gnomes? _____ **14,000** What will be the equilibrium price of garden gnomes? **$9.20** What rate of return will Deardwarf's cousin, Zwerg. make on his investment in a garden gnome that he ordered a year ago and for which he paid $1.000. **110%**

(b) Zwerg's neighbor, Munchkin, also makes garden gnomes and he has a gnome mold which is to be delivered on January 1. 1988. Zwerg, who is looking for a way to invest some more money, is considering buying Munchkin's new mold from Munchkin and installing it in his own plant. If the best rate of return that Zwerg can make on alternative investments of additional funds is 10%, how much should he be willing to pay for Munchkin's new mold? **$1,909**

(c) What do you think will happen to the number of garden gnomes ordered for delivery on January 1, 1989? Will it be larger, smaller, or the same as the number ordered the previous year? **larger**

_____After the passage of sufficient time, the industry will reach a new long run equilibrium. What will be the new equilibrium price of gnomes? **$7.20.**

23.3 (30) On January 1. 1988, there were no changes in technology or demand functions from that in our original description of the industry. but the government astonished the garden gnome industry by introducing a tax on the production of garden gnomes. For every garden gnome produced. the manufacturer must pay a $1 tax. The announcement came early enough in the day so that there was time for gnome producers to change their orders of gnome molds for 1989. Of course the gnome molds to be used in 1988 had been already ordered a year ago. Gnome makers had signed contracts promising to pay $1.000 for each gnome that they ordered and they couldn't back out of these promises.

INDUSTRY SUPPLY (Ch. 23)

(b) Suppose that you have exactly one newly installed gnome mold in your plant, what is your short run marginal cost of production if you produce up to 500 gnomes? **$7** What is your average variable cost for producing up to 500 gnomes? **$7** What is the cost in the short run of producing more than 500 gnomes? **not possible**

(c) If you have exactly one newly installed gnome mold. you would produce 500 gnomes if the price of gnomes is above **$7** dollars. You would produce no gnomes if the price of gnomes is below **$7** dollars. You would be indifferent between producing any number of gnomes between 0 and 500 if the price of gnomes is **$7** dollars.

(d) If you could sell as many gnomes as you liked for $10 each and none at a higher price, what rate of return would you make on your $1000 by investing in a gnome making machine? **50%** Is this higher than the return from putting your money in the bank? **yes** What is the lowest price for gnomes at which investing in a gnome mold gives the same rate of return as you get from the bank? **$9.20** Could the long run equilibrium price be lower than this? **no**

(e) At the price you found in the last section, how many gnomes would be demanded each year? **14,000** How many molds would be purchased each year? **28** Is this a long run equilibrium price? **yes**

23.2 (20) We continue our study of the garden gnome industry. Suppose that initially everything was as described in the previous problem. To the complete surprise of everyone in the industry. on January 1. 1988. the

INDUSTRY SUPPLY (Ch. 23)

(a) Recalling from previous problems the number of gnome molds ordered for delivery on January 1. 1988. we see that if gnome makers produce up to capacity in 1988, they will produce **14,000** gnomes. Given the demand function, we see that the market price would then have to be **$9.20**

(b) If you have a garden gnome mold, the marginal cost of producing a garden gnome, including the tax, is **$8.00** Therefore all gnome molds (would) (would not) be used up to capacity in 1988. **would**

(c) In 1988, what will be the total output of garden gnomes? **14,000** What will be the price of garden gnomes? **$9.20** What rate of return will Deardwarf's cousin Zwerg make on his investment in a garden gnome that he ordered a year ago and paid $1,000 for at that time? **−40%**

(d) Remember that Zwerg's neighbor, Munchkin, also has a gnome mold which is to be delivered on January 1, 1958. Knowing about the tax makes Munchkin's mold a less attractive investment than it was without the tax, but still Zwerg would buy it if he can get it cheap enough so that he makes a 10% rate of return on his investment. How much should he be willing to pay for Munchkin's new mold? **$546**

(e) What do you think will happen to the number of garden gnomes ordered for delivery on January 1, 1989? Will it be larger, smaller, or the same as the number ordered the previous year? **Smaller.**

(f) The tax on garden gnomes was left in place for many years and nobody expected any further changes in the tax or in demand or supply conditions. After the passage of sufficient time, the industry reached a new long run equilibrium. What was the new equilibrium price of gnomes? **$10.20**

(g) In the short run, who wound up paying the tax on garden gnomes, the producers or the consumers? **producers** In the long run, did the price of gnomes go up by more, less, or the same amount as the tax per gnome? **same amount**

(h) Suppose that early in the morning of January 1. 1988, the government had announced that there would be a $1 tax on garden gnomes. but that the tax would not go into effect until January 1. 1989. Would the producers of garden gnomes necessarily be worse off than if there were no tax? Why or why not?

No. The producers would anticipate the tax

increase and restrict supply, thereby raising prices.

(i) Is it reasonable to suppose that the government could introduce "surprise" taxes without making firms suspicious that there will be similar "surprises" in the future? Suppose that the introduction of the tax in January, 1988, makes gnome makers suspicious that there will be more taxes introduced in later years. Would this affect equilibrium prices and supplies? How?

No, because the producers could adjust supply

and pass on the taxes to consumers.

23.4 (40) Consider a competitive industry with a large number of firms, all of which have identical cost functions $c(y) = y^2 + 1$ for $y > 0$ and $c(0) = 0$. Suppose that initially the demand curve for this industry is given by $D(p) = 52 - p$. (The output of a firm does not have to be an integer number, but the number of firms does have to be an integer.)

(a) What is the supply curve of an individual firm? $S(p) =$ _____

$S(p) = p/2$ If there are n firms in the industry, what will be the industry supply curve? $Y = np/2$

(b) What is the smallest price at which the product can be sold? _____

$p^* = 2$

demand function for taxi rides be given by $D(p) = 1.100 - 20p$. where demand is measured in rides per day. and price is measured in dollars. Assume that the industry is perfectly competitive.

(a) What is the competitive equilibrium price per ride? 5

_____(Hint: In competitive equilibrium. price must equal marginal cost.) What is the equilibrium number of rides per day? _____

1,000 How many taxi cabs will there be in equilibrium? 50

(b) In 1990 the city council of Ham Harbor created a taxicab licensing board and issued a fixed number of licenses to each of the existing cabs. The board stated that it would continue to adjust the taxi cab fares so that the demand for rides equals the supply of rides, but that they will issue no new licenses in the future. In 1995 costs had not changed. but the demand curve for taxi cab rides had become $D(p) = 1.120 - 20p$. What was the equilibrium price of a ride in 1995? $6

(c) What was the profit per ride in 1995, neglecting any costs associated with acquiring a taxicab license? $1 What was the profit per taxicab license per day? 20 If the taxi operated every day, what was the profit per taxicab license per year? $7,300

(d) If the interest rate was 10% and costs, demand, and the number of licenses were expected to remain constant forever, what would be the market price of a taxicab license? $73,000

(e) Suppose that the commission decided in 1995 to issue enough new licenses to reduce the taxicab price per ride to $5. How many licenses would this take? 1

(f) Assuming that demand in Ham Harbor is not going to grow any more.

how much would a taxicab license be worth at this new fare? _____

Nothing.

(c) What will be the equilibrium number of firms in the industry? (Hint: Guess at $p^* = 2$. This gives $D(p) = 52 - 2 = n2/2$, which says $n^* = 50$

(d) What will be the equilibrium price? $p^* = 2$ What will be the equilibrium output of each firm? $y^* = 1$

(e) What will be the equilibrium output of the industry? $Y^* = 50$

(f) Now suppose that the demand curve shifts to $D(p) = 52.5 - p$. What Suppose that a new firm did enter in. Then there would be 51 firms, so that the demand equals supply equation would be: $52.5 - p = 51p/2$. Solving gives $p^* = 105/53$. This is less than 2, so the industry cannot support a new firm. The equilibrium number of firms is still $n^* = 50$.

(g) What will be the equilibrium price? _____ Solve $52.5 - p = 50p/2$ to get $p^* = 2.02$ What will be the equilibrium output of each firm? $y^* = 1.01$. What will be the equilibrium profits of each firm? Around .02.

(h) Now suppose that the demand curve shifts to $D(p) = 53 - p$. What will be the equilibrium number of firms? $n = 51$ What will be the equilibrium price? $p = 2$

(i) What will be the equilibrium output of each firm? $y = 1$ What will be the equilibrium profits of each firm? zero

23.5 (30) In 1990, the town of Ham Harbor had a more-or-less free market in taxi services. Any respectable firm could provide taxi service as long as the drivers and cabs satisfied certain safety standards.

Let us suppose that the constant marginal cost per trip of a taxi ride is $5, and that the average taxi has a capacity of 20 trips per day. Let the

(g) How much money would each current taxicab owners be willing to pay to prevent any new licenses from being issued? $73,000 each

What is the total amount that all taxicab owners together would be willing to pay to prevent any new licences from ever being issued? $3,650,000 The total amount that consumers of taxi rides would be willing to pay to have another taxicab license issued would be (more than), (less than), (the same as) this amount. more than

23.6 (20) In this problem, we will determine the equilibrium pattern of agricultural land use surrounding a city. Think of the city as being located in the middle of a large featureless plain. The price of wheat at the market at the center of town is $10 a bushel. and it only costs $5 a bushel to grow wheat. However, it costs 10 cents a mile to transport a bushel of wheat to the center of town.

(a) If a farm is located t miles from the center of town, write down a formula for its profit per bushel of wheat transported to market. _____ profit per bushel $= 5 - .10t$

(b) Suppose you can grow 1.000 bushels on an acre of land. How much will an acre of land located t miles from the market rent for? _____ rent $= 5000 - 100t$

(c) How far away from the market do you have to be for land to be worth zero? 50 miles

23.7 (10) Consider an industry with three firms. Suppose the firms have the following supply functions: $S_1(p) = p$, $S_2(p) = p - 2$. and $S_3(p) = 2p$ respectively. On the graph below plot each of the three supply curves. and the resulting industry supply curve.

Price

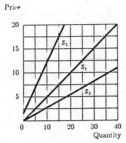

(a) If the market demand curve has the form, $D(p) = 10$. What is the resulting market price? **3** Output? **10**

_____ What is the output level for firm 1 at this price? **3**

_____ Firm 2? **1** Firm 3? **6.**

_____

23.8 (20) Suppose all firms in a given industry have the same supply curve given by $S_i(p) = p/2$. Plot and label the four industry supply curves generated by these firms if there are 1. 2. 3. or 4 firms operating in the industry.

Price

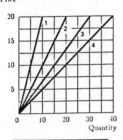

_____

(a) If all of the firms had a cost structure such that if the price was below \$3 they would be losing money, what would be the equilibrium price and output in the industry if the market demand was equal to $D(p) = 3.5$?

Answer: price = **\$3.50** , quantity = **3.5.**

How many firms would exist in such a market? **2.**

(b) What if the identical conditions as above hold except that the market demand was equal to $D(p) = 8 - p$. Now, what would be the equilibrium price and output? **\$3.20; 4.8**

_____ How many firms would operate in such a market? **3.**

_____

23.9 (30) A number of identical firms operate in a competitive industry. Each firm has a U-shaped average cost curve.

(a) On the diagram below draw a representative firm's average and marginal cost curves using blue ink, and indicate the long run equilibrium level of the market price.

Price

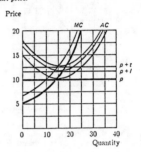

(b) Suppose the government imposes a tax, t, on every unit of output sold by the industry. Use red ink to draw the new conditions on the above graph. After the industry has adjusted to the imposition of the tax, the competitive model would predict the following: the market price would

(increase/decrease) by amount **Increase by t;** there would be (fewer) firms operating in the industry, and the output level for each firm operating in the industry would (**stay the same**).

(c) What if the government imposes a tax. l. on every *firm* in the industry. Draw the new cost conditions on the above graph using black ink. After the industry has adjusted to the imposition of the tax the competitive model would predict the following: the market price would (increase/), there would be (fewer) firms operating in the industry, and the output level for each firm operating in the industry would (increase).

23.10 (10) In many communities. a restaurant that sells alcoholic beverages is required to have a license. Suppose that the number of licenses is limited and that they may be easily transferred to other restaurant owners. Suppose that the conditions of this industry closely approximate perfect competition. If a restaurant's revenue is \$100,000 a year, and if a liquor license can be leased for a year for \$85,000 from an existing restaurant, what is the average total cost in the industry? **\$15,000.**

_____

23.11 (10) Consider a competitive market involving firms with identical U-shaped average cost curves that is in long run equilibrium. Suppose that the government imposes a lump sum tax on every firm in this industry. A firm can avoid this tax only if it stops production altogether.

(a) How will this tax affect the number of firms in the industry? _____
The number of firms will decrease.

(b) What will happen to the equilibrium price of the good? _____
The equilibrium price will increase.

(c) When long run equilibrium is re-established, how will each firm's output compare with the initial equilibrium output? _____
The equilibrium output of each firm remaining in the industry will increase.

Chapter 24

Market

24.1 (20) The Miss Manners Refinery in Dry Rock. Oklahoma. converts crude oil into gasoline. It takes 1 barrel of crude oil to produce 1 barrel of gasoline. In addition to the cost of oil there are some other costs involved in refining gasoline. Total costs of producing y barrels of gasoline are described by the cost function $c(y) = y^2/2 + p_o y$. where p_o is the price of a barrel of crude oil.

(a) Express the marginal cost of producing gasoline as a function of p_o and y. $\quad y + p_o$

(b) Suppose that the refinery can buy 50 barrels of crude oil for $5 a barrel. but must pay $15 a barrel for any more that it buys beyond 50 barrels. The marginal cost curve for gasoline will be $\quad y + 5 \quad$ up to 50 barrels of gasoline and $\quad y + 15 \quad$ thereafter.

(c) Plot Miss Manners' supply curve in the diagram below using blue ink.

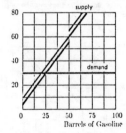

Price of Gasoline

(d) Suppose that Miss Manners faces a horizontal demand curve for gasoline at a price of $30 per barrel. Plot this demand curve on the graph above using red ink. How much gasoline will she supply? $\quad$ 25 barrels.

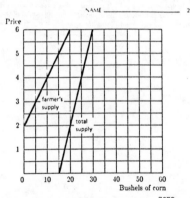

(e) If $p = \$2$, how many bushels of corn will he produce? zero output How many bushels will he get from the government stockpiles? the maximum PIK payment of 20 bushels.

(f) If $p = \$5$, how much corn will he supply? 15 bushels How many bushels of corn will he get from the government stockpiles, assuming he chooses to be in the PIK program? a PIK payment of 12.50.

(g) At any price between $p = \$2$ and $p = \$5$, write a formula for the size of the PIK payment. His supply curve is $S(p) = 5p - 10$, and his payment is $(40 - y)/2$. Thus the number of bushels he will supply in total is $25 - 2.5p$.

(h) How much corn will he supply to the market, counting both production and PIK payment, as a function of the market price p? Sum the supply curve and the PIK payment to get $TS(p) = 2.5p + 15$.

(e) If Miss Manners could no longer get the first 50 barrels of crude for $5, but had to pay $15 a barrel for all crude oil, how would her output change? It would decrease by 10 barrels to 15 barrels.

(f) Now suppose that an entitlement program is introduced that permits refineries to buy one barrel of oil at $5 for each barrel of oil that they buy for $15. What will Miss Manners' supply curve be now? $\quad S(p) = p - 10 \quad$ (Assume that it can buy fractions of a barrel in the same manner.) Plot this supply curve on the graph above using black ink. If the demand curve is horizontal at $30 a barrel, how much gasoline will Miss Manners supply now? 20 barrels.

24.2 (40) Suppose that a farmer's cost of growing y bushels of corn is given by the cost function $c(y) = y^2/20 + y$.

(a) If the price of corn is $5 a bushel, how much corn will this farmer grow? 40 bushels.

(b) What is the farmer's supply curve of corn as a function of the price of corn? $y = 10p - 10$.

(c) The government now introduces a Payment in Kind (PIK) program. If the farmer decides to grow y bushels of corn, he will get $(40 - y)/2$ bushels from the government stockpiles. Write an expression for the farmer's profits as a function of his output and the market price of corn, taking into account the value of payments in kind received. $py - c(y) + p(40 - y)/2 = py - y^2/20 - y + p(40 - y)/2$.

(d) At the market price p, what will be the farmer's profit maximizing output of corn? $S(p) = 5p - 10$ Plot a supply curve for corn in the graph below.

(i) Use red ink to illustrate the total supply curve of corn (including the corn from the PIK payment) in your graph above.

24.3 (40) In order to protect the wild populations of cockatoos. the Australian authorities have outlawed the export of these large parrots. An illegal market in cockatoos has developed. The cost of capturing an Australian cockatoo and shipping him to the U.S. is about $40 per bird. Smuggled parrots are drugged and shipped in suitcases. This is extremely traumatic for the birds and about 50% of the cockatoos shipped die in transit. Each smuggled cockatoo has a 10% chance of being discovered, in which case the bird is confiscated and a fine of $500 is charged. Confiscated cockatoos that are alive are returned to the wild. Confiscated cockatoos that are found dead are donated to university cafeterias.*

(a) When the market price of smuggled parrots is p. what is the expected return to a parrot-smuggler from shipping a parrot? $.45p - 90$

_____The supply schedule for smuggled parrots will be a horizontal line at the market price. $200 (Hint: At what price does a parrot-smuggler just break even?)

(b) The demand function for smuggled cockatoos in the U.S. is $D(p) = 7200 - 20p$ per year. How many smuggled cockatoos will be sold in the U.S. per year at the equilibrium price? 3,200 How many cockatoos must be caught in Australia in order that this number of live birds reaches U.S. buyers? 3200/.45 = 7111

(c) Suppose that the trade in cockatoos is legalized. Suppose that it costs about $40 to capture and ship a cockatoo to the U.S. in a comfortable cage and that the number of deaths in transit by this method is negligible. What would be the equilibrium price of cockatoos in the U.S.? $40 _____How many cockatoos would be sold in the U.S.? 6,400 _____How many cockatoos would have to be caught in Australia for the U.S. market? 6,400

---

* The story behind this problem is based on actual fact. but the numbers we use are just made up for illustration. It would be very interesting to have some good estimates of the actual demand functions and cost functions.

(d) Suppose that the instead of returning confiscated cockatoos to the wild, the customs authorities sold them in the U. S. market. The profits from smuggling a cockatoo do not change from this policy change. Since the supply curve is horizontal, it must be that the equilibrium price of smuggled cockatoos will have to be the same as the equilibrium price when the confiscated cockatoos were returned to nature. How many live cockatoos will be sold in the United States in equilibrium? __3,200__

_____ How many cockatoos will be permanently removed from the Australian wild? __3,520__

(e) In the equilibrium with smuggling, how many cockatoos are confiscated alive? (Assume that any cockatoos that are going to die in transit are already dead by the time the authorities find them.) __1,600__

24.4 (10) The horn of the rhinoceros is prized in Japan and China for its alleged aphrodisiac properties. This has proved to be most unfortunate for the rhinoceroses of East Africa. Although it is illegal to kill rhinoceroses in the game parks of Kenya, the rhinoceros population of these parks has been almost totally depleted by poachers. The price of rhinoceros horns in recent years has risen so high that a poacher can earn half a year's wages by simply killing one rhinoceros. Such high rewards for poaching have made laws against poaching almost impossible to enforce in East Africa. There are also large game parks with rhinoceros populations in South Africa. Since South Africa is much more of a police state than Kenya, game wardens have been able to prevent poaching almost completely. Therefore the rhinoceros population of South Africa has prospered. In a recent program from the television series *Nova*, a South African game warden explained that some rhinoceroses even have to be "harvested" in order to prevent overpopulation of rhinoceroses. "What then," asked the interviewer, "do you do with the horns from the animals that are harvested or that die of natural causes?" The South African game warden proudly explained that since international trade in rhinoceros horns was illegal, South Africa did not contribute to international crime by selling these horns. Instead the horns were either destroyed or stored in a warehouse.

(a) Suppose that all of the rhinoceros horns produced in South Africa are destroyed. Label the axes below and draw world supply and demand curves for rhinoceros horns with blue ink. Label the equilibrium price and quantity.

_____

(a) If the "street price" is p per ounce, what is the expected return to a dealer from selling an ounce of marijuana? __$p - 3$__ What then would be the equilibrium price of marijuana? __$8.__

(b) Suppose that the demand function for marijuana has the equation $Q = A - Bp$. If all confiscated marijuana is destroyed, what will be the equilibrium consumption of marijuana? __$A - 8B$__ Suppose that confiscated marijuana is not destroyed but sold on the open market. What will be the equilibrium consumption of marijuana? __$A - 8B$__

(c) The price of marijuana will (increase, decrease, stay the same)? __Stay the same.__

(d) If there were increasing rather than constant marginal cost in marijuana production, do you think that consumption would be greater if confiscated marijuana were sold than if it were destroyed? Explain

__Consumption will increase because the supply curve will shift to the right, lowering the price.__

_____

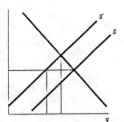

(b) If South Africa were to sell its rhinoceros horns on the world market, which of the curves in your diagram would shift and in what direction? __Supply curve to right__ Use red ink to illustrate the shifted curve or curves. If South Africa were to do this, would world consumption of rhinoceros horns be increased or decreased? __increased__ Would the world price of rhinoceros horns be increased or decreased? __decreased__ Would the amount of rhinoceros poaching be increased or decreased? __decreased.__

24.5 (20) The sale of rhinoceros horns is not prohibited because of concern about the wicked pleasures of sex-crazed aphrodisiac munchers, but because the supply activity is bad for rhinoceroses. Similarly, the Australian reason for restricting the exportation of cockatoos to the United States is not because having a cockatoo is bad for you. Indeed it is legal for Australians to have cockatoos as pets. The motive for the restriction is simply to protect the wild populations from being over-exploited. In the case of other commodities, it appears that society has no particular interest in restricting the supply activities but wishes to restrict consumption. A good example is illicit drugs. The growing of marijuana, for example, is a simple pastoral activity, which in itself is no more harmful than growing sweet corn or brussels sprouts. It is the consumption of marijuana to which society objects.

Suppose that there is a constant marginal cost of $5 per ounce for growing marijuana and delivering it to buyers. But whenever the marijuana authorities find marijuana growing or in the hands of dealers, they seize the marijuana and fine the supplier. Suppose that the probability that marijuana is seized is .3 and that the fine if you are caught is $10 per ounce.

Chapter 25

Monopoly

NAME_____

Introduction. The profit maximizing output of a monopolist can usually be found by solving for the output at which marginal revenue is equal to marginal cost. Having solved for this output, you find the monopolist's price by plugging the profit maximizing output into the demand function. In general, the marginal revenue function can be found by taking the derivative of the total revenue function with respect to the quantity. But in the special case of linear demand, it is easy to find the marginal revenue curve graphically. With a linear inverse demand curve, $p(y) = a - by$, the marginal revenue curve always takes the form $MR(y) = a - 2by$.

In this section, you will also find some problems about price discrimination. Remember that a price discriminator wants the *marginal revenue* in each market to be equal to the marginal cost of production. Since he produces all of his output in one place, his marginal cost of production is the same for both markets and depends on his *total* output. The trick for solving these problems is to write marginal revenue in each market as a function of quantity sold in that market and to write marginal cost as a function of the sum of quantities sold in the two markets. The profit maximizing conditions then become two equations which you can solve for the two unknown quantities sold in the two markets. Of course if marginal cost is constant, your job is even easier, since all you have to do is find the quantities in each industry for which marginal revenue equals the constant marginal cost.

25.1 (20) Professor Bong has just written the first textbook in Punk Economics. It is called *Up Your Isoquant.* Market research suggests that the demand curve for this book will be $Q = 2,000 - 100p$, where p is its price. It will cost $1000 to set the book in type. This setup cost is necessary before any copies can be printed. In addition to the setup cost, there is a marginal cost of $2 per book for every book printed.

(a) Write down the total revenue function $R(Q)$ for Professor Bong's book. $\underline{TR = Q(20 - Q/100) = 20Q - Q^2/100.}$

(b) Write down the total cost function $C(Q)$ for producing Professor Bong's book. $\underline{TC = 1000 + 2Q.}$

(c) Compute the marginal revenue and marginal cost functions. How many copies of the book should be printed in order to maximize Professor

NAME _____ 215

(a) If the supply schedule is horizontal at a price of $5,000 what will be the equilibrium number of Japanese cars sold in the U.S.? ____240____

_____thousand. How much money will Americans spend in total on Japanese cars? ____1.2____ billion dollars.

(b) Suppose that in response to pressure from American car manufacturers, the United States imposes an import duty on Japanese cars in such a way that for every car exported to the United States the Japanese manufacturers must pay a tax to the U.S. government of $2,000. How many Japanese automobiles will now be sold in the U.S.? ____236____

_____thousand. At what price will they be sold? ____7____ _____thousand dollars.

(c) How much revenue will the U.S. government collect with this tariff? ____472____ _____million dollars.

(d) On the graph below, the price paid by American consumers is measured on the vertical axis. Use blue ink to show the demand and supply schedules before the import duty is imposed. After the import duty is imposed, the supply schedule shifts and the demand schedule stays as before. Use red ink to draw the new supply schedule.

Price (thousands)

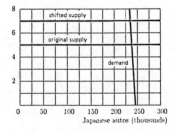

Bong's profits? $MR = \underline{\quad 20 - Q/50,}$ $MC = \underline{\qquad} = 2,$ $Q^* = \underline{\quad}$ = 900.

25.2 (10) Peter Morgan sells pigeon pies from a pushcart in Central Park. Morgan is the only supplier of this delicacy in Central Park. His costs are zero due to the abundant supplies of raw materials available in the park.

(a) When he first started his business, the inverse demand curve for pigeon pies was $p(y) = 100 - y$, where the price is measured in cents and y measures the number of pies sold. Use black ink to plot this curve in the graph below. On the same graph, use red ink to plot his marginal revenue curve.

Dollars

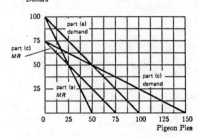

(b) What level of output will maximize Peter's profits? ____50 pies____

_____What price will Peter charge per pie? ____50 cents a pie.____

(c) After Peter had been in business for several months, he noticed that his demand curve had shifted to $p(y) = 75 - y/2$. Use blue ink to plot this curve in the graph above. Plot his new marginal revenue curve on the same graph with black ink.

(d) What is his profit maximizing output at this new price? ____75 pies____

_____What is the new profit maximizing price? ____37.5 cents____

25.3 (20) Suppose that the demand function for Japanese cars in the United States is such that annual sales of cars (in thousands of cars) will be $250 - 2P$, where P is the price of Japanese cars in thousands of dollars.

(e) Suppose that instead of imposing an import duty, the U.S. government persuades the Japanese governments to impose "voluntary export restrictions" on their exports of cars to the U.S. Suppose that the Japanese agree to restrain their exports by requiring that every car exported to the United States must have an export license. Suppose further that the Japanese government agrees to issue only 236,000 export licenses and sells these licenses to the Japanese firms. If the Japanese firms know the American demand curve and if they know that only 236,000 Japanese cars will be sold in America, what price will they be able to charge in America for their cars? ____7____ _____thousand dollars.

(f) How much will a Japanese firm be willing to pay the Japanese government for an export license? ____2____ _____thousand dollars. (Hint: Think about what it costs to produce a car and how much it can be sold for if you have an export license.)

(g) How much will be the Japanese government's total revenue from the sale of export licenses? ____472____ _____million dollars.

(h) How much money will Americans spend on Japanese cars?_____ ____1.652____ _____billion dollars.

(i) Why might the Japanese "voluntarily" submit to export controls?

Total revenue of Japanese companies and Japanese government is greater with voluntary export controls than it was without them. Since there is less output, Japanese costs must be lower. Hence their profits must be higher.

Calculus **25.4 (40)** Danny's Dump Trucks (the only producer of dump trucks) sells its output in both the domestic and the foreign markets. Because of import and export restrictions, there is no possibility that a purchase in one market could be sold in the other market. The demand and marginal revenue curves associated with each market are as follows.

$$P_d = 20,000 - 20Q \quad P_f = 25,000 - 50Q$$
$$MR_d = 20,000 - 40Q \quad MR_f = 25,000 - 100Q$$

Danny's production process exhibits constant returns to scale and he knows from past experience that it takes $1,000,000 to produce 100 trucks.

(a) What is the average cost of producing a truck? $10,000

_____What is the marginal cost? $10,000 ___Show the average and marginal cost curves on the graph.

(b) Draw the demand curve for the domestic market in blue ink and the marginal revenue curve for the domestic market in yellow ink. Draw the demand curve for the foreign market in red ink and the marginal revenue curve for the foreign market in black ink.

Dollars (1.000s)

(c) If Danny is maximizing his profits. he will sell _____ 250 _____trucks in the domestic market at _____ $15,000 _____dollars each and _____ 150 _____trucks in the foreign market at _____ $17,500 _____dollars each.

(d) What are Danny's total profits? $2,375,000.

(e) What is the price elasticity of demand in the domestic market? _____

_____ −3 _____What is the price elasticity of demand in the foreign market? _____ −2.33 _____What is true about the market in which the highest price is charged? less elastic.

profits be? $252,500

(b) If McSwill can charge a different price in each country, and wants to maximize profits. how many copies should it sell in the U.S.? _____ 23,000 _____What price should it charge in the U.S.? $13.50 _____How many copies should it sell in England? 4,500 _____What price should it charge in England? $11 _____How much will its total profits be? $255,000

25.6 (10) "Since the monopolist usually sets her output such that price is greater than marginal cost. all she has to do to increase profits is to sell one additional unit at a slightly lower price." What is fallacious about this argument?

In order to sell one additional unit at a lower price, the monopolist must lower her price on all of the units she is currently selling (unless we assume price discrimination). This lowering of the price may nullify the profits from the additional sale.

25.7 (20) A monopolist has a cost function given by $c(y) = y^2$ and faces a demand curve given by $P(y) = 120 - y$.

(a) What is his profit maximizing level of output? 30 _____What price will the monopolist charge? $90

(b) If you put a lump sum tax of $100 on this monopolist. what would his output be? 30

(c) If you wanted to choose a price ceiling for this monopolist so as to maximize consumer plus producer surplus, what price ceiling should you choose? $80

(f) Suppose the import and export restrictions change so that anybody who buys a dump truck in one market can immediately (and costlessly) resell it in the other. On the graph below. draw the new inverse demand curve (with blue ink) and marginal revenue curve (with black ink) facing Danny.

Dollars (1.000s)

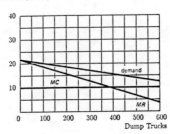

(g) Given that his costs haven't changed, how many dump trucks should Danny sell? 400 _____What price will he charge? _____ $15,714 _____How will Danny's profits change now that he can no longer practice price discrimination? decrease by $$9,400.

25.5 (20) Ferdinand Sludge has just written a disgusting new book, *Orgy in the Piggery*. His publisher, Graw McSwill estimates that the demand for this book in the U.S. is $Q_1 = 50.000 - 2.000 P_1$, where P_1 is the price in America measured in U. S. dollars. The demand for Sludge's opus in England is $Q_2 = 10.000 - 500 P_2$, where P_2 is its price in England measured in U.S. dollars. His publisher has a cost function $C(Q) = \$50,000 + \$2Q$, where Q is the total number of copies of *Orgy* that it produces.

(a) If McSwill must charge the same price in both countries. how many copies should it sell 27,500 _____and what price should it charge _____ $13 _____to maximize its profits, and how much will those

(d) How much output will the monopolist produce at this price ceiling? 30

(e) Suppose that you put a specific tax on the monopolist of $20 per unit output. What would his profit maximizing level of output be? _____ 25.

25.8 (30) Gargantuan enterprises has a monopoly in the production of antimacassars. Its factory is located in the town of Pantagruel. There is no other industry in Pantagruel and the labor supply equation there is $W = 10 + .1L$. where W is the daily wage and L is the number of person-days of work performed. Antimacassars are produced with a production function. $Q = 10L$. where L is daily labor supply and Q is daily output. The demand curve for antimacassars is $P = 41 - \frac{Q}{1,000}$, where P is the price and Q is the number of sales per day.

(a) Find the profit maximizing output for Gargantuan. 10,000

_____(Hint: Use the production function to find the labor input requirements for any level of output. Make substitutions so you can write the firm's total costs as a function of its output and then its profit as a function of output. Solve for the profit-maximizing output.)

(b) How much labor does it use? 1,000 _____What is the wage rate that it pays? $110

(c) What is the price of antimacassars? $31 _____How much profit is made? $200,000.

25.9 (10) Suppose that a monopolist faces an inverse demand curve given by $p(y) = 13/y$ and has a cost function of $c(y) = y^2$. What is his profit There is no profit maximizing level of output—the smaller amount of output he produces, the larger his profits.

25.10 (10) Suppose that a monopolist is able to sell to two different markets: one with a demand curve given by $y_1(p_1) = p_1^{-2}$ and the other with inverse demand curve given by $y_2(p_2) = p_2^{-3}$. He has constant marginal costs of production of 1.

(a) What is the profit maximizing price to charge in market 1? _____

$2.

(b) What is the profit maximizing price to charge in market 2? _____

$3/2

25.11 (20) Suppose that a monopolist faces an inverse demand curve given by $p(y) = 100 - 2y$. and that he has constant marginal costs of 20.

(a) What is his optimal level of output? ___20___ What price will the monopolist charge? ___$60.___

(b) What is the socially optimal price for this firm? ___$20.___

(c) What is the socially optimal level of output for this firm? ___40.___

(d) What is the deadweight loss due to the monopolistic behavior of this firm? ___400.___

(e) Now suppose that this monopolist could operate as a perfectly discriminating monopolist and sell each unit of output at the highest price it would fetch. The deadweight loss in this case would be ___0___

25.12 (20) A monopolist has an inverse demand curve given by $p(y) = 12 - y$ and a cost curve given by $c(y) = y^2$.

(a) What will be his profit maximizing level of output ___3___

(b) Suppose the government decides to put a tax on this monopolist so that for each unit he sells he has to pay the government $2.00. What will be his output under this form of taxation? ___2.5___

(e) If the *Daily Calumny* charges its profit maximizing price. and prints the profit maximizing amount of scandal. how many column inches of scandal should it print ___123.456 inches___ How many copies are sold ___49,383___ and what is the amount of profit for the Daily Calumny if it maximizes its profits? ___$1,235___

25.14 (20) The demand curve facing a monopolist is given by

$$D(p) = \begin{cases} 100/p & \text{for } p \leq 10 \\ 0 & \text{for } p > 10 \end{cases}$$

(a) Plot this demand curve in the graph below.

Price

(graph with axes Price from 0 to 8, Quantity from 0 to 200, curve plotted)

Quantity

(b) At what price is the (inverse) demand curve discontinuous? _____

$p = 10$

(c) Suppose that the monopolist has constant marginal costs of $1 per unit. What will its profits be if it charges a price of $2? ___$50___

(d) What will its profits be if it charges a price of $5? ___$80___

(e) What price maximizes its profits? ___$10___

(c) Suppose now that the government puts a lump sum tax of $10.00 on the profits of the monopolist. What will be his output? ___3___

25.13 (40) In Gomorrah, New Jersey, there is only one newspaper, the *Daily Calumny*. The demand for the paper depends on the price and the amount of scandal reported. The demand function is $Q = 15S^{1/2}P^{-3}$, where S is the number of column inches of scandal reported in the paper, Q is the number of issues sold per day, and P is the price. Scandals are not a scarce commodity in Gomorrah. However it takes resources to write, edit, and print stories of scandal. The cost of reporting S units of scandal is $10S$. These costs are independent of the number of papers sold. In addition it costs money to print and deliver the paper. These cost $.10 per copy and the cost per unit is independent of the amount of scandal reported in the paper. Therefore the total cost of printing Q copies of the paper with S column inches of scandal is $10S + .10Q$

(a) Calculate the price elasticity of demand for the *Daily Calumny*. ___−3___ Does the price elasticity depend on the number of scandals reported? ___no___ Is the price elasticity constant over all prices? ___yes___

(b) Calculate the profit maximizing price. ___$.15___ (Hint: What is the relation between the profit maximizing price, the marginal cost, and the price elasticity?) The difference between the profit maximizing price and the cost of printing and delivering the paper is ___$.05___

(c) If the *Daily Calumny* charges the profit maximizing price and prints 100 column inches of scandal, how many copies would it sell? (Round to the nearest integer) ___44,444___ Write a general expression for the ___$Q = 15S^{1/2}(.15)^{-3} = 4,444.44S^{1/2}$___

(d) Assuming that the paper charges the profit maximizing price, write an expression for profits as a function of Q and S. ___
Profits= $.15Q - .10Q - 10S$, Profits $= .05(4,444.44S^{1/2}) - 10S = 222.222S^{1/2} - 10S$.___

(f) What quantity maximizes its profits? ___10___

25.15 (20) In the graph below, use black ink to draw the inverse demand curve, $p_1(y) = 100 - y$.

(a) If the monopolist has zero costs, where on this curve will it choose to operate? ___At $y = 50$. $p = 50$.___

(b) Now draw another demand curve that passes through the profit maximizing point and is flatter than the original demand curve. Use a red pen to mark the part of this new demand curve on which the monopolist would choose to operate. (Hint: remember the idea of revealed preference?)

(c) The monopolist would have (larger, smaller) profits at the new demand curve than he had at the original demand curve. ___Larger.___

Price

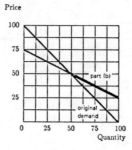

Quantity

Chapter 26

Oligopoly

26.1 (30) Carl and Simon are two rival pumpkin growers who sell their pumpkins at the Farmers' Market in Lake Whichisit, Minnesota. They are the only sellers of pumpkins at the market, where the demand function for pumpkins is $q = 3200 - 1600p$. The total number of pumpkins sold at the market is $q = q_C + q_S$ where q_C is the number that Carl sells and q_S is the number that Simon sells. The cost of producing pumpkins for either farmer is $.50 per pumpkin no matter how many pumpkins he produces.

(a) The inverse demand function for pumpkins at the Farmers' Market is

$p = a - b(q_C + q_S)$ where $a = $ ___**2**___ and $b = $ _____

___**−1/1600**___ The marginal cost of producing a pumpkin for

either farmer is ___**.5**___ .

(b) Every spring, each of the farmers decides how many pumpkins to grow. They both know the local demand function and they each know how many pumpkins were sold by the other farmer last year. In fact, each farmer assumes that the other farmer will sell the same number this year as he sold last year. So, for example, if Simon sold 400 pumpkins last year, Carl believes that Simon will sell 400 pumpkins again this year. If Simon sold 400 pumpkins last year, what does Carl think the price of

pumpkins will be if Carl sells 1200 pumpkins this year? ___**1**___

_____. If Simon sold q_S^{t-1} pumpkins in year $t - 1$, then in the spring of year t, Carl thinks that if he, Carl, sells q_C^t pumpkins this year,

the price of pumpkins this year will be ___**$2 - (q_S^{t-1} + q_C^t)/1600$**___

(c) If Simon sold 400 pumpkins last year, Carl believes that if he sells q_C pumpkins this year then the inverse demand function that he faces is $p = 2 - 400/1600 - q_C^t/1600 = 1.75 - q_C^t/1600$. Therefore, if Simon sold 400 pumpkins last year, Carl's marginal revenue this year will be $1.75 - q_C^t/800$. More generally, if Simon sold q_S^{t-1} pumpkins last year, then Carl believes that if he, himself, sells q_C^t pumpkins this year, his

marginal revenue this year will be ___**$2 - q_S^{t-1}/1600 - q_C^t)/800$**___

next period. Hint: Use the reaction functions.

$$q_s = 1200 - q_C/2 \quad q_C = 1200 - q_S/2$$

(i) Solve the two equations you wrote down in the last part for an equilibrium output for each farmer. Each farmer, in Cournot equilibrium,

produces ___**800**___ units of output. The total amount of

pumpkins brought to the Farmers' market in Lake Whichisit is _____

___**1600**___ . The price of pumpkins in that market is

___**$1**___ . How much profit does each farmer make? _____

___**$400**___

26.2 (30) Suppose that the pumpkin market in Lake Whichisit is as we described it in the last problem except for one detail. Every spring, the snow thaws off of Carl's pumpkin field a week before it thaws off of Simon's. Therefore Carl can plant his pumpkins one week earlier than Simon can. Now Simon lives just down the road from Carl and he can tell by looking at Carl's fields how many pumpkins Carl planted and how many Carl will harvest in the fall. (Suppose also that Carl will sell every pumpkin that he produces.) Therefore, instead of assuming that Carl will sell the same amount of pumpkins that he did last year, Simon sees how many Carl is actually going to sell this year. Simon has this information before he makes his own decision about how many to plant.

(a) If Carl plants enough pumpkins to yield q_C^t this year, then Simon

knows that the profit maximizing amount to produce this year is $q_S^t = $ _

___**$1200 - q_C^t/2$**___ . Hint: Remember the reaction functions you found in the last problem.

(b) When Carl plants his pumpkins, he understands how Simon will make his decision. Therefore Carl knows that the amount that Simon will produce this year will be determined by the amount that Carl produces. In particular, if Carl's output is q_C^t, then Simon will produce and sell

___**$1200 - q_C^t/2$,**___ and the total output of the two producers will be

___**$1200 + q_C^t/2$**___ . Therefore Carl knows that if his own output is

q_C, the price of pumpkins in the market will be ___**$1.25 - q_C^t/3200$**___

_____.

(d) Carl believes that Simon will never change the amount of pumpkins that he produces from the amount q_S^{t-1} that he sold last year. Therefore Carl plants enough pumpkins this year so that he can sell the amount that maximizes his profits this year. To maximize this profit, he chooses the output this year that sets his marginal revenue this year equal to his marginal cost. This means that to find Carl's output this year when Simon's output last year was q_S^{t-1}, Carl solves the following equation.

___**$2 - q_S^{t-1}/1600 - q_C^t/800 = .5$**___

(e) Carl's Cournot reaction function, $R_C^t(q_S^{t-1})$ is a function that tells us what Carl's profit maximizing output this year would be as a function of Simon's output last year. Use the equation you wrote in the last answer to

find Carl's reaction function, $R_C^t(q_S^{t-1}) = \dfrac{1200 - q_S^{t-1}/2}{}$ (Hint: This is a linear expression of the form $a - bq_S^{t-1}$. You have to find the constants a and b.)

(f) Suppose that Simon makes his decisions in the same way that Carl does. Notice that the problem is completely symmetric in the roles played by Carl and Simon. Therefore without even calculating it, we can guess

that Simon's reaction function is $R_S^t(q_C^{t-1}) = \dfrac{1200 - q_C^{t-1}/2}{}$ (Of course, if you don't like to guess, you could work this out by following similar steps to the ones you used to find Carl's reaction function.)

(g) Suppose that in year 1, Carl produced 200 pumpkins and Simon produced 1000 pumpkins. In year 2, how many would Carl produce? _____

___**700**___ How many would Simon produce? _____

___**1100**___ In year 3, how many would Carl produce? _____

___**650**___ How many would Simon produce? _____

___**850**___ Use a calculator or pen and paper to work out several more terms in this series. To what level of output does Carl's output

appear to be converging? ___**800**___ How about Simon's? _

___**800**___

(h) Write down two simultaneous equations that could be solved to find outputs q_S and q_C such that if Carl is producing q_C and Simon is producing q_S, then they will both want to produce the same amount in the

---

(c) In the last part of the problem, you found how the price of pumpkins this year in the Farmers' Market is related to the number of pumpkins that Carl produces this year. Now write an expression for Carl's total

revenue in year t as a function of his own output, q_C^t. ___**$1.25q_C^t - [q_C^t]^2$**___

___**/3200**___ Write an expression for Carl's marginal revenue in year t

as a function of q_C^t. ___**$1.25 - q_C^t/1600$**___

(d) Find the profit maximizing output for Carl. ___**1200**___

_____ Find the profit maximizing output for Simon. ___**600**___

_____ Find the equilibrium price of pumpkins in the Lake Which-

isit Farmers' Market. ___**$7/8**___ How much profit does Carl

make? ___**$450**___ How much profit does Simon make? _____

___**$225**___ An equilibrium of the type we discuss here is

known as a ___**Stackleberg**___ equilibrium

(e) If he wanted to, it would be possible for Carl to delay his planting until the same time that Simon planted so that neither of them would know the other's plans for this year when he planted. Would it be in Carl's interest to do so? Explain Hint: What are Carl's profits in the equilibrium above. How do they compare with his profits in Cournot equilibrium.

No. Carl's profits in Stackleberg equilibrium are larger than in Cournot equilibrium. So if the output when neither knows the other's output this year until after planting time is a Cournot equilibrium, Carl will want Simon to know his output.

26.3 (30) Suppose that Carl and Simon sign a marketing agreement. They decide to determine their total output jointly and to each produce the same number of pumpkins. To maximize their joint profits, how many

pumpkins should they produce in total? ___**1200**___ How

much does each one of them produce? ___**600**___ How much

profits does each one of them make? __$450__

26.4 (30) The inverse market demand curve for bean sprouts is given by $P(Y) = 100 - 2Y$, and the total cost function for any firm in the industry is given by $TC(y) = 4y$.

(a) The marginal cost for any firm in the industry is equal to _____ ____ __4__ ____ The change in price for a one unit increase in output is equal to __-2.__

(b) If the bean sprout industry were perfectly competitive, the industry output would be __48,__ and the industry price would be ____ __$4.__

(c) Suppose two Cournot firms operate in the market. The reaction function for Firm 1 would be $y_1 = 24 - y_2/2$. (Reminder: Unlike the example in your textbook, the marginal cost is not zero here.) The reaction function of Firm 2 will be $y_2 = 24 - y_1/2$. If the firms were operating at the Cournot equilibrium point, industry output would be __32,__ each firm would produce __16,__ and the market price would be __$36.__

(d) For the Cournot case draw the two reaction curves and indicate the equilibrium point on the graph below.

_____and price of __$28.__

26.5 (30) Grinch is the sole owner of a mineral water spring that costlessly burbles forth as much mineral water as Grinch cares to bottle. It costs Grinch $1 per gallon bottle to bottle this water. The inverse demand curve for Grinch's mineral water is $p = $10 - .10q$, where p is the price per gallon and q is the number of gallons sold.

(a) Write down an expression for profits as a function of q. $\Pi(q) = $ ___ __$9(10 - .10q) - q$.__ Find the profit maximizing choice of q for Grinch __45__

(b) What price does Grinch get per gallon of mineral water if he produces the profit maximizing quantity? __$5.50.__ How much profit does he make? __$202.50__

(c) Suppose, now, that Grinch's neighbor, Grubb finds a mineral spring that produces mineral water that is just as good Grinch's water, but it costs Grubb $3 a bottle to get his water out of the ground and bottle it. Total market demand for mineral water remains as before. Suppose that Grinch and Grubb each believe that the other's quantity decision is independent of his own.

(d) What is the Cournot equilibrium output for Grubb? __50/3__

(e) What is the price in the Cournot equilibrium? __$5.33__

26.6 (40) Albatross Airlines has a monopoly on air travel between Peoria and Dubuque. If Albatross makes one trip in each direction per day, the demand schedule for round trips is $q = 160 - 2p$, where q is the number of passengers per day. (Assume that nobody makes one-way trips.) There is an "overhead" fixed cost of $2,000 per day which is necessary to fly the airplane regardless of the number of passengers. In addition, there is a marginal cost of $10 per passenger. Thus, total daily costs are $2,000+10q$ if the plane flies at all.

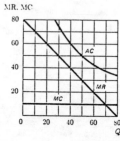

(e) If the two firms decided to collude, industry output would be _____ __24,__ and the market price would equal _____ __$52__

(f) Suppose both of the colluding firms are producing equal amounts of output. If one of the colluding firms assumes that the other firm would not react to a change in industry output, what incentive is there for the firm to increase its output by one unit? __An increase in profits of $35 $(13(51 - 4) - 12(52 - 4))$.__ What is the incentive if the smaller firm is producing only 2 units of the total industry production? __$45 $(3(51 - 4) - 2(52 - 4))$.__

(g) Suppose one firm acts as a Stackelberg leader and the other firm behaves as a follower. The maximization problem for the leader can be written as:
$$\max_{y_1}(100 - 2(y_1 + 24 - y_1/2))y_1 - 4y_1.$$

Solving this problem results in the leader producing an output of __24,__ and the follower producing __12.__ This implies an industry output of __36.__

(a) On the graph below, sketch and label the marginal revenue curve, and the average and marginal cost curves.

(b) Calculate the profit maximizing price and quantity and total daily profits for Albatross Airlines. $p = $ __45,__ $q = $ __70,__ $\pi = $ __$450 per day.__

(c) If the interest rate is 10% per year, how much would someone be willing to pay to own Albatross Airlines' monopoly on the Dubuque-Peoria route. (Assuming that demand and cost conditions remain unchanged forever.) __About $1.6 million.__

(d) If another firm with the same costs as Albatross Airlines were to enter the Dubuque-Peoria market and if the industry then became a Cournot duopoly, would the new entrant make a profit? __No; losses would be about $900 per day.__

(e) Suppose that the throbbing night life in Peoria and Dubuque becomes widely known and in consequence the population of both places doubles. As a result, the demand for airplane trips between the two places doubles to become $q = 320 - 4p$. Suppose that the original airplane had a capacity of 80 passengers. If AA must stick with this single plane and if no other airline enters the market, what price should it charge to maximize its output and how much profit would it make? $p = $ __60;__ $\pi = $ __2,000__

(f) Let us assume that the overhead costs per plane are constant regardless of the number of planes. If AA added a second plane with the same costs and capacity as the first plane, what price would it charge _____ $45; _____ how many tickets would it sell _____ 140; _____ and how much would its profits be? _____ $900 _____ If AA could prevent entry by another competitor, would it choose to add a second plane? _____ No. _____

(g) Suppose that AA stuck with one plane and another firm entered the market with a plane of its own. If the second firm has the same cost function as the first and if the two firms act as Cournot oligopolists, what will be the price. _____ $100/3; _____ quantities, _____ 280/3; _____ and profits _____ $1600/9 _____ ?

26.7 (20) Consider an industry with the following structure. There are 50 firms that behave in a competitive manner and have identical cost functions given by $c(y) = y^2/2$. There is one monopolist that has 0 marginal costs. The demand curve for the product is given by

$$D(p) = 1000 - 50p.$$

(a) What is the supply curve of one of the competitive firms? _____ $y = p$ _____

(b) What is the total supply from the competitive sector? _____ $y = 50p$ _____

(c) If the monopolist sets a price p, how much output will he sell? _____ $D_m(p) = 1000 - 100p$

(d) What is the monopolist's profit maximizing output? _____ $y_m = 500$ _____

(e) What will be the large firm's profits? _____ $937.50 _____
Finally suppose the large firm could force the competitive firms out of the business and behave as a real monopolist.

(f) What will be the equilibrium price? _____ 225/2 _____ What will be the equilibrium quantity? _____ 175/2 _____

(g) What will be the large firm's profits? _____ $(175/2)^2$ _____

Calculus 26.9 (30) In a remote area of the American Midwest before the railroads arrived, cast iron cookstoves were much desired, but people lived far apart, roads were poor, and heavy stoves were expensive to transport. Stoves could be shipped by river boat to the town of Bouncing Springs, Missouri. Ben Kinmore was the only stove dealer in Bouncing Springs. He could buy as many stoves as he wished for $20 each, delivered to his store. The only farmers that traded with Bouncing Springs lived along a road that ran east and west through town. Along that road, there was one farm every mile and the cost of hauling a stove was $1 per mile. There were no other stove dealers on the road in either direction. The owners of every farm along the road had a reservation price of $120 for a cast iron cookstove. That is, any of them would be willing to pay up to $120 to have a stove rather than to not have one. Nobody had use for more than one stove. Ben Kinmore charged a base price of $p for stoves and added to the price the cost of delivery. For example, if the base price of stoves was $40 and you lived 45 miles west of Bouncing Springs, you would have to pay $85 to get a stove, $40 base price plus a hauling charge of $45. Since the reservation price of every farmer was $120, it follows that if the base price were $40, any farmer who lived within 80 miles of Bouncing Springs would be willing to pay $40 plus the price of delivery to have a cookstove. Therefore at a base price of $40, Ben could sell 80 cookstoves to the farmers living west of him. Similarly, if his base price is $40, he could sell 80 cookstoves to the farmers living within 80 miles to his east, for a total of 160 cookstoves.

(a) If Ben set a base price of $p for cookstoves where $p < 120$, and if he charged $1 a mile for delivering them, what would be the total number of cookstoves he could sell? _____ $2(120-p)$

_____ (Remember to count the ones he could sell to his east as well as to his west.) Assume that Ben has no other costs than buying the stoves and delivering them. Then Ben would make a profit of $p - 20$ per stove. Write Ben's total profit as a function of the base price, $p, that he charges _____ $2(120-p)(p-20) = 2(140p - p^2 - 2000)$

(e) What is the monopolist's profit maximizing price? _____ $p = 5$ _____

(f) How much will the competitive sector provide at this price? _____ $y_c = 50 \times 5 = 250$

(g) What will be the total amount of output sold in this industry? _____ $Y = y_m + y_c = 750.$

26.8 (30) Consider a market with one large firm and many small firms. The supply curve of the small firms taken together is:

$$S(p) = 100 + p.$$

The demand curve for the product is:

$$D(p) = 200 - p.$$

The cost function for the one large firm is:

$$c(y) = 25y.$$

Suppose that the large firm is forced to operate at a zero level of output.

(a) What will be the equilibrium price? _____ 50 _____ What will be the equilibrium quantity? _____ 150 _____
Suppose now that the large firm attempts to exploit its market power and set a profit maximizing price. In order to model this we assume that customers always go first to the competitive firms and buy as much as they are able to and then go to the monopolist. In this situation,

(b) What will be the equilibrium price? _____ $37.50

(c) What will be the equilibrium quantity supplied by the monopolist? _____ 25

(d) What will be the equilibrium quantity supplied by the competitive firms _____ 137.5 _____

(b) Ben's profit maximizing base price is _____ $70 _____ . (Hint: You just wrote profits as a function of prices. Now differentiate this expression for profits with respect to p.) Ben's most distant customer would be located at a distance of _____ 50 _____ miles from him. Ben would sell _____ 100 _____ cookstoves and make a total profit of _____ $5,000

(c) Suppose that instead of setting a single base price and making all buyers pay for the cost of transportation, Ben offers free delivery of cookstoves. He sets a price $p and promises to deliver for free to any farmer who lives within $p - 20$ miles of him. (He won't deliver to anyone who lives further than that, because it then costs him more than $p to buy a stove and deliver it.) If he is going to price in this way, how high should he set p.

_____ $120 _____ How many cookstoves would Ben deliver? _____ 200 _____ How much would his total revenue be? _____ $24,000 _____ How much would his total costs be (including the cost of deliveries and the cost of buying the stoves.) _____ $14,000

_____ (Hint: What is the average distance that he has to haul a cookstove?) How much profit would he make? _____ $10,000 _____

When Ben pays for delivery, he is able to price discriminate between the nearby farmers and the far away ones. This way he charges a higher price net of transportation cost to nearby farmers who have a high willingness to pay net of transportation cost and a lower price net of transportation costs to those who live far away and whose willingness to pay above transportation cost is smaller.

Calculus 26.10 (30) Perhaps you wondered what Ben Kinmore, who lives off in the woods quietly collecting his monopoly profits, is doing in this chapter on oligopoly. Well, unfortunately for Ben, before he got around to selling any stoves, the railroad built a track to the town of Deep Furrow, just 40 miles down the road, west of Bouncing Springs. The storekeeper in Deep

Furrow. Huey Sunshine, was also able to get cookstoves delivered by train to his store for $20 each. Huey and Ben were the only stove dealers on the road. Let us concentrate our attention on how they would compete for the customers who lived between them. We can do this, because Ben is able to charge different base prices for the cookstoves he ships east from the prices he charges for the cookstoves he ships west. So is Huey.

Suppose that Ben sets a base price, p_B, for stoves he sends west and adds a charge of $1 per mile for delivery. Suppose that Huey sets a base price, p_H, for stoves he sends east and adds a charge of $1 per mile for delivery. Farmers who live between Ben and Huey would buy from the seller who is willing to deliver most cheaply to them (so long as the delivered price does not exceed $120). If Ben's base price is p_B and Huey's base price is p_H, somebody who lives x miles west of Ben would have to pay a total of $p_B + x$ to have a stove delivered from Ben and $p_H + (40 - x)$ to have a stove delivered by Huey.

(a) If Ben's base price is p_B and Huey's is p_H, write down an equation that could be solved for the distance x^* to the west of Bouncing Springs that Ben's market extends. $\underline{p_B + x^* = p_H + (40 - x^*)}$
If Ben's base price is p_B
and Huey's is p_H, then Ben will sell $\underline{20 + (p_H - p_B)/2}$ cookstoves
and Huey will sell $\underline{20 + (p_B - p_H)/2}$ cookstoves.

(b) Recalling that Ben makes a profit of $p_B - 20$ on every cookstove that he sells, Ben's profits can be expressed as the following function of p_B
and p_H. $\underline{(20 + (p_H - p_B)/2)(p_B - 20)}$

(c) Suppose that Ben thinks that Huey's price will stay at p_H, no matter what price Ben chooses, what choice of p_B would maximize Ben's
profits? $\underline{p_B = 20 + p_H/2}$ Hint: Set the derivative of Ben's profits with respect to his price equal to zero. Suppose that Huey thinks that Ben's price will stay at p_B, no matter what price Huey chooses,

what choice of p_H would maximize Huey's profits? $\underline{p_H = 20 + p_B/2}$

_____ Hint: From the symmetry of the problem and the answer to the last question, it should be easy to see the answer.

(d) Can you find a base price for Ben and a base price for Huey such that each is a profit maximizing choice given what the other guy is doing? Hint: Find prices p_B and p_H that simultaneously solve the last two

equations. $\underline{p_B = p_H = 40}$ How many cookstoves does Ben sell

---

function of how far west he lives from Ben.

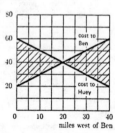

Dollars

(f) With the pricing policies you just graphed, which farmers get stoves delivered most cheaply, those who live closest to the merchants or those

who live midway between them? $\underline{\text{live midway}}$ On the graph you made, shade in the area representing each merchant's profits. How

much profits does each merchant make? $\underline{\$400}$ If Ben and Huey are pricing in this way, is there any way for either of them to increase his profits by changing the price he charges to some farmers?

$\underline{\text{No.}}$

---

to farmers living west of him? $\underline{20}$ How much profits does he make on these sales? $\underline{\$400}$

(e) Suppose that Ben and Huey decided to compete for the customers who live between them by price discriminating. Suppose that Ben offers to deliver a stove to a farmer who lives x miles west of him for a price equal to the maximum of Ben's total cost of delivering a stove to that farmer and Huey's total cost of delivering to the same farmer less 1 penny. Suppose that Huey offers to deliver a stove to a farmer who lives x miles west of Ben for a price equal to the maximum of Huey's own total cost of delivering to this farmer and Ben's total cost of delivering to him less a penny. For example, if a farmer lives 10 miles west of Ben, Ben's total cost of delivering to him is $30, $20 to get the stove and $10 for hauling it 10 miles west. Huey's total cost of delivering it to him is $50, $20 to get the stove and $30 to haul it 30 miles east. Ben will charge the maximum of his own cost, which is $20, and Huey's cost less a penny, which is $49.99.

The maximum of these two numbers is $\underline{\$49.99}$ Huey will charge the maximum of his own total cost of delivering to this farmer, which is $50, and Ben's cost less a penny, which is $19.99. Therefore Huey

will charge $\underline{\$50.00}$ to deliver to this farmer. This farmer

will buy from $\underline{\text{Ben}}$ whose price to him is cheaper by one penny. When the two merchants have this pricing policy, all farmers

who live within $\underline{20}$ miles of Ben will buy from Ben

and all farmers who live within $\underline{20}$ miles of Huey will buy from Huey. A farmer who lives x miles west of Ben and buys

from Ben must pay $\underline{60 - x}$ dollars to have a cookstove delivered to him. A farmer who lives x miles east of Huey and buys from

Huey must pay $\underline{60 - x}$ for delivery of a stove. On the graph below, use blue ink to graph the cost to Ben of delivering to a farmer who lives x miles west of him. Use red ink to graph the total cost to Huey of delivering a cookstove to a farmer who lives x miles west of Ben. Use pencil to mark the lowest price available to a farmer as a

---

Chapter 27

Game Theory

27.1 (25) Maynard's Cross is a trendy bistro that specializes in carpaccio, and other uncooked substances. Most people who come to Maynard's come to see and be seen by other people of the kind who come to Maynard's. There is however, a hard core of 10 customers per evening who come for the carpaccio and don't care how many other people come. The number of additional customers who appear at Maynard's depends on how many people they expect to see. In particular, if people expect that the number of customers at Maynard's in an evening will be X, then the number of people who actually come to Maynard's is $Y = 10 + .75X$. In equilibrium, it must be true that the number of people who actually attend the restaurant is equal to the number who are expected to attend.

(a) What two simultaneous equations must one solve to find the equilibrium attendance at Maynard's.

$y = 10 + .75x$ and $x = y$.

(b) What is the equilibrium nightly attendance? __40__

(c) On the axes below, draw the lines that represents each of two equations you mentioned in part (a). Label the equilibrium attendance level.

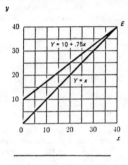

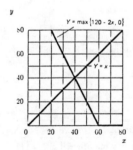

(b) Suppose that people expect the number of customers on any given night to be the same as the previous night's attendance. Suppose that 50 customers show up at Yogi's on the first day of business. How many will

show up on the second day? __20;_____the third day? _____

__80;_____the fourth day? _____0;_____the

fifth day? _____120;_____the ninety-ninth day? _____0;_____

_____the hundredth day? _____120._____

(c) What would you say is wrong with this model if at least some of Yogi's customers have memory spans of more than a day or two?

Customers would notice that last night's attendance is not a good predictor of tonight's attendance. In fact, if the cycle were to persist, they would notice that attendance is low on odd numbered days and high on even numbered days. Noticing this, they would tend to come on odd numbered days.

27.3 (20) Consider the following game matrix.

(d) Suppose that one additional carpaccio enthusiast moves to the area. Like the other 10, he eats at Maynard's every night no matter how many others eat there. Write down the new equations determining attendance at Maynard's and solve for the new equilibrium number of customers.

$y = 11 + .75x$ and $y = x$.

(e) Use a different color ink to draw a new line representing the equation that changed. How many additional customers did the new steady customer attract? __44__

(f) Suppose that everyone bases expectations about tonight's attendance on last night's attendance and that last night's attendance is public knowledge. Then $X_t = Y_{t-1}$, where X_t is expected attendance on day t and Y_t is actual attendance on day $t - 1$. At any time t, $Y_t = 10 + 3/4X_t$. Suppose that on the first night that Maynard's is open, attendance is 20.

What will be attendance on the second night? __25__

(g) What will be the attendance on the third night? __28.75__

_____

(h) Attendance will tend toward some limiting value. What is it? _____

__40__

27.2 (20) Yogi's Bar and Grill is frequented by unsociable types who hate crowds. If Yogi's regular customers expect that the crowd at Yogi's will be X, then the number of people who show up at Yogi's, Y, will be the larger of the two numbers, $120 - 2X$ and 0. Thus $Y = \max\{120 - 2X, 0\}$.

(a) Solve for equilibrium attendance at Yogi's. Draw a diagram depicting equilibrium on the axes below.

A game matrix.

		Player B	
		Left	Right
Player A	Top	a, b	c, d
	Bottom	e, f	g, h

(a) If (top, left) is a dominant strategy equilibrium, then we know that

$a >$ __e__, $b >$ __d__, _____ __c__, _____ $> g$, and _____

__f._____$> h$.

(b) If (top, left) is a Nash equilibrium, then which of the above inequalities must be satisfied? __$a > e; b > d$.__

(c) If (top, left) is a dominant strategy equilibrium must it be a Nash equilibrium? __Yes._____Why?

If the conditions for a dominant strategy are fulfilled, the conditions for a Nash equilibrium are also fulfilled.

27.4 (25) This problem is based on an example developed by the biologist, John Maynard Smith, to illustrate the uses of game theory in the theory of evolution. Males of a certain species frequently come into conflict with other males over the opportunity to mate with females. If a male runs into a situation of conflict, he has two alternative "strategies." A male can play "Hawk" in which case he will fight the other male until he either wins or is badly hurt. Or he can play "Dove," in which case he makes a display of bravery but retreats if his opponent starts to fight. If an animal plays Hawk and meets another male who is playing Hawk, they both are seriously injured in battle. If he is playing Hawk and meets an animal who is playing Dove, the Hawk gets to mate with the female and the Dove slinks off to celibate contemplation. If an animal is playing Dove and meets another Dove, they both strut around for awhile. Eventually the female either chooses one of them or gets bored and wanders off. The expected payoffs to each of two males in a single encounter depend on which strategy each adopts. These payoffs are depicted in the box below.

The Hawk-Dove game.

		Animal B	
		Hawk	Dove
Animal A	Hawk	−5, −5	10, 0
	Bottom	0, 10	4, 4

(a) Now while wandering through the forest, a male will encounter many conflict situations of this type. Suppose that he can not tell in advance whether another animal which he meets will behave like a Hawk or like a Dove. The payoff to adopting either strategy oneself depends on the proportion of the other guys that are Hawks and the proportion that are Doves. For example, suppose all of the other males in the forest act like Doves. Any male that acted like a Hawk would find that his rival always retreated and would therefore enjoy a payoff of ___10___

_____ on every encounter. If a male acted like a Dove when all other males acted like Doves, he would receive an average payoff of ___4___

(b) If strategies which are more profitable tend to be chosen over strategies that are less profitable, explain why there cannot be an equilibrium in which all males act like Doves.

If you know that you are playing opposite a Dove, then the payoff from playing a Hawk will dominate the payoff from playing a Dove. Therefore, everyone playing a Dove is not a Nash equilibrium.

(c) If all the other males acted like Hawks, then a male who adopted the Hawk strategy would be sure to encounter another Hawk and would get a payoff of ___−5.___ If instead, this male adopted the Dove strategy, he would again be sure to encounter a Hawk, but his payoff would be ___0___

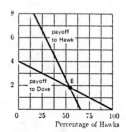

(i) If the proportion of Hawks is slightly greater than E, which strategy does better? ___Hawk___ If the proportion of Hawks is slightly less than E, which strategy does better? ___Dove___

_____ If the more profitable strategy tends to be adopted more frequently in future plays, then if the strategy proportions are out of equilibrium, will changes tend to move the proportions back towards equilibrium or further away from equilibrium? ___further away___

27.5 (15) Evangeline and Gabriel met at a freshman mixer. They want desperately to meet each other again, but they forgot to exchange names or phone numbers when they met the first time. There are two possible strategies available for each of them. These are Go to the Big Party or Stay Home and Study. They will surely meet if they both go to the party and they will surely not otherwise. The payoff to meeting is 1,000 for each of them. The payoff to not meeting is zero for both of them. The payoffs are described by the matrix below.

Close Encounters of the Second Kind

		Gabriel	
		Go To Party	Stay Home
Evangeline	Go To Party	1000, 1000	0, 0
	Stay Home	0, 0	0, 0

(d) Explain why there could not be an equilibrium where all of the animals acted like Hawks.

If everyone plays Hawk, it would be profitable to play Dove.

(e) Since there is not an equilibrium in which everybody chooses the same strategy, we might ask whether there might be an equilibrium in which some fraction of the males chose the Hawk strategy and the rest chose the Dove strategy. Suppose that the fraction of a large male population that chooses the Hawk strategy is p. Then if one acts like a Hawk, the fraction of one's encounters in which he meets another Hawk is about p and the fraction of one's encounters in which he meets a Dove is about $1 - p$. Therefore the average payoff to being a Hawk when the fraction of Hawks in the population is $p \times (-5) + (1 - p) \times 10 = 10 - 15p$. Similarly, if one acts like a Dove, the probability of meeting a Hawk is about p and the probability of meeting another Dove is about $(1 - p)$. Therefore the average payoff to being a Dove when the proportion of Hawks in the population is p will be $p \times 0 + (1 - p) \times 4$.

(f) Write an equation that states that when the proportion of the population that acts like Hawks is p, the payoff to Hawks is the same as the payoffs to Doves. $4 - 4p = 10 - 15p$

(g) Solve this equation for the value of p such that at this value Hawks do exactly as well as Doves. This requires that $p =$ ___6/11.___

(h) On the axes below, use blue ink to graph the average payoff to the strategy Dove when the proportion of the male population who are Hawks is p. Use red ink to graph the average payoff to the strategy, Hawk, when the proportion of the male population who are Hawks is p. Label the equilibrium proportion in your diagram by E.

(a) Find all of the dominant strategy equilibria for this game. _____
The only dominant strategy equilibrium is (Top, Left).

(b) Find all of the pure Nash equilibria for this game. ___(Top, Left)___ and (Bottom, Right).

(c) Of the pure Nash equilibria that you found, do any of them seem to be "more reasonable" than others? Why or why not?
Although (Bottom, Right) is a Nash equilibrium it seems a silly one since if either player believes that there is even the slightest chance that the other will go to the party, he or she will want to go himself. The only way it can make sense to stay home is if you are absolutely certain the other person is staying home.

(d) Let us change the game a little bit. Evangeline and Gabriel are still desperate to find each other. But now there are two parties that they might go to. There is a little party at which they would be sure to meet if they both went there and a huge party where they might never see each other. The expected payoff to each of them is 1,000 if they both go to the little party. Since there is only a 50-50 chance that they would each other at the huge party, the expected payoff to each of them is only 500. If they go to different parties, the payoff to both of them is zero. The payoff matrix for this game is:

More Close Encounters

		Gabriel	
		Little Party	Big Party
Evangeline	Little Party	1000, 1000	0, 0
	Big Party	0, 0	500, 500

(e) Does this game have a dominant strategy equilibrium? ___No.___

_____ What are the two Nash equilibria in pure strategies?
The Nash equilbria are: both go to the little party, and both go to the big party.

(f) One of the Nash equilibria is Pareto superior to the other. Suppose that each person thought that there was some slight chance that the other would go to the little party. Would that be enough to convince them both to attend the little party? __No__ Can you think of any reason why the Pareto superior equilibrium might emerge if both players understand the game matrix. and both know that the other understands it. and each knows that the other knows that he or she understands the game matrix.

_____ If both know the game matrix and each knows

that the other knows it, then each might predict that

the other will think that it is more likely that both will

go to the little party

27.6 (10) This is a famous game. know to game theorists as "The Battle of the Sexes." The story goes like this. Two people, let us call them Roger and Michelle. although they greatly enjoy each others' company. have very different tastes in entertainment. Roger's tastes run to ladies' mud wrestling, while Michelle prefers the Italian opera. They are planning their entertainment activities for next Saturday night. For each of them. there are two possible actions. go to the wrestling match or go to the opera. Roger would be happiest if both of them went to see mud wrestling. His second choice would be for both of them to go to the opera. Michelle would prefer if both went to the opera. Her second choice would be that they both went to see the mud wrestling. They both think that the worst outcomes would be that they don't agree on where to go. If this happens, they both stay home and sulk.

Battle of the Sexes

		Michelle	
		Wrestling	Opera
Roger	Wrestling	2.1	0.0
	Opera	0.0	1.2

(a) Is this a zero sum game? __No__ Does this game have

a dominant strategy equilibrium? __No__

_____

(a) Suppose that the coin is unbalanced and lands on heads 80% of the

time and tails 20% of the time. Now what is your best strategy? _____

Always call heads.

(b) What if the coin lands 50% of the time on heads and 50% on tails? What is your best strategy?

_____ It doesn't matter—you can either always call

heads, always call tails, or randomize your calls. since

the expected value will be the same in any of these cases.

(c) Now, suppose that I am able to choose the type (i.e., the probability that the coin will land on heads) of coin that I will toss, and that you will know my choice. What type of coin should I choose to minimize my

losses? __I should choose a fair coin (probability of landing

on heads equal to 50%).

(d) What is the Nash mixed strategy equilibrium for this game? (It may help to recognize that a lot of symmetry exists in the game.)

we both randomize 50:50

27.9 (20) Ned and Ruth love to play "Hide and Seek." It is a simple game, but it continues to amuse. It goes like this. Ruth hides upstairs or downstairs. Ned can either look upstairs or downstairs but not in both places. If he finds Ruth, Ned gets 1 scoop of ice cream and Ruth gets none. If he does not find Ruth, Ruth gets 1 scoop of ice cream and Ned gets none. Fill in the payoffs in the matrix below.

Hide and Seek

		Ruth	
		upstairs	downstairs
Ned	upstairs		
	downstairs		

(a) Is this a zero sum game? __Yes.__ What are the Nash equilibria in pure strategies?

_____ No pure Nash equilibria exist for this game.

(b) Can you find a Nash equilibrium in mixed strategies for this game? __Yes, each choice is played with probability 1/2.__

(b) Find two Nash equilibria in pure strategies for this game? __Both go

to the opera. Both go to the mud wrestling.

(c) Find a Nash equilibrium in mixed strategies

Each person plays each strategy with probability 1/2.

27.7 This is another famous two-person game. known to game theorists as "Chicken." Two teenagers in souped up cars drive towards each other at great speed. The first one to swerve out of the road is "chicken." The best thing that can happen to you is that the other guy swerves and you don't. Then you are the hero and the other guy is the chicken. If you both swerve. you are both chickens. If neither swerves. you both end up in the hospital. A payoff matrix for a chicken-type game is the following.

Chicken

		Leroy	
		Swerve	Don't Swerve
Joe Bob	Swerve	1.1	1.2
	Don't Swerve	2.1	0.0

(a) Does this game have a dominant strategy? __No.__

_____ Does it have any Nash equilibria in pure strategies? __Yes.__

_____ There are two Nash equilibria in pure

strategies. Each of these equilibria has one teenager

swerving and the other not swerving.

(b) Find a Nash equilibrium in mixed strategies for this game. __Play

each strategy with probability 1/2.

27.8 (15) I propose the following game: I flip a coin and while it is in the air you call either heads or tails. If you call the coin correctly. you get to keep the coin. Suppose that the coin always lands on heads, what is the

best strategy for you to pursue? __Always call heads.

(c) After years of playing this game. Ned and Ruth thought of a way to liven it up a little. Now if Ned finds Ruth upstairs. he gets 2 scoops of ice cream but if he finds her downstairs. he gets 1 scoop. If Ned finds Ruth. she gets no ice cream but if he doesn't find her she gets 1 scoop. Fill in the payoffs in the graph below.

Advanced Hide and Seek

		Ruth	
		upstairs	downstairs
Ned	upstairs		
	downstairs		

(d) Are there any Nash equilibria in pure strategies? __No__

_____ Is there a Nash equilibrium in mixed strategies? _____

Yes, Ned looks upstairs with probability $\frac{1}{2}$, downstairs with

probability $\frac{1}{2}$. Ruth hides upstairs with probability $\frac{1}{3}$

downstairs with probability $\frac{2}{3}$.

27.10 (60) Economic ideas and equilibrium analysis have many fascinating applications in biology. Popular discussions of natural selection and biological "fitness" often take it for granted that animal traits are selected for the "benefit of the species." Modern thinking in biology emphasizes that individuals (or strictly speaking, genes) are the unit of selection. A mutant gene that induces an animal to behave in such a way as to help the species at the expense of the individuals that carry that gene will soon be eliminated. no matter how beneficial that behavior is to the species.

A good illustration is a paper in the *Journal of Theoretical Biology*, 1979, by Brockmann, Grafen, and Dawkins called "Evolutionarily Stable Nesting Strategy in a Digger Wasp." They maintain that natural selection results in behavioral strategies that maximize an individual animal's expected rate of reproduction over the course of its lifetime. According to the authors. "Time is the currency which an animal spends. "

Females of the digger wasp *Sphex ichneumoneus* nest in underground burrows. Some of these wasps dig their own burrows. After she has dug her burrow. a wasp goes out to the fields and hunts katydids. These she stores in her burrow to be used as food for her offspring when they hatch. When she has accumulated several katydids. she lays a single egg in the burrow, closes the food chamber, and starts the process over again. But digging burrows and catching katydids is time-consuming. An alternative strategy for a female wasp is to sneak into somebody else's burrow while she is out hunting katydids. This happens frequently in digger wasp colonies. A wasp will enter a burrow that has been dug by another wasp and partially stocked with katydids. The invader will start catching katydids. herself. to add to the stock. When the founder and the invader finally meet, they fight. The loser of the fight goes away and never comes back. The winner gets to lay her egg in the nest.

Since some wasps dig their own burrows and some invade burrows begun by others, it is likely that we are observing a biological equilibrium in which each strategy is as effective a way for a wasp to use its time for producing offspring as the other. If one strategy were more effective than the other, then we would expect that a gene that led wasps to behave in the more effective way would prosper at the expense of genes that led them to behave in a less effective way.

We now consider some possible descriptions of equilibrium. These are similar in spirit, but not in detail, to alternatives posed by the authors of the original paper.

Suppose the average nesting episode takes 5 days for a wasp that digs its own burrow and tries to stock it with katydids. Suppose that the average nesting episode takes only 4 days for invaders. Suppose that when they meet, half of the time the founder of the nest wins the fight and half of the time the invader wins. Let D be the number of wasps that dig their own burrows and let I be the number of wasps that invade the burrows of others. The fraction of the digging wasps that are invaded will be about $\frac{5}{4}\frac{I}{D}$. (Assume for the time being that $\frac{5}{4}\frac{I}{D} < 1$.) Half of the diggers who are invaded will win their fight and get to keep their burrows. The fraction of digging wasps who lose their burrows to other wasps is then $\frac{1}{2}\frac{5}{4}\frac{I}{D} = \frac{5}{8}\frac{I}{D}$. Assume also that all of the wasps who are not invaded by other wasps will successfully stock their burrows and lay their eggs.

(a) Then the fraction of the digging wasps who do not lose their burrows is just _____ $1 - \frac{5}{8}\frac{I}{D}$.

Therefore over a period of 40 days, a wasp who dug her own burrow every time would have 8 nesting episodes. Her expected number of successes would be _____ $8 - 5\frac{I}{D}$

(b) In 40 days, a wasp who chose to invade every time she had a chance would have time for 10 invasions. Assuming that she is successful on the average half the time, her expected number of successes would be _____ 5. _____ Write an equation that expresses the condition that wasps who always dig their own burrows do exactly as well as wasps who always invade burrows dug by others.

$8 - 5\frac{I}{D} = 5$

invaders, it might be that the expected number of eggs that a founder gets to lay is an increasing rather than a decreasing function of the number of invaders. On the axes below, show an equilibrium in which digging one's own burrow is an increasingly effective strategy as $\frac{I}{D}$ increases and in which the payoff to invading is constant over all ratios of $\frac{I}{D}$. Is this equilibrium stable? _____ Yes.

(f) Explain.

If the ratio $\frac{I}{D}$ is greater then the equilibrium ratio, there is a bigger payoff to digging than to invading. If $\frac{I}{D}$ is less than the equilibrium ratio, the payoff to invading exceeds the payoff to digging. In each case the responses move toward equilibrium.

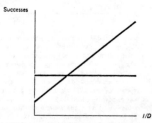

(g) The authors of the study investigated whether the average number of successful nestings per season for a digger was higher or lower if the digger was invaded more often. The answer turned out to be "lower". Therefore the story told in the last section, though it might be interesting for some species that share nests, does not apply to digger wasps. The authors proposed a more elaborate explanation involving burrows that were abandoned because of invasions by ants and centipedes. Rather than pursue that explanation in detail, we will consider a simplified version. So far, while the payoff to the diggers has depended on $\frac{I}{D}$, the return to invaders has been independent of this ratio. But suppose invaders have to spend time searching for a likely burrow to invade. The more invaders there are relative to diggers, the longer it will take an invader to find a promising burrow. Furthermore, if there are many invaders relative to diggers, it becomes probable that more than one invader will enter some burrows and the invaders may have to compete among themselves

(c) The equation you have just written should contain the expression $\frac{I}{D}$. Solve for the numerical value of $\frac{I}{D}$ that just equates the expected number of successes for diggers and invaders. The answer is $\frac{3}{5}$. _____

_____

(d) Just when you may have thought you were getting somewhere, we come upon a snag. The problem is that the equilibrium we have found doesn't appear to be stable. To see this, let us draw a diagram. On the axes below, use blue ink to graph the expected number of successes in a 40-day period for wasps that dig their own burrows every time where the number of successes is a function of $\frac{I}{D}$. Use black ink to graph the expected number of successes in a 40-day period for invaders. Notice that this number is the same for all values of $\frac{I}{D}$. Label the point where these two lines cross and notice that this is equilibrium. Just to the right of the crossing, where $\frac{I}{D}$ is just a little bit bigger than the equilibrium value, which line is higher, the blue or the black? black _____

_____ At this level of $\frac{I}{D}$, which is the more effective strategy for any individual wasp? invade _____ Suppose that if one strategy is more effective than the other, the proportion of wasps adopting the more effective one increases. If, after being in equilibrium, the population got joggled just a little to the right of equilibrium, would the proportions of diggers and invaders return toward equilibrium or move further away?

further away

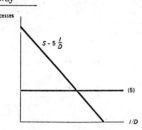

(e) The authors of the study cited above noticed this likely instability and cast around for possible changes in the model that would lead to stability. They observed that an invading wasp does help to stock the burrow with katydids. This may save the founder some time. If founders win their battles often enough and get enough help with katydids from

as well as with the original occupant. We can expect, then, that the payoff to invading will also be less profitable as the ratio of diggers to invaders increases. Suppose that a wasp who always chooses to invade other burrows succeeds in producing $\frac{2D}{I}$ viable eggs per 40-day period and that a wasp who always digs her own burrow succeeds in producing $8(1 - \frac{3I}{D})$ viable eggs per 40-day period. Denote the ratio $\frac{I}{D}$ by x. Write an equation in terms of x that states the condition that wasps who dig their own burrows, will on the average do just as well as wasps who invade burrows dug by others. _____ $\frac{3}{x} = 8 - 5x$

(h) Solve this equation for x. This should be a quadratic equation with two solutions for x. The solutions are _____ 1 _____ and _____ 3/5 _____

(i) On the axes below, graph the average payoff to diggers and the average payoff to invaders as a function of x. (Hint: One of these lines will be a hyperbola, and the other one will be a straight line.)

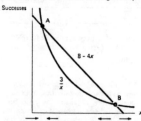

(j) in the graph you have just drawn, the lines cross twice, representing two possible equilibrium situations where diggers are just as well off as invaders. Label the equilibrium with the smaller ratio, x, of invaders to diggers with the label A and label the other equilibrium B. If x is just slightly bigger than A, which kind of wasp does better? Invaders _____

_____

(k) If x is just slightly smaller than A, which kind of wasp does better? Assuming that the kind of wasp that is doing better reproduces more than the kind that is doing worse, is there a tendency to move back to equilibrium after a small deviation from A? Diggers _____ *(l)* If x is just slightly bigger than B. which kind of wasp does better?___

_____Diggers_____

(m) If x is just slightly smaller than B. which kind of wasp does better?

_____Invaders_____

(n) Again assuming that the kind of wasp that is doing better reproduces more than the kind that is doing worse, is there a tendency to move back

to equilibrium after a small deviation from B?_____Yes._____

Chapter 28

Exchange

28.1 (20) Mutt and Jeff are going to trade corned beef and cabbage. Mutt has 4 pounds of cabbage and no beef, and Jeff has 4 pounds of beef and no cabbage. Mutt is indifferent between corned beef and cabbage. Jeff always consumes corned beef and cabbage in fixed proportions of 1:1.

(a) Illustrate the endowment in the following Edgeworth box. Use blue ink to draw some indifference curves for each person in the Edgeworth box. Use red ink to show the locus of Pareto efficient allocations.

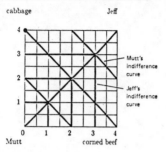

(b) If Mutt and Jeff were to trade using a competitive market, what would be the equilibrium ratio of the price of corned beef to the price of cabbage? _____1_____ What would be the equilibrium consumption bundle for Jeff? _____(2, 2)_____

28.2 (5) Consider a pure exchange economy with two consumers and two goods. At some given Pareto efficient allocation it is known that both consumers are consuming both goods and that consumer A has a marginal rate of substitution between the two goods of 2. What is consumer B's marginal rate of substitution between these two goods? ___2___

(b) In the same diagram, use a red pencil to draw in the competitive equilibrium budget line. What is p_2/p_1 in equilibrium? $p_2/p_1 = 1$

28.5 (20) Remember Tommy Twit from Chapter 3? Tommy is happiest when he has 8 cookies and 4 glasses of milk per day and his indifference curves are concentric circles centered around (8,4). Tommy's mother, Mrs. Twit, has strong views on nutrition. She believes that too much of anything is as bad as too little. She believes that the perfect diet for Tommy would be 8 glasses of milk and 2 cookies per day. In her view, a diet is healthier the smaller is the sum of the absolute values of the differences between the amounts of each food consumed and the ideal amounts. For example, if Tommy eats 6 cookies and drinks 6 glasses of milk, Mrs. Twit believes that he has 4 too many cookies and 2 too few glasses of milk, so the sum of the absolute values of the differences from her ideal amounts is 6. On the axes below, plot some other combinations of milk and cookies that Mrs. Twit thinks are no better or worse for Tommy than (6,6).

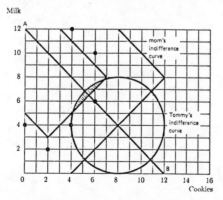

On the same graph you used for Tommy's indifference curves, use blue ink to draw an indifference curve representing the locus of consumption combinations that Mrs. Twit thinks are exactly as healthy for Tommy as 7 cookies and 8 glasses of milk. Also draw her indifference curve representing consumptions that she thinks are exactly as good for Tommy as 8

28.3 (20) Suppose that Mutt and Jeff have 4 cups of milk and 4 cups of juice to divide between themselves. Each has the same utility function given by $u(m, j) = \max\{m, j\}$, where m is the amount of milk and j is the amount of juice that each has. That is, each of them cares only about the larger of the two amounts of liquid that he has and is indifferent to the liquid of which he has the smaller amount.

(a) Sketch an Edgeworth box for Mutt and Jeff. Use blue ink to show a couple of indifference curves for each. Use red ink to show the locus of Pareto optimal allocations. (Hint: Look for boundary solutions.)

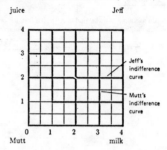

28.4 (20) Al has a utility function given by $u_A(x_A^1, x_A^2) = \min\{x_A^1, x_A^2\}$, and Bob has a utility function given by $u_B(x_B^1, x_B^2) = x_B^1 + x_B^2$. Al initially has 10 units of good 1 and none of good 2. Bob initially has 10 units of good 2 and none of good 1.

(a) In the Edgeworth box below, illustrate a few of each person's indifference curves and the endowment. Mark the endowment with the letter W.

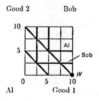

cookies and 4 glasses of milk. Use red ink to sketch Tommy's indifference curve running through all combinations that he thinks are exactly as good as 7 cookies and 8 glasses of milk.

(a) On the graph, shade in the area consisting of combinations of cookies and milk that both Tommy and his mother agree are better than 7 cookies and 8 glasses of milk where "better" for Mrs. Twit means she thinks it is healthier, and "better" for Tommy means he likes it better.

(b) Use black ink to sketch the locus of combinations of cookies and milk that have the property that it is impossible to change the combination in such a way as to make Tommy like it better without his mother thinking the change is bad for Tommy. Label the endpoints of this locus A and B.

28.6 (20) Consider a small exchange economy with two consumers, Astrid and Birger, and two commodities, herring and cheese. Astrid's initial endowment is 4 units of herring and 1 unit of cheese. Birger's initial endowment has no herring and 7 units of cheese. Astrid's utility function is $U(H_A, C_A) = H_A C_A$. Birger is a more inflexible person. His utility function is $U(H_B, C_B) = \min\{H_B, C_B\}$. (Here H_A and C_A are the amounts of herring and cheese for Astrid and H_B and C_B are amounts of herring and cheese for Birger.)

(a) Draw an Edgeworth box, showing the initial allocation, and sketching in a few indifference curves. Measure Astrid's consumption from the lower left and Birger's from the upper right. In your Edgeworth box, draw two different indifference curves for each person, using blue ink for Astrid's and red ink for Birger's.

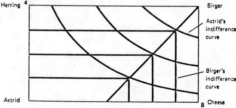

(b) Use black ink to show the locus of Pareto optimal allocations. (Hint: Since Birger is kinky, calculus won't help much here. But notice that because of the rigidity of the proportions in which he demands the two goods, it would be inefficient to give Birger a positive amount of either good if he had less than that amount of the other good. What does that tell you about where the Pareto efficient locus has to be?)

Pareto efficient allocations must be on boundary of box.

28.7 (30) Dean Foster Z. Interface and Professor J. Fetid Nightsoil exchange bromides and platitudes. Dean Interface's utility function is

$$U_I(B_I, P_I) = B_I + 2\sqrt{P_I}.$$

Professor Nightsoil's utility function is

$$U_N(B_N, P_N) = B_N + 4\sqrt{P_N}.$$

Dean Interface's initial endowment is 6 bromides and 2 platitudes. Professor Nightsoil's initial endowment is 8 platitudes and 4 bromides.

(a) Label the initial endowment E in the following Edgeworth box.

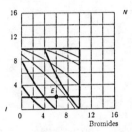

Platitudes

Bromides

(b) If Dean Interface consumes P_I platitudes and B_I bromides, his marginal rate of substitution will be $\underline{P_I^{-1/2}}$. If Professor Nightsoil consumes P_N platitudes and B_N bromides, his marginal rate of substitution will be $\underline{2P_N^{-1/2}}$.

(c) On the contract curve, Dean Interface's marginal rate of substitution equals Professor Nightsoil's. Write an equation that states this condition.

$\underline{\sqrt{P_I} = \sqrt{P_N}/2}$ This equation is especially simple because each person's marginal rate of substitution depends only on his consumption of platitudes and not on his consumption of bromides.

(d) From this equation we see that $P_I/P_N = \underline{1/4}$ at all points on the contract curve. This gives us one equation in the two unknowns P_I and P_N.

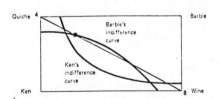

(b) Use blue ink to draw an indifference curve for Ken that shows allocations in which her utility is 4. Use red ink to draw an indifference curve for Barbie that shows allocations in which his utility is 6.

(c) Write an expression for each person's marginal rate of substitution between quiche and wine as a function of that person's consumption of each good. For Ken, $\underline{W_K/Q_K}$. For Barbie, $\underline{W_B/Q_B}$.

(d) At a Pareto optimal allocation in which each person gets some of each good, what must be true of the two people's marginal rates of substitution?

They must be equal.

(e) Write an equation that states this condition in terms of the consumptions of each good by each person. On your graph, show the locus of points that are Pareto efficient. (Hint: If two people must each consume two goods in the same proportions as each other, and if together they must consume twice as much wine as quiche, what must those proportions be?)

$$W_B/Q_B = W_K/Q_K$$

(f) Is the allocation where Ken gets 3 quiches and 6 containers of wine Pareto efficient? Yes.

(g) Calculate each person's marginal rate of substitution at this point.

The MRS for Ken is $\underline{2}$ and the MRS for Barbie is $\underline{2}$.

(e) But we also know that along the contract curve it must be that $P_I + P_N = \underline{10}$, since the total consumption of platitudes must equal the total endowment of platitudes.

(f) Solving these two equations in two unknowns, we find that everywhere on the contract curve, P_I and P_N are constant and equal to _____

$\underline{P_I = 2}$ and $\underline{P_N = 8}$.

(g) Therefore the contract curve is a (vertical) (horizontal) (diagonal) line in the Edgeworth box. Horizontal

(h) Dean Interface has thick gray penciled indifference curves. Professor Nightsoil has red indifference curves. Draw a few of these in the Edgeworth box you made. Use blue ink to show the locus of Pareto optimal points.

(i) Find the competitive equilibrium prices and quantities. You know what the prices have to be at competitive equilibrium because you know what the marginal rates of substitution have to be at every Pareto optimum. $\underline{P_I = 2 \text{ and } P_N = 8}$

28.8 (35) A little exchange economy contains just two consumers, named Ken and Barbie, and two commodities, quiche and wine. Ken's initial endowment is 3 units of quiche and 2 units of wine. Barbie's initial endowment is 1 unit of quiche and 6 units of wine. Ken and Barbie have identical utility functions. We write Ken's utility function as $U(Q_K, W_K) = Q_K W_K$ and Barbie's utility function as $U(Q_B, C_B) = Q_B W_B$, where Q_K and W_K are the amounts of quiche and wine for Ken and Q_B and W_B are amounts of quiche and wine for Barbie.

(a) Draw an Edgeworth box below, to illustrate this situation. Put wine on the horizontal axis and quiche on the vertical axis. Measure goods for Ken from the lower left corner of the box and goods for Barbie from the upper right corner of the box. (Be sure that you make the length of the box equal to the total supply of wine and the height equal to the total supply of quiche.) Locate the initial allocation in your box and label it W. On the sides of the box, label the quantities of quiche and wine for each of the two consumers in the initial endowment.

(h) Show that in this example, Ken's marginal rate of substitution between quiche and wine is equal to 2 at all Pareto optimal allocations.

At a Pareto optimum, we must have $W_B/Q_B = W_K/Q_K$, $Q_B + Q_K = 4$, and $W_B + W_K = 8$. This implies $W_B/Q_B = W_K/Q_K = 2$.

(i) What must be the relative prices of quiche and wine at a competitive equilibrium? $\underline{p_q/p_w = 2}$

(j) We know that a competitive equilibrium must be Pareto optimal and that in competitive equilibrium, each person's marginal rate of substitution between quiche and wine must be equal to the ratio of the price of quiche to the price of wine. Since demand and supply depend only on *relative* prices, there is a competitive equilibrium in which the price of wine is 1 and the price of quiche is $\underline{2}$.

(k) What must be Ken's consumption bundle in competitive equilibrium? $\underline{2 \text{ quiche, } 4 \text{ wine.}}$ How about Barbie's consumption bundle? $\underline{2 \text{ quiche, } 4 \text{ wine.}}$ (Hint: You found competitive equilibrium prices above. You know Ken's initial endowment and you know the equilibrium prices. In equilibrium Ken's income will be the value of her endowment at competitive prices. Knowing her income and the prices, you can compute her demand in competitive equilibrium. Having solved for Ken's consumption and knowing that total consumption by Ken and Barbie equals the sum of their endowments, it should be easy to find Barbie's consumption.)

(l) On the Edgeworth box for Ken and Barbie, draw in the competitive equilibrium allocation and draw Ken's competitive budget line (with black ink).

28.9 (50) This problem combines equilibrium analysis with some of the things you learned in the chapter on intertemporal choice.

On the planet Drongo, there is just one commodity, cake, and two time periods. There are two kinds of creatures, "old" and "young." Old creatures have an income of I units of cake in period 1 and no income in period 2. Young creatures have no income in period 1 and an income of I^* in period 2. There are N_1 old creatures and N_2 young creatures. The consumption bundles of interest to creatures are pairs (c_1, c_2), where c_1 is cake in period 1 and c_2 is cake in period 2. All creatures, old and young, have identical utility functions, representing preferences over cake in the two periods. This utility function is $U(c_1, c_2) = c_1^a c_2^{1-a}$, where a is a number such that $0 \leq a \leq 1$.

(a) If current cake is taken to be the *numeraire*, (that is, its price is set at 1), write an expression for the present value of a consumption bundle (c_1, c_2). $\underline{c_1 + c_2/(1+r)}$ Write down the present value of income for old creatures $\underline{I;}$ for young creatures $\underline{I^*/(1+r)}$. The budget line for any creature is determined by the condition that the present value of its consumption bundle equals the present value of its income. Write down this budget equation for old creatures $\underline{c_1 + c_2/(1+r) = I:}$ for young creatures $\underline{c_1 + c_2/(1+r) = I^*/(1+r)}$.

(b) If the interest rate is r, write down an expression for an old creature's demand for cake in period 1 $\underline{c_1 = a\,I}$ and in period 2 $\underline{c_2 = (1-a)(1+r)I}$. Write an expression for a young creature's demand for cake in period 1 $\underline{c_2^* = \dfrac{aI^*}{(1+r)}}$ in period 2 $\underline{c_2^* = (1-a)I^*}$. (Hint: remember that if someone has a budget line $p_1 c_1 + p_2 c_2 = W$ and a utility function of the form proposed above, then that individual's demand function for good 1 is $c_1 = aw/p$ and demand for good 2 is $c_2 = (1-a)w/p$.) If the interest rate is zero, how much cake would a young creature choose in each period? $\underline{c_1^* = aI^*}$ and $\underline{c_2^* = (1-a)I^*}$ For what value of a would it choose the same amount in each period if the interest rate is zero? $\underline{a = .5}$ If $a = .55$, what would r have to be in order that young creatures would want to consume the same amount in each period.

(c) The total supply of cake in period 1 equals the total cake earnings of all old creatures, since young people earn no cake in this period. There are N_1 old creatures and each earns I units of cake, so this total is $N_1 I$. Similarly, the total supply of cake in period 2 equals the total amount

earned by young creatures. This amount is $\underline{N_2 I^*}$.

(d) At the equilibrium interest rate, the total demand of creatures for period 1 cake must equal total supply of period 1 cake, and similarly the demand for period 2 cake must equal supply. If the interest rate is r, then the demand for period 1 cake by each old creature is $\underline{aI,}$ and the demand for period 1 cake by each young creature is $\underline{aI^*/(1+r)}$ Since there are N_1 old creatures and N_2 young creatures, the total demand for period 1 cake at interest rate r is $\underline{N_1 aI + N_2 aI^*/(1+r)}$.

(e) Using the results of the last section, write an equation that sets the demand for period 1 cake equal to the supply. Write a general expression for the equilibrium value of r, given N_1, N_2 I_1, and I_2. $\underline{N_1 aI + N_s aI^*/(1+r) = N_1 I}$. Solution is $r = \underline{\dfrac{N_2 I^* a}{N_1 I(1-a)} - 1}$. For special case, $r = 10\%$.

Solve this equation for the special case when $N_1 = N_2$ and $I_1 = I_2$ and $a = 11/21$.

(f) In the special case at the end of the last section, show that the interest rate that equalizes supply and demand for period 1 cake will also equalize supply and demand for period 2 cake.

Supply equals demand for period 2 cake if $N_1(1-a)I(1+r) + N_2(1-a)I^* = N_2 I^*$. If $N_1 = N_2$ and $I = I^*$, this implies $(1-a)(1+r) + (1-a) = 1$. If $a = 11/21$, then we must have $r = .1$.

(g) Why does this happen?

Because of Walras' law.

Chapter 29

Production

29.1 (30) Tip and Spot finally got into college. Tip has found that he can write term papers at the rate of ten pages per hour and solve workbook problems at the rate of three per hour. Spot on the other hand, can write term papers at the rate of six pages per hour. and solve problems at the rate of two per hour. Like all good students. both Tip and Spot only work six hours per day.

(a) If Tip spends zero hours working on term papers. how many problems can he solve in a day?_____18_____If Tip works two hours on term papers, he can produce _____20_____pages and solve _____12_____workbook problems. If Tip spends six hours working on term papers how many pages can he write?___60.___

(b) In the graph below draw and label Tip's production possibility curve. Draw Spot's production possibility curve (you might want to use a technique similar to that used for Tip above.) If you could hire either Tip or Spot at no charge, which one of them would you employ?___Tip.___

29.2 Assume a Robinson Crusoe economy. For each of the following situations give either graphical or verbal explanation of the economics involved.

(a) An economy with constant returns to scale where the firm makes positive profits is not a competitive equilibrium.

If the firm is making positive profits under constant returns to scale, then the profit maximizing firm can increase its profits by expanding output. However, this implies that it must have additional labor, but since the amount of labor is finite, the firm will demand more labor than is forthcoming, and thus there will be excess demand in the labor market.

(b) A production function exhibiting increasing returns to scale is incompatable with a competitive equilibrium.

In order to increase its profits the firm can always produce more output (a vertical shift in the isoprofit line). However, in order to produce more output the firm must use more labor, but since labor is finite, the demand for labor by the firm will exceed the supply.

(c) It is possible to have a competitive equilibrium, even though the firm has increasing returns to scale over some small initial range of production. (Hint: draw a graph that illustrates the possibility.)

Draw the standard picture and add a small region of increasing returns at small elvels of output.

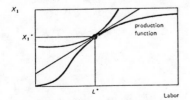

Problems

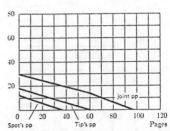

(c) What is Tip's marginal rate of transformation between pages and problems?_____−3.33_____What is Spot's marginal rate of transformation?_____−3_____Which of the two has a comparative advantage in the production of term papers?_____Tip._____

(d) Tip and Spot decide to work together (gasp!). On the above graph plot their joint production possibility curve. Whenever they need to write a term paper. (Tip   ) always works on the paper until over _____60,_____pages are needed. at which time (Spot) begins to help.

(e) True or False? Since Tip can solve three workbook problems in the

False. Even though Tip is more productive than Spot doing workbook problems, Tip's comparative advantage is in term papers. The marginal rates of transformation imply that for every workbook problem Tip does he can't do 3.33 pages of term papers, while Spot only gives up 3 pages of term papers. Thus, if they need to do both, Tip should always work on the term papers.

(d) (20) Assuming a standard production function (see for example the

We already know that the labor demand function is decreasing the wage rate from our study of firms, so this essentially provides the answer.

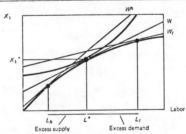

(e) It is possible to have a competitive equilibrium even with a non-

Part *(c)* illustrates that this can happen.

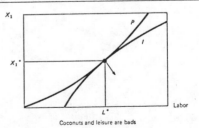

Coconuts and leisure are bads

29.3 (30) Recall our friends the Mungoites of Chapter 2. They have a strange two-currency system consisting of Blue Money and Red Money. Originally, there were two prices for everything. a blue money price and a red money price. The blue currency prices are 1 bcu per unit of ambrosia and 1 bcu per unit of bubblegum. The red currency prices are 2 rcu's per unit of ambrosia and 4 rcu's per unit of bubblegum.

(a) Harold has a blue income of 9 and a red income of 24. If he has to pay in *both* currencies for any purchase, draw his budget set in the graph below. (Hint: you answered this question a few months ago.)

Bubblegum

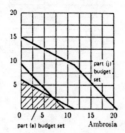

part (j)
budget
set

part (a) budget set   Ambrosia

(b) The Free Choice party campaigns on a platform that Mungoites should be allowed to purchase goods at *either* the blue money price or the red money price, whichever they prefer. We want to construct Harold's budget set if this reform is instituted. To begin with, how much bubblegum could Harold consume if he spent all of his blue money and his red money on bubblegum? 15 units of bubblegum.

(c) How much ambrosia could he consume if he spent all of his blue money and all of his red money on abrosia? 21 units of ambrosia.

(d) If Harold were spending all of his money of both colors on bubblegum and he decided to purchase a little bit of ambrosia, which currency would he use? The red currency.

(e) How much ambrosia could he buy before he ran out of that color money? 12 units of ambrosia.

(f) What would be the slope of this budget line before he ran out of that kind of money? The slope would be $-\frac{1}{2}$.

(g) If Harold were spending all of his money of both colors on ambrosia and he decided to purchase a little bit of bubblegum, which currency would he use? The blue currency.

(h) How much bubblegum could he buy before he ran out of that color money? He could buy 9 units of bubblegum.

(i) What would be the slope of this budget line before he ran out of that kind of money? The slope would be -1.

(j) Use your answers to the above questions to draw Harold's budget set if he could purchase bubblegum and ambrosia using either currency in the above graph.

Chapter 30

Welfare

30.1 (20) One possible method of determining a social preference relation is the *Borda count* also known as rank order voting. Each voter is asked to rank all of the alternatives. If there are 10 alternatives, you give your first choice a 10, your second choice a 9, and so on. The individual scores for each alternative are then added over all individuals. The total score for an alternative is called its Borda count. The social preference relation is defined so that x is "socially at least as good as" y if x has at least as high a Borda count as y. Suppose that there is only a finite number of alternatives to choose from and that every individual has complete, reflexive, and transitive preferences. For the time being, let us also suppose that individuals are never indifferent between any two different alternatives but always prefer one to the other.

(a) Is the social preference ordering defined in this way complete?_____

_____Yes,_____, reflexive?_____yes._____. transitive?___

_____yes,_____

(b) If everyone prefers x to y, will the Borda count rank x as socially preferred to y? Explain your answer.

Yes. If everybody ranks x ahead of y then everyone must give x a higher rank than y. Then the sum of the ranks of x must be larger than the sum of the ranks of y.

(c) Suppose that there are two voters and three candidates, x, y, and z. Suppose that Voter 1 ranks the candidates, x first, z second, and y third. Suppose that Voter 2 ranks the candidates, y first, x second, and z third.

What is the Borda count for x?_____5,_____, for y?_____

_____4,_____, for z?_____3_____Now suppose that

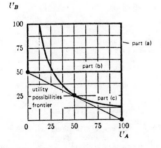

(a) Assume that we want to maximize social welfare. If we have a Nietzschian social welfare function, $W(U_A, U_B) = \max\{U_A, U_B\}$, the maximum will have U_A equal to _____100_____and U_B equal to

_____0._____

(b) If instead we use a Rawlsian criterion, $W(U_A, U_B) = \min\{U_A, U_B\}$, then the social welfare function is maximized where U_A equals _____

_____33.33_____and U_B equals _____33.33._____

(c) Suppose that social welfare is given by $W(U_A, U_B) = U_A^{0.5}U_B^{0.5}$. In this case, social welfare is maximized where U_A equals _____50_____

_____and U_B is _____25._____ (Hint: you might want to think about the similarities between this maximization problem and the consumer's maximization problem with a Cobb-Douglas utility function.)

(d) Show the three social maxima on the above graph. Use black ink to draw a Nietzschian isowelfare line through the Nietzschian maximum. Use red ink to draw a Rawlsian isowelfare line through the Rawlsian maximum. Use blue ink to draw a Cobb-Douglas isowelfare line through the Cobb-Douglas maximum.

30.4 (20) A parent has two children named A and B and she loves both of them equally. She has a total of $1,000 to give to them.

it is discovered that candidate z once lifted a beagle by the ears. Voter 1, who has rather large ears himself, is appalled and changes his ranking to x first, y second, z third. Voter 2, who picks up his own children by the ears, is favorably impressed and changes his ranking to y first, z second, x third. Now what is the Borda count for x?_____4,_____, for y?_____5,_____ for z?_____3_____

(d) Does the social preference relation defined by the Borda count have the property that social preferences between x and y depend only on how people rank x versus y and not on how they rank other alternatives. Explain.

No. The example in the previous section illustrates this. The ranking of z changed but nobody changed his mind about whether x was better than y or *vice versa*. Before the change in the ranking of z, the Borda count of x was greater than that of y. After the change, the Borda count of y was greater than that of x.

30.2 (10) Another possible way to make a social ordering is to put the names of all of the alternatives in a hat, draw the names out at random one at a time, and number them by the order in which they are drawn. The proposed social ranking will then be x is "socially preferred to" y if x is drawn before y. Which of the Arrow axioms are satisfied and which are violated by this ranking?

The Pareto rule is violated: even if everyone prefers x to y, the social ranking will depend on the order in which they are drawn.

30.3 (20) Suppose the utility possibility frontier for two individuals is given by $U_A + 2U_B = 100$. On the graph below plot the utility frontier.

(a) The parent's utility function is $U(a, b) = \sqrt{a} + \sqrt{b}$, where a is the amount of money she gives to A and b is the amount of money she gives to B. How will she choose to divide the money? _____$a = b = \$500$_____

(b) Suppose that her utility function is $U(a, b) = -\frac{1}{a} - \frac{1}{b}$. How will she choose to divide the money? _____$a = b = \$500$_____

(c) Suppose that her utility function is $U(a, b) = \log a + \log b$. How will she choose to divide the money? _____$a = b = \$500$_____

(d) Suppose that her utility function is $U(a, b) = \min\{a, b\}$. How will she choose to divide the money? _____$a = b = \$500$_____

(e) Suppose that her utility function is $U(a, b) = \max\{a, b\}$. How will she choose to divide the money? _____$a = \$1,000, b = 0$, or vice versa_____

(Hint: In the above three cases, we notice that the parent's problem is to maximize $U(a, b)$ subject to the constraint that $a + b = 1,000$. This is just like the consumer problems we studied earlier. It must be that the parent sets her marginal rate of substitution between a and b equal to one since it costs the same to give money to each child.)

(f) Suppose that her utility function is $U(a, b) = a^2 + b^2$. How will she choose to divide the money equally between her children._____She gives everything to one of the children; this is a corner solution._____Explain why she doesn't set her marginal rate of substitution equal to 1 in this case.

Her preferences are not convex, her indifference curves are quarter circles.

30.5 (20) In the previous problem, suppose that A is a much more efficient shopper than B so that A is able to get twice as much consumption goods as B can for every dollar that he spends. Let a be the amount of consumption goods that A gets and b the amount that B gets. We will measure consumption goods so that one unit of consumption goods

costs \$1 for A and \$2 for B. Thus the parent's budget constraint is
$a + 2b = 1000$.

(a) If the mother's utility function is $U(a, b) = a^2 + b^2$, which child will
get more money?____A____Which child will get to consume
more?____A____

(b) If the mother's utility function is $U(a, b) = \log a + \log b$, which child will
get more money?____They get the same amount of money.____

Which child will get to consume more?____A consumes more.____

(c) If the mother's utility function is $U(a, b) = -\frac{1}{a} - \frac{1}{b}$, which child will
get more money?____B will.____Which child will get to consume
more?____The consumption will be the same.____

(d) If the mother's utility function is $U(a, b) = \max\{a, b\}$, which child will
get more money?____A will.____Which child will get to consume
more?____A will consume more.____

(e) If the mother's utility function is $U(a, b) = \min\{a, b\}$, which child will
get more money?____B will.____Which child will get to consume
more?____Their consumption will be the same.____

30.6 Calc (20) Norton and Ralph have a utility possibility frontier which
is given by the following equation, $U_R + U_N^2 = 100$ (where R and N signify
Ralph and Norton respectively).

(a) If we set Norton's utility to zero, what is the highest possible utility
Ralph can achieve?____100.____If we set Ralph's utility to
zero, what is the best Norton can do? ____10____

(b) What are the fair allocations in this case? ____See diagram.____

30.8 (20) Paul and David consume apples and oranges. Paul's utility
function is $U_P(A_P, O_P) = 2A_P + O_P$ and David's utility function is
$U_D(A, O) = A_D + 2O_D$, where A_P and A_D are apple consumption for
Paul and David and O_P and O_D are orange consumption for Paul and
David. There are a total of 12 apples and 12 oranges to divide between
Paul and David. Paul has blue indifference curves. David has red ones.
Draw an Edgeworth box showing some of their indifference curves. Mark
the Pareto optimal allocations on your graph.

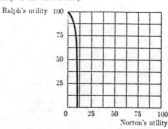

(a) Write one inequality that says that Paul likes his own bundle as well
as he likes David's and write another inequality that says that David likes
his own bundle as well as he likes Paul's.

____$2A_P + O_P \geq 2A_D + O_D$ and $A_D + 2O_D \geq A_P +$____

____$2O_P$____

(b) Use the fact that at feasible allocations, $A_P + A_D = 12$ and $O_P + O_D =$
12 to eliminate A_D and O_D from the first of these equations. Write the
resulting inequality involving only the variables A_P and O_P. Now in your
Edgeworth box, use blue ink to shade in all of the allocations such that
Paul prefers his own allocation to David's. ____$2A_P + O_P \geq 18$____

(c) Use a procedure similar to that you used above to find the allocations
where David prefers his own bundle to Paul's. Describe these points with
an inequality and shade them in on your diagram with red ink.

____$A_D + 2O_D \geq 18$____

(b) Plot the utility possibility frontier on the graph below (put Ralph's
utility on the vertical axis).

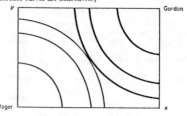

(c) Derive an equation for the slope of the above utility possibility curve.____
$\frac{dU_R}{dU_N} = -2U_N$.____

(d) Both Ralph and Norton believe that the ideal allocation is given by
____$W = U_R + 10U_N$.____

(e) Norton, on the other hand, believes that $U_R = 19$, $U_N = 9$ is the
best distribution. What is the social welfare function Norton presents?
____$W = U_R + 18U_N$.____

30.7 (20) Roger and Gordon have identical utility functions. $U(x, y) =$
$x^2 + y^2$. There are 10 units of x and 10 units of y to be divided between
them. Roger has blue indifference curves. Gordon has red ones.

(a) Draw an Edgeworth box showing some of their indifference curves and
mark the Pareto optimal allocations with black ink. (Hint: Notice that
the indifference curves are nonconvex.)

(d) On your Edgeworth box, mark the fair allocations.

30.9 (30) Romeo loves Juliet and Juliet loves Romeo. Besides love, they
consume only one good, spaghetti. Romeo likes spaghetti, but he also likes
Juliet to be happy and he knows that spaghetti makes her happy. Juliet
likes spaghetti, but she also likes Romeo to be happy and she knows that
spaghetti makes Romeo happy. Romeo's utility function is $U_R(S_R, S_J) =$
$S_R^a S_J^{1-a}$ and Juliet's utility function is $U_J(S_J, S_R) = S_J^a S_R^{1-a}$, where
S_J and S_R are the amount of spaghetti for Romeo and the amount of
spaghetti for Juliet respectively. There is a total of 24 units of spaghetti
to be divided between Romeo and Juliet.

(a) Suppose that $a = 2/3$. If Romeo got to allocate the 24 units of
spaghetti exactly as he wanted to, how much would he give himself?____
____8____How much would he give Juliet?____16____

____(Hint: Notice that this problem is formally just like
the choice problem for a consumer with a Cobb-Douglas utility function
choosing between two goods with a budget constraint. What is the budget
constraint?)

(b) If Juliet got to allocate the spaghetti exactly as she wanted to, how
much would she take for herself? ____16____How much
would she give Romeo?____8____

(c) What are the Pareto optimal allocations? (Hint: An allocation will
____The Pareto optimal allocations are all of the al-
locations in which each person gets at least 8 units of
spaghetti.

(d) When we had to allocate two goods between two people, we drew an
Edgeworth box with indifference curves in it. When we have just one good
to allocate between two people, all we need is an "Edgeworth line" and
instead of indifference curves, we will just have indifference dots. Draw an
Edgeworth line below. Let the distance from left to right denote spaghetti
for Romeo and the distance from right to left denote spaghetti for Juliet.

(e) On the Edgeworth line you drew above, show Romeo's favorite point
and Juliet's favorite point.

(f) Suppose that $a = 1/3$. If Romeo got to allocate the spaghetti, how much would he choose for himself? ____$(9, 16)$____ If Juliet got to allocate the spaghetti, how much would she choose for herself? _____$(16, 8)$._____ Draw an Edgeworth line below showing the two people's favorite points and the Pareto optimal points.

(g) When $a = 1/3$, at the Pareto optimal allocations what do Romeo and Juliet disagree about?

Romeo wants to give spaghetti to Juliet, but Juliet does not want to accept it. Juliet wants to give spaghetti to Romeo but Romeo does not want to accept it. Both still like spaghetti for themselves but each prefers to give it to the other.

30.10 (20) Hatfield and McCoy hate each other but love corn whiskey. Because they hate for each other to be happy, each wants the other to have less whiskey. Hatfield's utility function is $U_H(W_H, W_M) = W_H - W_M^2$ and McCoy's utility function is $U_M(W_M, W_H) = W_M - W_H^2$, where W_M is McCoy's daily whiskey consumption and W_H is Hatfield's daily whiskey consumption (both measured in quarts.) There are 4 quarts of whiskey to be allocated.

(a) If McCoy got to allocate all of the whiskey, how would he allocate it? ____$W_M = 4$____ If Hatfield got to allocate all of the whiskey, how would he allocate it? ____$W_H = 4$____

(b) If each of them gets 2 quarts of whiskey, what will the utility of each of them be? ____2____ If a bear spilled 2 quarts of their whiskey and they divided the remaining 2 quarts equally between them, what would the utility of each of them be? ____0____ If it is possible to throw away some of the whiskey, is it Pareto optimal for them each to consume 2 quarts of whiskey? ____no____

(c) If it is possible to throw away some whiskey and they must consume equal amounts of whiskey, how much should they throw away? _____3 quarts._____

Chapter 31

Externalities

31.1 (20) Horsehead, Massachusetts, is a picturesque village on a bay which is inhabited by the delectable crustacean, *homarus americanus*, also known as the lobster. Horsehead issues permits to trap these creatures, and is trying to determine how many permits to issue. The economics of the situation are this:

1. It costs $2,000 dollars a month to operate a lobstering boat.
2. If there are x boats operating in Horsehead Bay, the total revenue from the lobster catch per month will be $f(x) = 10x - x^2$, measured in thousands of dollars.

(a) In the graph below, plot the average product, $AP(x) = f(x)/x$, and the marginal product $MP(x) = 10 - 2x$ curves. In the same graph plot the line indicating the cost of operating a boat.

AP,MP

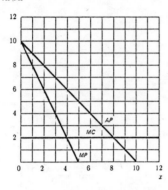

(b) If the permits are free of charge, how many boats will trap lobsters in Horsehead, Massachusetts? (Hint: How many boats must enter before there are zero profits?) Set AP equal to cost to give $10 - x = 2$, or $x = 8$ boats.

(a) If an individual can choose how many hours per day he wants to drive and if he believes that the amount of driving he does won't affect the amount that others drive, how many hours per day will he choose to drive? ____8____ (Hint: What value of d maximizes $U(m,d,t)$.)

(b) If everybody chooses his best d, then what is the total amount, t, of driving by other persons? ____8,000____ (Hint: If everyone drives d hours, then each citizen will find that the total driving by others is $1,000d$.)

(c) What will be the utility of each individual? ____26____

(d) Suppose that everybody drives 6 hours a day, what will be the utility level of a typical citizen of El Carburetor? ____106____

(e) Suppose that the citizens decided to pass a law restricting the total number of hours that any one is allowed to drive. What amount of driving should everyone be allowed if the objective is to maximize the utility of the typical citizen. ____5____ (Hint: Rewrite the utility function, substituting $1,000d$ for t, and maximize with respect to d.)

(f) Could the same objective be achieved with a tax on driving? Yes.

(g) If so, how much would the tax have to be per hour of driving? (Hint: We want to maximize $16d - d^2 - td$, which gives first-order condition $16 - 2d - t$. The optimal d is 5, so we need to set $t = 6$.

31.4 (30) Tom and Jerry are roommates. Tom likes raucous music, while Jerry likes peace and quiet. Every week, Tom and Jerry each get two dozen chocolate chip cookies sent from home. Draw an Edgeworth box depicting the possible allocations of cookies and hours of music played in their room. On the vertical axis put hours of music. On the horizontal axis, measure cookies for Tom from left to right and cookies for Jerry from right to left. (Notice that both must get the same amount of music, while they can get different amounts of cookies.)

(c) What number of boats maximizes total profits? Set MP equal to cost to give $10 - 2x = 2$, or $x = 4$ boats.

(d) If Horsehead, Massachusetts, wants to restrict the number of boats Let p be the price of the permit. Then we want $10 - 4 = 2 + p$, which says that the average product with 4 boats equals 2 plus the price of a permit. Solving, we have $p = 4$ thousand dollars a month.

31.2 (20) Suppose that a honey farm is located next to an apple orchard, and each acts as a competitive firm. Let the amount of apples produced of honey produced will be ____100____ and the equilibrium amount of apples produced will be ____150____

(a) Suppose that the honey and apple firms merged. What would be the profit maximizing output of honey for the combined firm? ____150____ What would be the profit maximizing amount of apples? ____150____

(b) What is the socially efficient output of honey? ____150____ ____If the firms stayed separate, how much would honey production have to be subsidized to induce an efficient supply? $1 per unit

31.3 (20) In El Carburetor, California, population 1,001, there is not much to do except to drive your car around town. Everybody in town is just like everybody else. While everybody likes to drive, the citizens all complain about the congestion, noise, and pollution caused by traffic. A typical citizen's utility function is $U(m,d,t) = m + 16d - d^2 - 6t/1,000$, where m is the citizen's consumption of Big Macs, d is the number of hours per day that he, himself, drives and t is the total amount of driving (measured in person hours per day) done by all of the other citizens of El Carburetor. Each individual can afford 10 Big Macs. To keep our calculations simple, suppose it costs nothing to drive a car.

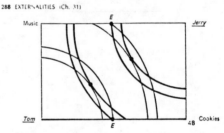

(a) Suppose the dorm's policy is that you must have your roommate's permission to play music. If this is the case, label the initial endowment points in the above diagram. Draw the highest indifference curves Tom and Jerry can possibly achieve without any trade. Shade in all of the allocations that would make both roommates better off than their initial endowments. If trade was allowed, indicate the potential final allocations.

(b) Now suppose the dorm's policy is "rock-n-roll is good for the soul," and thus you don't require your roommate's permission to play music. Complete the steps described above for this new case.

(c) Under the policy of getting your roommate's permission to play music, what is the highest level of utility Jerry can achieve if he is an astute trader? ____What is the highest level Tom can achieve if he is a shrewd trader? ____Under the rock-n-roll policy what are the two utility levels? Illustrate these points on your graph.

(d) Which dorm policy would Tom prefer? Rock-n-roll ____Which policy does Jerry prefer? roommate's permission ____Could it ever happen that this was not the case? this is always the case if preferences are convex.

(e) Suppose Jerry is indifferent to the amount of music Tom plays (this may be due to a profound hearing loss caused by listening to loud music while in high school). In the diagram below draw the new Edgeworth diagram.

(f) In the above diagram label the following: (1) the endowment point if you need your roommate's permission. (2) the endowment point if you don't need your roommate's permission. (3) the potential endowments which would make both roommates better off under each set of property rights. and (4) the pareto optimial trades under each set of property rights.

(g) Which property right distribution does Tom prefer? _____

Tom would probably prefer the rock-n-roll distribution; however, it is possible that he achieves the same utility under the permission distribution.

Which one does Jerry prefer? _____ Jerry would probably be better off if music isn't allowed, although, it is again the case that he could be indifferent to the final allocation under rock-n-roll.

What is the intuition behind these results? The basic intuition is that since Jerry is indifferent to the level of music, he can never be induced to trade some of his food for a reduction in the level of music. Even when Tom does not have the property rights, he may be able to convince Jerry to allow the full amount of music, given that Jerry doesn't care about it. In this case Tom is as well off as in the case of being given full music rights. However, even though Jerry is indifferent, when he has the property rights, he may use them to achieve additional food in exchange for allowing some more music (which Jerry doesn't even care about!).

_____

31.5 (20) The cottagers on the shores of Lake Invidious are an unsavoury bunch. There are 100 of them and they live in a circle around the lake.

(a) Calculate his utility level. _____ 0 _____

(b) Suppose that each consumer consumes only 3/4 of a unit. Will all individuals be better off or worse off? _____ Better off. _____

(c) What is the best possible consumption if all are to consume the same amount? _____ 1/2 _____

(d) Suppose that everybody around the lake is consuming 1 unit. can any two people make themselves both better off either by redistributing consumption between them or by throwing something away? _____ No. _____

_____

(e) How about a group of three people? _____ No. _____

(f) How large is the smallest group that could cooperate to benefit all of its members? _____ 100 _____

Chapter 32

Public Goods

32.1 (20) Bob and Ray are two hungry economics majors who are sharing an apartment for the year. In a flea market they spot a 25 year old sofa that would look great in their living room.

Bob's utility function for money and sofas is $u_B(S, M_B) = (1+S)M_B$ and Ray's utility function for money and sofas is $u_R(S, M_R) = (2+S)M_R$. In these expressions M_B and M_R are the amounts of money that Bob and Ray have to spend on other goods. $S = 0$ when the sofa is not available, and $S = 1$ when the sofa is available. Bob has W_B dollars to spend, and Ray has W_R dollars.

(a) What is Bob's reservation price for the sofa?
Using the definition of reservation price, we want to solve $1W_B = 2(W_B - p)$, or $p_B = W_B/2$.

(b) What is Ray's reservation price for the sofa?
In this case, we want to solve $W_R = 3(W_R - p)$, which gives $p_R = 2W_R/3$.

(c) If the sofa costs $10, shade in the combinations of (W_B, W_R) for which
Shade in all values of (M_B, M_R) for which $M_B/2 + 2M_R/3 \geq 10$.

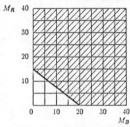

32.2 (10) Cowflop, Wisconsin, has 1,000 people. Every year they have a fireworks show on the fourth of July. The citizens are interested in only two things -- drinking milk and watching fireworks. Fireworks cost 1 gallon of milk per unit. People in Cowflop are all pretty much the same.

(c) Suppose that everyone in town pays an equal share of the cost of the skating rink. Total expenditure by the town on its skating rink will be $10Y. Then the tax bill paid by an individual citizen to pay for the skating rink is $10Y/1,000 = $Y/100$. Every year the citizens of Muskrat vote on how big the skating rink should be. Citizens realize that they will have to pay their share of the cost of the skating rink. Knowing this, a citizen realizes that if the size of the skating rink is Y, then the amount of Labatt's ale that he will be able to afford is $1,000 - Y/100$.

(d) Therefore we can write a voter's budget constraint as $X_i + Y/100 = 1,000$. In order to decide how big a skating rink to vote for, a voter simply solves for the combination of X_i and Y that maximizes his utility subject to his or her budget constraint and votes for that amount of Y. How much Y is that in our example? $Y = 100$.

(e) If the town supplies a skating rink that is the size demanded by the voters will it be larger than, smaller than, or the same size as the Pareto optimal rink? The same.

(f) Suppose that the Ontario cultural commission decides to promote Canadian culture by subsidizing local skating rinks. The provincial government will pay 50% of the cost of skating rinks in all towns. The costs of this subsidy will be shared by all citizens of the province of Ontario. There are hundreds of towns like Muskrat in Ontario. It is true that to pay for this subsidy, taxes paid to the provincial government will have to be increased. But there are hundreds of towns from which this tax is collected, so that the effect of an increase in expenditures in Muskrat on the taxes its citizens have to pay to the state can be safely neglected. Now, approximately how large a skating rink would citizens of Muskrat vote for. $Y = 100\sqrt{2}.$ (Hint: Rewrite the budget constraint for individuals observing that local taxes will be only half as large as before and the cost of increasing the size of the rink only half as much as before. Then solve for the utility maximizing combination.)

(g) Does this subsidy promote economic efficiency? No.

32.4 (20) Ten people have dinner together at an expensive restaurant and agree that the total bill will be divided equally among them.

(a) What is the additional cost to any one of them of ordering an appetizer that costs $20.

$2.

In fact, they have identical utility functions. The utility function of each citizen i is $U_i(x_i, y) = x_i + \sqrt{y}/20$, where x_i is the number of gallons of milk per year consumed by citizen i and y is the number of units of fireworks exploded in the town's Fourth of July extravaganza. (Private use of fireworks is outlawed)

(a) Solve for each citizen's marginal rate of substitution between fireworks and milk. $1/(40\sqrt{y})$

(b) Find the Pareto optimal amount of fireworks for Cowflop.

625.

32.3 (30) Muskrat, Ontario, has 1,000 people. Citizens of Muskrat consume only one private good, Labatt's ale. There is one public good, the town skating rink. Although they may differ in other respects, inhabitants have the same utility function. This function is $U_i(X_i, Y) = X_i - 100/Y$, where X_i is the number of bottles of Labatt's consumed by citizen i and Y is the size of the town skating rink, measured in square meters. The price of Labatt's ale is $1 per bottle and the price of the skating rink is $10 per square meter. Everyone who lives in Muskrat has an income of $1,000 per year.

(a) Write down an expression for the marginal rate of substitution between skating rink and Labatt's ale for a typical citizen. $100/Y^2$
What is the marginal cost of an extra square meter of skating rink (measured in terms of Labatt's ale.)? 10.

(b) Since there are 1,000 people in town, all with the same marginal rate of substitution, you should now be able to write an equation that states the condition that the sum of marginal rates of substitution equals marginal cost. Write this equation and solve it for the Pareto efficient amount of Y.

$1,000\frac{100}{Y^2} = 10$. Solution is $Y = 100$.

(b) Explain why this may be an inefficient system.

Since each person pays less than the social cost, he will tend to overindulge.

32.5 (20) Bonnie and Clyde are business partners. Whenever they work, they have to work together. Their only source of income is profit from their partnership. Their total profits per year are $50H$, where H is the number of hours that they work per year. Since they must work together, they both must work the same number of hours. Bonnie's utility function is $U_B(C_B, H) = C_B - .02H^2$ and Clyde's utility function is $U_C(C_C, H) = C_C - .005H^2$, where C_B and C_C are the annual amounts of money spent on consumption for Bonnie and for Clyde and where H is the number of hours that they both work.

(a) If the number of hours that they both work is H, what is Bonnie's marginal rate of substitution between private and public goods (that is, the ratio of her marginal utility of public goods to her marginal utility of private goods.)? $-.04H$ What about Clyde's? $-.01H$

(b) Write an expression for the sum of their marginal rates of substitution. $-.05H$

(c) What is the marginal cost in terms of public good of reducing their work effort by one unit? 50.

(d) Write an equation that can be solved for the Pareto optimal number of hours for Bonnie and Clyde to work. $.05H = 50$

(e) Now solve this equation for the Pareto optimal H _____ $H = 1,000$

_____(Hint: This model is formally the same as a model with one public good H and one private good, income.)

32.6 (20) Lucy and Melvin share an apartment. They spend some of their income on private goods like food and clothing that they consume separately and some of their income on public goods like the refrigerator, the household heating, and the rent which they share. Lucy's utility function is $2X_L + Y$ and Melvin's utility function is $X_M Y$, where X_L and X_M are the amounts of money spent on private goods for Lucy and for Melvin and where Y is the amount of money that they spend on public goods. Lucy and Melvin have a total of $8,000 per year between them to spend on private goods for each of them and on public goods.

(a) What is Lucy's marginal rate of substitution between private and public goods? ____ $1/2$ ____ What is Melvin's? ____ X_M/Y

(b) Write an expression for the efficiency condition for provision of the Pareto efficient quantity of the public good. ____ $1/2 + X_M/Y = 1$

(c) Suppose that Melvin and Lucy each spend $2,000 on private goods for themselves and they spend the remaining $4,000 on public goods. Is this a Pareto efficient outcome? ____ Yes.

(d) Give an example of another Pareto optimal outcome in which Melvin gets more than $2,000 and Lucy gets less than $2,000 worth of private goods. ____ One example would be Melvin gets $2500, Lucy gets $500 $Y = \$5,000$.

Give an example of another Pareto optimum in which Lucy gets more than $2,000. ____ Lucy gets $5,000, Melvin gets $1,000 $Y = \$2,000$.

(b) More generally, when everybody pays the same amount of taxes, if x lessons are provided by the government to each creature, the total cost to the government is ____ 6 million fondas ____ times x and the taxes that one creature has to pay is ____ 2 ____ times x.

(c) Since aerobics lessons are going to be publically provided with everybody getting the same amount and nobody able to get more lessons from another source, each creature faces a choice problem that is formally the same as that faced by a consumer, i, who is trying to maximize a Cobb-Douglas utility function subject to the budget constraint $2A + B = I$. where I is its income. Explain why this is the case.

If A lessons are provided, you pay taxes equal to $2A$ fondas. After taxes, you will have $I - 2A$ fondas to spend on B which costs 1 fonda per unit.

(d) Suppose that the aerobics lessons are paid for by a head tax and all lessons are provided by the government in equal amounts to everyone. How many lessons would the rich people prefer to have supplied? ____ 25 ____ How many would the poor people prefer to have supplied? ____ 12.5 ____ (Hint: In each case you just have to solve for the Cobb-Douglas demand with an appropriate budget.)

(e) If the outcome is determined by majority rule, how many aerobics lessons will be provided? ____ 12.5 ____ How much bread will the rich get? ____ 75 ____ How much bread will the poor get? ____ 25

(f) Suppose that aerobics lessons are "privatized" so that no lessons are supplied publically and no taxes are collected. Every creature is allowed to buy as many lessons as it likes and as much bread as it likes. Suppose that the price of bread stays at 1 fonda per unit and the price of lessons stays at 2 fondas per unit. How many aerobics lessons will the rich get? ____

(e) Describe the set of Pareto optimal allocations. ____ The allocations that satisfy the two equations $X_M/Y = 1/2$ and $X_L + X_M + Y = \$8,000$.

(f) The Pareto optima that treat Lucy better and Melvin worse will have (more of, less of, the same amount of) public good as the Pareto optimum that treats them equally. ____ Less of.

32.7 (20) On the planet Jumpo there are two goods, aerobics lessons and bread. The citizens all have Cobb-Douglas utility functions of the form $U_i(A_i, B_i) = A_i^{1/2}B_i^{1/2}$, where A_i and B_i are i's consumptions of aerobics lessons and bread. Although tastes are all the same, there are two different income groups, the rich and the poor. Each rich creature on Jumpo has an income of 100 and every poor creature has an income of 50 fondas (the currency unit on Jumpo). There are two million poor creatures and one million rich creatures on Jumpo. Bread is sold in the usual way, but aerobics lessons are provided by the state despite the fact that they are private goods. The state gives the same amount of aerobics lessons to every creature on Jumpo. The price of bread is 1 fonda per loaf. The cost to the state of aerobics lessons is 2 fondas per lesson. This cost of the state-provided lessons is paid for by taxes collected from the citizens of Jumpo. The government has no other expenses than providing aerobics lessons and collects no more or less taxes than the amount needed to pay for them. Jumpo is a democracy and the amount of aerobics to be supplied will be determined by majority vote.

(a) Suppose that the cost of the aerobics lessons provided by the state is paid for by making every creature on Jumpo pay an equal amount of taxes. On planets, such as Jumpo, where every creature has exactly one head, such a tax is known as a "head tax". If every citizen of Jumpo gets 20 lessons, how much will be total government expenditures on lessons? ____ 120 million fondas ____ How much taxes will every citizen have to pay? ____ 40 fondas ____ If 20 lessons are given, how much will a rich creature have left to spend on bread after it has paid its taxes? ____ 60 fondas ____ How much will a poor creature have left to spend on bread after it has paid its taxes? ____ 10 fondas

____ 25 ____ How many will the poor get? ____ 12.5 ____
____ How much bread will the rich get? ____ 50 ____
____ How much bread will the poor get? ____ 25 ____

(g) Suppose that aerobics lessons remain publically supplied but are paid for by a proportional income tax. The tax rate will be determined so that tax revenue pays for the lessons. Suppose that if A aerobics lessons are offered to each creature on Jumpo, the tax bill for a rich person will be $3A$ fondas and the tax bill for a poor person will be $1.5A$ fondas. If any number, A, of lessons are given each creature, show that with this tax scheme the total tax revenue collected will be equal to the total cost of A lessons. ____ Since there are 2,000,000 poor and 1,000,000 rich, total revenue is equal to $2,000,000 \times 1.5A + 1,000,000 \times 3A = 6,000,000A$. There are 3,000,000 people in all. If each gets A lessons and one lesson costs 2 fondas, the total cost would be $6,000,000A$.

(h) With the proportional income tax scheme discussed above, what budget constraint would a rich person consider in deciding how many aerobics lessons to vote for? ____ $3A + B = 100$ ____ What is the relevant budget constraint for a poor creature? ____ $1.5A + B = 50$ ____ With these tax rates, how many aerobics lessons per creature would the rich favor? ____ $50/3$ ____ How many would the poor favor? ____ $50/3$ ____ What quantity of aerobics lessons per capita would be chosen under majority rule? ____ $50/3$ ____ How much bread would the rich get? ____ 50 ____ How much bread would the poor get? ____ 25.

(i) Calculate the utility of a rich creature under a head tax ____ $\sqrt{937.5}$ ____ under privatization ____ $\sqrt{1250}$, ____ under

a proportional income tax._____ $\sqrt{833.3}$ _____ (Hint: In each case, solve for the consumption of bread and the consumption of aerobics lessons that a rich person gets and plug these into the utility function.)

Now calculate the utility of each poor creature under the head tax_____

_____ $\sqrt{312.5}$, _____ privatization _____ $\sqrt{312.5}$, _____. and under the proportional income tax _____ $\sqrt{833.3}$ _____. (Express these utilities as square roots rather than calculating out the roots.)

(j) Is privatization Pareto superior to the head tax? _____ Yes _____

_____ Is a proportional income tax Pareto superior to the head tax?

_____ Yes _____ Is privatization Pareto superior to the proportional income tax? Explain this last answer

_____ No. The rich prefer privatization to

the proportional income tax, the poor prefer the pro-

portional income tax to privatization. _____